'GREEK' THOMSON

'GREEK'

EDINBURGH UNIVERSITY PRESS

THOMSON

EDITED BY GAVIN STAMP AND SAM McKINSTRY

© Edinburgh University Press, 1994

Transferred to digital print 2015

Edinburgh University Press Ltd
22 George Square, Edinburgh

Designed by Geoff Green

Typeset in Linotype Plantin
by Nene Phototypesetters Ltd,
Northampton, and
printed and bound by CPI Group (UK) Ltd
Croydon, CR0 4YY

A CIP record for this book is available from the British Library

ISBN 978 0 7486 1345 8

The publisher wishes to
acknowledge subsidy from the
Scottish Arts Council
towards the publication of this volume

CONTENTS

URBANISM

INTERIORS

THE INTERNATIONAL DIMENSION

PERSPECTIVE

    GAVIN STAMP

    Select Bibliography   243
    Index   245

LIST OF ILLUSTRATIONS

LIST OF CONTRIBUTORS

MARK BAINES is a tutor and lecturer at the Mackintosh School of Architecture in Glasgow, from which he qualified in 1975. He subsequently worked for Gillespie, Kidd & Coia and other architectural practices in Glasgow. He was co-organiser of the Greek Thomson exhibition held in Glasgow in 1984.

BRIAN EDWARDS was Senior Lecturer in the Department of Architecture and Building Science at Strathclyde University and is now Professor of Architecture at the University of Huddersfield. His interest is in cities and how they are created, nurtured and changed. He is the author of *Scottish seaside Towns* and *London Docklands: Urban Design in an Age of De-regulation*.

ANDOR GOMME has a personal chair in English Literature and Architectural History at the University of Keele. He is a former Chairman of the Society of Architectural Historians of GB and has written (jointly with others) books on the architecture of Glasgow and Bristol. He is currently putting together a book on Francis Smith and spends what time is left over listening to, editing and writing about music.

IAN GOW was educated at George Heriot's School, Edinburgh, and Trinity College, Cambridge. After a brief spell in the London branch of the Inspectorate of Ancient Monuments he returned home to the National Monuments Record of Scotland, where he is now Curator of the Architectural Collections. He has published extensively on the decorative arts and architecture of Scotland, and his most recent book (also published by EUP) is *The Scottish Interior*.

JULIET KINCHIN now lectures in Historical and Critical Studies at the Glasgow School of Art. She original-ly came to Glasgow in 1980 to work in the Decorative Arts Department of Glasgow Museums before moving to the University of Glasgow where she set up the Christie's postgraduate course in Decorative Arts.

JAMES MACAULAY is Senior Lecturer in Architectural History at the Mackintosh School of Architecture, Glasgow. He has been Chairman of both the Society of Architectural Historians of Great Britain and the Architectural Heritage Society of Scotland. He is the author of *The Gothic Revival, 1745–1845*, *The Classical Country House in Scotland, 1660–1800* and *Architecture in Detail: Glasgow School of Art*.

CHARLES MCKEAN has been Secretary and Treasurer of the Royal Incorporation of Architects in Scotland since 1989. He is the author of a number of architectural books and papers relating to the rediscovery of the real architectural history of Scotland and was the founder/editor of the RIAS/Landmark Trust series of illustrated architectural guides to Scotland.

JOHN MCKEAN trained as an architect at the Glasgow School of Architecture and then studied history at Essex University, writing a graduate thesis on Alexander Thomson. Since then he has written about Thomson and lectured on him occasionally at the Glasgow School of Art, the Architectural Association and in Europe. He is the author of 'Fear and Loathing in the Office of Architecture' (in *Studio International*) and 'Dark and Light in the Personality of Glasgow' (in B. Bocchi (ed.), *Glasgow: Forma e Progetto della Citta*, Venice, 1990). He now teaches at the University of Brighton.

SAM MCKINSTRY is a Senior Lecturer at the University of Paisley and the author of the recent standard monograph on the Scottish architect Sir Robert Rowand Anderson (also published by EUP), based on his Ph.D. thesis for the University of St Andrews. He is a guest lecturer in architectural history at the Universities of Edinburgh and Strathclyde.

ANDREW MACMILLAN is Professor of Architecture at the University of Glasgow and Head of the Mackintosh School of Architecture, having been a Senior Partner in the firm of Gillespie, Kidd & Coia. As a Glaswegian, he has been an enthusiast for Greek Thomson since 1945. He recently published *Six Scottish Burghs*.

JANE PLENDERLEITH was born in Glasgow and completed her Ph.D. at Glasgow University in 1991. She lectures in German at Paisley University and her research interests range from Goethe and the German eighteenth century to the literature of the former German Democratic Republic.

SALLY JOYCE RUSH first became interested in the applied arts, in particular stained glass, as a History of Art student at Edinburgh University. Since then she has become a specialist in the neglected subject of nineteenth-century stained glass in Scotland and is currently completing a Ph.D. thesis at the Mackintosh School of Architecture.

GAVIN STAMP was born in Kent, brought up in the suburbs of London and educated at Gonville and Caius College, Cambridge. Having been a freelance architectural writer in London, he became a lecturer at the Mackintosh School of Architecture in 1990. He was the founder of the Alexander Thomson Society, is Chairman of the Twentieth Century Society, and is the author of, amongst other things, *Telephone Boxes*.

ALEXANDER STODDART was born in Edinburgh and is a neoclassical architectural sculptor who lives and works in Paisley. While at the Glasgow School of Art, he was profoundly impressed by Thomson's observations in the Haldane Lectures on the finish of the Elgin Marbles. He has recently completed sculpture on the Italian Centre in Glasgow, and was responsible for the Cynico-Stoic Athena in the new development behind Burnet's Athenaeum façade in St George's Place.

DAVID M. WALKER was born in 1933 at Dundee, the subject of his earliest architectural researches, and studied at the College of Art there. In 1958–9 he began investigating Glasgow; his appointment to the Historic Buildings staff of the Scottish Office in 1961 enabled him to extend his researches to Edinburgh and Aberdeen. He was until 1993 Chief Inspector of Historic Buildings, a post he had held under different titles since 1975.

DAVID WATKIN is the author of monographs on Thomas Hope, C. R. Cockerell and 'Athenian' Stuart, and (with Tilman Mellinghoff) of *German Architecture and the Classical Ideal: 1740–1840* (1987). He is a Fellow of Peterhouse and Reader in the History of Architecture at the University of Cambridge.

PREFACE

This book is a response to the growing interest in and research into the second great architect of international stature associated with the city of Glasgow. At present, the literature about 'Greek' Thomson is small compared to that devoted to the other supreme Glaswegian designer, Charles Rennie Mackintosh. There are some articles in journals, but the essential biographical information is supplied in Ronald McFadzean's standard and indispensable work, *The Life and Work of Alexander Thomson* – published in 1979 and now difficult to obtain.

In recent years, however, investigation has begun into the wider aspects of Thomson's achievement, both in terms of his place in the context of mid-Victorian Glasgow and his involvement in all the arts associated with architecture. For there is the growing realisation that, like Mackintosh, Thomson was also a designer concerned with ironwork, decoration and furniture. The foundation of the Alexander Thomson Society in 1991 confirmed the serious revival of interest in the long-neglected architecture of the Glaswegian talent whom Sir Nikolaus Pevsner considered to be 'a national figure in British architecture'. And so it occurred to both editors independently that a publication adding to our understanding of Thomson's genius was overdue. This book is the result.

The chapters are widely divergent and often innovative in approach. In them, we see Thomson in his role as the architect of urban renewal, self-consciously contributing to the cityscape of a burgeoning Glasgow, as well as disposer of façades, co-ordinator of trades, and patron of the sister arts of sculpture and interior and furniture design. Evident, too, in these studies is the international stature of Thomson as intellectual, theorist, theologian, Romantic, and as the focus of critics past and present. This is a collection illuminating the current state of knowledge about one of the deepest and most creative minds in Scottish architectural history.

We are particularly pleased that Sir John Summerson agreed to contribute to this collection with a short essay, written in 1991, which confirms that, for some, the greatness of Alexander Thomson was never forgotten. Sadly, he did not live to see it even in proof, so that this introduction is now a last, posthumous publication by the finest British architectural writer of our century.

GAVIN STAMP AND SAM MCKINSTRY
Strathbungo and Paisley
April 1994

ACKNOWLEDGEMENTS

Thanks are due, above all, to all those who have given up their time and knowledge to contribute to this book, for none has received nor will receive any financial recompense for their efforts. Any royalties such that interest in the work of Greek Thomson may generate will go to the Alexander Thomson Society.

We are greatly in debt to the National Monuments Record for Scotland (NMRS) for providing a large proportion of the illustrations in this book, so demonstrating the transcendent importance of that visual archive. We are also most grateful to the Libraries Department of Glasgow City Council for permitting the reproduction of drawings by Thomson in the Mitchell Library collection. Thanks are also due to Strathclyde Regional Archives, the Scottish Record Office, the Irish Architectural Archive, Glasgow Museums & Art Galleries and to the Glasgow School of Art for making visual material available. Charles McKean's essay is illustrated with material partly in the collection of the Royal Incorporation of Architects in Scotland (RIAS), and David Walker's essay uses early photographs in his own collection, some of which came from the late Alfred G. Lochead. Mark Baines' essay is illustrated by his own photographs and drawings and by measured drawings prepared by Paul Bell, Robert Clarke, Gerry Grams, Peter Smith and Stephen Wong, all students – past and present – at the Mackintosh School of Architecture. Dr Ronald McFadzean, Thomson's biographer, generously made available Thomas Annan photographs in his own collection, as well as the copy he prepared of the much-damaged drawing of the Albert Memorial design in the Glasgow School of Art, while Alexander Thomson's great-grand-daughters, Ann Hutchison and Catherine Rentoul, assisted by lending material for reproduction, as well as with information and encouragement. We are also most grateful to Olive Cook for allowing us to use the magnificent photographs taken by her late husband, Edwin Smith. All other modern photographs were taken by Gavin Stamp.

To those many others, too numerous to mention individually, who assisted the seventeen contributors to this book in many different ways, we can only offer our thanks.

INTRODUCTION

FIGURE I.I   The St Vincent Street church in *c.*1930.

Chapter One

.

ON DISCOVERING 'GREEK' THOMSON

John Summerson

I first saw Edinburgh and Glasgow in 1926, the year of that disturbing episode in the history of democracy, the General Strike. I was one of a number of Bartlett (University College, London) students who enlisted as porters at King's Cross, 'for the duration'. The work was mostly trundling milk-churns from the trains to the collecting bay but I usually found time to watch the *Flying Scotsman* steaming majestically from Platform 10 at 10.00 a.m., with gallant black-leg driver and fireman on the footplate. The famous train never missed a day, and I was so impressed by the ritual that I resolved that when the strike was over, the *Flying Scotsman* would carry me to Scotland. Which, a few weeks later, it did, and I spent my porter's wages on the fare and modest hotel accommodation in the two great cities of the north.

I took my sketch-book (see FIGURE 1.2) and the contents remind me today how I reacted first to Edinburgh and then to Glasgow. Edinburgh, the 'Modern Athens', was glorious, of course, but the Greek Revival had broken its back on the Calton Hill, leaving the spectral Parthenon fragment to remind us of the fact. In Glasgow, how different! The Greek Revival had turned itself into a new style, still mostly Greek but also romantically abstract. Alexander Thomson was the man behind this and he had shown how a measure of abstraction could produce intrinsically classical solutions to the problems of the 1860s and 1870s – churches, villas, tenements, office blocks, etc. I had not yet heard of Le Corbusier and nobody thought much of that eccentric upstart, Frank Lloyd Wright. As for Mackintosh, the man himself was still alive and his works were remembered, if at all, only as something

quite out-moded and not worth a thought or a glance. Thomson was Glasgow's architect hero.

Today, of course, the position is reversed and we are taught to concede that Mackintosh was the greater innovator of the two. Well, I wonder . . .

It was Sir Albert Richardson, in his epoch-making book on *Monumental Classic Architecture* published in 1914, who opened my eyes to Thomson's 'predilection for abstract form in its enthralling mystery and dramatic intensity'. Notwithstanding his passion for the Greek and the Egyptian, it is these abstract qualities which mark Thomson out as an exceptional figure in nineteenth-century architecture. A feeling for the abstract comes and goes through the nineteenth century. It was strong around 1800, with Ledoux in France, Friedrich Gilly in Prussia and Soane in England. In the 1820s and 1830s it was overwhelmed by the new eclecticism, and by mid-century it was dead – *except in Glasgow*. Thomson picked it up in an odd way – mostly from the world of painting and, as he himself admitted, from John Martin in particular. Those apocalyptic scenes – *The Fall of Babylon* (1819) (see FIGURE 1.3), *Belshazzar's Feast* (see PLATE 1) (1820) and *Pandemonium* (1841) – were furnished with buildings of the most powerful kind: vast cubic masses playing against each other, interminable colonnades of some unacknowledged order, temples of inconceivable solemnity and exotic style.

Martin got something from Schinkel, something from Turner and something perhaps from J. M. Gandy. Thomson, a generation younger than Martin, took these apocalyptic forms and – what is so surprising – *made them work*. He raised two of his Glasgow

3

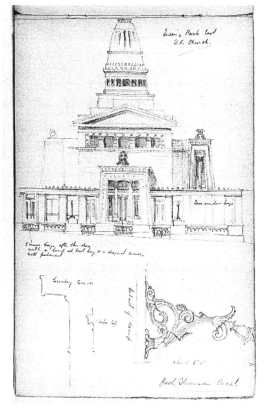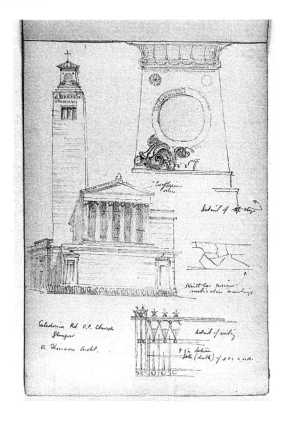

FIGURE 1.2   Pages from Sir John Summerson's 1926 sketchbook showing the Queen's Park and Caledonia Road churches.

churches on vast cubic pedestals (just what Gilly did in his design for a monument to Frederick the Great, which Thomson cannot, I think, have seen). His terraces of housing have a three-dimensional sublimity which makes Nash's Regent's Park look poverty-stricken. Even quite humble blocks of tenements are given a bizarre primitivism which makes them alive and interesting. His villas have a generous broad-eaved nobility, foreign to most things of the kind in the 1850s and 1860s.

It is this apocalyptic vision and the way in which Thomson succeeds in realising it in Victorian Britain which is the wonder. There is nothing like Thomson anywhere outside Glasgow. Edinburgh never caught the magic germ, neither did Aberdeen; and I cannot think of anything in continental Europe which is comparable. One has to cross the Atlantic and look at Frank Lloyd Wright's creations of 1900–10 (see FIGURE 16.5) to find an equivalent handling of form. There is some-

thing wildly 'American' about Thomson – a 'New World' attitude. You can see it in the villas with their spreading eaves – a sort of primitivism, ultra-Tuscan. Compare, for instance, Thomson's double villa at Langside with, say, the William G. Fricke house, Oak Park, Illinois (1902) and the other Wright houses of the period. Then there is something very like Frank Lloyd Wright in the big cubic interiors of the churches. Look at the Unity Church in Oak Park (1906) (see FIGURE 16.8) and then at the interior (in the few – alas! – surviving photographs) of the Queen's Park church in Glasgow.

'Discoveries' made in years of adolescence are nearly always moving in old age (and it is now sixty-five years since I 'discovered' Thomson). European architecture has taken several curious twists and turns in those years but, to me, Thomson's work comes as freshly as ever as an illuminator of urban and suburban forms.

FIGURE 1.3   *The Fall of Babylon*, mezzotint by John Martin,
1831.

BACKGROUND

FIGURE 2.1   151–7 Queen Street, 1834, designed for
Archibald McLellan, probably by David Hamilton, photo
1965.

Chapter Two

.

IN SEARCH OF PURITY

GLASGOW 1849–56

Charles McKean

The title 'Second City of the Empire', grumped the Scottish *Building Chronicle* wryly in July 1854, accords ill with a city 'with a roofless Post Office and asking in vain for a Museum'. Not untypically, for Glasgow's (and Scotland's) uncertainties and problems rather than its achievements dominated that magazine and others of the period. Somewhat short, you might think, of the confidence that the Whig theory of history might have led one to expect from the boom town of Victorian Britain.

This chapter focuses upon Glasgow and its architects in the years leading up to the formation of the practice A & G Thomson in 1856, in order to approximate the *Zeitgeist* within which Thomson reached architectural maturity. The *Building Chronicle*, launched by architect James Maclaren (of Maclaren Soutar Salmond), first appeared on 10 May 1854, 'to record the progress in this portion of the Empire'.[1] Generally following the lines of the (London) *Builder* – at which it sniped at the lack of coverage of Scots matters – it appeared monthly for just over three years. The technical, architectural and aesthetic debates which flit across its pages may fairly be represented as reflecting contemporary architectural preoccupations; and the very first issue carries an extensive advertisement for a 'proposed architectural exhibition' in Bath Street. Since that exhibition and its doings are covered *in extenso*, a formal link between the two may be inferred.

MID-CENTURY GLASGOW

Times were curious. Extraordinary volumes of new construction faced unlet property; the gracious streets and squares of Blythswood fronted mews so thickly spread with dung as to render them as noisome as the High Street;[2] improved tenements for the working classes made no impression upon the waves of what John Buchanan called the 'Irish Huns'[3] settling in the High Street, Gallowgate and Calton – at least a better fate than facing the 'Great Hunger' back home. Tentative steps toward smoke and sewage control were overwhelmed by pollution.

Architecture was hesitant in direction – as the Glasgow Architectural Exhibition was to exemplify with its Grecian, Italian and Renaissance Courts and Gothic Library. The *Chronicle* was in search of certainty: '[We] would fain discover, in the present mania of fashions and conflicts of styles, some symptom of a *principle* which may hereafter be worked out in the ultimate production of a distinct national architecture'[4] (my italics). Maclaren's editorial plea was one of many – in addresses to the Liverpool Architectural Society, the Architectural Institute of Scotland, or to the Glasgow Architectural Society – urging the necessity of a new synthesis leading to an architecture appropriate to the time. Physically and metaphorically, there was a search for purity.

The practicalities of Glasgow life were far from pure. As the Blythswood New Town marched north and westward, up hill and down valley with the relentlessness of Roman legions (possibly to the designs of the superannuated James Craig),[5] Glasgow glanced moodily over its shoulder at its abandoned ancestor. Nostalgia had blossomed from 1824 with books and engravings antiquarian in intent – in stark contrast to James Denholm's praise of his 'modern' city in 1798 and 1804,[6] proud of its new arcaded streets, its public buildings, charities, and achievements – easily the

FIGURE 2.2   'The Modern Architecture', new architecture
in Paris, from the *Building Chronicle*.

FIGURE 2.3   'American Villa Architecture' and Claypotts,
Forfarshire, from the *Building Chronicle*.

FIGURE 2.4   The *Illustrated London News* panorama of
Glasgow in 1864.

FIGURE 2.5   Sauchiehall Street looking west, *c.*1860. The
three-bay villa still stands in Scott Street; Thomson's Grecian
Chambers would soon rise to its left.

measure of those in Edinburgh (naturally!). William
Simpson, in particular, undertook an extensive series
of watercolours of vanishing Glasgow, some of which
were later engraved in *Views and Notices of Glasgow in
Ancient Times*.[7]

Progressives were faced with a dilemma: whilst
appreciating the city's fine heritage of rickety buildings, they could not impede progress. Weekly, John
Buchanan recorded Dean of Guild Court decrees of
demolition: the roofs of Fiddler's Close were in such a
state of decomposition that they were carted to the
dung heap of a cowfeeder's premises 'after having for
years protected a most degraded and wretched population from the bitterness of the weather'.[8] The worst
conditions in the High Street, Gorbals and Calton
offered no normal remedy, for there remained no
residual value in the properties: 'Mr McTear, the
Auctioneer, very accurately remarked that in these
halcyon times, it was almost possible for the beggar on

the Bridge to become the owner of fixed property in the
shape of stone and lime.'[9] After 1849, wholesale clearance had become unavoidable.

The loss of history caused lamentation. Buchanan
bewailed the replacement of jaunty crow-stepped and
arcaded buildings by dull rebuilding: 'Look at our
Trongate, High Street and Saltmarket, and see what
modern architecture and utilitarianism has done for
them. No broken outline, no variety, but the hard
unpicturesque horizontal line which pleases only by its
extent, not by its beauty.'[10] Rochead's first entry into
the Trongate, Nos. 42–70, had been just such a building, which his peers considered typically skilful Italianate. The effect of the new antiquarianism upon him,
however, was soon visible across the street, where he
sought 'to emulate the architecture of that ancient
locality'. The *Chronicle* took an instant dislike: 'an
attempt is made to treat the subject in the picturesque style of the old Scottish, but we cannot call it a

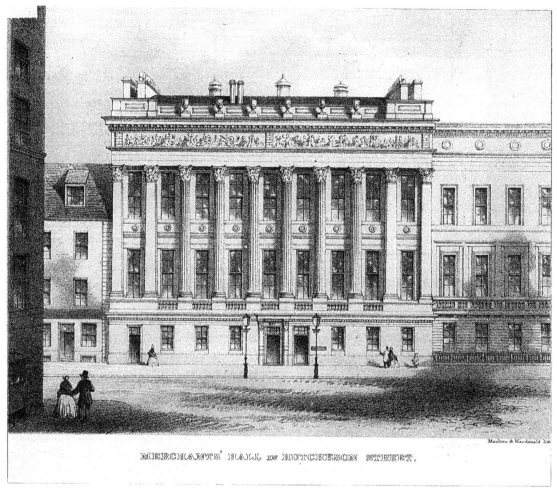

FIGURE 2.6   The new Merchants' Hall in Hutcheson Street
by Clarke & Bell, lithograph from *View of the Merchants'*
House of Glasgow, 1866.

successful one'.[11] Four months of reflection (or lobby-ing) later, it reconsidered the design in a fulsome eulogy of how the proposed City of Glasgow Bank (see FIGURE 2.7) had corbelled wall turrets after the 'much admired' Glamis Castle, 'imparting to the whole line of building that grace, ease and picturesque fashion of outline which gives so much interest and beauty to this pecu-liar cast of architecture. From the description we have given, our readers will be prepared to hear that we admire his [Mr Rochead's] design.'[12]

Maclaren, it may be observed, also admired Roc-head's (now vanished) Pitt Street chapel, 'one of the finest specimens of classical architecture Mr Rochead

has produced',[13] the proposed suburbs with 'boule-vards à la Française' north of Great Western Road,[14] the splendid Gothic design with which he trumped the Hays of Liverpool for the West End Park church and the Italianate Sailors' Home in the Broomielaw.[15] Yet, however brilliant even a J. T. Rochead (the Oliver Hill of his day) might be in his eclecticism, this was insuf-ficiently serious in intent to match the achievements of the Second City.

The city's leadership appears to have passed to entre-preneurs from the Council whose lack of effectiveness is satirised in the *Chronicles of Gotham*[16] in a savage por-trayal of indecision and ineffectuality. The anonymous

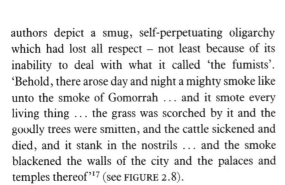

FIGURE 2.7　The City of Glasgow Bank in Trongate by J. T. Rochead, 1855, from the *Building Chronicle*.

FIGURE 2.8　*Territory of the Giants of Rollox, Clear day*, from the *Chronicles of Gotham*, 1856.

authors depict a smug, self-perpetuating oligarchy which had lost all respect – not least because of its inability to deal with what it called 'the fumists'. 'Behold, there arose day and night a mighty smoke like unto the smoke of Gomorrah ... and it smote every living thing ... the grass was scorched by it and the goodly trees were smitten, and the cattle sickened and died, and it stank in the nostrils ... and the smoke blackened the walls of the city and the palaces and temples thereof'[17] (see FIGURE 2.8).

Into the mouth of Ruler John (the Lord Provost) the chronicler put: 'And I shut my ears to the wailings of the people because of the poisoned waters and filthy things which they drank daily. Also shut I my nostrils and felt not the stinks of the Giants of Rollox by reason of their riches.'[18] That conditions were truly appalling, much attributable to the Tennants' St Rollox Works, could be gauged by their ecological consequence. In 1850, Buchanan noted: 'breathing a smoky vapour is not the only grievance of which the public complains. During the whole of last summer many of the formerly

fine umbrageous trees on Glasgow Green were blackened as if they had been struck by lightning's bolt, and just now we observe that many of them have been grabbed out as useless and blasted trunks.'[19]

If smoke would be controlled adequately in Liverpool, why not in Glasgow – unless the Provost had a vested interest? Smoke remained a matter of the first significance. The *Chronicle* believed it to be the principal motive behind the city's westward flight into Park:

Glasgow with its suburbs resembles one of the hedgehog flower-pots to be seen in the windows of our seedsmen ... as the plan in one of these contrivances feels its way to be air holes in its clay covering, so have our builders to dodge the bone boiling, chemical and smoke producing establishments in our suburbs until they reach a spot where their tenants can open their windows without the risk of asphyxia ... their linen turning yellow and their rounds of beef blue.[20]

Eventually, an 1827 Act designed to protect the

amenity of Glasgow Green was deployed to compel industrialists to raise chimneys to 300 feet and ensure that their furnaces combusted more efficiently.

Disconcertingly persistent diseases like cholera proved capable of withstanding the covering-over of the foul Molendinar Burn, and enjoyed endemic residence in the city from 1830 at least – being rampant by the 1850s. Residence near the Clyde during hot summer months could be seriously unpleasant. Two thundering editorials in the *Chronicle* in June and July 1857 blamed civic inaction, poor planning and inadequate ventilation of the sewers for disasters such as this one:

During Tuesday [June] that portion of the city, including a large part of Buchanan Street drained by St Enoch's Burn, was rendered almost uninhabitable by a sickening sulphurous vapour and smell which worked their way upwards from the sewers. The effluvia fairly drove people from their places of business, and the state of those confined to dwelling houses was pitiable. Silver plate and brass were dimmed by the pollution, and painting and room paper were defaced'.[21]

Nor was the problem confined to the old downtown. Buchanan excoriated the wealthy denizens of Blythswood Hill for bringing 'the malarious influence of cholera into the very midst of welcome comfort' by the filthy state of their back lanes and, the following week, excoriated the 'appearance of the vacant ground west of Blythswood Square, with its open ditches, stagnant water, and remains of defunct cats and dogs'.[22]

'Plagues' wrote the chronicler of Gotham 'go over the City even to the West-End, and the tender and weakly, the aged, yea also the strong men sicken and die'.[23] He satirised the plan of *the Philanthropists* to buy the lands around the Kelvin – 'a mighty sewer filled with all manner of corruption' – for public benefit; and would not, presumably, have in any way been assuaged by the appointment of Sir Joseph Paxton to lay out what became the West End Park. Plague touched Thomson whilst he stayed in South Apsley Place (see FIGURE 2.9) in the professional quarter of the Gorbals, with the death of his first daughter in March 1854, his fourth child in February 1855, his youngest son George in December 1856, and his elder son Alexander in January 1857.[24]

Early Victorian Glasgow might well have given the onlooker the sensation of marking time; that it was building, demolishing, sweating and asphyxiating was indisputable. But the first phases were complete; and the next phase not fully apparent. The Blythswood estate, thought the *Chronicle*, conveyed 'aristocratic dullness'.[25] They had a point. The handsome Blythswood estate was – as the engravings by Joseph Swan of St Vincent, West George and Buchanan Streets reveal only too clearly – without highlight. Not even No. 196 West George Street, the most delightful of all, is more than pretty. Furthermore, Blythswood had failed to carry its inexorable rectangularity much west of the hill, and its outer edge was severely criticised for permitting a narrow vennel (widened to Elmbank Street) and for the narrow and unrelieved tediousness of Sauchiehall Street.

The last and most influential of the old guard, David Hamilton (see also FIGURE 2.1) (expired 1843) had departed in glory with the Western Club in Buchanan Street – 'a palace which at once bespeaks the taste of him who planned it and the wealth of those who raised funds to rear and furnish it'. Dr John Strang lamented his friend: 'Perhaps no one has contributed more to the architectural adornment of Glasgow than that gifted and tasteful individual. ... Like most men of true genius, he possessed great modesty, and from his kind and convivial habit endeared himself to a large circle of attached friends, who valued his talents and bewailed his loss.'[26] Strang's praise of the grandiosely Italianate Western reveals the extent to which taste now required richer fare than the neo-Soane delicacy of Hamilton's earlier work. Thus also did A. Williams address the Glasgow Architectural Association in April 1857:

Let us select, for sake of contrast, Hutchesons' Hospital and place it beside the Exchange or the Western Club. We have a sufficiently striking example of this advancement [in the art of architecture]. The quaint forms, the stringy ornament and miserable detail of the Hospital are so widely separated from the masterly and elegant treatment of the last two mentioned edifices that one, unaware of the fact, would never for a moment suppose them the offspring of the same mind.'[27]

It was, perhaps, nor surprising that little outcry had arisen at the demolition of Alexander 'Picture' Gordon's

FIGURE 2.9   Apsley Place, Hutchesonstown, in the 1950s.
Thomson and his family lived at No. 3 South Apsley Place
from *c.*1847 until 1856.

splendid 1804 mansion in Buchanan Street seven
years before, whose design Bolton attributes to Soane
himself. Brash and both Bairds were comfortable but
not commanding architects (John Baird I's genius in
Gardner's Warehouse attracted the *Chronicle*'s censure
for defects 'traceable to the circumstance that the
architect, in detailing his elevation, has not been able to
get rid of the idea that he has stone to work upon').[28]

THE NEW WAVE OF ARCHITECTS

Alexander Thomson was one of a new generation of
Scots architects – John Burnet, William Clarke,
Charles Wilson and J. T. Rochead in Glasgow; and
David Rhind, David Cousin, John Lessels and J. Dick
Peddie in Edinburgh – all Fellows of the Architectural
Institute of Scotland, all giving papers to it. In-
furiatingly, Thomson's seemingly contentious paper

(the *Glasgow Herald* reported the debate as 'lively') on
'The Sources and Elements of Art Considered in Connexion with Architectural Design', delivered on 24
March 1853 in St Mary's Hall Renfield Street, escaped
publication in the *Proceedings of the Architectural Institute of Scotland*. Rochead, Burnet and Wilson nomin-
ated merrily for Associate Membership; Thomson and
his partner Baird but once – J. Connell, joiner. Whereas Rochead, Wilson and Burnet all served on the
Institute's Council, Thomson left that to his partner.

Historical and technical papers given before the
Institute were generally unexceptionable – on Roman
monuments (Alexander Thomson of Banchory), restoration of old buildings (Lessels), and castle comparisons (Rochead); on new materials, the uses of iron,
ventilation, sewers, fires, grates, and dwellings for the
working classes. Papers on matters of aesthetics,
however, reveal deep cultural uncertainty. Against a

FIGURE 2.10   'Iron-Fronted Building' in Jamaica Street by Barclay & Watt, from the *Building Chronicle*.

new theory of the beautiful by Cousin who, in the Aesthetic Club, had invented a system of proportion to which he designed the Reid School of Music, Edinburgh, there was set the predominantly historicist influence of Billings and Fergusson.

Leaving aside Ruskin (almost universally loathed, the arguments used in an anonymous letter from Crito so closely approximating to Thomson's later Haldane Lectures as to imply Crito's identity), architect after architect returned to the question of the correct deployment of new materials, of appropriateness and of 'an architecture of the time'. It comes as something of a shock that John Graham's 1860 retrospective of William Playfair to the AIS[29] felt casually able to categorise the works of that great man into Greek, Roman, modern Italian, Gothic, Tudor and Scottish Baronial in almost equal quantities.

'Appropriateness' was of greater consequence than the imposition of a universal style. A bank, a shop, a church, a club – or a warehouse might wish to signal their differences to the others rather than subsume them. The *Chronicle*, inveighing against what it called 'mask architecture' (what we would now call façade architecture), sought to discover a universal principle or style, and believed that if only 'a universal popular zeal and confidence' would emerge, great architects would appear as they always had for great occasions.[30] Others were not so trusting. On 2 November 1855, Mr (presumably Thomas) Gildard, of Gildard and Macfarlane, harangued the annual *conversazione* of the Glasgow Architectural Association:

> *The modern architect puts free trade commerce into feudal warehouses, shelters in our villainous villas from rain, if not sunshine, by Italian verandahs, and, irrespective either of absolute fitness or association of ideas, gives Congregational-Unionists their choice in Bath Street of a Gothic Cathedral or a Grecian temple ... The circumstances of the age imperatively demand some new and* suitable *application or development of architectural principles.*[31]

Gildard thought it reprehensible that Christian congregations should meet in pagan temples. Lord Neaves, by contrast, argued that the classical form was expressly suited to Presbyterian worship since it allowed the minister to communicate with his audience. In March 1855, the *Chronicle* welcomed Dick Peddie's Pollock Street church in pure Roman temple form: 'Once Glasgow church goers recover from the shock which may be created by this innovation upon the prevailing style of their Church architecture, we make no doubt they will admire Mr Dick Peddie's design all the more.'[32] And they did: particularly the United Presbyterians – that intelligent, disputatious Church for the non-conforming managerial classes for whom Glasgow architects designed a superb collection of classical temples; and Thomson some of his finest achievements.

A curiosity emerges from the pages of the *Chronicle*: the notion of purity as applied to architecture. The word is sparingly and carefully deployed. Pure Gothic was a nonsense, since it depended upon the type; pure Italian likewise (it was no use Charles Wilson founding upon Sansovino); pure Egyptian was somewhat beyond reach; and pure Roman a contradiction in terms. 'Pure' was used almost without exception in the form of a Homeric epithet, no less: *pure Greek*. Baird and Thomson's Blackfriars parish school the *Chronicle* pronounced Jacobean, whereas the epithet first leaps out attached to Baird and Thomson's sculpture workshop for John Mossman in Cathedral Street in a 'pure Greek style'.[33]

Twó years later, the editor's fancy had developed sufficiently to laud Baird and Thomson's new Caledonia Road church (see FIGURE 5.1) since the architects, not 'trammelled by a rigid adherence to ancient examples' had 'skilfully adapted the style to the requirements of Presbyterian worship'.[34] It is as though Thomson's genius had responded to the architectural debate by developing an approach to architecture founded upon an effective synthesis of appropriate materials and technology, in which the exterior was an expression of the volumes and purposes within – reached by a reductive analysis of the nearest to which architecture could approach to purity.

THE GLASGOW ARCHITECTURAL EXHIBITION

Rediscovering the Glasgow Architectural Exhibition of 1854–7 is like tracking a ghost. Direct evidence, by way of papers, minutes, drawings or other illustrations, has yet to turn up. Instead, we have the chimeras from the *Building Chronicle*, the (London) *Builder*, and from the records of the Architectural Institute. Even they let us down: in 1853, for example, William Clarke (of Clarke & Bell) addressed the Institute on the subject of the proposed exhibition in Glasgow, but since it was not published in the 1853–4 papers, we do not know what he had in mind.

In the 5th Annual Report (30 November 1854), AIS Chairman David Cousin commended the desire of 'a few gentlemen resident in Glasgow' – impatient that the commercial capital of Scotland, so remarkable for its wealth, energy and intelligence, should as yet have so little to boast of in respect of collections of art, and that so little should have been done towards the cultivation of the Fine Arts –

determined to take the initiative. They have united to purchase ground, to erect an exhibition gallery, and be at the whole expense of the exhibition: and they even contemplate the possibility, should their efforts meet with the sympathy and support of their fellow towns- *men, of founding a permanent Museum of Art and School of Architecture, and to give permanent accommodation to the Institute at a modest rent.*[35]

In short, the Glasgow architects had decided to force the city's hand into providing a museum almost fifty years before it was to appear at Kelvingrove. Regretting it could do no more, the AIS voted a contribution of £50 followed, in October, by Glasgow Town Council's miserly vote of just double that sum toward the cost of transporting the exhibits. To put this into context, the organising committee held itself responsible for £3000 (independent of a heritable bond for £4000).[36]

The *Chronicle* reported that the exhibition's intent was 'to excite emulation amongst architects by bringing their designs into competition before a public tribunal; second, to encourage artists to advances in every branch of art relating to architecture'.[37]

The Institute appointed a committee on 24 November 1853, to assist the promoters in the collection of exhibits. Chaired by William Clarke, members consisted of James Ballantine (presumably the stained-glass man), Alexander Allan (cabinetmaker), Walter Davidson, Alexander Gray, and architects George Bell (Clarke's partner), Alexander Thomson (then the Institute's auditor), James Brown, John Burnet, David Cousin, J. Dick Peddie, J. T. Rochead, James Salmon, Charles Wilson and Charles Heath Wilson (Superintendent or Head Master of the Government School of Art in Glasgow, who may have been the *onlie begetter* of the entire affair).

It is not clear which architects had pledged to pay, but the following were involved in duties: James Collie (drawings or models of original designs); Charles Heath Wilson (views of architectural buildings (*sic*), engravings, painting or sun pictures); George Bell (architectural models and building machinery); James Brown (sculptured and carved ornament); Charles Wilson (wall and ceiling decorations in relief); William Clarke (wall and ceiling decorations in paint and paper); John Burnet (painted, stained and embossed glass); James Salmon (metallic castings, wrought iron, etc.); Alexander Thomson (marbles, mosaics, fountains and vases); John Baird (ornaments in porcelain, silver, cast and cut glass); Charles Heath Wilson (upholstery, carpets, tapestry and paper hangings); and J. T. Rochead (furniture). The architects for the exhibition hall were Baird & Thomson[38] and – to judge by the *Chronicle*'s comparisons between it and the Caledonia Road church – Thomson himself.

In Christmas week 1854, the Lord Provost of Glasgow received his Edinburgh counterpart, and the Provost and magistrates of Dundee, Lanark, Kilmarnock and ten other towns to an opening of speeches, choral music, a prayer from Dr Norman MacLeod, and a musical promenade.[39] He welcomed the 'magnificent hall, decorated in the most beautiful architectural style, and therein collected works of art worthy of a palace'. Edinburgh, in reply, congratulated Glasgow 'on the success which had attended this effort to provide a place of refined enjoyment, an exhibition which could not fail to lead to the most important result' (i.e. Glasgow would have the burden of a museum to carry before the capital did, hence the Lord Provost of Edinburgh's enthusiasm). In a vote of thanks to Glasgow architects, Sir James Campbell trusted that 'the result would be an improvement of our streets and buildings in Glasgow, and the general advancement of architectural art over the country'.

Heath Wilson, replying for the organising committee, urged that the collection 'might form a permanent museum where the taste might still be further cultivated and improved'. For all its wealth, Glasgow had no museum of its own, the revenues of his School of Design had been cut by 25 per cent, and the city's architects were jealous of London's Brompton Road exhibition. On 21 January 1855, Heath Wilson inaugurated the AIS's presence in the exhibition with a triumphal lecture on 'The Formation of Provincial Museums for Works of Art'. Hailing this 'auspicious day for the progress' for such ideas, he rejoiced that the Glasgow profession had 'placed before our countrymen an example of what might be undertaken'.[40] It was planned to have a life of three months.

Events were rescheduled to take place within this 'home for architecture and architects', and the AIS relocated its sessional programme to the Exhibition's Gallery (although the Glasgow Architectural Association remained sternly aloof in Angus's Temperance Coffee Rooms). There were soirées and tea meetings, and – following the lead of the McLellan Galleries, which had opened the previous year – cheap-price openings on Friday and Saturday, 12 and 13 October 1855, which attracted the largest single attendances of the exhibition's life.

The ground plan of the 'Scottish Exhibition' is shown on the first (1859) edition of the 1:500 Ordnance Survey of the city (see FIGURE 2.11), but no other drawings have yet been discovered of the building into which the Glasgow architectural profession invested its substance.[41] A retrospective analysis has to be based on letterpress descriptions. The Exhibition Hall lay on the south side of Bath Street, near the junction of Hope Street, upon a rectangular site 69 ft wide and 108 ft deep, with light entering from the east, but otherwise toplit. Thomson's façade was 'plain': an uphill door led into a spacious lofty two-storeyed top-lit saloon 'in which great pains had been taken and a considerable sum expended to embellish' – separated from aisles by square columns. The elegance of the brilliantly painted open timberwork of its roof – very much in the manner of Baird & Thomson's Caledonian Road church[42] – was much admired. Principal exhibits – a stupendous chimney-piece by Thomson, a statue of Wallace, immense pieces of glasswork and sculpture – lay in the saloon. Up spacious stairs were rooms for architectural models, photography, brass-rubbings and, along the east flank, the Great Gallery in which meetings took place.[43]

The east (downhill) aisle beneath the gallery was divided at ground level into four courts. No. 1 offered a miscellany, containing a pair of highly ornate chimney-pieces by Baird & Thomson, stained glass by Ballantine, and a 32-panelled ceiling with coloured scrolls on a white ground, painted with the names of celebrated architects by David Ramsay Hay. But it failed to attract the *Chronicle*'s enthusiasm. No. 2 was Greek; its designer Thomson. Reviewed (two months after opening) even in its unfinished state, the *Chronicle* admired the dwarf pilasters of the upper part of its walls (with a dash of Moorish), and the heavy, deep-moulded enriched capitals against a dark-blue background on which honeysuckle ornaments stood out. The coffers of the ceiling were touched with red and blue against a blue ceiling powdered with gilt stars. (Was it coincidence that Heath Wilson had given a lecture on 23 February 1854, in which he noted that 'the Greeks, a people incapable of bad taste' painted their temples externally as well as internally – 'glowing with vermilion, blue and gold'?) There was another fine chimney-piece, and a door with cap supported on slender detached pilasters.

The third court, by William Clarke, was Italian – 'a

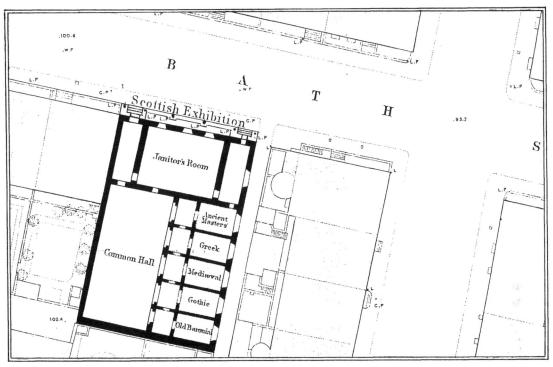

FIGURE 2.11   Ground plan of the Scottish Exhibition in Bath Street, from the first 1:500 Ordnance Survey, surveyed in 1858.

gay style of colour and decoration carried out very successfully' in contrast to John Burnet's sober Gothic library with its oaken ceiling and woodwork, green carpet with small white flowers, and green-and-crimson wallpaper. The Renaissance court by Hugh Bogle & Company contained only packing cases at the time of visit. In addition to the plaster casts so assiduously prepared and collected by Charles Heath Wilson, the architectural content was increased by the collection of architectural drawings from Dr Puttrich of Leipzig, which illumined the history of architecture. Of architectural photography – thought to be the coming thing – there was a profusion.

The Glasgow Architectural Exhibition earned the *Builder*'s encomium that Glasgow was 'the most go-ahead city in Great Britain'.[44] James Hay, President of the Liverpool Architectural Association, reported to his members how impressed he had been by the apartment 'in the Grecian character [which] particularly interested me as possessing a freshness and an originality of handling which exhibit the artist as thoroughly imbued with the chaste and classic feeling of that highly civilised and polished nation'.[45] He regretted that this 'very creditable exhibition ... has not met with the encouragement it so eminently merits, besides a prospect of its terminating in pecuniary loss to the projectors'.

Less animated by the architectural models and drawings (the *Chronicle* concurred, dismissing the brass-rubbings as a 'chamber of horrors' and the model room as poorly stocked – relieved only by the two models lent by Prince Albert), Hay bewailed the prominence of foreign examples to Scots – as might be expected from an architect who had built so well and so successfully in Scotland.

In the 6th AIS Annual Report, David Rhind, Chairman, was proud to claim patronage of the exhibition for the Institute:

the Council have every reason to believe it has been attended with much advantage in the way of spreading a knowledge and improving the taste, in the details of those branches of the arts which may be considered more immediately accessory to architectural study.

The exhibition was worthy of public countenance and support ... The Council confidently trust that the example thus given by their fellow countrymen in Glasgow may be followed in other localities.[46]

The Institute's countenance took the form of a promenade in the Exhibition Building on 21 January 1856, enlivened by Mr Agnew's band, after which members retired to the Gallery to listen to the different papers.

But what was a three-month exhibition doing still open in January 1856? Why had new machinery, drawings and models been added to it? It should have closed the previous April. One can only surmise that the Glasgow architects hung on as long as they could in trying to persuade the Council to take it over. Strenuous efforts were made to keep it alive, sometimes by adding new exhibits, sometimes simply by rearranging the deck-chairs.

It was all in vain. On 1 January 1857, the *Chronicle* reported that 'It is well known that the attempt to make this exhibition permanent has not been successful, and that the undertaking has involved its spirited and praiseworthy projectors in considerable pecuniary loss ... We understand that it has now been determined to wind up the whole affair, and dispose of the property in Bath Street. ...'[47]

The building was subsequently used as showrooms and then offices before giving way, in 1875, to another building by Thomson: the office block at 87–97 Bath Street (see FIGURE 2.12), which was itself demolished in 1970.

Unwise as it was for professionals to overreach themselves, Glasgow's architects knowingly accepted a financial risk in the hope that they would be bailed out either by overwhelming public attendance or by civic contribution. Unfortunately, irrespective of the stunning quality of the building, exhibits and events, their attempt to compel the authorities to a museum – decades before its time – failed.

Some interesting comparisons can be made between the Glasgow Architectural Exhibition in 1855–6, Glasgow's Glasgow in 1990, and the Environment Show Pavilion erected by the architectural profession in the Glasgow Garden Festival in 1988. All three attempted to communicate with the public, to offer education and an understanding of the history of architecture and of Glasgow, and to hold other events to increase their civic

purpose. The Glasgow Architectural Exhibition, however, enjoyed a main street frontage, and lasted eight times longer than its allotted span. In its stylistic promiscuity, it represented the uncertainties of the period – framed within the tight discipline of a Thomson building – as compared to the eclectic promiscuousness of the others.

A last dying echo of the building – and a penultimate item in the *Building Chronicle* itself – is a sour note of the meeting held in June 1857 in the (presumably empty) exhibition rooms to consider 'the state of the affairs of the Institute in Glasgow'. Attendance at meetings had been so poor that papers had been cancelled, and the Institute was suffering arrears from Glasgow members alone of £453 12s.[48] Although a Committee was appointed to consider grievances, the final issue of the *Building Chronicle*, August 1857, contains a letter from AIS Hon. Secretary, William Millar, refuting the statement that although Glasgow furnished one half of the AIS membership, it received little benefit as 'erroneous and contrary to the fact'.[49]

The *Building Chronicle* vanished from sight and, before long, so did the Architectural Institute's Glaswegian limb; the Scottish exhibition rooms also eventually disappeared, but not before they had been the birthplace of a new organisation in Glasgow which would eventually become the Glasgow Institute of Architects. Its founding members were the Glasgow members of the AIS and had all, with the exception of Honeyman, been deeply involved in the exhibition. It was called the Glasgow Architectural Society, and Alexander Thomson was soon to be its President.[50]

NOTES

1. The *Building Chronicle – a Journal of Architecture and the Arts*, Edinburgh, vol. 1, no. 1 (10 May 1854), p. 1.
2. Ibid., p. 23.
3. J. B., Aliquis, Senex, etc. (J. B. is John Buchanan), *Glasgow Past and Present*, Glasgow, 1851, p. 31: 'The Irish Huns, with their usual attendants, the piggeries, have defiled the side of the hill.'
4. The *Building Chronicle*, vol. 1, no. 8 (9 Nov. 1854), p. 99.
5. C. McKean, F. A. Walker, D. Walker, *Central Glasgow*, Edinburgh, 1989, p. 116.
6. Denholm James, *History of Glasgow*, Glasgow, 1798 and 1804.
7. *Views and Notices of Glasgow in Ancient Times*, Allan & Ferguson, Glasgow, 1847.

FIGURE 2.12 Thomson's office building at 87–97 Bath
Street on the site of the Scottish Exhibition, built in 1875 and
demolished in 1970.

8. Buchanan, *Glasgow*, p. 91.

9. Ibid., p. 12.

10. Ibid., p. 18.

11. The *Building Chronicle*, vol. 1, no. 4 (26 July 1854), p. 52.

12. Ibid., vol. 1, no. 8 (9 Nov. 1854), p. 108.

13. Ibid., vol. 1, no. 20 (1 Nov. 1855), p. 259.

14. Ibid., vol. 2, no. 23 (1 Feb. 1856), p. 20.

15. Ibid., vol. 2, no. 24 (1 Mar. 1856), p. 32.

16. Anon., *Chronicles of Gotham*, Glasgow, 1856.

17. Ibid., p. 24 ff.

18. Ibid., p. 73.

19. Buchanan, *Glasgow*, p. 142.

20. The *Building Chronicle*, vol. 1, no. 20 (1 Nov. 1855), p. 259.

21. The *Building Chronicle*, vol. 2, no. 41 (Aug. 1857), p. 238.

22. Buchanan, *Glasgow*, p. 9.

23. *Chronicles of Gotham*, p. 48.

24. Ronald McFadzean, *Life and Work of Alexander Thomson*, London, 1979, p. 62.

25. The *Building Chronicle*, vol. 1, no. 10 (1 Jan. 1855), p. 000.

26. Dr John Strang, *Glasgow and its Clubs*, Glasgow, 1856, p. 567.

27. The *Building Chronicle*, vol. 2, no. 37 (Apr. 1857), p. 185.

28. The *Building Chronicle*, vol. 2, no. 35 (1 Feb. 1857), p. 157.

29. Architectural Institute of Scotland, *Transactions*, Edinburgh, 1860, p. 3, Session Tenth and Eleventh Read to the Institute on 16 February 1860.

30. The *Building Chronicle*, no. 3 (1 Jan. 1854), p. 29.

31. Ibid., vol. 1, no. 21 (1 Nov. 1855), p. 268.

32. Ibid., vol. 1, no. 12 (1 Mar. 1855), p. 163.

33. Ibid., vol. 1, no. 4 (26 July 1854), p. 52.

34. Ibid., vol. 2, no. 25 (1 Apr. 1856), p. 44, Baird & Thomson. 'Those who have observed the roof of the galleries of the Bath Street exhibition will have an idea of its appearance when we say that the roofs of both buildings are by the same architects'.

35. Architectural Institute of Scotland, *Transactions*, Edinburgh, 1854, 5th Report of Council of Management, p. 7.

36. The *Building Chronicle*, vol. 1, no. 18 (1 Sept. 1855), p. 18.

37. Ibid., vol. 1, no. 1 (10 May 1854), p. 7.

38. Ibid., vol. 2, no. 25 (1 Apr. 1856), p. 44; ibid., vol. 1, no. 11 (1 Feb. 1855), p. 142.

39. Ibid., vol. 1, no. 18 (1 Sept. 1855), p. 228.

40. The *Building Chronicle*, vol. 1, no. 12 (Mar. 1855), pp. 154–6.

41. Ibid., vol. 2, no. 25 (1 Apr. 1856), p. 44.

42. Ibid., vol. 1, no. 11 (1 Feb. 1855), p. 142. Principal descriptions of the Exhibition and its buildings are to be found in the *Building Chronicle* as follows: vol. 1, no. 9 (5 Dec. 1854), pp. 114–5; vol. 1, no. 10 (1 Jan. 1855), p. 128; vol. 1, no. 11 (1 Feb. 1855), pp. 142–3; vol. 1, no. 12 (1 Mar. 1855), p. 157; vol. 1, no. 13 (1 Apr. 1855), pp. 169–70. Costs and administration are touched on in vol. 1, no. 18 (1 Sept. 1855), p. 229. Comment by the Glasgow Architectural Association, vol. 1, no. 21 (1 Dec. 1855), p. 268.

43. Ibid., vol. 1, no. 20 (1 Nov. 1855), p. 255.

44. *Builder*, 14 Apr. 1855, p. 172.

45. The *Building Chronicle*, vol. 1, no. 20 (1 Nov. 1855), p. 255.

46. Architectural Institute of Scotland, *Transactions*, Edinburgh, 1855, 6th Report of Council of Management, p. 7.

47. The *Building Chronicle*, vol. 2, no. 34 (1 Jan. 1857), p. 146.

48. Architectural Institute of Scotland, *Transactions*, Edinburgh, 1857, 8th Report of Council of Management, pp. 6 and 11.

49. The *Building Chronicle*, vol. 2, no. 41 (Aug. 1857), p. 243.

50. A. M. Doak, *The First Hundred Years of the Glasgow Institute of Architects*, 1968. After 1867, D. & J. Mclellan & Co. used the exhibition rooms as showrooms, and from 1872 to 1874 the building was the head office of John E. Walker, funeral director, before being demolished. In a letter to his brother George in the Cameroons dated 20 September 1872, Thomson recorded that, 'John E Walker sold his stables in Cambridge Street to the Tramways Company and bought the Exhibition Buildings in Bath Street which I converted into Coach House below and stables for about 70 horses above which is now in full operation . . .'

.

Chapter Three

THE DEVELOPMENT OF THOMSON'S STYLE
THE SCOTTISH BACKGROUND

David M. Walker

Neither Alexander Thomson in his own writings nor Thomas Gildard in his recollections of him give much hint of how Thomson built up the elements of his mature style. We know that he admired Harvey Lonsdale Elmes's St George's Hall, Liverpool and the architecture in the paintings of John Martin; that he was interested in the publications of James Fergusson; and very little more. But however much of Thomson's inspiration came from German sources, and in particular Schinkel's *Sammlung*, at least some of his ideas were developed from the work of architects much nearer home.

When Thomson's family moved into Glasgow from Balfron in 1825, much of the architecture of the seventeenth- and earlier eighteenth-century city remained and was to survive for most of his lifetime. Of these earlier buildings only those of Allan Dreghorn (1706–64) are likely to have been of more than antiquarian interest to him. St Andrew's church (1739–56)[1] he is likely to have respected for its sheer scale and absolutely regular temple-like form. Unlike those of the comparable London churches of the same generation, the portico at St Andrew's was of the same width as the church. Its steps were contained within massive retaining walls extruded from the plinth of the pilastraded flank elevations, suggesting that Dreghorn knew of the Maison Carrée at Nîmes. Dreghorn's Town Hall (1737) as extended from its original Old Somerset House-like five bays to ten in 1758–60[2] – a composition sufficiently unusual for Dreghorn to have demonstrated what the effect would be in a fine elevational model carved in wood[3] – had the same absolutely logical treatment as St Andrew's, its even repetition of Ionic pilastered bays, differentiated only by the alter-

nating pediments of the first-floor windows, forming the original prototype of Glasgow's pilastered commercial façades of the next century, not least Thomson's own (see FIGURE 3.2). It certainly had something of 'the mysterious power of the horizontal element' he so admired. Dreghorn's other known work, his seven-bay pedimented mansion on Clyde Street (1752),[4] which he modelled on Colen Campbell's Shawfield Mansion,[5] is unlikely to have had any particular lesson for him, although the way in which it and its eastern giant-order neighbour – probably also Dreghorn's work – each formed a symmetrical composition between three pavilions, the central pavilion being mutual, must have appealed to his ingenious mind.[6] Of the fourteen other great five- and seven-bay pedimented villas of the tobacco era the only one likely to have been of particular interest to him was the mansion of James Ewing of Strathleven, the site of which is now occupied by Queen Street Station. Its doorpiece, re-erected in the walled garden at Blair Tummock (see FIGURE 3.3), is remarkable in that its Corinthian columns are set not in antis but in a rich architrave frame, a device favoured not only by Thomson but also by the younger Burnet well into the present century. Although similar in its robust Roman character to Dreghorn's work, it was built long after Dreghorn's death for Baillie George Crawford in 1778–80.[7]

Thomson's thoughts on Robert and James Adam's late Glasgow public buildings of the 1790s are not recorded. Neither the Infirmary with its canted and domed centrepiece nor the Trades House, with its elevation cut up into single-bayed elements, seems likely to have had much appeal for him.[8] The more unified and monumental columnar treatment of the

FIGURE 3.1   St Jude's Episcopal Church, West George
Street, Glasgow, by John Stephen, 1840.

FIGURE 3.2 Town Hall, later the Tontine Hotel, Trongate,
Glasgow, by Allan Dreghorn, 1737–60, demolished, photo
c. 1890.

Assembly Rooms, and the logical pediment-gabled
roof treatment of the University residences on High
Street are more likely to have impressed.[9]

The early years of the nineteenth century were
dominated by David Hamilton (1768–1843), Peter
Nicholson (1765–1844) and the slightly younger William Stark (1770–1813). Hamilton's early work was
markedly influenced by Robert Adam, for whom he
must have worked in some capacity, since the folios of
his drawings – now in the University of Glasgow
collection – show that he had access to unpublished
projects. There is no evidence of him in the surviving
Adam correspondence, and his acquaintance with
them may have been as stonecarver rather than as
architectural assistant, his father William having been a
stonemason; David himself was admitted to the Incorporation of Masons in 1800. Somehow he also acquired
a knowledge of Sir John Soane's practice which ex-

tended far beyond what could have been gleaned from
the short-lived house that master designed in 1798 for
Robert Dennistoun on Buchanan Street,[10] and of late
eighteenth-century French work. Most of these early
works of Hamilton's, several of which demonstrated
considerable ingenuity in the late Adam idiom, have no
real significance in relation to the development of
Thomson's style and need not be discussed here. The
most influential for the future was his Theatre Royal
of 1805 in Queen Street.[11] It had a five-bay front, the
upper façade of which had distyle porticos – presumably derived from those of Adam's Assembly Rooms –
framing a distyle in antis colonnade. With the order at
the central bays reduced to pilasters, it was to provide
the basic concept for David Bryce's Edinburgh and
Leith Bank in Edinburgh (1841), a building which, as
will be set out later, was to have some relevance to the
development of Thomson's style.

FIGURE 3.3   Doorpiece from the Glasgow house of James
Ewing of Strathleven, as re-erected in the walled garden at
Blair Tummock.

Peter Nicholson arrived in Glasgow from London in
1800 and stayed only eight years.[12] He seems to have
been largely self-taught and his career was more significant for its contribution to building science than to
architecture. Nevertheless he has a particular place in
any account of the development of the Greek Revival in
Scotland and had a direct link with Thomson. The
pedimented central houses of his Carlton Place development (1802) were the first pure Greek in Glasgow,
pedimented with a giant heptastyle anta order and
Greek Doric columned porches which expressed the
twin three-bay houses behind them – an unorthodox
but absolutely logical arrangement which Nicholson
probably considered to have sufficient authority in
antiquity from the Choragic Monument of Thrasyllus.
Their austere monumental concept contrasts strangely
with the splendours of the rich plasterwork of late
eighteenth-century character in the Laurie houses at
Nos. 51–2.[13] Similarly Greek Doric, with an attached
tetrastyle portico at first-floor level, was Nicholson's

Hamilton Building at the Old College, not executed
until 1811–13, some years after he had left Glasgow, by
John Brash who made some minor modifications to the
design.[14]

Thomson would certainly have owned the most
relevant, if not all, of Nicholson's books. As Howard
Colvin has observed, Nicholson 'used his great ability
as a mathematician to simplify many old formulae used
by architectural draughtsmen as well as devise new
ones' which led to his publications being widely acquired by practices unimpressed by their author's
architecture.

Several of Nicholson's books had illustrations by his
son Michael Angelo Nicholson (c.1796–1841) whose
daughters Jane and Jessie married Alexander Thomson
and his partner to be, John Baird (who was unrelated to
Thomson's employer of the same name), respectively,
on 21 September 1847, some six years after their
father's death and three after their grandfather's. It is
unlikely that Thomson had any direct contact with
either of them.[15]

Presumably initially trained by his father, Michael
Angelo was sent to study architectural drawing in the
school run by Richard Brown in London before being
articled to the distinguished practice of John Foulston
in Plymouth.[16] Thereafter he must have spent some
time with William Burn, as he was able to publish the
drawings of Burn's Carstairs House for Sir Henry
Monteith, which he claimed as his own; it can only be
assumed that it was executed under his supervision and
that he made many of the detail drawings.[17]

Of the other designs published in his father's *New
Practical Builder* his 'Church in the Grecian Style'
reflected in geometrically elaborated and spired form
the Inwoods' St Pancras church, conveniently near his
drawing academy off Euston Square. Its door and
window openings have the rosetted Erechtheum
architraves favoured by both Stephen and Thomson. A
second church design ('A Chapel') with a recessed
distyle in antis Greek Doric portico in the centre of a
three-bay pedimented front provided the model for
John Dick Peddie's fine Greek Corinthian Sydney
Place UP Church in Glasgow's Duke Street in 1857.[18]
More relevant to Thomson was Michael Angelo's
scheme for 'Mausoleum P' (see FIGURE 3.4) in which
Greek Ionic porticos were set high on a wider substructure of channelled rustication. In it one can perhaps see

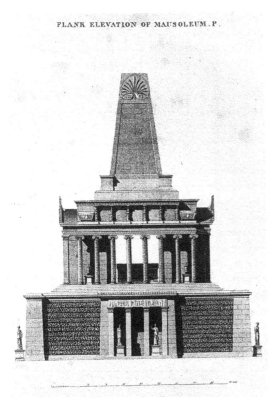
FLANK ELEVATION OF MAUSOLEUM.P.

FIGURE 3.4 Side elevation of the design for 'Mausoleum P' by Michael Angelo Nicholson, engraving from Peter Nicholson's *New Practical Builder*, 1825.

the germ of the idea for both Caledonia Road church and St Vincent Street church.

Particular relevance also attaches to the work of William Stark, the son of a minor Midlothian landowner with linen interests in Dunfermline and Glasgow. Of his professional training we know all too little despite the existence of a family memoir and several contemporary references to his genius.[19] From his Calton report of 1813 we learn that he had apparently seen Amsterdam,[20] probably *en route* to St Petersburg where he was resident in 1798 and which gave him a unique view of international classicism as practised there by Paul I's French, Italian and Russian architects. By 1803 he had settled in Glasgow and in 1804 he successfully competed against David Hamilton for the Hunterian Museum. Its deep Roman Doric portico, approached by steps contained between massive walls as at St Andrew's, won the admiration of his contemporaries

but had little discernible influence on the development of Thomson's style.[21] Much more relevant was his St George's Tron church on Buchanan Street, designed in 1807.[22] English baroque sources have been suggested for the diagonally buttressed tower with obelisk finials flanking a peristyle rising into an open-work crown capped by a further obelisk. The origins of the design are at least as likely to be Russian, which would perhaps have been more evident had the obelisks been statues as originally intended, or possibly Dutch. Although Thomson invariably preferred the lower stages of his towers to be uncompromisingly simple and square, St George's probably provided the basic idea for the upper stages of the tower of his St Vincent Street church. Stark may also have provided the profile of its pointed domical top in the glazed dome of his extraordinary radial-plan Glasgow Asylum (1810)[23] even if the influence of James Fergusson's illustrations of Hindu architecture should certainly not be discounted.

As a Greek Revivalist, Stark was later in the field than Nicholson, but his work was to be more significant for the future. In 1805 he made a design for a school at Greenock. It combined a Greek Doric portico with rather Soanic round-arched openings and a low dome, the drum of which was to have had a somewhat Roman swagged frieze.[24] It remained on paper, but in 1809 he designed and built the Judiciary Buildings and South Prison at Glasgow Green, following some sort of limited competition with David Hamilton and Robert Reid.[25] Its façade was much more correctly Greek than the Greenock design, eschewing arched openings entirely. Channelled in the French manner, it had a hexastyle Greek Doric portico – the first use of that order in giant form in Scotland and the second in the United Kingdom. The portico was no doubt suggested by that of Smirke's Covent Garden Theatre in London, built in the previous year,[26] but the composition as a whole derived mainly from Thomas Harrison's Assize Courts at Chester Castle, the corresponding section of which had been completed in 1801.[27] Chester also provided the main feature of the internal plan, a colonnaded hemicycle courtroom immediately behind the portico. Whether Stark had visited Chester or obtained plans of it from the City Surveyor, James Cleland – who made a tour of English and Irish courthouses and 'principal jails' in 1808 – is not known.

The west elevation of the prison seems to have been

of an extraordinary monumentality which challenged comparison with George Dance's Newgate, having a three-bay centrepiece of shallow receding arches between massive pylons.[28] One may be reasonably confident that Thomson admired the marked horizontality and purity of Stark's main elevation even though he himself never used the Doric order; he certainly praised the portico in his 1866 lecture.[29]

David Hamilton's parallel design, one of three submitted by him of which the other two were three-storeyed with similar centrepieces at the two upper storeys, was surprisingly similar in elevation to Stark's.[30] The main differences were at the end pavilions which were less wide and emphatic, and at the central pavilion which was to have had a tetrastyle Greek Doric portico projected from flanking bays of antae in place of Stark's full-width hexastyle portico. Returning the portico on to the façade in pilastered form for one bay only on either side was to be a recurring theme in Hamilton's work, to be seen at St Enoch's church and the Normal School late in his career. In certain respects, Hamilton's design was an even purer Grecian than Stark's, the channel-jointing being omitted and the openings emphasised by corniced architraves. The design was repeated in reduced form in his competition design for the County Buildings at Ayr[31] where he was again unsuccessful, the Ionic design submitted by the London Scottish architect Robert Wallace being preferred. Greek Doric also was Hamilton's Town Building, Port Glasgow (1815–16), where his scheme superseded one by William Burn.[32] It bears a spire similar to his Town Steeple at Falkirk (1813–14)[33] which in turn was quite remarkably similar to Burn's at North Leith church (1813–16),[34] inaugurating a tenuous and somewhat impenetrable stylistic link between their practices which was to be in evidence again in the 1840s. Whose design the spire was in the first instance, beyond a certain affinity with Francis Johnston's St George's Dublin (1802–14), is difficult to establish for certain.

By the time Thomson was apprenticed, these Greek designs were almost twenty years old. Graeco-Roman had begun to supersede Greek in Glasgow in the late 1820s and from 1840 onwards mainstream Glasgow architecture was Italian, whether Germanic cinquecento like Charles Wilson's or Barryesque like J. T. Rochead's. To his Glasgow contemporaries in the mid-

1850s Thomson must have seemed to be seeking inspiration more than a decade in the past. But in Edinburgh – even though the architecture of Burn, Bryce and Rhind had become progressively more Barryesque from 1834 onwards – Thomas Hamilton and William Henry Playfair had kept the Hellenic light burning late into the 1840s with their schemes for the National Gallery, and there was in fact rather more contact between the Glasgow and Edinburgh architects than the marked divisions in their clientele would seem to suggest. When David Hamilton died in 1843, William Henry Playfair wrote his son James a touching letter of condolence referring to his 'most excellent father' which leaves one in no doubt that he knew them at first hand. From 1850, when the failed (and very much Edinburgh-based) Institute of Architects in Scotland was refounded as the Architectural Institute of Scotland of which Thomson was a member, there was regular contact between the premier Edinburgh and Glasgow practitioners with, perhaps, the opportunity to see unpublished projects on visits to each other's offices.[35]

Although it was from the work of these premier practices that Thomson's individual style developed, it was by observation rather than direct contact. Thomson received his professional training in the offices of Robert Foote (d. 1854) and John Baird (1798–1859). Foote was the son of David Foote & Son, plasterers and stucco merchants. Soon after he became sole partner in 1827, he set up practice as an architect as well. The Footes were well off and, alone among Scottish architects of the time, Robert had not only made the Grand Tour but had reached Greece. He had also built up a large collection of classical casts and an important library which may have included the German publications from which much of Thomson's style derived. Only one building by Foote, a three-storey astylar block at 82–90 Buchanan Street, is known. A photograph of 1884 at the People's Palace shows it to have been dated 1832 and a much more interesting design than it is generally given credit for, with a very deep plain parapet under the still surviving central block pediment. The detail was simple but refined, with inclined Graeco-Egyptian Vitruvian architraves (original and not inserted as the *Buildings of Scotland: Glasgow* volume suggests)[36] very close-spaced at the outer bays with just a hint of the close-ordered

Thomson rhythms to come. Foote suffered from a disease of the spine and withdrew from practice in 1836, when Thomson was placed with Baird to complete his apprenticeship. Foote's influence extended far beyond that date, however, as Thomas Gildard recorded accounts of Thomson's visits to his house at Helensburgh and of excursions on which Foote had to be carried. Foote reopened his practice in 1842, only to close it permanently in 1847.[37]

In Baird's office Thomson's experience is more likely to have been practical than theoretical. Baird's own professional training was amongst the shortest on record since he inherited the practice of an uncle, Shepherd, at the age of 20 in 1818.[38] Nevertheless he was a very competent classicist: his Roman Doric Greyfriars United Presbyterian Church on Albion Street (1821),[39] a galleried rectangle with a tetrastyle portico of fluted and filleted columns, was finely designed and executed, if not particularly imaginative. Much the same could be said of his Wellington United Presbyterian Church (1825) (see FIGURE 14.2),[40] very similar in concept but pure Greek with an Ilissus Ionic order as at William Burn's North Leith church a decade earlier. The flank elevation had a giant order of antae at the end bays only, a Smirke device frequently adopted by Burn. Thomson evidently thought well of it as it is referred to in his 1866 lecture.

By the time Thomson entered Baird's office, Wellington church was eleven years in the past. A much more austere work which may have had some relevance to Thomson's own style was Anderston United Presbyterian Church (1839) (see FIGURE 3.5),[41] again similar in basic concept but with a pedimented tetrastyle frontispiece, the close-spaced antae of which framed three doors with the severest of entablatures threaded through the pilaster shafts. In it we can perhaps see a hint of the bay design of Thomson's warehouse on Dunlop Street and his Washington Hotel on Sauchiehall Street. In 1842 Baird designed Claremont House, a three-storey and basement five-bay mansion with a porch of coupled Ionic columns, subsequently expanded into Claremont Terrace, a shallow crescent of terrace houses, in 1847.[42] The porches of the later houses are rather more imaginative than that of the original house, with a bolder projection from the façade. Although Thomson probably worked on them, the Ionic order is of the same Ilissus type as at Welling-

FIGURE 3.5   Anderston United Presbyterian Church, by John Baird I, 1839, demolished, photo from Aikman, *Historical Notices of the United Presbyterian Congregations in Glasgow*, 1875.

ton church with a single face to the architrave rather than the three Thomson more usually adopted in his own practice. Thomson used the Ilissus order only in his later years at Great Western Terrace and, with a still more simplified entablature, at Westbourne.

Much of Thomson's time in his later years at Baird's is known to have been spent on the various Jacobean schemes for the unbuilt University buildings on Woodlands Hill.[43] No doubt he also worked on Cairnhill, Airdrie (1841)[44] and the additions to Stonebyres[45] of about the same date, both also Jacobean in style; and less profitably on Baird's old-fashioned Burn-type Tudor houses at Birkwood[46] and Urie.[47] Baird's work after Thomson's departure was perhaps more significant. In his *Victorian City*, Francis Worsdall ascribes to him the remarkable three-storey two-bay commercial building at 66 Buchanan Street of about 1851.[48] This has hints of David Hamilton's late style and of Thomson's own style about it, particularly at the second-floor windows which have inclined architraves and are divided by slim Thomson-like cast-iron columns answered by half shafts inset in the architraves, a treatment repeated at the wider pilastered first-floor openings beneath. One is left wondering if perhaps it was designed rather earlier than 1851 while Thomson was still in the office, or whether, as newly set-up architects then often did, he took in work from his former employer. Perhaps Thomson's most useful contact from Baird's office was the ironfounder Robert

McConnel, whose patent beams Baird and his partner-to-be James Thomson (1835–1910) used at the iron-façaded building at 36 Jamaica Street (1855).[49] McConnel's beams made Thomson's Buck's Head buildings on Argyle Street and Dunlop Street (1862–3) possible, and it may well be that – as first built – his Gordon Street building (1859) had them also.

The key to Thomson's commercial façade designs lies not with Baird but with the later work of David Hamilton and of his son James (1818–61). From 1822 onward David Hamilton was engaged on the enlargement and reconstruction of Hamilton Palace for Alexander, 10th Duke of Hamilton who had succeeded in 1819. In greatly enlarged and neoclassicised form it implemented the scheme for a Corinthian porticoed north front planned by William Adam some eighty years earlier[50] and superseded a late Adam-school design with a castle-type plan made by Hamilton for the previous Duke shortly after he succeeded in 1799.[51] The 10th Duke had been ambassador to St Petersburg and from 1810 was the son-in-law of William Beckford who had forsaken gothic for neoclassic in his old age. In 1804 the Duke had obtained designs for a riding-school and a Turkish *Khiosk* from Giacomo Quarenghi, and in 1810 appears to have commissioned from him a scheme for the north front of the palace itself. In 1819 he commissioned further designs for the palace from Luigi Poletti and Francesco Saponeri in Rome. Of these, Saponeri's design has survived to show that it was essentially the selected design, enlarged by end pavilions which in some degree anglicised its Alexandrian empire character. The final drawings for the façade are undated but the carcass of the building seems to have been complete by about 1826. The completion of the interior, for which the Duke obtained designs by Charles Percier in Paris from September 1827, continued into the 1840s. In the event, Percier's designs were not used, but their detailing greatly extended Hamilton's repertoire of neoclassical detail. In the fitting-out of the interior, Hamilton worked in association with the London decorator and dealer Robert Hume, who had already been used by Beckford, from at least 1829. Hume's long-standing involvement with the palace, in the end apparently more as contractor than as designer since what existed related to his designs only at the reworking of Percier's scheme for the tribune, has already been detailed by Professor

Tait and need not be repeated here.[52] Sufficient is it to say that the Great Entrance Hall (1834–6) and the Black Marble Stair (1838 onwards) were unmistakably in Hamilton's style while the Dining-Room (1833) had elements of both.

At first sight, Hamilton Palace (see FIGURE 3.6) might not seem to have any bearing on the development of Thomson's style. But at the elevation behind the hexastyle portico, two columns deep with 25 ft monoliths of polished Dalserf stone, was a façade treatment which did not appear in the Saponeri design and was to be very significant for the future. Threaded through the giant pilasters was a subsidiary pilastrade framing the central door and main-floor windows of the great entrance hall. Within, as executed by Hamilton, the treatment of the great double-height entrance hall was consistent with the portico except that the giant pilasters were fluted, the subsidiary pilastrade framing doors, chimney-pieces and niches on the internal walls.

At the reconstruction of the Cunninghame mansion on Glasgow's Queen Street as the Royal Exchange in 1827–9 the elements of the Hamilton Palace portico were developed further. The main portico was even bigger and richer than that at the Palace, although similarly of the Castor and Pollux order with capitals sculpted by James Fillans.[53] Within, the Corinthian columned hall has a richly coffered segmental ceiling which is clearly a by-product of schemes for Hamilton. But the main interest of the design in relation to Thomson lies in the refacing of the Cunninghame mansion behind the portico. A giant order of pilasters of Soanic 'picturesque period' character was applied to it, the ground-floor openings being formed by a subsidiary order of pilasters threaded through it while the upper windows were set in heavily pedimented architrave frames. Thereafter the use of the giant and subsidiary pilaster motif developed rapidly. It appeared again nearby, now at first- and second-floor levels, at the Corinthian pilastered McLellan building at 151–7 Queen Street (1834) (see FIGURE 2.1), not documented but unmistakably in Hamilton's style; at the Ionic pilastered corner pavilions of Royal Exchange Square which appear to be a David Hamilton and James Smith redesign of the Archibald Elliot II and Robert Black scheme between 1830 and 1839;[54] and again at the Corinthian centre and end pavilions of Robert Black's Adelaide Place scheme on Bath Street of 1839.[55] In

FIGURE 3.6   Hamilton Palace, reconstructed by David
Hamilton, 1822–6, photo *c*.1895.

Edinburgh, probably thanks to his links with Glasgow through his brother John, it appeared in David Bryce's Corinthian pilastered Edinburgh and Leith Bank at the corner of George and Hanover Streets in 1841,[56] and, set back as a continuous pilastrade behind a free-standing colonnade, at the same architect's Caledonian Insurance Building of 1839, also on George Street.[57] The last also provided the general arrangement of the Merchants' House (see FIGURE 2.6) section of his ex-draughtsmen William Clarke and George Bell's City and County Buildings of 1844 – of which more later – and Bryce's own Dublin Standard Assurance Building of 1853 on O'Connell Street.[58]

The pilastered versions of these designs provided the basic bay arrangement of Thomson's Dunlop Street (see FIGURE 3.7) and Washington Hotel, Sauchiehall Street, buildings and – in a much more developed form – the germ of the concept of his Gordon Street and Union Street buildings. Now that the discovery of McConnel patent beams (when the Dunlop Street building was demolished) has confirmed Dr Ronald McFadzean's conclusion that it was not the building

which caused the Dean of Guild Court so much deliberation in 1849 – despite having flues in the pilasters venting into ornamental chimney pots seemingly as described[59] – we know that the progression of Thomson's façade design is not as straightforward as Andor Gomme and the present writer had supposed it to be in 1968. One is left to conclude that Dunlop Street was a later reworking of the original idea to meet the requirements of a much lower budget for façading.

Thomson's Dunlop Street and Washington Hotel elevations were of course much more ruthlessly logical than those of Hamilton, Black and Bryce in that at second-floor level the glazing was from pilaster to pilaster, without any intervening masonry to form a conventional window opening. But there can be little doubt that it was from Hamilton, and from his Queen Street building in particular, that he developed the concept. Where Hamilton originally got the idea from is far from clear. In his unexecuted designs for the enlargement of Grosvenor House, London, Smirke proposed an exactly similar treatment of the portico elevation to that of Hamilton Palace, but unless there

FIGURE 3.7   Thomson's Dunlop Street warehouse, c.1859, largely demolished, photo 1961.

was a very late redesign at Hamilton, the date, 1827, seems too late to be helpful.[60] Smirke did, however, use giant and subsidiary orders in a much less consistent way as incidents in the overall design, as at the Royal College of Physicians (now Canada House), London (1822–5)[61] and at the Council House, Bristol (1824),[62] while the three-bay sections of superimposed pilastrades set in pilaster strips at Normanby Park (1825–30)[63] suggest that he was familiar with Schinkel's published designs for the Berlin Schauspielhaus of 1819.

Smirke apart, the motif was uncommon in English architecture at the time despite its use by Palladio at the Palazzo Valmarana, Vicenza; by Michelangelo at the Capitoline Palaces in Rome; and nearer home, by Wren at Winchester Palace, by Vanbrugh at Blenheim and by Dr Clarke at Christ Church Library, Oxford. It appears in the context of an attached Greek Doric tetrastyle portico at Richard Lane's Salford Town Hall

of 1825,[64] and in a more vestigial form at the attached Greek Ionic porticos of Decimus Burton's Grove House (1822)[65] and James Lansdown's Stratherne Lodge (1828)[66] in Regent's Park, London. Much closer to David Hamilton's use of it at Queen Street is John Pinch's block on the west side of Queen Square, Bath (1830).[67] It does not, however, quite have the absolute logic of his Queen Street building as the central bays have attached Ionic columns rather than pilasters, while the ground floor is of conventional channelled rustication. At Charles Underwood's excellent Worcester Terrace, Clifton, Bristol,[68] the same consistently pilastered and trabeated treatment as at the Queen Street building was achieved. At 1851 it is much too late to have any relevance to Hamilton's work, but it is possible that Thomson may have been aware of it. Other late examples of the motif tend to be the work of secondary rather than leading figures, notably Henry Briant at the Greek Ionic Royal Berkshire Hospital at Reading (1837) where it is used behind a free-standing portico.[69]

In 1835, David Hamilton and his son James designed the Normal – later Dundas Vale – School, in New City Road, the original proportions of which have been somewhat masked by a later dormered mansard attic.[70] It was not perhaps a masterpiece but marked the beginning of a still more individualistic approach to style. The main block was of two storeys and five bays with round-arched keyblocked windows and a bracket cornice, flanked by pyramid-roofed three-bay pilastered pavilions again with keyblocked arched windows which suggest that he had had a look at Thomas Hamilton's Dean Orphanage, Edinburgh, of two years earlier.[71] The most interesting feature of the design was, however, the couple-columned portico which – as at his rebuilding of St Enoch's church, Glasgow as a severe classic rectangle in 1827[72] – is integrated with the pilasters framing the flanking windows. But at the Normal School the Doric columns were not merely square as at Thomas Hamilton's Arthur Lodge, Edinburgh[73] but intaken some distance below the capitals to produce a telescopic profile. The main roof was originally also of the same low pyramidal form as those of the wings, but truncated by the tower, the consoled top and Lysicrates finial of which showed an interest in the possibilities of picturesque classical profiles. Its inspiration may again derive from Thomas

Hamilton, who incorporated a tower of similar picturesque classic profile in his school of 1829 at
Kinghorn.[74]

In 1839–43 Hamilton and his son James designed
the Western Club House and four banks in Glasgow, all
of individual design and some of them at least probably
related to an extensive continental tour made by James
in or about 1840.[75] Of these, the British Linen Bank at
110 Queen Street[76] had astylar Italianate façades linked
by a boldly circled corner. As at their Cleland Testimonial Building at the corner of Buchanan and
Sauchiehall Streets in 1835,[77] the drum turning the
corner was recessed to achieve considerably more than
half a circle within the line of the façades. It differed
from the London and Newcastle drum corners of the
period which curved outwards over the line of the
pavement, and from the Edinburgh and Aberdeen
circled corners which never achieved more than a third
of a circle. Hamilton's treatment of the bowed angle
was paralleled in a number of German designs of the
period[78] and in one of Simpson's alternative designs for
the North of Scotland Bank in Aberdeen.[79] It was a
proportion of bow Thomson himself was to favour even
if in a quite different context.

Related in design were the Clydesdale Bank on
Queen Street (see FIGURE 3.8) and the Western Bank on
Miller Street, which had boldly corniced three-storey
and basement cube façades of rather similar proportion. The Clydesdale[80] was the more orthodox in its
architecture. It was three bays wide with shallow rectangular tripartites, Roman Doric pilastered at ground-
floor level to answer the central portico into which they
were integrated, an arrangement developed – as at the
Normal School – from his portico at St Enoch's church.
These tripartite bays differed from conventional late
Georgian tripartite windows in having lights of equal
width, and rose through two storeys only against the
otherwise severe three-storey façade. Although frequently adopted by Burn in his neo-Jacobean country
houses, such rectangular bays were uncommon in
classical architecture at the time and still more so in
commercial buildings. Even if of much shallower projection, they were probably the precursors of Thomson's rectangular bays. The general concept of the
Clydesdale Bank, in a much more developed three-
dimensional form, was adopted by Thomson in his end
elevations at Great Western Terrace. Whether Hamil-

FIGURE 3.8   Clydesdale Bank, Queen Street, Glasgow, by
David & James Hamilton, 1840, demolished, photo c. 1895.

ton developed the idea from Playfair's country house
designs, of which more below, or possibly from some
German source, is difficult to say. David Bryce, ever

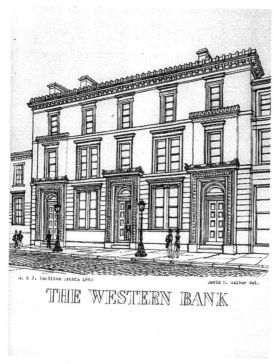

THE WESTERN BANK

FIGURE 3.9   The Western Bank in Miller Street, Glasgow, by D. & J. Hamilton, 1840, demolished.

quick to adopt a useful idea, incorporated a pilastered rectangular bay, more of Playfair than Hamilton type, into the ground-floor frontage of his Insurance Company of Scotland Building at 95 George Street, Edinburgh in 1840,[81] skilfully combining it with a boldly consoled balcony as at Burn's New Club of 1834 in the same city.[82]

Hamilton's Western Bank (see FIGURE 3.9),[83] of five bays, was even more individual than the Clydesdale, both in composition and in detail. The centre and end bays had huge architraved doorpieces with *diamanté* ornaments. Above the outer doorpieces were shallow battered projecting bays with single windows which died into the wall at second-floor level. At the ground- and first-floor levels of the second and fourth bays were two-light windows formed by a central anta pilaster dividing an architrave frame, a motif presumably of German origin and one subsequently adopted by Thomson. At the top floor, as at the Clydesdale, identical single-light top-floor windows ran in an even rhythm unifying the façade beneath, a Thomson device seen at Westbourne Terrace and elsewhere.

Somewhat similar in concept to these was the much larger Western Club[84] on Buchanan Street, which exemplified a very different approach to Italianate design from Barry's. As at the Western Bank the rhythm of its five bays is uneven: the centre three are regular, but the broad minimally advanced end bays have late classical tripartites through two storeys. The lower tripartites rise into cantilever brackets bearing balconies, a device seen in Playfair's houses of the late 1820s – discussed below – but richer in detail. Their projection answers that of the portico which has square coupled columns with Graeco-Roman Corinthian capitals emphasising the massive rectangularity and robust character of the overall design. Above, identical single-light second-floor windows with baroque architraves and a deep bracketed crowning entablature containing an attic – derived, as Elizabeth Williamson has pointed out, from the entablature of the Palazzo Doria Pamphilii at Genoa – unify the façade beneath as at the Western Bank.[85] Hamilton's interior was largely reconstructed by John Honeyman in 1871[86] but photographs taken just before it was gutted indicate at least one ceiling of similar character to those at Hamilton Palace.[87]

The Hamiltons' last major building was the refronting of the Virginia mansion on Ingram Street as the Union Bank (see FIGURE 3.19).[88] A five-bay Roman Doric portico of American plantation house-like proportions was stretched across the building with statuary punctuating the balustraded balcony at second-floor level. It acted as a screen to the main façade rather on the principle of that of Playfair's Surgeons' Hall in Edinburgh, the central three bays being balustraded off from the pavement between elevated plinths, and the end bays gated. Within were architraved openings of the Erechtheum type favoured by both Stephen and Thomson. The top floor had a dwarf pilastraded treatment, Schinkel fashion, advanced and pedimented at the three central bays. It may have been less original in detail than the Clydesdale Bank and the Western Club, but its singular concept and sheer grandeur were a tribute to the experimental approach of the Hamilton practice.

Of James Hamilton's contemporaries in Glasgow, John Stephen (c.1807–50) had the most original mind. Nothing is recorded of his professional training, but by 1834, at the age of 27, he was a partner in the

FIGURE 3.10 The Union Bank in Ingram Street, Glasgow, refronted by D. & J. Hamilton, 1841.

FIGURE 3.12 Flanking wings of the Blythswood Testimonial School, photo 1966.

FIGURE 3.11 Blythswood Testimonial School, Renfrew, by John Stephen, 1840, demolished, photo 1966.

architectural and civil engineering practice of Scott, Stephen and Gale. Robert Scott, his senior partner, described as of 'The Architectural Academy' Glasgow, had first appeared as a subscriber to Nicholson's *Architectural Dictionary* in 1819, and it may be that Stephen had been one of his pupils.[89] In 1840 he won the competition for the Blythswood Testimonial School in Renfrew (see FIGURES 3.11 and 3.12).[90] Its central pavilion with a tetrastyle Greek Doric portico surmounted by a tower composed of superimposed variations on the themes of the Choragic Monument of Lysicrates and the Tower of the Winds – a slimmed and simplified version of the Inwoods' tower at St Pancras – was relatively orthodox, the total effect being reminiscent of some of Michael Angelo Nicholson's designs. Stephen's individual approach to design was more evident in the flanking wings which had window pilastrades, severe uncorniced block entablatures and dramatic Egyptian doorpieces at the end elevations. The slightly earlier lodge at Sighthill Cemetery (1839)[91] had developed these themes further. A single-storey rectangular building of temple-like form, it anticipated a number of Thomson motifs. The entrance gable had a recessed distyle Greek Doric portico set in a severe broad architrave frame crowned by a pedimental block entablature; that towards the cemetery a similar arrangement with an anta-pilastered window

FIGURE 3.13 St Jude's Episcopal Church, West George Street, Glasgow, by John Stephen, 1840, photo c.1880.

peristyle. The themes of the main elevation were echoed in miniature at the small porches on its return elevations while the windows of the flanking bays had the same exaggeratedly tall proportions and inclined architraves of the central doorpiece, the anta order again bearing block entablatures which oversailed the line of the pilaster shafts. The flank elevations were severe but distinctive, the upper windows having plain architraves which drop to contain the cills. The glazing was of distinctive proportion throughout with margin panes.

Although Hamilton had used small-scale block pediments at his Cleland Testimonial Building, Stephen's Egyptic Greek had rather more in common with that of the older Dumfries architect Walter Newall who similarly favoured pedimental block entablatures, if never on quite so bold a scale, as can be seen at his Observatory of 1834 (now the Museum) there,[93] and in a lesser degree in his houses of which the most important seems to be the central clerestory-towered Granton House, near Moffat. Whether or not there was any connection between Newall and Stephen remains to be established. By 1845, Stephen had abandoned Greek for a round-arched neoclassical manner at his Gartsherrie School, Coatbridge (see FIGURE 3.14), designed for the Bairds of ironworks fame.[94] Its main entablature was of orthodox form, but was borne on massive console brackets at the recessed centre, a motif which may well have provided Thomson with the idea for his consoled eaves galleries at the Grosvenor Building and the Alexandra Hotel. Above the block pediment motif reappeared, recessed between sections of solid parapet. His Tron Free Church on Glasgow's Dundas Street, built in the later 1840s, was remarkable for its giant recessed arch portico but was of a tamer classical orthodoxy in both proportion and detail.[95]

Another architect of whom we know too little was David Bryce's younger brother John, who died at the early age of 46 in 1851. Like his brother he was interested in the possibilities of the baroque as can be seen at his McGavin Monument of 1834 in Glasgow Necropolis[96] and the façade of the intended catacombs of 1836 there.[97] His largest building, long gone and inadequately recorded in Pagan's engraving, was the Glasgow House of Refuge[98] which had a central octagon, probably deriving in plan from Burn's asylum at Dumfries, from which projected a tetrastyle Roman

instead of a portico. Clasping these were lower pylons of coupled antae bearing uncorniced block entablatures which framed flank elevations of five-light window bands. His St Jude's Episcopal Church in West George Street (see FIGURES 3.1 and 3.13) (also 1840)[92] exploited the same block entablature theme on a much larger scale. The central bay of its three-bay street frontage projected boldly with an Egyptian version of the Erechtheum doorpiece recessed between slim coupled antae. These bore a pedimental block entablature and a Choragic Monument of Lysicrates open

Doric pilastered front. It bore a Choragic Monument of Lysicrates tower, evidently similar in character to Stephen's at St Jude's, but set on a clock stage. His domestic architecture in the Queen's Crescent and West Princes Street area of Woodside, Glasgow (1840 onwards)[99] is remarkable only for the use of square columns at the Roman Doric doorpieces, a detail which suggests that he assisted Alexander Kirkland at St Vincent Crescent in 1850,[100] as at the more orthodoxly classical 2–26 Bothwell Street in the previous year.[101]

Somewhat similar in character to Stephen's work, though less imaginative, was a single work by James Smith (1808–63), the Glasgow Collegiate School on Hill Street in Garnethill, Glasgow (1840) (see FIGURE 3.15)[102] – elements of which still survive in modified form as the ground floor of Archibald Macpherson's great palazzo of St Aloysius College. It had a distyle Ionic portico set between plain masses of masonry with Soanic incised ornaments, and seven-bay flanks of closely spaced windows between pylon angles, an arrangement reminiscent of the Sighthill lodge, albeit in plainer form with architraved openings. Whether Smith was capable of such a design at that date is somewhat uncertain as his initial background was builder rather than architect. His father had moved in 1826 from Alloa to Glasgow where he became contractor for the Royal Bank and the builder of much of the north side of Royal Exchange Square. The younger Smith had set up office as architect as well as builder by 1837 when he designed the rather undistinguished Victoria Baths at 106 West Nile Street.[103] Having married David Hamilton's daughter, he formed a disastrous partnership with his son James on David's death in 1843 which was terminated by sequestration in the following year. It is thus possible that, although not then in partnership, assistance was obtained from the Hamilton office as the incised Soanic ornaments, paralleled at the western façade of the Royal Exchange, would indeed suggest.

An architect of some importance, one of whose works also has stylistic links with Stephen's, was George Murray. His Fever Hospital at the Infirmary (1825–32)[104] was plain with a giant anta order through three identical storeys, but the Albion Street façade of his City Hall (1840)[105] had points of interest. An unbroken channelled ground floor bore an upper façade of five bays, the centre three of which were

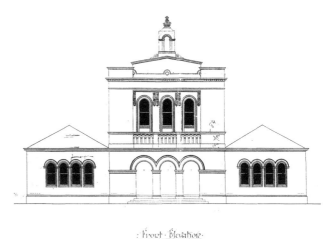

: Front · Elevation ·

FIGURE 3.14   Elevation of Gartsherrie School, Coatbridge, by John Stephen, 1845, measured drawing c.1890.

recessed with a pilastrade of windows at first-floor level, Vitruvian architraved windows at second-floor level and consoles bearing a massive entablature which, like the ground floor, was on a continuous plane: it probably provided the idea for Stephen's bolder treatment of the same idea at Gartsherrie School and in turn for Thomson's eaves galleries with console brackets. As in Stephen's work the windows of the end bays were mildly Egyptian in character with inclined architraves. Of particular interest was the dwarf-pilastered treatment of the antae and deep plain Thomson-like entablature of the first-floor pilastrade. Even if the proportions of some of the elements were deliberately awkward, it was a design of considerable originality. Whether its originality was Murray's own, or whether he bought in help – perhaps from Stephen – for this more prestigious civic commission is a question unlikely to be resolved.

Although William Stark had moved to Edinburgh about 1811, that city had initially been slower to adopt the Greek Revival. Richard Crichton (1771–1817) and Robert Reid (1774–1856) were both architects of the post-Adam school, although the latter was quick to adopt his own very personal interpretation of the Greek Revival at his Doric Leith Custom House in 1811[106] following his humiliating eclipse by Stark and Hamilton in the limited competition for Glasgow's Judiciary

GLASGOW COLLEGIATE SCHOOL.

FIGURE 3.15   Glasgow Collegiate School, Hill Street,
Glasgow, lithograph by James Smith, 1840.

FIGURE 3.16   Midlothian County Buildings, Parliament
Square, Edinburgh, by Archibald Elliot, 1817, demolished,
c.1900.

Buildings. Stark himself had died in October 1813, leaving in hand only the brilliant interiors of the Signet and Advocates' Libraries,[107] the latter precociously anticipating the Graeco-Roman of the late 1820s, 1830s and 1840s. The key figures were initially Archibald Elliot (1761–1823) and William Burn (1789–1870) whose North Leith church of 1813 has already been discussed in relation to David Hamilton's Port Glasgow Town Buildings, and whose Greek Ionic Merchant Maiden Hospital of 1816–19 closely followed the manner of his master Sir Robert Smirke in both composition and detail.[108] Executed in droved ashlar rather than the polished ashlar Burn had intended, old photographs show that the Merchant Maiden lacked the precision Thomson admired. Of greater interest to him must have been the work of Archibald Elliot who, although almost thirty years older than Burn, was well abreast of the Greek Revival in London thanks to his office there. If his Waterloo Place buildings of 1815–19[109] still followed older fashions in having an arched ground floor, the tetrastyle Ionic porticos and Miletus-capitaled antae of its upper façades had the refinement of execution Thomson sought as did his Midlothian County Buildings of the same date on Parliament Square (see FIGURE 3.16).[110] One of the capital's saddest losses, old photographs show that the latter challenged comparison with William Wilkins in purity of detail.

Of more direct relevance to Thomson's development were Thomas Hamilton (1784–1858), five years older than Burn but in practice some three years later, and William Henry Playfair (1790–1857) who did not return from London until 1816. Thomas Hamilton, some of whose works have already been referred to, has already been the subject of an essay by Ian Fisher and a short monograph by Joe Rock[111] and his career need not be outlined again here. Sufficient must it be to observe that the concept of Thomson's competition design for South Kensington owes something to Hamilton's High School – which he considered to be one of 'unquestionably the two finest buildings in the Kingdom'[112] – as did Honeyman's neo-Greek competition design for Kelvingrove much later. Other Hamilton designs which are likely to have been of particular interest to Thomson are 93 George Street (1833) (see FIGURE 3.17)[113] with its use of cast-iron columns with richly detailed bracket capitals which may have pro-

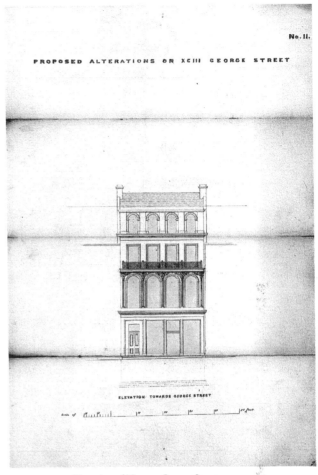

FIGURE 3.17   Elevation of No. 93, George Street, Edinburgh, by Thomas Hamilton, 1833.

vided the initial idea for the Buck's Head Building even if Thomson's much more daring structural system was entirely his own; Arthur Lodge (c.1829)[114] with its square-columned porch and elegant use of incised ornament; and his scheme for Edinburgh's National Gallery (1847–8)[115] which may have had some influence on the massing of Thomson's designs for St Vincent Street church and St Mary's Free, Albany Street, Edinburgh. At a more detailed level the console-cantilever capitals at the flanking porches of the National Gallery scheme anticipated Thomson's use of this very uncommon feature at the first-floor pilastrade of Thomson's Egyptian Halls. It was a motif John Dick Peddie (1824–91) had been quick to adopt in the porch of his United Presbyterian Synod Hall at 5 Queen

FIGURE 3.18   Baingle Brae House, Tullibody, by Alexander
Taylor, 1834, demolished, photo 1966.

Street, Edinburgh, built in the same years (1847–8):
Thomson may have seen it at second rather than first
hand.

Joe Rock has established a link between Hamilton
and Alexander Taylor, an Edinburgh architect who
settled in Glasgow in the 1830s. His villa at Baingle
Brae, Tullibody (1834) (see FIGURE 3.18)[116] developed
the general arrangement of Arthur Lodge into a more
fantastic profile with a central chimney lantern inspired
by Hamilton's twin chimney towers at Dean Orphanage (1833),[117] interesting only in relation to Thomson
as a fairly early attempt to introduce richly picturesque
profiles into classical architecture. More directly relevant to Thomson's work was his design for Clarendon
Place, Glasgow[118] (1840–1), which Thomson cited as
an imaginative adaptation of Greek detail. The tetrastyle Tower of the Winds portico of its narrow gusset
façade was originally intended to have been answered
by that of a corresponding block as at Elliot's Waterloo
Place in Edinburgh. Above the portico the façade rises
up into chimney blocks punctuated by diminutive
arched recesses and crowned by tall Greek fireclay pots
flanking a block pediment. A feature which must have
particularly interested Thomson was the pilastraded
attic, a feature he himself was to adopt at Walmer
Crescent. Details of interest in relation to Thomson's
work are also to be seen at the attic of his Royal
Crescent on Sauchiehall Street (1839),[119] where the
two-light dormers have block pediments, some of them
distinctly Thomsonesque with antae recessed between
pylon-like chimney blocks.

Playfair's major neo-Greek buildings appear to have

a certain relevance to the development of Thomson's
ideas on composition. Even if the elements are quite
different – Greek Doric columns rather than antae – the
concept of long unbroken colonnades stretched between pedimented end projections at the Royal Institution (now the Royal Scottish Gallery) on the Mound in
Edinburgh, as enlarged in 1831–6, is echoed in the
general outline of Moray Place. At Playfair's Surgeons'
Hall in Nicolson Street in the same city (1829) the
relationship is perhaps more obvious: the concept of an
Ionic portico elevated on a blind screen wall of unbroken banded masonry with monumental entrances
to either side is echoed, albeit in different proportions,
at Caledonia Road church. Playfair's Museum Hall,
with its anta pilastered piers and compartmented ceiling, and even more the old Graduation Hall (redesigned 1826, now regrettably remodelled with a mezza-
nine as the Public Office) of the University's Old
College, have much in common with the austere anta
pilastered Greek interiors of Smirke's British Museum
and the Old General Post Office at St Martin's-le-
Grand in London. While Thomson himself preferred
open timber roofs to compartmented ceilings for large
spaces, their simple logical treatment anticipates to
some extent Thomson's interior at Caledonia Road.

Although Playfair's relentlessly pilastraded and
tunnel-vaulted library hall at the Old College certainly
carries the mind away into space and speculations upon
infinity, the relevance of Playfair's work to Thomson's
lies not so much in his great public buildings as in the
Germanic classical-Italianate houses he designed in
1828–9 – Belmont, Corstorphine, Dunphail, Morayshire and Drumbanagher, Armagh, only the first of
which Thomson is likely to have seen – and the Italianate villa of Dalcrue farmhouse on the Lynedoch estate
in Perthshire, designed in 1832 (see FIGURE 3.19).

Dr Ronald McFadzean has already drawn attention
to the relationship between the window arrangement of
the end bays of Drumbanagher to those of Thomson's
Grecian Building on Sauchiehall Street,[120] but more
might be said about them. It can safely be assumed that
they relate directly to Playfair's acquisition of the
earlier parts of Schinkel's *Sammlung* although they
have no direct counterparts there, while some elements, particularly at Dunphail (see FIGURE 3.20), also
relate to the English picturesque school publications of
J. B. Papworth, J. M. Gandy and others in his library.

FIGURE 3.19 Dalcrue farmhouse, Lynedoch, Perthshire, by
W. H. Playfair, 1832.

FIGURE 3.20 Dunphail House, Morayshire, by W. H.
Playfair, 1828 photo, prior to 1960s' alterations.

FIGURE 3.21   Drumbanagher, Armagh, Ireland, by W. H.
Playfair, 1828, largely demolished, photo c.1930.

At the time, these houses were unique in British
country-house architecture with features which did not
become common currency until the 1840s. Belmont[121]
and the slightly later Drumbanagher (see FIGURE
3.21)[122] were essentially similar in profile – two-
storeyed between advanced three-storey bookend
blocks – but Drumbanagher was much the larger,
having façades of equal importance whereas Belmont
was a single-aspect house with a Smirke-type arched
porte-cochère (cf. Smirke's Newton Don) projecting
from one end. The composition of the bookend façades
is quite remarkably similar to Johann Matthis Hansen
and Ole Jorgen Schmidt's Landhaus Baur, Hamburg-
Blankinese of 1829–30[123] which suggests that there
must be a common German source. On the garden
front of Drumbanagher the ground-floor elevations of
the bookends were projected as tripartite rectangular
bays of square antae surmounted by Schinkel-type
flower urns, although such features appear as porticos
and pergolas rather than window bays in the *Sammlung*. Playfair's immediate source for this feature
seems to have been Schloss Glienicke, as indeed it was
for the tower which flanked the main block.[124] Thomas
Hope and William Atkinson had introduced the pilastraded rectangular bay at The Deepdene in 1818,[125]
but otherwise the anta-pilastered window bay was to
remain a rare feature until Decimus Burton's Grim-
ston, Yorkshire,[126] in the late 1830s and was not common currency until the 1840s. Still more unusual,
Dunphail[127] introduced the idea of rectangular bays
carried up through two storeys. In both Dunphail and
Drumbanagher there are elements of Thomson's picturesque grouping with broad-eaved pyramid roofed
towers, particularly at Dunphail, but at both houses
the main block was strictly symmetrical. Although
much smaller and more simply detailed, the Dalcrue
farmhouse[128] comes still closer to the Thomson villa
model in its combination of two-storey low-pitched

FIGURE 3.22 Aberlour House, Banffshire, by William Robertson, 1838.

gable-fronted main block with rectangular bay and a single-storey wing with a pyramid-roofed tower in the angle, all with broad-eaved roofs. Picturesque elements are also to be found in Playfair's unexecuted classical design for Brownlow House, Lurgan (1833),[129] which was to have had a stepped main façade interpenetrating a Corinthian temple centrepiece. As at Belmont, the entrance was to have been an arched *porte-cochère* projected from the end elevation. Schinkel's influence on Playfair's work is still evident in the 1840s, most notably in the awesomely logical design for the Edinburgh National Galleries which omitted the present central porticos, the perspective drawing of which might have come straight from the *Sammlung*.[130]

Somewhat similar in spirit to Playfair's work were the late buildings of the Elgin-based architect William Robertson (1786–1841). Robertson had originally settled in the area at Cullen in 1822, his town hall there bearing such a resemblance to John Paterson's Seafield Baths at Leith that the probability must be that he was a pupil.[131] But in 1838 he designed the enlargement of Dochfour, Inverness,[132] to a house of distinctly similar character to Dunphail – which he had probably seen –

albeit with the composition reversed, and in the same year the very advanced neoclassical mansion of Aberlour (see FIGURE 3.22).[133] Whether Robertson actually designed Aberlour or was the executant architect is perhaps arguable since the central Greek Doric porch (extended to a *porte-cochère* by his nephews A. & W. Reid in 1855–7) and superimposed square anta-order column portico were quite remarkably similar to those of Laleham House, Middlesex, designed by John Buonarotti Papworth in 1839.[134] It rather looks as if Laleham was a reduced version of a design provided for Aberlour. Markedly of the Playfair–Schinkel school are the rectangular tripartite bays of the end elevations, but these were not added until 1854, again by A. & W. Reid.[135]

It is unlikely that Thomson knew of Robertson, or of Aberlour, but if only from engravings and lithographs he was probably familiar with the work of Archibald Simpson (1790–1847) and John Smith (1781–1852) of Aberdeen. Smith had returned from an unknown office in London in 1805; and Simpson from those of Robert Lugar and David Laing, followed by study in Rome, in 1813.[136]

Simpson approached the Hamiltons and Playfair in sheer sophistication. His work is, however, less easy to relate to Thomson's. His Crimonmogate House (c.1822),[137] Murtle House (1823),[138] Stracathro House (1827),[139] Letham Grange (1827),[140] Anderson's Institution, Elgin (1831–2),[141] Old Infirmary, Aberdeen (1832–9)[142] and Mrs Elmslie's Institution, later the High School for Girls (1837–9)[143] all feature columned or pilastered frontages recessed between two- or three-bay projecting pavilions, as did his sadly unexecuted classical design for Marischal College.[144] His North of Scotland Bank on the corner of Castle Street and King Street, Aberdeen (1839–40)[145] was of a somewhat different order, with channel-pilastered elevations linked by a quadrant Corinthian portico which suggest an acquaintance with the work of C. R. Cockerell, in particular the London and Westminster Bank on Lothbury, London, of 1837[146] and the Literary and Philosophical Institution, Bristol of 1821–3.[147] His classical and Italianate churches are all of a severe temple-like form: St Giles at Elgin[148] with its Choragic Monument of Lysicrates tower and hexastyle Doric portico develops themes from Porden's St Matthew's, Brixton with greater sophistication, while Inverbrothock, Arbroath (1828)[149] has a razor-sharp anta-pilastered front in the shallowest of relief. If Thomson actually saw any of these works, what must have struck him was the supreme refinement of the execution and the quality of the interior work. Simpson excelled in the design of severely trabeated interiors with classical friezes and woodwork, particularly doors, which in sheer originality anticipated Thomson's experiments later.

Like Playfair, Simpson was skilled in broad-eaved Italianate, notably at Linton House (1835),[150] Glenferness, Nairn (1844)[151] and Thainstone (1847)[152] but it is unlikely that Thomson had any opportunity to see them. Although earlier in the field, Smith's best work in many respects echoed Simpson's, as at the Town's Schools in Little Belmont Street, Aberdeen (1841),[153] the portico of which echoed that of Crimonmogate, and the outstandingly fine North Church, Aberdeen (1830), whose Choragic Monument of Lysicrates tower echoed Simpson's at Elgin.[154]

The work of contemporaries and near-contemporaries of Thomson, whose architectural practices ran more or less parallel to his, lies outside the scope of this chapter, but a few works by architects who set up in business earlier, and which have a special relevance, call for some discussion. Of particular interest is the early work of two Edinburgh men, William Clarke (1809–89) and George Bell (1814–87) who settled in Glasgow after winning the competition for the City and County Buildings on Wilson Street and the adjacent Merchants' House on Hutcheson Street in 1844.[155] Bell was a pupil of the younger Archibald Elliot but at, or possibly before, Elliot's death in 1843 moved to the office of Burn and Bryce where he met Clarke. At first sight the Wilson Street façade of the City and County Buildings, with its Greek Ionic portico raised high on a screen wall might seem to owe something to Playfair's Surgeons' Hall with the important difference that the area behind the screen wall is enclosed. Both parts of the composition are, however, more likely to have drawn inspiration from Harvey Lonsdale Elmes's original design for the Assize Courts of 1839 at Liverpool,[156] especially in respect of the podium at the City and County Buildings with its sculptured frieze by Walter Buchan. The concept of the rather American-looking Corinthian colonnade of the Merchants' House presumably comes from the elevated Ionic colonnade Elmes proposed for the Assize Courts, but strengthened by squaring the columns at the end bays. Behind the colonnade the first-floor windows are treated as a continuous pilastrade as at Bryce's Edinburgh Caledonian Insurance Building (1839) referred to earlier. In its general massing at least there is something of the columnar grid of Thomson's major warehouse designs, while the vestibule behind the podium of the City and County Buildings, toplit through rooflights in the portico floor, provided the idea for Thomson's vestibules at Caledonia Road and St Vincent Street.

Although less obviously related, mention should also be made of the early work of David Hamilton's pupil and chief draughtsman, Charles Wilson (1810–63) to whose office Alexander Thomson was at least an occasional visitor – as Thomas Ross, an assistant of Wilson's, recorded that Wilson took care that the assistants had the chance to see him.[157] Although Wilson was essentially an Italian Renaissance designer whose inspiration lay in France (which he visited in 1841) and even more in Germany, he designed at least one building in pure Greek, the Parliamentary Road United Presbyterian Church in Pladda Street (1839) (see FIGURE 3.23),[158] a small chaste temple, which had a

FIGURE 3.23   Parliamentary Road UP Church, Pladda
Street, Glasgow, by Charles Wilson, 1839, demolished,
photo 1875 from Aikman.

tetrastyle anta-pilastered front with finely proportioned
windows and an anthemion frieze worthy of Playfair
himself. Some of his early villa designs also have a
certain relevance to the development of Thomson's
style, notably in their use of antae recessed from the
wall plane at the openings.

It would, of course, be rash indeed to suggest that the
developments in Scottish neoclassical design outlined
in this chapter are all directly relevant to Thomson's
style, although many of them would be at the back of
his inquiring mind if only from daily familiarity. At the
most, they represented ideas which could be developed
more imaginatively. It should always be remembered
that, like Playfair, Thomson had a copy of Schinkel's
Sammlung. But while the sale catalogue of Playfair's
wonderfully comprehensive library – which included
Percier & Fontaine and Durand – has been preserved,
Thomson's has not. It will take much time and effort to
establish what he had beyond Schinkel and Fergusson
and, no less importantly, we do not know what the
Robert Foote and David and James Hamilton libraries
contained. The appearance on the market in recent
years of German folios from the library of Thomson's
contemporary, James Salmon, is an indication that
even the less familiar continental folios had found their
way to the more prosperous Scottish architectural practices to a greater degree than one might otherwise have
expected. Rather, we must see what was developing in
the 1820, 1830s and 1840s as only partly interrelated
parallel developments drawn from a mix of observation
and a wider variety of published sources than hitherto
supposed. While certain aspects of the stylistic developments of Thomson and his predecessors can be
accepted as self-evident, it is an area which requires
much more research.

ACKNOWLEDGEMENTS

This chapter has its origins in a paper given some thirty years ago to the Society of Architectural Historians. Sadly several of those who helped in its preparation at the time have long gone but it is right that their assistance should be remembered: Alfred G. Lochhead, Professor William J. Smith, Professor Andrew McLaren Young, George Emslie and, more recently, Colin McWilliam, at whose suggestion the paper was given. Miss Catherine H. Cruft and Professor Ian Hodkinson, happily still with us, also helped. The original paper has been much refined over the years since and, among many others, I particularly wish to acknowledge the assistance in various details of Mr Ian Gow, Mr Aonghus MacKechnie, Mr Philip McWilliams, Professor Frank A. Walker and Dr Gavin Stamp.

NOTES

1. Disused, made redundant in 1992. See James Thomson, *History of St Andrew's Parish Church, Glasgow*, Glasgow, 1905; Renwick (ed.), *Extracts from the Records of the Burgh of Glasgow*, Glasgow, 1912, vol. vi, pp. 72–3; G. Hay, *The Architecture of Scottish Post-Reformation Churches*, Oxford, 1957, p. 102.

2. Subsequently reconstructed as the Tontine Hotel, 1781, demolished 1911 after a fire. See Renwick, *Extracts*, vol. v, p. 495 and 1912, vol. vi, p. 14; J. Cowan, *From Glasgow's Treasure Chest*, Glasgow, 1951, p. 392ff.

3. Recently acquired by the National Museum of Scotland.

4. Façade overlaid 1857, completely demolished 1976. See *The Regality Club of Glasgow*, 1st ser., Glasgow, 1889, pp. 54–73, with measured drawing of chimney-piece; illustrations in Renwick, *Extracts*, vol. vii (frontispiece) and R. Stuart, *Views and Notices of Glasgow in Former Times*, Glasgow, 1848, plate opposite p. 55.

5. Demolished 1792. Colen Campbell, *Vitruvius Britannicus*, London, 1715–25, vol. II, pl. 51; G. L. M. Goodfellow, 'Colen Campbell's Shawfield Mansion in Glasgow', *Journal of the Society of Architectural Historians* (USA), vol. XXIII (1964), no. 3, pp. 123–8.

6. See J. Denholm, *The History of the City of Glasgow*, 3rd edn, Glasgow, 1804, frontispiece.

7. Demolished 1838. See *The Regality Club of Glasgow*, 1st ser., pp. 106–28, drawing not accurate but shows a five-bay front with a three-bay pediment which bore urns, one of which has been refixed over the surviving doorpiece.

8. The infirmary was altered in 1850 when the basement area was removed and demolished in 1907; the Trades House, Glassford Street is still extant, but has been enlarged at several dates, and substantially rebuilt to the rear by James Sellars in 1887–8. See A. T. Bolton, *The Architecture of R. & J. Adam*, London, 1922, section on Glasgow in vol. ii, pp. 193–7; F. Worsdall, *The City that Disappeared*, Glasgow, 1951, pp. 52–3.

9. The Assembly Rooms were demolished in 1889–1911 to make way for the Post Office extension on Ingram Street, and the College residences at the corner of High Street and College Street for inadequate reasons as late as 1973. See Worsdall, *The City that Disappeared*, pp. 44 and 65; Bolton, *The Architecture of R. & J. Adam*, vol. ii, p. 194; G. Richardson, *New Vitruvius Britannicus*, London, 1802–10, vol. i, plates 8–9; Denholm, *The History of the City of Glasgow* and other sources. The central part of the upper façade of the Assembly Rooms survives re-erected as a triumphal arch on Glasgow Green.

10. Demolished. Drawings Soane Museum; D. Stroud, *The Architecture of Sir John Soane*, London, 1961, p. 161. For Hamilton, see A. MacKechnie (ed.), *David Hamilton, Architect 1768–1843, Father of the Profession*, Glasgow, 1993.

11. Burnt 1829 and inadequately recorded. Engraved elevation in Denholm, *The History of the City of Glasgow*; perspective view in *Glasgow Delineated*, Glasgow, University Press, 1827; lithograph of façade in ruins in Stuart, *Views and Notices*. The NE pavilion of Royal Exchange Square stands on the site.

12. H. M. Colvin, *Dictionary of British Architects 1600–1840*, London, 1978; *Dictionary of National Biography*; memoir in P. Nicholson, *Builder and Workman's New Directory*, London, 1824.

13. P. Nicholson, *Architectural Dictionary*, London, 1812–29, vol. ii, p. 912.

14. J. Coutts, *History of the University of Glasgow*, Glasgow, 1909, p. 357.

15. See R. McFadzean, *The Life and Work of Alexander Thomson*, London, 1979, pp. 16–18.

16. See Colvin, *Dictionary of British Architects*, article on M. A. Nicholson: date of death not accurately given, but includes many details not given by McFadzean.

17. P. Nicholson, *The New Practical Builder and Workman's Companion*, 1823.

18. Later Trinity Duke Street church, converted to Kirkhaven Day Centre 1975. Illustrated in J. L. Aikman, *Historical Notices of United Presbyterian Congregations in Glasgow*, Glasgow, 1877.

19. Colvin, *Dictionary of British Architects*; typescript memoir by R. Gordon Stark at National Library of Scotland; S. Nicholls (ed.), *Dictionary of National Biography, Missing Persons*, Oxford, 1993.

20. W. Stark, *Report on the Plans for Laying out the Grounds of Buildings between Edinburgh and Leith*, Edinburgh, 1814, quoted in A. J. Youngson, *The Making of Classical Edinburgh*, Edinburgh, 1966, p. 152.

21. Demolished some time after 1887. See Worsdall, *The City that Disappeared*, p. 99 and photographs at the

present Hunterian Museum, Glasgow.

22. Only the frontal section is to Stark's design, the remainder was redesigned by James Cleland. See Markus (ed.), *Order in Space and Society*, p. 197, quoting Town Council and committee minutes.

23. Demolished 1908: latterly the Barony Poorshouse, Parliamentary Road. See Markus, *Order in Space and Society*, p. 94 ff.

24. G. Williamson, *Old Greenock*, 2nd ser., Greenock, 1888, p. 250 (id).

25. The planning of the interior was found inconvenient and was partly remodelled by Clarke & Bell in 1845; finally in 1910–13, J. H. Craigie rebuilt it completely, retaining only the portico but apparently reusing some original material internally. For the original building history see Markus, *Order in Space and Society*, p. 50 ff.

26. See J. Britton and A. C. Pugin, *The Public Buildings of London*, London, 1828, vol. i, pp. 193–226, illustrations A. T. Bolton (ed.), *Sir John Soane RA: Lectures on Architecture*, London, 1929.

27. Markus, *Order in Space and Society*, p. 50. For Chester Castle see J. M. Crook in *Country Life*, 15 Apr. 1971, and J. M. Crook, *The Greek Revival*, London, 1972, plates 171 and 172.

28. Markus, *Order in Space and Society*, p. 63.

29. Haldane Lecture, III (1874), p. 8.

30. Markus, *Order in Space and Society*, p. 56.

31. Photographs of original plans, National Monuments Record of Scotland.

32. W. F. McArthur, *History of Port Glasgow*, Glasgow, 1932, p. 179; information from Town Council Minutes per J. R. Hume.

33. *Royal Commission on the Ancient and Historical Monuments of Scotland: Stirlingshire*, Edinburgh, 1963, no. 311.

34. Drawings, National Monuments Record of Scotland; Hay, *Post-Reformation Churches*, p. 111 ff.

35. See J. Frew (ed.), *Scotland and Europe*, St Andrews, 1991, p. 17 and its published *Transactions* (copies in Edinburgh Architectural Association Library, 15 Rutland Square, Edinburgh).

36. E. Williamson, A. Riches, M. Higgs, *The Buildings of Scotland: Glasgow*, London, 1990, p. 221.

37. T. Gildard, 'An Old Glasgow Architect on Some Older Ones', *Proceedings of the Royal Philosophical Society of Glasgow*, vol. XXVI (1895), pp. 97–123; *Some Old Glasgow Architects*, MS biography of Alexander Thomson and related MSS, Mitchell Library, Glasgow; McFadzean, *Alexander Thomson*, pp. 6–9.

38. James Maclehose, *One Hundred Eminent Glasgow Men*, Glasgow, 1886, pp. 22–4.

39. Demolished *c.*1968. See Aikman, *Historical Notices*; Worsdall, *The City that Disappeared*, p. 82.

40. Secularised and subsequently demolished, 1884. See Aikman, *Historical Notices*.

41. Demolished 1967. See Aikman, *Historical Notices*.

42. Maclehose, *Glasgow Men*, pp. 21–2.

43. Plans, University of Glasgow archives. See also Anne Ross in *The College Courant*, vol. 26 (1974), pp. 25–30.

44. Demolished 1991. H. M. Nisbett and S. C. Agnew, *Cairnhill*, Edinburgh, 1949, p. 201.

45. Demolished 1934. J. B. Greenshields, *Annals of the Parish of Lesmahagow*, Glasgow, 1864, p. 83.

46. Greenshields, Annals, p. 101.

47. Maclehose, *Glasgow Men*, p. 23.

48. F. Worsdall, *Victorian City*, p. 53.

49. Wyatt Papworth (ed.), *Architectural Publication Society's Dictionary 1852–1892*, article on Glasgow and numerous subsequent references.

50. W. Adam, *Vitruvius Scoticus*, Edinburgh, 1812, pl. 11.

51. Photograph of drawing in National Monuments Record of Scotland.

52. Demolished 1925. See A. A. Tait, 'The Duke of Hamilton's Palace', in *Burlington Magazine*, vol. CXXV (July 1983), pp. 394–402; Ian Gow, *The Scottish Interior*, Edinburgh, 1992, pp. 104–5; *Country Life*, 7, 14 and 21 June 1919; G. Walker, *Hamilton Palace, a Photographic Record*, Hamilton, n.d.

53. Latterly Stirling's Library. *Architectural Publication Society's Dictionary*, articles on David Hamilton and Glasgow; C. C. Brewsher, *The Glasgow Royal Exchange Centenary 1827–1927*, Glasgow, 1927, and numerous other references.

54. See Brewsher, *Glasgow Royal Exchange*. The final responsibility is far from clear. The latest state of knowledge is summarised by Elizabeth Williamson in Williamson, Riches and Higgs, *Buildings of Scotland: Glasgow*.

55. *The Architects and Civil Engineers' Directory*, London, 1868.

56. V. Fiddes and A. J. Rowan, *Mr David Bryce*, Edinburgh, 1976, p. 93, pl. 6.

57. Ibid., p. 92, pl. 9.

58. Ibid., pl. 10.

59. Demolished 1974. See Senex, *Glasgow Past and Present*, vol. i, Dean of Guild Reports.

60. Illustrated in Christopher Simon Sykes, *Private Palaces*, London, 1985, p. 250, and David Pearce, *London's Mansions*, London, 1986, pl. 124.

61. Illustrated before reconstruction as Canada House in A. E. Richardson, *Monumental Architecture in Great Britain*, London, 1914, pp. 58–9.

62. Illustrated in A. H. Gomme, M. Jenner and B. Little, *Bristol: An Architectural History*, London, 1979, p. 238; and Richardson, *Monumental Architecture in Great Britain*, pl. xxxvii.

63. Illustrated in *Country Life*, 17 Aug. 1961; Crook, *The Greek Revival*, pl. 142.

64. Illustrated in Cecil Stewart, *The Stones of Manchester*, London, 1953, p. 29.

65. Illustrated in J. Elmes, *Metropolitan Improvements*, London, 1831, pp. 30–2.

66. Exhibited Royal Academy 1828: Colvin, *Dictionary of British Architects*.
67. Illustrated in Bryan Little, *The Building of Bath*, London, 1947, pl. 112.
68. Illustrated in Gomme, Jenner and Little, *Bristol*, pp. 255–6.
69. Illustrated in N. Pevsner, *The Buildings of England: Berkshire*, Harmondsworth, 1966 and later edns, pl. 54.
70. Pagan, *Sketch of the History of Glasgow*, pp. 126–7; plate showing original form of main roof.
71. Now Dean College. See Joe Rock, *Thomas Hamilton, Architect*, Edinburgh, 1984, pp. 51–3.
72. Demolished 1925; stood in St Enoch Square, incorporating an earlier steeple by J. Jaffrey of 1780: illustrated J. M. Leighton, *Select Views of Glasgow*, Glasgow, 1829; Worsdall, *The City that Disappeared*, p. 80.
73. Dalkeith Road/Blacket Place, Attribution. See Rock, *Thomas Hamilton*, pp. 45–7.
74. Colvin, *Dictionary of British Architects*; original reference *Edinburgh Evening Courant*, 6 Aug. 1829.
75. Undated 19th-century newspaper cutting, recording reminiscences of an ex-assistant of Hamilton's in a discussion of his church at Ascog.
76. Demolished 1968. Pagan, *Sketch of the History of Glasgow*, p. 104. Illustrated in Worsdall, *The City that Disappeared*, p. 114.
77. T. Gildard, 'An Old Glasgow Architect', p. 104.
78. See David Watkin and Tillman Mellinghoff, *German Architecture and the Classical Ideal*, London, 1987, e.g. The Theaterverwaltung, Brunswick, c.1840, p. 213.
79. Illustrated in Nic Allen (ed.), *Scottish Pioneers of the Greek Revival*, Edinburgh, 1984 (cover).
80. Pagan, *Sketch of the History of Glasgow*, pp. 180–1. A similar treatment of the rectangular bay, but with a bolder projection and a pediment, was to be found at D. & J. Hamilton's Hutchesons' Boys' School (1839) but it is not yet known whether these were modified in any way by John Burnet senior when he reconstructed it. See illustration of the building in its final state in Worsdall, *The City that Disappeared*, p. 103.
81. Fiddes and Rowan, *Mr David Bryce*, p. 95. A larger similar building with plain tripartite bays, probably also by Burn and Bryce, formerly existed at the east end of George Street, see pl. 149 in *Thomas Begbie's Edinburgh*, Edinburgh, 1992.
82. Plans, National Monuments Record of Scotland; photo as first built, *Thomas Begbie's Edinburgh*, pl. 7.
83. Demolished. Most of the façade survived until c.1960, incorporated into Woolworth's store on Argyle Street. Illustrated in Pagan, *Sketch of the History of Glasgow*, p. 178.
84. Gutted and Honeyman's additions removed 1968. *Architectural Publication Society's Dictionary*, articles on Glasgow and Hamilton.
85. Williamson, Riches and Higgs, *Buildings of Scotland: Glasgow*, p. 222.
86. John Honeyman's office books.
87. Copies in National Monuments Record of Scotland.
88. Refronted by John Burnet in 1875–7 and now Lanarkshire House. Parts of the Hamilton design remain on the flank elevations. The portico was reused at the Royal Princess's Theatre, 121 Gorbals Street, where it survived until the 1970s. See R. S. Rait, *History of the Union Bank of Scotland*, Glasgow, 1930; Worsdall, *The City that Disappeared*, pp. 115 and 146.
89. Colvin, *Dictionary of British Architects*, see under both Scott and Stephen.
90. Largely demolished. Stephen won a competition held in Feb. 1840 (information from minutes of building committee, Blythswood Papers TD 234.98 in Strathclyde Regional Archives per Professor Frank A. Walker. See also his *The South Clyde Estuary: An Illustrated Architectural Guide to Inverclyde and Renfrew*, Edinburgh, 1986, p. 97, quoting the minutes).
91. *Architectural Publication Society's Dictionary*, 'Glasgow'.
92. Latterly St Jude's Free Presbyterian Church, now disused, details simplified and tower demolished in 1960s. See Pagan, *Sketch of the History of Glasgow*, p. 181.
93. Walter Newall's archive of drawings has recently been acquired by the Museum. Aonghus MacKechnie has drawn my attention to the fact that Newall did have a link with Stephen in that his partner, Gale, worked with him on the Dumfries water supply.
94. Allan Peden, *The Monklands: An Illustrated Architectural Guide*, Edinburgh, 1992, p. 39, quoting research by Philip McWilliams.
95. Demolished c.1960. See reference in David Thomson, 'The Works of the Late Charles Wilson', in the *Proceedings of the Philosophical Society of Glasgow* (1882), pp. 552–69.
96. Pagan, *Sketch of the History of Glasgow*, p. 182.
97. G. Blair, *Sketches of Glasgow Necropolis*, Glasgow, 1857, p. 34; *Architectural Publication Society's Dictionary*, 'Glasgow'.
98. Stood on Duke Street, at Whitehill. Pagan, *Sketch of the History of Glasgow*, p. 180.
99. Sasines.
100. Senex, *Glasgow Past and Present*, pp. 26–8; F. Worsdall in *Scottish Field*, Mar. 1965, pp. 26–8.
101. Originally Eagle Buildings: *Architectural Publication Society's Dictionary*; F. Worsdall in *Scottish Field*, Mar. 1965, pp. 26–8.
102. *Architectural Publication Society's Dictionary*, 'Glasgow'; Williamson, Riches, Higgs, *Buildings of Scotland: Glasgow*, p. 299 (date misprinted 1866).
103. For James Smith, see F. Worsdall, 'Poor Mr Smith', in *Scottish Field*, Dec. 1963, pp. 50–1.
104. *Architectural Publication Society's Dictionary*, 'Glasgow'.
105. Ibid.
106. T. H. Shepherd, *Modern Athens*, London, 1829. The building was considerably reordered by William Burn in 1824 when the perron was built. See J. Gifford, C.

McWilliam and D. Walker, *The Buildings of Scotland: Edinburgh*, Harmondsworth, 1984, p. 462.

107. The Advocates Library was subsequently acquired by the Writers to the Signet. See Youngson, *The Making of Classical Edinburgh*, pp. 134–134.

108. Demolished *c.*1930, after being much added to as George Watson's Hospital. Illustrated in Shepherd, *Modern Athens*. For William Burn's Greek Revival work see David Walker in Allen, *Scottish Pioneers of the Greek Revival*, pp. 3–5.

109. Youngson, *The Making of Classical Edinburgh*, pp. 142–7.

110. Illustrated in Shepherd, *Modern Athens*, p. 74.

111. Allen, *Scottish Pioneers of the Greek Revival*; Rock, *Thomas Hamilton*.

112. Thomson, 'An Inquiry as to the Appropriateness of the Gothic Style …', in *Proceedings of the Glasgow Architectural Society* (1865–7), p. 58.

113. Façade altered 1900, restored to its original form 1980s; Dean of Guild plans, 6 Aug. 1833.

114. Rock, *Thomas Hamilton*, pp. 45–7.

115. Ibid., pp. 72–3.

116. Adam Swan, *Clackmannan and the Ochils: An Illustrated Architectural Guide*, Edinburgh, p. 56.

117. See note 71.

118. Gildard, 'An Old Glasgow Architect', p. 116.

119. Ibid.; Pagan, *Sketch of the History of Glasgow*, p. 181.

120. McFadzean, *Alexander Thomson*, p. 154.

121. Plans, Edinburgh University Library.

122. Demolished after the Second World War and a new house built. Only fragments remain on the site. Plans, Edinburgh University Library; Mark Bence-Jones, *Burke's Guide to Country Houses, vol. 1 Ireland*, London, 1978, p. 112.

123. Watkin and Mellinghof, *German Architecture*, p. 138.

124. K. F. Schinkel, *Sammlung Architektonischer Entwürfe*, plates 137–9.

125. David Watkin, *Thomas Hope and the Neo Classical Ideal*, London, 1968, pl. 70.

126. Christopher Hussey, *English Country Houses: Late Georgian*, London, 1958, p. 230 ff.

127. Altered, most recently in 1960s. Plans, Edinburgh University Library: modern line rendering of Playfair's elevation in C. McKean, *The District of Moray: An Illustrated Architectural Guide*, Edinburgh, 1987, p. 50.

128. Plans, Edinburgh University Library.

129. Plans, Edinburgh University Library, and Royal Incorporation of Architects in Scotland.

130. Plans, Edinburgh University Library. Perspective. Illustrated in Youngson, *The Making of Classical Edinburgh*, pp. 284–5.

131. Elizabeth Beaton, *William Robertson: Architect in Elgin*, Elgin, 1984.

132. Ibid.

133. Ibid., pl. 6.

134. John Harris, *The Design of the English Country House 1620–1920*, London, 1985, pp. 182–3.

135. Plans, Forres Museum, per Elizabeth Beaton.

136. For a detailed account of Simpson's career see G. M. Fraser's serial, 'Archibald Simpson, Architect and His Times', in *Aberdeen Weekly Journal*, 5 Apr.–11 Oct. 1918, and for illustrations, see Aberdeen Civic Society, *Archibald Simpson: Architect of Aberdeen, 1790–1847*, Aberdeen, 1978.

137. Fraser, 'Archibald Simpson', ch. xi, mansard roof added 1875, but interior largely intact.

138. Ibid., ch. x, interior gutted as Rudolph Steiner School.

139. Ibid., ch. x; *Forfarshire Illustrated*, Dundee, 1843, p. 137.

140. Fraser, 'Archibald Simpson', ch. x; *Forfarshire Illustrated*, p. 71. Altered and enlarged with tower by Alexander Ross of Inverness.

141. *Architectural Publication Society's Dictionary*, 'Simpson'; illustrated in McKean, *The District of Moray*, p. 17; Aberdeen Civic Society, *Archibald Simpson*.

142. Fraser, 'Archibald Simpson', ch. xv and ch. xxiii.

143. Ibid., ch. xix.

144. Illustrated in W. Brogden, *Aberdeen: An Illustrated Architectural Guide*, Edinburgh, 1986, p. 32.

145. Fraser, 'Archibald Simpson', ch. xx.

146. Illustrated in Watkin, *The Life and Works of Charles Robert Cockerell*, London, 1978, plates 136 and 137; Richardson, *Monumental Architecture in Great Britain*, pl. xxxvii.

147. Illustrated in Watkin, *C. R. Cockerell*, pl. 35.

148. Fraser, 'Archibald Simpson', ch. x.

149. *Aberdeen Journal Notes and Queries*, vol. I (1908), pp. 168–9.

150. Ibid., p. 169.

151. Fraser, 'Archibald Simpson', ch. xxiii.

152. *The Builder*, vol. V (1847), p. 217.

153. *Aberdeen Journal*, 4 Mar. 1840 (contracts, illustrated in Brogden, *Aberdeen*, p. 34.

154. Now Aberdeen Arts Centre, King Street: interior gutted. Illustrated in Hay, *Post-Reformation Churches*, pl. 17.

155. Original perspective in National Monuments Record of Scotland; Richardson, *Monumental Architecture in Great Britain*, p. 73, pl. xxxv.

156. Illustrated in Crook, *The Greek Revival*, RIBA Drawings Series, London, 1968, plates 37 and 38.

157. David Breeze (ed.), *Studies in Scottish Antiquity* (presented to Stewart Cruden), Edinburgh, 1984, p. 398.

158. Aikman, *Historical Notices*.

FIGURE 4.1   The St Vincent Street church from the south,
photo *c.*1900.

Chapter Four

·

'GREEK' THOMSON'S LITERARY AND PICTORIAL SOURCES

James Macaulay

One of the curiosities in the literature pertaining to 'Greek' Thomson is that no one hitherto has examined why he used the Greek Revival style for his four churches. It may have been a matter of personal preference in that he was not prepared to use arcuated forms – whether Roman, Gothic or Renaissance; or he may have been following a current fashion. Yet, given what is known of Thomson, that explanation is too trite; it does not carry conviction.

It is known that Thomson was deeply devoted to his Presbyterian faith; he was an elder in his church and family prayers were said each evening in his household. How then could Christianity, no matter how cerebral, be celebrated in churches whose stylistic origins were inextricably associated with the polytheism of classical Greece? A general answer to this question is provided by Thomson himself in his Haldane Lectures, which are examined in detail in another chapter. However, the design of the St Vincent Street United Presbyterian Church (see FIGURE 4.1) may provide additional insights.

In 1916, a short account of that church was published, in which it is stated that Thomson was 'imbued with the thought that the classic style which was in use for all sacred structures when Paul preached was that best fitted for a Presbyterian place of worship'. There was the rub that dictated – since the Presbyterian service was essentially auditory – not a rectangular plan but a square one, which could only be achieved 'by the addition of aisles – a method borrowed from the Gothic by the architect. The Solomonic Temple appears to have had a similar arrangement.'[1] If these words, written more than forty years after Thomson's death, are a correct summation of his views – and they may

well be if they were approved, as has been suggested, by the architect's son[2] – then it would be interesting to study how Thomson came to equate the plan of Solomon's Temple with that of a Greek temple.

While it could be assumed that Thomson would have possessed an extensive architectural and possibly theological library, nothing was known of its extent. However, it has now been discovered that in 1934 Thomson's granddaughter bequeathed to the Mitchell Library in Glasgow drawings and a collection of 880 books, including old schoolbooks, some of which belonged to Thomson's son John. The architectural library, it seems, went to the Glasgow Philosophical Society, the collections of which were subsequently dispersed.[3] Nevertheless, there are enough clues in Thomson's lectures and in his built works to indicate which published texts he would have consulted, while others – more textual than illustrative – were important enough in the expanding knowledge of the antique world not to be overlooked, and the more so if they could prove useful in the polemical struggle between advocacy of the superiority of the Greek and earlier styles over all later ones.

A Greek Revivalist would begin with Stuart and Revett's *Antiquities of Athens*. The first volume had been published in 1762, but volume three did not appear until 1795. In the preface to volume one there was set out the argument that was to sustain the Greek against other classical styles: 'The ruined Edifices of Rome ... have generally been considered as the Models and Standard of regular and ornamental Building ... [yet] as Greece was the great Mistress of the Arts, and Rome, in this respect, no more than her disciple, it may be presumed, all the most admired Buildings ... were but

FIGURE 4.2 The Ionic order from the Erechtheum in volume II of the *Antiquities of Athens*.

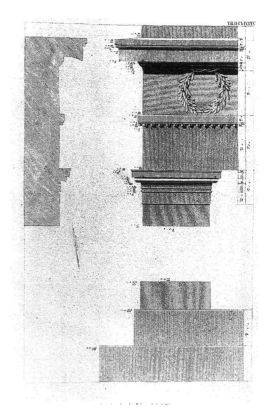

FIGURE 4.3 The Doric order of the Choragic Monument of Thrasyllus in volume II of the *Antiquities of Athens*.

imitations of Grecian originals.' To support that contention it was considered relevant to introduce 'accurate Representations of these Originals' since architecture 'at present appears to be founded on too partial and too scanty a system of ancient Examples'.[4] Yet, the examples illustrated in this first volume were not the major monuments on the Acropolis, but the small Ionic temple on the Ilissos, 'the buildings of which ... are extremely simple, yet withal so elegant'.[5] Even so, details which may have interested Thomson could be found in the plate of the Tower of the Winds, Athens, showing pseudo-isodomic masonry which Thomson favoured and which he used, first at Caledonia Road church (see FIGURE 14.1) and again at the St Vincent Street church. In the latter, the pulpit is flanked by lamps set on tripods, which Stuart and Revett described as prizes in games and festivals as 'the Reward of superior Force, Address and Genius'.[6]

Volume two of the *Antiquities of Athens* was pub-

lished in 1787 and contains a clue to a disturbing element in two of Thomson's church compositions: the introduction of a tall square tower or campanile alongside the main temple-like form (see FIGURE 5.1). Although the design of these towers has been commented on and their sources seen in Italian vernacular and Romanesque architecture, these are no justifications for a tower in an antique composition. So, did Thomson look at the plate of the Acropolis, where a tall crenellated tower stands to the left and overtops the Parthenon? It was this same volume that included the Erechtheum (see FIGURE 4.2), the most ornamental and most complete of all the Ionic temples. An important view, because it is so early, shows the inside of the west wall where the three window openings – reminiscent of the south wall of the St Vincent Street church – have inward–sloping jambs and lugged architraves. Finally, Thomson was to make much use of the Choragic Monument of Thrasyllus (see FIGURES 4.3 and 14.4), where

FIGURE 4.4 The northern end of Thomson's Eton Terrace,
Oakfield Avenue, 1865; photograph c.1955.

54 'Greek' Thomson

FIGURE 4.5   General view of the Acropolis at Athens; from
Picturesque Views of the Antiquities of Pola by Thomas
Allason, 1819.

the use of a central pier allowed Thomson to accommodate a pair of doorways within one porch – as at Oakfield Avenue (see FIGURE 4.4).

Another series, which was first published in the eighteenth century and continued into the next, was the *Antiquities of Ionia*, sponsored by the Society of Dilettanti. In part two, attention was drawn to two facets for those interested in Greece. First, there were 'the vast remains of splendour and power in the mouldered ruins of their public buildings; not only in the great ruling states, such as Athens, Corinth and Syracuse, but in little obscure republics, such as Paestum, Segesta and Selinus.'[7] More importantly, however, in the diffusion of archaeological knowledge was the statement, remarkable for the year 1797, that 'In the Temples of the Upper Egypt, many traces of a style of Architecture, ornament, and construction, similar to that adopted by the Greeks in their own country, may be discovered.'[8]

In 1819, Thomas Allason's *Picturesque Views of the Antiquities of Pola* – which has a general view of the Acropolis at Athens (see FIGURE 4.5), including the high square tower by the Parthenon – not only criticises Stuart and Revett for the inadequacy of their views, especially 'those of the Acropolis at Athens, which are extremely imperfect', but drew attention to their omission of the entasis 'or swelling, in the columns of the Parthenon, the Temple of Theseus, the Propylea, etc. etc. when it is so very apparent, not only in those structures, but in all the remaining Antiquities of Greece.'[9] Perhaps the exaggeration as to the widespread use of entasis was considered justifiable when criticising another author.

Allason's work could have been useful to Thomson by showing a view of two Roman temples (see FIGURE 4.6) which – with the engaged columns at the angles, and entablatures, pediments and low pitched tiled roof behind and foliage in front – are comparable to an

FIGURE 4.6 Two Roman temples, a plate from Allason's
Picturesque Views of the Antiquities of Pola, 1819.

unkempt and dilapidated Thomson villa, while the view of the Temple of Augustus (see FIGURE 4.7) with an adjacent house inevitably brings to mind Thomson's linking of the Caledonia Road and St Vincent Street (see FIGURE 1.1) churches with tenements.[10]

The first text devoted to a single Greek monument was Inwood's *The Erectheion at Athens*, published in 1827, with the subscribers including all the leading Greek Revival practitioners – all of whom were London-based. Two sections of the text could have been of particular interest to Thomson: reference was made to the temple at Jerusalem and to the passage of the Israelites from Egypt into Sinai, where 'a second sanctuary was commenced ... the most ancient certain instance of temple now known' with 'ten supports in front and twenty at the sides'.[11] In addition, 'it may be surmised that the labrum, whose stand was of copper, placed before the temple at Sinai, resembled a tripod, from which the tripods in [the] temple of Apollo at

Thebes with Phoenician characters may have originated, and thus its form made known in Greece.'[12]

While it can be accepted in such a work that 'There is perhaps no effort of Athenian architecture that in a higher degree excites our admiration than the Ionic capitals',[13] there was praise, too, for Ionic doorways with their consoles and diminution of the openings.[14] Useful also perhaps to an imaginative architect was the 'View of the Ancient Walls and Keep Tower of Aegisthaeana, a City of Megara' (see FIGURE 4.8).[15] The square tower has a shallow pitched roof below which are three vertical openings which compare with the topmost stages of the tower of Caledonia Road church.

With the publication of the supplementary fourth volume of the *Antiquities of Athens*, the list of subscribers widened to include not only all the well-known London architects, but others such as Ignatius Bonomi of Durham, and William Burn and Thomas Hamilton of Edinburgh. Among the Glasgow names were David

FIGURE 4.7   The Temple of Augustus, a plate from Allason's
Picturesque Views of the Antiquities of Pola, 1819.

Hamilton, a stylish and inventive classicist, and John
Baird, in whose office Thomson worked. The most
interesting name is that of Robert Foote, who first set
Thomson on an architectural path and of whom it is
recorded that 'having had the benefit of foreign travel,
[he] had realised the beauties of Greek architecture,
which influenced the career of his pupil'.[16]

Today one views the ruins of the Grecian world
while forgetting that not so long ago their appearance
was very different. For example, the west front of the
propylaea on the Athenian Acropolis shows that the
intercolumniations were walled up, with occasional
small openings, so that the Doric columns read as being
half engaged.[17] Such a mass of walling with few openings is a reminder perhaps of the podium of the St
Vincent Street church and, on a lesser scale, of portions
of the Double Villa. It should also be borne in mind
that antique ruins were not always looked on with a
scholarly eye but rather in relation to nineteenth-
century visual concepts. Thus, in the siting of temples,
especially in the countryside, 'One of the constituent

properties of architectural effect, the principle of the
picturesque, seems powerfully to have been felt by
them.'[18] And not only by the Greeks but also by Thomson, whose asymmetrical compositions led Hitchcock
to describe his churches as 'Romantic Classical'.[19]

Possibly the most scholarly text of the nineteenth
century was *Prolusiones Architectonicae* by William Wilkins – famous as the architect of the National Gallery,
London, and the University of London buildings – but
on the title-page accredited as 'Formerly a Senior
Fellow of Caius College, in the University of Cambridge; Regius Professor of Architecture in the Royal
Academy'. In his text, Wilkins examined the construction of the Erechtheum and, like others before him,
singled out the north doorway for which he gives the
dimensions. When it comes to roofs, he adduced 'that
some temples were embellished with ornamental ceilings below the framework of timber which supported
the tiles', and not only does he cite Pausanias but 'In the
sacred writings there is an ample description of a ceiling of this description.'[20] He then goes on to compare

FIGURE 4.8   'View of the Ancient Walls and Keep Tower of
Aegisthaeana, a City of Megara', from *The Erectheion at
Athens* by H. W. Inwood, 1827.

the temple at Jerusalem with Greek examples in which
'a resemblance will be found to exist, that can only
be attributed to the adoption of the same principles
by the architects of Palestine and Greece'.[21] Indeed,
the biblical account of the temple is enough 'to con-
vince an architect of the present day, that it relates
to a mode of building which prevailed amongst the
Greeks at a later period'.[22] Clearly, the details of Greek
architecture as well as the concept of a connection
between Solomon's Temple in Jerusalem and Greek
models were well documented and had passed into
general architectural thinking by the time Thomson
had begun practice.

It was then that the Society of Dilettanti published
*An Investigation into the Principles of Athenian
Architecture*, possibly the single most original text. In
the introduction it was explained 'That it had been
recently ascertained that traces of the most refined
thought and subtile [sic] optical principles were to be
found in the Parthenon and the Greek buildings of the
best time; the most important of these being the curvature of the horizontal lines and the inclination of the
columns.'[23] The curvature had been discovered by
John Pennethorne in 1837, 'When much of the rubbish
which encumbered the stylobate of the Parthenon had
been removed', with T. L. Donaldson elucidating the
inclination of the columns.[24] After the historical description followed chapters on the jointing of stones,
curvature, the inclination of columns and entasis. In
the chapter 'On the Polychromy of the Parthenon', it

stated that, when taking measurements, 'it was impossible not to be attracted by the evident though
generally faint traces of ancient colouring which occasionally met the eye'.[25] The text concluded with some
reflections on the current state of the Greek Revival,
the products of which were described as 'cold and
hard'. Indeed, 'a rigid adherence to precedent has often
proved fallacious, when persisted in contrary to that
universal rule of commonsense, which requires that
architecture shall be suited to the manners, habits, and
wants of the people, and worthy of the science of the
day'.[26] This was the challenge that Thomson was to
accept.

What, however, gave Thomson's architectural creations the emotive power was the combination of the
literary research and careful measured drawings of
cognoscenti and architects with the visual imagery of the
painter. It is known that Thomson admired the work
of J. M. W. Turner (1775–1851), with *Decline of the
Carthaginian Empire* (1817), being cited as one example; and that of John Martin (1789–1854) in particular.[27] Although it has been stated that Martin offered
'little or nothing in terms of original research',[28] it can
be demonstrated from his own accompanying descriptions and other internal evidence that his architectural
compositions were constructed from a scholarly basis.[29]
From the numerous prints of Martin's work that were
available, Thomson would have gleaned an appreciation of gigantic scale, of elements heaped one upon the
other on podia, of colonnades of limitless extent, of
ornate capitals and of towers looming in the background, as well as of the rich colourings of the East.
Subjects such as *Seventh Plague of Egypt* (1823) (see
FIGURE 14.3) or *Belshazzar's Feast* (1820) demonstrate
why 'Martin was most admired for his convincingly
staged narratives, for the dramas of decline and fall,
failure and salvation',[30] all of which would have struck
a chord with Thomson, whose religious beliefs were
much shaped by the Old Testament.

It is to be regretted that Thomson's modern biographer gave no attention to the architect's use of colour
in either his domestic or ecclesiastical work, when it is
recorded by Thomson's earliest biographer that 'In
some instances he painted the figure with his own
hand, and in many he drew all the stencils.'[31] Yet an
interest in colour must have determined much of
Thomson's thinking, for not only were there the

provoking comments about the Parthenon, but in 1856 – when Thomson was working on the Caledonia Road church – Owen Jones's *The Grammar of Ornament* appeared. Once again, there is no proof that Thomson read the book but, looking at the vibrant illustrations and reading the text, one can only assume that he did. Jones, writing of the 'General Principles in the Arrangement of Form and Colour in Architecture', enunciated propositions such as: 'The Decorative Arts arise from, and should properly be attendant upon, Architecture ... Construction should be decorated.' That was standard stuff. What is more novel is Jones's analysis of ancient ornamentation and its line of descent':

> *The architecture of the Egyptians is thoroughly polychromatic ... They dealt in flat tints, and used neither shade nor shadow, ... We are strongly inclined to believe that the Assyrian is not an original style, but was borrowed from the Egyptian, ... Greek art ... though borrowed partly from the Egyptian and partly from the Assyrian ... rose rapidly to a high state of perfection ... It carried the perfection of pure form to a point which has never since been reached.*[32]

That Thomson was aware of Egyptian art is evident from his own lectures, in which he cites publications by J. C. Wilkinson, David Roberts and James Fergusson, all of whom were influential in bringing a knowledge of the Egyptian and Assyrian styles to the fore.[33] Although Wilkinson's *Manners and Customs of Ancient Egypt* (1837) had aroused much interest, it was the deft and captivating renderings of the Pharaonic temples and funerary monuments in Roberts's *Egypt and Nubia* (1846–9)[34] that would have given Thomson a vocabulary of ideas with a theoretical hypothesis for their use being provided in two texts by James Fergusson: *The Palaces of Nineveh and Persepolis Restored* (1851) and the more widely read *The Illustrated Handbook of Architecture* of four years later. In the first, Fergusson puts forward the claim that 'it is a fact that it is now impossible to doubt, that all that is Ionic in the arts of Greece is derived from the valleys of the Tigris and Euphrates';[35] while in the second he is more specific, stating that

> *the architecture of Assyria was that of a Semitic people, and especially interesting as exhibiting actual examples of that style with which we have long been familiar from the descriptions in the Bible of the buildings of Solomon ... Till, however, the palaces of Assyria were disinterred, and those of Persepolis examined, we had but little to guide us in our restorations, but now it requires only a little more time and patient industry to make all clear.*[36]

Steeped as he must have been in the Old Testament, Thomson responded to such writings by creating churches which are markedly different in composition and decoration from those by other Greek Revival architects; for unlike their ascetic studies, Thomson's religious compositions are personifications of his Presbyterian faith.

NOTES

1. R. McFadzean, *The Life and Work of Alexander Thomson*, London, 1979, p. 97.
2. Ibid., p. 96.
3. Personal communication between Dr Gavin Stamp and author, 1993.
4. J. Stuart and N. Revett, *The Antiquities of Athens*, London, 1762, vol. I, p. 1.
5. Ibid., p. 7.
6. Ibid., p. 29.
7. *Antiquities of Ionia*, London, 1797, pt. II, p. ix.
8. Ibid., p. 19.
9. T. Allason, *Picturesque Views of the Antiquities of Pola*, London, 1819, p. 3.
10. Ibid., pp. 15 and 21.
11. H. W. Inwood, *The Erectheion at Athens*, London, 1827, p. 4.
12. Ibid., p. 36.
13. Ibid., p. 106.
14. Ibid., pp. 111 and 113.
15. Ibid., p. 158.
16. The manuscript notes of a talk by Thomas Gildard are in the Mitchell Library, Glasgow. See also McFadzean, *Alexander Thomson*, pp. 6–7.
17. C. R. Cockerell, W. Kinnaird, T. L. Donaldson, W. Jenkins and W. Railton, *Antiquities of Athens and Other Places in Greece, Sicily, etc* (Suppl. to the *Antiquities of Athens*), London, 1830, vol. IV, pl. I: 'A View of the West Front of the Propylaea at Athens'.
18. T. L. Donaldson, 'The Temple of Apollo Epicurius at Bassae', ibid., p. 3.
19. H.-R. Hitchcock, *Architecture: Nineteenth and Twentieth Centuries*, Harmondsworth, repr. 1967, p. 61.
20. W. Wilkins, *Prolusiones Architectonicae*, London, 1837, p. 85.
21. Ibid., p. 101.

22. Ibid., p. 128.

23. F. C. Penrose, *An Investigation into the Principles of Athenian Architecture*, London, 1851, introduction.

24. Ibid., p. 20.

25. Ibid., p. 55.

26. Ibid., p. 83.

27. McFadzean, *Alexander Thomson*, pp. 59–60.

28. W. Feaver, *The Art of John Martin*, Oxford, 1975, p. 40.

29. N. Monckton, 'Architectural Backgrounds in the Pictures of John Martin', *Architectural Review* CIV (Aug. 1948), pp. 81–8.

30. Feaver, *John Martin*, p. 86.

31. Obituary by T. Gildard for *The British Architect* (1875). (Gildard's notes, Mitchell Library, Glasgow.) There seems to be some dispute about the internal colouring of the St Vincent Street church. In his obituary notice of Thomson, Gildard says that the interior decoration was not completed. However, in J. Logan Aikman (ed.), *United Presbyterian Congregations in Glasgow*, Glasgow, 1875, it is stated that St Vincent Street church had been painted and decorated. In 1888 Gildard, in speaking about Thomson, says that the decoration was not by him.

32. O. Jones, *The Grammar of Ornament*, London, 1856, Thomson, of course, would have long known that Greek temples were coloured. The first volume of the *Transactions of the Institute of British Architects* (1835–6) carried an article, translated from the German, by Dr Kugler, 'On the Polychromy of Greek Architecture', pp. 73–99, which listed the various published works by Hittorff and others who had investigated the colouring of ancient monuments.

33. McFadzean, *Alexander Thomson*, pp. 59 and 214.

34. J. S. Curl, *The Egyptian Revival*, London, 1982, p. 182.

35. J. Fergusson, *The Palaces of Nineveh and Persepolis Restored*, London, 1851, p. 340.

36. J. Fergusson, *The Illustrated Handbook of Architecture*, London, 1855, vol. I, pp. 162 and 201.

THEORY AND IDEALS

FIGURE 5.1   The Caledonia Road church from the south-
east, c. 1860, before the construction of the City of Glasgow
Union Railway viaduct. The Caledonian Railway's Southside
terminus lay to the left of the lamp-post.

Chapter Five

·

THOMSON'S ARCHITECTURAL THEORY

Sam McKinstry

Religion has been the soul of art from the beginning.
(Alexander Thomson, Haldane Lectures, II (1874), p. 6)

While the work of Alexander 'Greek' Thomson has at last begun to receive the international recognition it deserves, its theoretical underpinnings have not as yet been seriously investigated. As a result, the popular conception of Thomson as a latter-day neoclassicist persists, bordering on useless cliché, and explaining little or nothing of the architect's intentions as a designer. McFadzean, in *The Life and Work of Alexander Thomson*, provides readers with what they would expect from his book's title: a factual guide to Thomson, indeed, an indispensable one.[1] In contrast, he has little to say about Thomson's architectural theory, apart from venturing the view that Thomson should be seen as a proto-functionalist who failed, ultimately, to cast off the shackles of historical style.

In his functionalist interpretation of Thomson, McFadzean follows Pevsner, who emphasised the architect's preference for trabeated styles and commented on his rational objections to arcuated forms.[2] As might be expected from a writer of this persuasion, Thomson's biographer concludes his book with comparisons between his subject, Frank Lloyd Wright and Le Corbusier, noting elsewhere that 'He [Thomson] had forged his own style of modern architecture and stood looking into the future seeing a new architecture based on functions, structure (the recent 1851 exhibition still fresh in his mind), and the elimination of extraneous ornament.'[3]

John McKean, in a paper written in 1985, takes issue with McFadzean's view of Thomson as proto-modernist.[4] By way of alternative explanation,

McKean draws attention to Thomson's 'obvious delight in manipulating visual and spatial effects', which is clear from studies of Thomson's architectural details, in particular the interior of the demolished Queen's Park church (see FIGURE 13.1). Here McKean examines the contrast between this and the massive pillars of the façade, which, viewed externally, appear to support the masonry of the tall dome. Old photographs confirm that this was illusory. The mass above is supported on slender cast-iron columns, skirted by a clerestory of frosted glass. His justification for this interpretation is not only empirical: McKean makes occasional references to Thomson's writings, where the architect refers to the ancient Egyptian and Greek practice of expressing 'in symbols and in abstract forms ... ideas of beauty and grandeur'. For McKean, Thomson's architecture pursues 'eternal qualities'. 'Fragments extracted from their contexts were made to convey whatever abstracted reactions his taste demanded: grandeur, mystery or majesty.' In practice, McKean does not advocate the complete rejection of McFadzean's functionalist and rationalist interpretation of Thomson's theory, arguing earlier in his paper that Thomson may have derived from Laugier, directly or indirectly, the desire to express 'both the apparent and actual solidity of trabeated construction'. However, it is obvious that such concerns only partially explain Thomson's theoretical approach, a point McKean makes well.

While his paper is a timely and necessary supplement to McFadzean, it was not intended as a complete picture of Thomson's architectural theory, nor even as a summary. In particular, it only touches on the relationship between Thomson's evangelicalism and his aesthetics, which is central to an understanding of his thought. Thomson was, it must be remembered, an elder of the United Presbyterian Church, a denomination renowned for its devout evangelicalism, which he wholeheartedly espoused.

Fortunately, there is no shortage of evidence for a deeper analysis of Thomson's theoretical position. In 1866, he published his well-known 'Inquiry as to the Appropriateness of the Gothic Style for the Proposed Buildings for the University of Glasgow', his critique of Scott's designs; and in 1874, four lectures on architecture – subsequently published – were given to the Glasgow School of Art and Haldane Academy.[5] In total this material runs to some ninety pages of architectural discussion, densely typeset, closely argued, and punctiliously expressed. It is difficult to read, although the fault lies mainly at the door of time. There are several drawbacks which accentuate the difficulties. The critique is polemical and overstates its case; the lectures were not intended as an exposition, pure and simple, of the architect's theoretical principles, although they perhaps inevitably take a tendentious direction.[6]

In the first of the Haldane Lectures, Thomson sets out his basic aesthetic presuppositions. Significantly, he rejects those definitions of art, or approaches to it, which rely on the replication of nature alone. Nature is flawed, for one thing; beauty in natural objects is not uniform, or it may even be completely absent. Ruskin, whose 'exquisitely refined mind seems to imbibe from all the springs of truth' insists on 'artists taking nature as they find it'. This makes little allowance for man's 'higher powers'. As well as placing Thomson in the ranks of the many architects who so clearly noticed Ruskin's inconsistencies, his observations here reveal an aesthetic which sets out to exhibit truth 'in its purest and most beneficial forms'. 'Mere feats of dexterity [in the replication of nature] may astonish or amuse us; they do not elevate our minds.' Examples of the approach approved by Thomson are the drawings of Flaxman or the paintings of Turner, the latter attracting the paradoxical praise of Ruskin in spite of their lack of naturalistic detail.

Next to be identified in his lecture are the three endowments possessed by man: the perceptive, the selective and the creative faculties. The perceptive 'recognises and enjoys the beautiful in a general and almost passive way', the selective 'acts like a palate or conscience distinguishing and discriminating between what is truly and purely beautiful from what is not so', while the creative is explained in wholly Christian terms:

Some say that man can never get beyond his experiences. Whence then come Music and Architecture? There is nothing in Nature like either; for although they may have been slow of growth the fact is before us that they are something that by man or through his agency has been added to the work of God, and that, not presumptuously or sinfully, as some would tell us, but by destiny and duty; for being made in the image of God, man was made partaker of the divine nature so far as to become a fellow-worker with God – in however humble a sense, a co-Creator.[7]

His stance is unambiguous. An architect's duty is to create, under God, works which elevate the mind of man. Such, then, was Thomson's personal aim. But how is the mind to be elevated, and what are these 'ideas of beauty and grandeur', on which Thomson insists so much? A great deal of the answer emerges in the three remaining lectures, in his analysis of the Egyptian, Greek and Roman styles, which were being examined to 'show how far man has succeeded in this [co-Creatorial] department of duty'.

Central to Thomson's analysis of the architectural achievements of Egypt and Greece was the assumption that the process of divine revelation, culminating in the advent of Christ, had been progressively at work in history. God, in his Providence, had first revealed Himself gradually through nature, 'the Elder Scriptures', and then through the nations. The Greek civilisation, in particular, had prepared mankind for the Christ and His teachings. This was, and is, theologically orthodox; shortly after Thomson's death in 1875, Westcott, the Bishop of Durham, would write that 'the work of Greece . . . lives for the simplest Christian in the New Testament'. Westcott saw Aeschylus as a 'preparation' for Plato, and Euripides as a religious teacher representing a further 'distinct stage in the preparation . . . for Christianity'.[8] But for Thomson, divine truth had been discerned much earlier in Egypt, where 'some great hearted, far-seeing man had in the beginning instilled into the minds of his people the idea of immortality and of the resurrection of the dead'. This was followed by the proposition, indispensable to an understanding of his thought, that 'Religion has been the soul of art from the beginning'. It was the strongest impulse that art was called upon to express. Indeed, Thomson concludes that 'striving after the permanent seems to be the soul of Egyptian art. It is an endeavour to realise the idea of eternity.'

How this actually works is demonstrated in Thomson's examination of Egyptian architectural forms, especially the obelisk. He observes that 'We have the idea of duration repeated in the hardness of the granite of which it is composed.' In its carefully adjusted proportion and its perfect – seemingly weightless – poise, it appears 'as an imperishable thought, a symbol of truth or justice'. The principle becomes clearer when Thomson states that 'There are various modes of impressing the mind with a sense of greatness. That which most readily presents itself is actual bulk; and we find this mode resorted to in Egyptian art more than in any other.'[9] Thus pyramids and temples expressed greatness, stability and duration, the columns and capitals of the latter, softened by shadow, contributing to a sense of 'perfect repose'. Finally, Thomson quotes de Quincey's response to the Memnon's head, which he had studied in the British Museum, and which for him was not human, but symbolic:

what it symbolised to me were – 1st, the peace which passeth all understanding; 2nd, the eternity which baffles and confounds all faculty of computation – the eternity which had been, the eternity which was to be; 3rd, the diffusive love, not such as rises and falls upon waves of life and mortality, not such as sinks and swells by undulations of time, but a procession, an emanation from some mystery of endless dawn.[10]

Thomson's analysis of Greek art, in his third lecture, operates along similar lines. As a preliminary, he examines the linkages between the Egyptian and Greek cultures, which, he concludes, might have been numerous, but do not explain Greek genius. This was expressed in 'beauty and symmetry of form, and harmony of relative proportion'. Its greatness 'was of the intellectual rather than the material kind', since Greek buildings were not, on the whole, large. Thomson next praised the 'picturesque' grouping of the Erechtheum, and observed that the style, properly understood and contrary to what its detractors said, was flexible enough

for modern needs. After noting the principal attractions and detailed features of the most well-known Greek buildings, Thomson finally turned his attention to the Parthenon, which he asked his audience to imagine 'when Greece was the light of the world'.

A great rock rises from amidst the widespread city. Its battlemented walls follow the irregularities of the precipice, here assuming the shape of a tower or bastion, there some form of grace which suggests a sacred purpose. But the chief objects are the Parthenon and its companions. And now let us ... gaze with the eye of the soul on the wonderful sight. John saw 'the Holy City, New Jerusalem, coming down from God out of Heaven, prepared as a bride adorned for her husband'. What do we see here? A group of beautiful forms, so full of thought that they seem to think. They seem possessed of some high contemplative, rapturous kind of life altogether different from any of the ordinary or natural sorts. ... they neither move nor are moved, but sit upon that rock as upon a throne, high and lifted up in the sight of all the people, in the sight of all the gods.[11]

In Thomson's mind's eye, these 'angelic forms' stood 'as mediators between heaven and earth, sending upwards the prayers and praises of men, and drawing downwards the approbation and blessing of the eternal gods'. Confirming his conception of the whole as a coalescence of the aesthetic and religious dimensions, he exhorts his audience to imagine 'the colossal figure of Minerva ... standing in the midst with her hand raised pointing to heaven'. This, he felt, must surely have been one of the most glorious sights given to man, never to be seen again 'in this world'. Once again, as in Egypt, architectural forms were employed to evoke emotional, intellectual and even spiritual responses.

If Thomson's enthusiasm for the architecture of the past reaches its zenith when he speaks of the halls of Karnak or the stones of the Parthenon, it touches its nadir in his final lecture on the architecture of Rome. Roman architecture represents a downward step from the Greek 'because its motive is totally different'. For the Romans, 'their worldly business ... [was] of greater importance than the temples of their gods'. Their architecture 'did not look upwards for inspiration' and 'mystery was henceforth abolished'. Clearly, a civilisation lacking in moral and spiritual fibre could not engender architecture of permanent worth. It was 'fleshly', never 'sanctifying religion with any holy ray of spiritual truth'. The Colosseum was 'tremendously ugly', and was invested with the spirit of the 'cruel hearted people' who thronged it out of 'an intense thirst for blood'. The Pantheon, however, possessed a portico 'of very great beauty' but this was out of sympathy with its rotunda. Inside, Thomson admitted that it 'commanded the admiration of all beholders', but that he did not like the 'trifling' detailing on the lower reaches of the walls. The single event, which, more than any other, had turned architecture away from the 'settled tranquillity which rests on the perfect law of God' had been Rome's 'adoption of the arch as an architectural feature'. Thomson's objection was twofold. 'In its aesthetic, as in its constructive capacity, the arch never sleeps.' It was structurally unsound, and had left Europe strewn with ruins: aesthetically, its contemplation produced restlessness, reflecting the spiritual shortcomings of Roman civilisation.

While events denied Thomson the opportunity to comment at length on Gothic architecture, the few remarks he spared it in the last of his lectures – together with his observations on Scott's University design – make it clear that he considered it an inferior genre. From the standpoint of stability, Thomson had ventured that 'Stonehenge is more scientifically constructed than York Minster'. From an aesthetic standpoint, the 'restlessness' produced by the arch called out for a focal point, hence the evolution in the Gothic style of complex window traceries. This led to 'dissipation and dispersion', rather than repose. In his critique of the University designs, Thomson makes an attempt at even-handedness. The style's variety and tree-like qualities could be 'pleasing', calling as they did for the pleasurable exercise of the imagination in an effort to unravel and arrange. This was as much as he could muster, however, in support of a style produced at the time of Christendom's decadence. How could 'earnest and intelligent Protestants' support the 'impudent assertion' that it was the 'Christian style'? In his attitude to Gothic, Thomson's inseparable blend of aesthetics and theology is again apparent.

His writings, and indeed much of what has been said above, reveal a further major strand in his thinking: the Sublime. Dixon and Muthesius note that the Picturesque and the Sublime 'permeate Victorian architecture

and architectural writing'.[12] The literature of Scottish high-Victorian architecture, including the *Building Chronicle* of the 1850s and the *Transactions of the Architectural Institute of Scotland*, is sprinkled with references to the Picturesque. This found its visual expression in the Scots Baronial movement popularised by David Bryce. The Sublime, however, seldom emerges, but in Thomson it is all-pervasive. Its most stunning manifestation is a passage in the first Haldane Lecture which appears as Thomson makes the case for the 'subjective', rather than the copyist approach to the representation of nature in art:

To illustrate this, let us suppose an example. We shall lay the scene in the Highlands – at midwinter – at the dead hour of night. Several weeks of intense frost have turned all water into ice as solid as the rocks; the snow, which had been falling all day, has now ceased; a solitary pedestrian is toiling up the slippery steep, striving bravely against the drowsiness and stupefaction which are often experienced in such circumstances. But he has reached the summit and pauses to recover breath; and as he stands, he gazes with wonder at the strange scene around him. The moon has set, but through the clear cold air myriads of stars, in all degrees of brightness . . . look down on him in radiant beauty. There is neither light nor shade, mere whiteness as far as the eye can follow . . . There is no sound of waterfall, or trickling rill, or whispering breeze; no moving thing . . . A painful feeling of oppression, deepening into fear, creeps over his senses from the deathlike stillness which reigns around him. But this gives place to something else – an indescribable strange consciousness, which every instant becomes more intense, that he is standing there alone, the only living thing before God. . . . his terror melts into ecstatic joy; and now, exulting in the love of God, he finds new strength, and passes on his way.[13]

Thomson's point is to emphasise that 'Although all this could not be painted, much of it might.' In making it, he lays bare the Sublime artistic vision with which he so closely identified: his admiration for Turner can now be fully understood.

Even if he had not mentioned his name in the lecture, the above passage makes it obvious that Thomson was deeply influenced by Edmund Burke, who had stated in the *Sublime and Beautiful* that 'The passion

FIGURE 5.2 *Belshazzar's Feast*, steel engraving by
J. Horsburgh after John Martin, from *Blackie's Imperial
Family Bible*, 1845.

caused by the great and sublime in nature, when those causes operate most powerfully, is astonishment; and astonishment is that state of the soul, in which all its motions are suspended, with some degree of horror.'[14] Just as Thomson's prose is full of Burkean language, so his architectural prescriptions reflect those of Burke, whose nostrum that 'Greatness of dimension is a powerful cause of the sublime' is echoed in Thomson's statement (quoted above) that greatness may be conveyed through bulk. Thomson also refers to the 'principle of repetition', equivalent to Burke's 'Succession and uniformity of parts', which suggested infinity. Burke had noted that, on these principles, 'the grand appearance of the ancient heathen temples, which were generally oblong forms, with a range of uniform pillars on every side, will be easily accounted for'.[15] So too on this basis is Thomson's stated admiration for 'the magnificent architectural compositions of the late John Martin' (see FIGURE 5.2), whose Sublime colonnaded

panoramas of Greece, Egypt and the Holy Land had graced the drawing-rooms of evangelicals over the previous half century.

Other aspects of Thomson are completely explained by reference to Burke. Since light, or its absence, is a cause of the Sublime, Burke advocates a 'well managed darkness', hence Thomson's manipulation of light at St Vincent Street or Queen's Park churches, a device which is also based on his admiration for the mysterious clerestories of Egyptian temples. A further ground principle of Burke's aesthetics is 'that no work of art can be great, but as it deceives'. Visual deception in the pursuit of the Sublime or the Beautiful was acceptable. The utilitarian dimension should never be allowed to destroy aesthetic effect, and it certainly, according to Burke, cannot create it; 'fitness is not tantamount to beauty'. The study of 'the wedge-like snout of a swine' is sufficient to demonstrate that its eminent suitability to its purpose does not make it beautiful. And so it is with Thomson. In discussing the University designs, he had observed that Scott's stated primary objective was practical: 'he had devoted his attention chiefly to ... concocting the plans and dealing out to each of the Professors the exact kind and amount of accommodation which the business of his class required ...'.[16] This task Thomson describes as 'very humble business'. In a different context, he was to state on biblical grounds that the design of Solomon's Temple 'was not controlled by any utilitarian consideration'.[17] While structural and functional integrity were important, these dimensions should never usurp the greater aims of architecture. This approach is again consistent with Burke, and explains precisely why the elevations of Thomson's great churches, for example, do not correspond with their internal layouts, or why, in some of his lesser buildings, he is neglectful of rear elevations.[18]

The debt to Burke is as massive as it is obvious. It is clear from the lectures, though, that Thomson was well aware of the developments in aesthetic theory that had succeeded Burke's book. Hussey, in the first chapters of *The Picturesque*, picks out as significant the contribution of Uvedale Price, who, in 1794 proposed that 'the picturesque' was quite different to the 'sublime' and the 'beautiful', and deserved to be classified separately.[19] In the first Haldane Lecture, Thomson states that 'the sublime and the beautiful ... properly expressed only two branches of his [Burke's] subject', revealing his familiarity with this point of view. Hussey next notes the contribution of Alison, whose 'Essay on Taste' accounted for beauty in terms of the association of ideas, mentioned specifically by Thomson in his first lecture. In spite of his knowledge of these subsequent developments in aesthetics, it was clearly to Burke that Thomson remained most indebted. The reasons are not hard to find: Uvedale Price's 'picturesque' category was of subordinate if still significant interest to Thomson, who stated that 'There are two terms used in speaking of art, the picturesque and the ideal', but was to say of the variety and flexibility offered by the former that 'neither is essentially of the things which are "a joy forever"'. Thomson much preferred the classical qualities of 'symmetry of form' and 'harmony of relative proportion', both of which conformed more closely to Burke's idea of 'the beautiful'. Thomson, however, agreed to some extent with Alison, stating that 'The

pleasure we derive from objects of sight arises *partly* [my emphasis] from the associations they suggest, and partly from their own inherent beauty.'[20] That notwithstanding, there must also have been an emotional attachment to Burke for his biblicism. The highest illustrations of the Sublime were to be found in 'Scripture alone', Burke had written, and were in evidence whenever God was represented as appearing or speaking, and throughout the Psalms. For both men the Sublime was an integral part of their Christian worldview, and scripture an indispensable tool of verbal expression.[21]

There is evidence that Thomson was by no means the only member of the United Presbyterian Church to be influenced by Burke's notion of the Sublime. Woodside, in *The Soul of a Scottish Church*, deals with that denomination's contribution to the literature of Scotland, drawing attention to the poet Michael Bruce, of Kinnesswood near Lochleven.[22] Bruce was 'a man of simple piety as well as of high intelligence', born in 1746 in a village nestling in the shade of the beautiful Lomond Hills, 'surroundings ... fitted to aid the development of a Christian poet'. He was 'very susceptible to the sublime influences of external scenery ... and Nature led him up to Nature's God'. It is likely that he would hear of Burke's recently published *Sublime and Beautiful* whilst at theological college. His life was tragically short, lasting a mere twenty-one years. During that time he paraphrased a number of Psalms for congregational singing, including 'O God of Bethel, by whose hand' and 'Where high the heavenly temple stands'. The quality and character of his work are well captured in the first verse of his paraphrase of Isaiah, 2:

> *Behold the mountain of the Lord,*
> *In latter days shall rise,*
> *On mountain tops above the hills,*
> *And draw the wondering eyes.*[23]

A Church which virtually revered the Psalms and paraphrases must often – in all the sonority of its primitive, unaccompanied praise – have been conscious of the Sublime.

Thomson's debt to Burke is matched by an equally obvious debt to James Fergusson. At a superficial level, Fergusson's descriptions of the temple at Karnak and the Choragic Monument of Lysicrates – uplifted from *The Illustrated Handbook of Architecture* – are quoted in the Haldane Lectures, where his opinions on the evolution of various stylistic elements are discussed at length, mostly with Thomson's approval.[24] More importantly, Fergusson's Introduction to the above work is an attempt to enumerate the 'true principles which ought to guide us in designing or criticising architectural objects'. Sound construction is essential, if not sufficient. The Egyptians and the Greeks never deviate from 'the perpendicular wall or prop, supporting a horizontal beam', half the effect of their buildings arising from this. They knew of the arch, but 'wisely' rejected it as it would cause 'complexity and confusion' in their designs. For the Hindus, 'An arch never sleeps', he observes, which – as has been noted – Thomson was not to forget. Fergusson goes on to describe the importance, for good architecture, of the careful disposition of form, good proportion, restrained use of ornament, and the selective use of uniformity, or variety, depending on circumstances. This carefully reasoned formula was intended as a corrective to the over-reliance on pictorial effects which he perceived on every hand, and all of it is broadly consistent with Thomson's position. So, too, is Fergusson's use of the term 'sublime' or its derivatives twelve times in his Introduction, and the plentiful use of Burkean ideas throughout. At face value, the two men's positions could not be distinguished, but in practice, the use of the arch and the styles which carried it were acceptable to Fergusson, although he admits in the body of his work that the ancients who avoided it 'probably showed more science and discrimination than we do'. For the mature Thomson, its prohibition was almost literally an article of faith. One intriguing aspect remains: to what extent was his final abandonment of the arch, evident in his work from the mid-1850s onwards, sparked off by his studies of Fergusson? It is not impossible to judge with finality, but his respect for that writer means that his influence cannot be ruled out.

In summary, then, this study has sought to show that the theoretical roots of Thomson's mature architectural style are for the most part discernible in his surviving writings, and that his theory was constructed within a framework of theological conviction. The key is Thomson's concept of progressive divine revelation in history, which he saw reflected in the aesthetic flowerings of Egypt and Greece. This he readily and ingeniously

FIGURE 5.3   Detail of the Pitt Street entrance of the St Vincent Street church.

reconciled with ideas of the Sublime derived from Edmund Burke, whose descriptions and characterisations of the same phenomena were suitably Christian, and had inspired several generations of artists, architects and critics. Thomson's 'theology of Beauty' or 'Christian aesthetic' appears all the more remarkable when contrasted with the 'architectural morality' and functionalism of Pugin, also born of deep Christian conviction, and propagated in the high-Victorian period by Scott, Street, Butterfield and their followers. By the time Thomson was writing his Haldane Lectures, this latter movement had spread to Scotland and had found its champion in the young Robert Rowand Anderson, a Scott pupil whose persuasive powers

FIGURE 5.4 Interior of the Caledonia Road church looking towards the entrance, photo 1964.

combined with economic circumstances to bring an end to the Picturesque-influenced Scots Baronial movement.[25] Undoubtedly, though, Thomson's remarkable temperament was influenced by his ecclesiastical roots; he and his forebears were secessionists, nonconformists, belonging to a denomination marked out, according to Woodside, for 'the value that it put upon the individual'. Thomson was its aesthetic epitome.

His principal aims were undoubtedly affective: to elevate men's minds through an architecture that, so often, borders on worship in stone. Who could fail, even today, to be touched by feelings of awe and eternity while standing before the shell of Caledonia Road church? And what Sublime emotions must have been experienced inside, in the hearts of the faithful, as Dr Jeffrey, Thomson's own minister, spoke on 'Voices from Calvary' in surroundings of such evocative magnificence?[26] (see FIGURES 5.4 and 5.5)

NOTES

1. Ronald McFadzean, *The Life and Work of Alexander Thomson*, London, 1979.
2. Nikolaus Pevsner, *Some Architectural Writers of the Nineteenth Century*, Oxford, 1972, pp. 183–7. Pevsner, in a brief summary of Thomson's 'An Inquiry as to the Appropriateness of the Gothic Style of the Proposed Buildings for the University of Glasgow' (see n. 16), alights on Thomson's condemnation of the arch.
3. Ronald McFadzean, 'The Villas of Alexander Thomson', unpublished RIAS prize essay, 1971.
4. John Maule McKean, 'The Architectonics and Ideals of Alexander "Greek" Thomson', *Annals of the Architectural Association School of Architecture*, (1985), no. 3, pp. 31–44.
5. The Haldane Lectures were subsequently published piecemeal in the *British Architect*. Thomson's own copies of the offprints, annotated with detailed corrections to the spelling and grammar, were preserved by Thomas Gildard and have been deposited in the Mitchell Library, Glasgow.

FIGURE 5.5 The ceiling of the Caledonia Road church,
photo taken in 1964.

6. 'Greek Thomson', paper presented to the Glasgow Architectural Association, 30 January 1888, by Thomas Gildard, Mitchell Library, Glasgow.

7. Haldane Lectures, I (1874), Mitchell Library, Glasgow, p. 16.

8. R. Jenkyns, *The Victorians and Ancient Greece*, London, 1973, p. 71.

9. Haldane Lectures, II (1874), Mitchell Library, Glasgow, p. 11.

10. Ibid., II, p. 14.

11. Ibid., III, pp. 19–20.

12. Roger Dixon and Stefan Muthesius, *Victorian Architecture*, London, 1978, p. 20.

13. Haldane Lectures, I (1874), Mitchell Library, Glasgow, pp. 7–8.

14. Edmund Burke, *A Philosophical Inquiry into the Origins of our Ideas of the Sublime and Beautiful*, Glasgow, 1818, p. 58 (first published in 1759).

15. Ibid., p. 81.

16. Alexander Thomson, 'An Inquiry as to the Appropriateness of the Gothic Style for the Proposed Buildings for the University of Glasgow, with Some Remarks upon Mr. Scott's Plans', *Proceedings of the Glasgow Architectural Society* (7 May 1866), p. 18.

17. Haldane Lectures, II (1874), p. 6.

18. This point with justification concerned McFadzean, since he claimed that Thomson's functionalism and rationalism were the dominating influences in his architecture.

19. Christopher Hussey, *The Picturesque*, London, 1927, pp. 55–82.

20. Thomson, 'University of Glasgow Buildings', p. 3.

21. Burke's Whig politics may also have endeared him to Thomson, who, as an elder of a nonconformist Church (the United Presbyterian Church), would probably hold similar views.

22. David Woodside, *The Soul of a Scottish Church*, Edinburgh, n.d. (c.1915), pp. 169–72.

23. *The Church Hymnary*, Oxford, 1973, no. 312.

24. James Fergusson, *The Illustrated Handbook of Architecture*, 2 vols, London, 1855.

25. Sam McKinstry, *Rowand Anderson: The Premier Architect of Scotland*, Edinburgh, 1991.

26. R. T. Jeffrey, *Voices from Calvary*, Edinburgh, 1860. This book contains sermons preached in Caledonia Road church in the late 1850s – with Thomson, doubtless, in attendance.

FIGURE 6.1   The pulpit in the Caledonia Road church,
photo 1964.

Chapter Six

THOMSON AND SCHLEIERMACHER

Sam McKinstry and Jane Plenderleith

The relationship between Thomson's design and the architectural style of Karl Friedrich Schinkel is discussed elsewhere in this book. This chapter will propose that a second Teutonic influence helped shape Thomson's intellectual and theoretical perspectives and hence his design: Friedrich Daniel Ernst Schleiermacher (1763–1834) (see FIGURE 6.2). Contrary to the general ignorance among non-specialists which surrounds his achievement today, this German theologian has been described by one biographer as representing 'a turning point in the history of Christendom' and by another as having 'dominated the theological thought of the last century'.[1]

Born in 1768 in Breslau in Silesia (since 1945 Polish territory), the son of a Reformed chaplain, Schleiermacher's intellectual precocity confirmed his suitability for a clerical career, and under the tutelage of the Moravians at Niesky, he trained for ordination. The emphasis throughout the Pietistic religious training he received was on the cultivation of a personal, experiential, Christocentric faith, in which warmth and feeling – in the individual's relationship with God and with fellow human beings – were paramount. After a two-year spell, Schleiermacher moved to the Moravian seminary at Barby. Here, the students exploited the more relaxed academic atmosphere to gain access to works of contemporary philosophy, which were officially proscribed by the Barby authorities. Liberal periodicals and the works of writers such as Kant, Lessing and Herder stimulated the questing intellect of the young theologian. An unofficial philosophical club of 'free-thinkers' was formed, and Schleiermacher too was much influenced by these philosophies and their manifest incompatibility with the official doctrines of

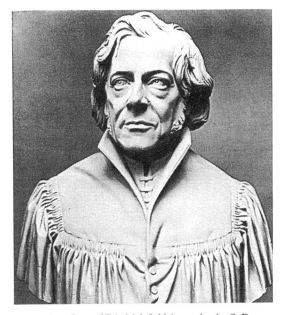

FIGURE 6.2 Bust of Friedrich Schleiermacher by C. D. Rauch.

his chosen faith. He rapidly, and perhaps inevitably, felt the inadequacy of a purely Pietistic Christian outlook to operate effectively in a world of questing intellectualism, and struggled to formulate a philosophically defensible theory which could counter the cold deistic tendencies of the Enlightenment as exemplified in the writings of Voltaire, Diderot, Helvétius or even Frederick the Great.

With his attempt to reconcile the calls of rationality and of faith in a revealed Christian God, Schleiermacher joined the tradition of what has to be seen as a peculiarly German response to deism and Enlightened philosophy, where the relationship between reason and revelation, between philosophy and religion, was considerably less polemical than in France. The impetus in Germany was towards a reconciliation of rational and religious tempers in the propagation of a 'reasonable religion' acceptable to philosophers and Churchmen alike.[2] It was this tradition which sparked Schleiermacher's interest in the philosophical defence of theology and the faith it attempts, as a science, to explain. He left Barby in 1787, to the mutual relief of all concerned, and read philosophy at Halle for two years. It is worth noting, however, that despite this evidence of an apparent rejection of some of the major tenets and claims of Pietism in the light of rational philosophy, the subsequent course of Schleiermacher's life, work and theology was in fact to be characterised by those virtues of warmth, fellow-feeling and vivid awareness of the nearness of God which typify Pietist faith and its manifestations.

In 1790, with his theological position still developing, Schleiermacher was licensed as a preacher in the Reformed Church. His first post-licentiate appointment was as tutor for three happy and productive years to the family of a Prussian count. By the end of 1793, he was appointed to a curacy at Landsberg on the Warthe, subsequently acting as a hospital chaplain in Berlin and as court preacher at Stolpe in Pomerania, before moving back to Halle in 1804. During these years, friendships with some of the most prominent figures in Germany's intellectual world were established and maintained. His circle in Berlin included the Schlegels, the von Humboldts, Moritz, the Spaldings, the composer Reichardt (Director of the Berlin *Akademie der Künste*), the sculptor Schadow and other leading intellectuals. Undoubtedly, some of the Romantic influences apparent in his theological works owe their genesis to the debates of this circle. Schleiermacher's credibility as an intellectual was gradually established, and a potentially influential figure in the history of German theology and philosophy was in the making.

In 1799, Schleiermacher published anonymously the work that would thrust him into prominence, *On Religion: Speeches to its Cultured Despisers*.[3] The general character of Schleiermacher's philosophical circle of friends at the time would indicate unequivocally that it was the more sceptically inclined of these who formed his intended audience, but the work may be read as a defence of religion against the whole school of rational-

ism, the prime product of his earlier struggles. The *Speeches* lay strong emphasis on the supremacy of human religious experience, and feeling over reason. Most significantly, they are to be seen as a defence of religion *as a whole* rather than Christianity in particular. While the work draws on Schleiermacher's philosophical knowledge – not least on the law of moral absolutism expounded by Kant, whom Schleiermacher met briefly in 1791 – it is suffused with the spirit of Romanticism and also by the warm Pietism he absorbed during his Moravian education. A revision of the work appeared in 1806, more consistent with the evangelical Christian stance that was to characterise him for the rest of his life.

The *Speeches* are five in number. The first, entitled 'Defence', calls on the reader to look deep into her or his own soul and inward emotions, to that point at which every feeling and conception known to humanity finds its form and its impetus. Schleiermacher's conclusion is that there piety, or faith, is to be found, and that this force has an existence independent of the experiencing individual, but relies on the individual to bring it out to fruitful productivity in the world: 'I maintain that in all better souls piety springs necessarily by itself; that a province of its own in the mind belongs to it, in which it has unilateral sway; that it is worthy to animate most profoundly the noblest and best and to be fully accepted and known by them.'[4] In concluding thus his first *Speech*, Schleiermacher clarifies both his intended audience and his authorial goal. In a language instinct with the vocabulary and images of Pietism, he claims that 'piety' has an independent existence in the minds and psyches of all people, that from this impulse all religious activity springs. Here the influence and adaptation of Kant is obvious: Schleiermacher supplants the moral law – which for Kant is, or should be, the font of all human actions – with the pietistic impulse of faith.[5] His intention in this work is to make apparent the potential awakening of faith and religious impulse which is latent in all human beings. Schleiermacher argues for the liberating effect on the soul of an experience of oneness with the Infinite. Those who saw the need for neither divinity nor eternity are challenged by the alleged persistence and consistency of human religious experience to acknowledge the existence and potential function of their own latent piety and to find evidence of the existence and ongoing function of God therein: a principal theme in the justification of faith, which forms the rest of Schleiermacher's book.

It is in the fifth *Speech*, in which Schleiermacher discusses the claims and relative veracity of all religions, that the relevance of Schleiermacher's theology for students of Alexander Thomson is most acute. As one writer has put it: 'Out of this [i.e. the fifth *Speech*] the Study of Comparative Religion has come'.[6]

In the *Speeches* as a whole, and the fifth in particular, the validity of 'positive religions' is upheld. Broadly speaking, these are religions of revelation in the world by a God who demands belief in His works and the continuation of these works in the world by those of faith. There is thus an explicit comparison with 'natural religions' such as deism which attempt mechanistically to explain the workings of the universe and subvert 'faith' to the claims and refutations of reason:

The so-called natural religion is usually so much refined away, and has such metaphysical and moral graces, that little of the peculiar character of religion appears. It understands so well to live in reserve, to restrain and to accommodate itself that it can be put up with anywhere. Every positive religion, on the contrary, has certain strong traits and a very marked physiognomy, so that its every movement, even to the careless glance, proclaims what it really is.[7]

Schleiermacher's reputation as the father of comparative religion rests mainly on his perception of an underlying unity in all manifestations of faith, transcending not just credal but also national–traditional bounds. To be religious, for Schleiermacher, is not simply to adhere to the outward forms and proclaimed tenets of a particular creed, but to acknowledge and to possess in oneself the very essence of the Infinite. The sense of oneness with the Infinite which all individuals may experience in themselves is itself an intuition of a universal, all-determining basis to all religions: 'Is there not in all religions more or less of the true nature of religion, as I have presented it to you? Must not, therefore, each religion be one of the special forms which mankind, in some region of the earth and at some stage of development, has to accept?'[8] It is this perceived unity in all the many different and varied manifestations of faith in a supreme Godhead which forms the main focus of Schleiermacher's attack on the mechanistic world-view put forward by 'natural religions' like deism: 'But why do those who respect natural religion at once distrust everyone who introduces any characteristic feature into his religion? They also would have uniformity, though at the opposite extreme from sectarianism, the uniformity of indefiniteness.'[9] Despite his acknowledgement of the inherent value of all manifestations of religions, with all their attendant characteristics and peculiarities, Schleiermacher is at pains to point out the overriding worth of what he first refers to as 'the highest stage of religion', which for him is Christianity. All other world religions are to be seen as prefigurations of this:

How you may succeed in deciphering the rude and undeveloped religions of remote peoples, or in unravelling the manifold, varied religious phenomena of Greece and Rome, I care very little. May your gods guide you! But when you approach the holiest in which the Universe in its highest unity and comprehensiveness is to be perceived, when you would contemplate the different forms of the highest stage of religion which is not foreign or strange, I cannot be indifferent as to whether or not you find the right point of view.[10]

The highest of all 'positive religions' for Schleiermacher is Christianity, its supremacy arising from its founder and central focus, Jesus, 'who has been the author of the noblest that there has yet been in religion'.[11] This shows a Christocentric tendency in Schleiermacher's thought which was to solidify in subsequent works, notably *The Christian Faith (Der Christliche Glaube)* of 1821. Here in the *Speeches* Schleiermacher's appreciation of Christianity in this context is based on what he perceives as this religion's glorious origins, manifestations and ongoing function: 'The original intuition of Christianity is more glorious, more sublime, more worthy of adult humanity, penetrates deeper into the spirit of systematic religion and extends itself further over the whole Universe.'[12]

But Judaism, especially but not exclusively through its anticipation and prefiguration of Christianity, comes in for particular praise: 'the beautiful childlike character of Judaism charms me. ... Regard only its strictly religious elements, and then say what is the human consciousness of man's position in the Universe and his relation to the Eternal that everywhere shines through.'[13] That, despite Schleiermacher's repeated rhetorical and semantic insistence in the *Speeches* that he is offering a defence of 'religion' in general, and perceiving an underlying and overriding unity in all religious manifestations, he still proclaims the supremacy of Christianity inheres in the reconciliation of the finite and worldly with the Infinite, which is demonstrated in the life, works and repercussions of the founder of the Christian religion. In its quest for universal and eternal purity, Christianity recognises that it must take the impure, determined aspects of worldly life into itself and purify them, imbue them too with a sense and an intuition of the Infinite: 'And just because the ungodly is everywhere operative, because all actuality together appears unholy, an infinite holiness is the aim of Christianity. Never content with its attainments, it seeks, even in its purest productions, even in its holiest feelings, traces of irreligion and of the tendency of all finite things to turn away from the unity of the Whole.'[14] This is, for Schleiermacher, the essence of Christianity and the significance of Christianity as a world religion: 'Never forget that the fundamental intuition of a religion must be some intuition of the Infinite in the finite, some one universal religious relation, found in every other religion that would be complete, but in this one only placed in the centre.'[15] It is, moreover, an observation which, it could be argued, comes into its own in the architectural creations of Alexander Thomson.

Schleiermacher's construction of a history of religions in which Christianity takes the highest place in the highest kind of religion had far-reaching repercussions for the development of the philosophy of religion. Hegel's opening of the way to an understanding of the history of religion based on the dialectic of universal laws of humanity and particular impulses in individuals owes much to Schleiermacher's comparison of religions and his proclamation of the supremacy of Christianity as a reconciliation of the particular and finite with the universal Infinite.[16] It is demonstrable that Schleiermacher's reputation as 'the father of liberal Protestantism'[17] rests on his apology of Christianity as the culmination, not the contradiction, of all other religions. After Schleiermacher, faiths formerly dismissed as 'heathen' could not be so summarily despatched by students of religion. Their serious study was given a specific theological basis and justification

which greatly enhanced the promulgation of new theories and the search for an underlying commonality in a specifically theological context.

Clearly, Thomson's sense of the validity of certain elements of the so-called 'pagan' religions, and his conception of progressive revelation through time and historical manifestation – which he stated plainly in his Haldane Lectures, and on which his architectural interpretation of history so much depended – bear a strong resemblance to the theology expounded by Schleiermacher.

However, it seems unlikely that Thomson would have had any direct knowledge of these works. He did not know German, and Schleiermacher's theological works were late in translation.[18] An atmosphere of orthodoxy surrounds the religious activity of the Thomson family as a whole. Descended from Covenanters and Dissenters, deeply missionary in orientation, the Thomsons appear at first sight improbable recipients of theological ideas from Germany with more than a whiff of liberalism about them. An examination of Alexander's own beliefs leads to the same conclusion: family papers make it clear that 'The Book' was accorded a high place in his own home, and in the Haldane Lectures Christ is referred to as 'He who had no sin'. An incident recounted by Thomson's nephew in his biography of George Thomson, Alexander's missionary brother, gives a contrary insight, however. The two brothers attended a lecture in one of the Glasgow churches in the 1850s, where the speaker examined evolutionism and the Darwinian worldview. Shortly afterwards, the two men were engaged in nature study by the side of a stream in Strathbungo, coming upon a piece of stone which split to reveal fossilised insects and raindrops. From this point onwards, it appears, mental adjustments were made in their faith to let it accommodate evolution, widening rather than destroying their conception of the divine order. This is quite consistent with the fine intellect expressed in the Haldane Lectures, and, indeed, in Thomson's architecture. It is also consistent with the progressive tone and high intellectual quality of the best United Presbyterian thought from Thomson's period, with which he was undoubtedly familiar. In this respect, a parallel may be drawn between Thomson's search to reconcile his received orthodoxy with evolutionary science and Schleiermacher's struggle

FIGURE 6.3 *The Crucifixion*, steel engraving by
W. Richardson after John Martin, from *Blackie's Imperial
Family Bible*, 1845.

with the claims of Pietism and rationalism. For
Schleiermacher, this resulted in a liberal theological
treatise with far-reaching consequences; Thomson's
response was in the formation of stone structures proc-
laiming a sense of the Infinite.

The two outstanding examples of that United Presbyterian thought were John Ker (1819–86) (see FIGURE
6.4) and John Cairns (1818–92) (see FIGURE 6.5). Ker
was a brilliant student in moral and natural philosophy
while at Edinburgh University. In 1838 he entered
the divinity hall of the United Presbyterian Church
(then the United Secession Church), studying French
and German and 'getting the whole German dictionary
by heart'. He also learned Hebrew and Arabic, spending six months in Halle under Tholuck, and then
attending the lectures of Neander, a Jew converted to
Christianity under the preaching of Schleiermacher, in
Berlin. Ker was inducted minister of East Campbell
Street church in Glasgow in 1851, acquiring a reputa-

FIGURE 6.4 The Revd John Ker.

tion as a preacher of high oratorical skill. He transferred to a new and larger church in Sydney Place, Glasgow, in 1857. Ker's writings, mostly on mainstream Christian topics, reveal little of his philosophical and linguistic inclinations, and, indeed, when he was awarded a professorship in the United Presbyterian Theological Hall in 1876, it was in 'practical training'. Nevertheless, he is an outstanding example of the intellectual calibre of the best United Presbyterian divines, a direct link with the school of Schleiermacher, and evidently known to and respected by Alexander Thomson.

John Cairns is an even more significant figure in this context. The son of a shepherd, he became the 'most distinguished student of his day' while at Edinburgh University. His philosophical, literary and scientific opinions were admired and discussed by his professors. Cairns entered the Presbyterian Secession Hall in 1840, officiating for a month in an English independent chapel in Hamburg at the end of 1843, prior to spending the winter and spring of 1843–4 in Berlin 'ardently studying the German language, philosophy and theology'. Licensed as a preacher in 1845, he quickly became one of Scotland's foremost divines, basing himself at Golden Square church, Berwick-upon-Tweed. In 1867, he became Professor of Apologetics in the United Presbyterian Theological Hall. Cairns produced many works on Christian themes which, as was not the case for Ker, allowed him ample scope to express his philosophical inclinations and great erudition. He travelled widely, represented Scottish church interests abroad, and was a polyglot. In due course he became Principal of the United Presbyterian Theological College.

In his writings, Cairns frequently takes up the opportunity to compare and contrast other religions with Christianity. For example, in *Christ and the Christian Faith*, he notes that 'even the Gentile world, with the gropings of its superstition and the struggles of its philosophy, does not lie beyond . . . this preparation for Christ'. In the same work, he observes that 'There is a belief in the supernatural; a faith in things unseen and future before either Moses or Christ.'[19] In his 1877 work *The Jews in Relation to the Church and the World*, the superiority of Christianity is stressed: 'Other religions . . . have been successful in some sort – Buddhism in China, Mahometanism both in the East and in the West – while ancient Rome, with all its tolerance, spread its gods. . . . But with every abatement, Christ-

FIGURE 6.5   The Revd John Cairns.

ianity has been the most successful religion in history.'[20]

These observations by Cairns offer a clear link from Thomson's religious background to a milieu which both illuminates and legitimises the theological perspectives of the Haldane Lectures, and which points back to Schleiermacher. Indeed, Cairns knew the works of the German theologian very well. In his *Outlines of Apologetical Theology* (1867), he speaks approvingly of Schleiermacher as having refuted in anticipation the demythologised Christ of Lévi-Strauss.

Whether Thomson read Schleiermacher or even knew his name is really irrelevant. Schleiermacher's theology greatly influenced the world of ideas, and directly or indirectly, Thomson fed on these ideas as the tradition in which he operated also fed on them. The two men were linked in any case in mining the gold of post-Enlightenment Romanticism. That the one influenced the other is especially intriguing.

Nor should it be forgotten that there were more prosaic reasons underpinning Thomson's interest in pagan religions: it is not surprising to find such an interest among Christians with missionary inclinations, if only to delimit the points of agreement and disagreement in each instance. Romanticism flourished, too, at a time of expanding imperial power and improved transportation and with it, geographical, historical and archaeological discovery. New revelations of distant peoples, shores and faiths percolated back to Western Europe, and the response of the 'civilised' world to these alien ideas is arguably epitomised, in discrete but implicitly linked modes of expression, by such as Schleiermacher and Thomson. Assimilation of the cultures of the 'New World' was greatly enhanced by a correspondingly facilitated intensification of links among the peoples and cultures of the 'Old'. If Schinkel was influenced by the Romantic atmosphere of Scotland during his tour of 1826, the compliment was returned in subsequent decades.

NOTES

1. See George Cross, *The Theology of Schleiermacher*, Chicago, 1911, Preface, p. vii, and J. Arundel Chapman, *An Introduction to Schleiermacher*, London, 1932, p. 13.
2. This is evidenced in the very titles of some of the prominent 'theological' works of the time. See, for example, Lessing's *Das Christentum der Vernunft* (The Christianity of Reason) of 1784; Fichte's *Versuch einer Kritik aller Offenbarung* (Attempt at a Critique of all Revelation) of 1791; and especially Kant's *Religion innerhalb der Grenzen der bloßen Vernunft* (Religion within the Bounds of Reason Alone) of 1793. A full account of the 'rational religion' promulgated by the major exponents of enlightened philosophy in Germany is given in Ernst Cassirer, *The Philosophy of the Enlightenment*, trans. Fritz C. A. Koelln and James P. Pettigrove, Princeton, 1951.
3. The German title reads: *Über die Religion: Reden an die Gebildeten unter ihren Verachtern.*
4. Schleiermacher, *On Religion: Speeches to its Cultured Despisers*, trans. John Oman, New York, 1958, p. 21.
5. The Second Speech, 'The Nature of Religion' develops the theme of the differences between piety and morality: 'Is religion incorporated into morality and subordinated to it, as a part to the whole? Is it, as some suppose, special duties towards God, and therefore a part of all morality which is the performance of all duties? But, if I have rightly appreciated or accurately reproduced what you say, you do not think so. You rather seem to say that the pious person has something entirely peculiar, both in his doing and leaving undone, and that morality can be quite moral without therefore being pious', ibid., pp. 28 f.
6. See T. A. Burkill, *The Evolution of Christian Thought*, New York, 1966, p. 381.
7. Schleiermacher, *On Religion*, p. 214.
8. Ibid., p. 216.
9. Ibid., p. 231.
10. Ibid., p. 238.
11. Ibid., p. 246.
12. Ibid., p. 241. A detailed account of Schleiermacher's overriding preference for the Christian faith is to be found in Karl Barth, *The Theology of Schleiermacher*, ed. Dietrich Ritschl, trans. Geoffrey W. Bromiley, Michigan, 1982, esp. pp. 224 f.
13. Schleiermacher, *On Religion*, pp. 238 f.
14. Ibid., pp. 243 f. See Burkill, *Christian Thought*, p. 382.
15. Schleiermacher, *On Religion*, p. 237.
16. See E. O. James, *Comparative Religion*, London, 1961, pp. 17 f.
17. Burkill, *Christian Thought*, p. 382.
18. The *Speeches* first appeared in translation (of Schleiermacher's third, revised edition) in London in 1893. *Der Christliche Glaube* did not appear in English until after the Second World War: *The Christian Faith*, trans. H. R. Mackintosh and J. S. Stewart, Edinburgh, 1948.
19. John Cairns, *Christ and the Christian Faith*, London, 1904, p. 67. (Most of Cairns's important texts were first published in Thomson's lifetime.)
20. John Cairns, *The Jews in Relation to the Church and the World*, London, 1877, pp. 22 f.

FIGURE 7.1   Detail of the tower of the St Vincent Street
church with herms probably by John Mossman.

Chapter Seven

·

THOMSON, MOSSMAN AND ARCHITECTURAL SCULPTURE

Alexander Stoddart

> He impresses on the hard marble the beauty of the form which nature failed to achieve in a thousand attempts, and he places it before her, exclaiming as it were, 'This is what you desired to say!'
>
> (Arthur Schopenhauer, *The World as Will and Representation*, book 3, §45)

It is a source of intense frustration that Alexander Thomson did not engage to a greater extent the services of Glasgow's pre-eminent nineteenth-century sculptor John Mossman (1817–90) (see FIGURE 7.1). Both in biography and in architectural history, much would have been gained from a consistently substantial series of collaborative essays, 'written' by the two – one possibly Scotland's greatest architectural visionary; the other its most committed architectural statuary. Yet, despite the very close friendship known to have existed between Thomson and Mossman, and despite their equality of class and professional reputation, they met as it were *on the parapets*, but rarely.

If we crave a taste of what a full-blown Thomson–Mossman collaboration might have amounted to, we can only look to James Sellars' 'Thomsonesque' St Andrew's Halls, Glasgow, thoroughly fused into the façade of which the Mossman family's supreme architectural sculpture scheme resides (see FIGURE 7.12). But a rather more intense analysis of the material that does exist in the tender nexus between the architect and the sculptor, together with an estimation from the sculptural point of view of Thomson's unexecuted, colossal designs, disclose a surprisingly rich vein of glyptic consciousness. Put this into the company of Thomson's brilliant Haldane Lectures, so much devoted to matters of adornment, and you have proof that, far from being

sculpturally illiterate, Thomson emerges as an authority on the use of sculpture in architecture. The material void in Thomson's actual use of anthropomorphic decoration serves only to brighten the light of his theoretical capacities in this field, and sustains what must be but a circumstance thrown up by the rolling orb of Fortuna.

John Mossman was born in London in 1817, the son of an accomplished artisan stonemason, William Mossman the elder (1793–1851). William's forebears had been well established in Edinburgh, first as goldsmiths (owning, for a period, John Knox's house on the Royal Mile), then as printers in the early part of the eighteenth century. William commenced his trade in the stone-lodges of the capital's New Town sites, then removed to London where he worked as an assistant of Sir Francis Chantrey, Britain's leading portrait sculptor. By the early 1830s William Mossman had set up his works in Glasgow's Barony district, capitalising upon the newly founded 'hygienic cemetery' of the Necropolis on Craig Park (opened 1833). This burial ground cannot be overestimated as the mainstay of Glasgow's achievements in the prosecution of the glyptic art, functioning as a voracious consumer of finely cut, and sublimely conceived monuments, and collecting statuary from the hands of the humblest masons (Galbraith, Peter Lawrence, M'Lean) together with works by pupils of Thorvaldsen (Ritchie, Park). John Mossman served his apprenticeship on works for Glasgow's Necropolis, and here performed the almost formulaic metamorphosis which his father had failed to achieve under Chantrey, namely the change from artisan to artist – so characteristic of the progress towards eminence in sculpture throughout the nineteenth century.

FIGURE 7.2 Hall chimney-piece at Holmwood with a cherub holding a barometer, probably carved by George Mossman (the chimney-piece *without* the cherub was illustrated in *Villa and Cottage Architecture*).

were changing at this time; Thorvaldsen had only four years to live and neoclassicism, in its most limpid form, was giving way to a more heavily draped, Victorian, Romantic quantity. Breadth of handling was now tolerable, and G. F. Watts was firmly fixed on the horizon.

It is important to intimate that the name 'Mossman' refers to a family of sculptors, and so to credit John's brothers William (1824–84) and George (1823–63). George Mossman's (see FIGURE 7.2) regrettably few surviving works assist in estimating the effect of change of taste upon the Mossman operation, since, as an exceptionally talented provincial, he had gained a place at the Royal Academy Schools upon the recommendation of William Behnes. When in London, he worked both with Behnes and with the Foley brothers, which sculptors are now believed to have had a significant part in the genesis of a Pre-Raphaelite school of sculpture. George Mossman was at the RA at the same time as Millais and Hunt, and the two pre-eminent PRB sculptors Thomas Woolner and Alexander Munro were likewise present in London. Both George and William Mossman worked under John Thomas on the decoration of Barry's Houses of Parliament during the late 1840s, where they are sure to have met with Munro, who had been introduced to Barry by Harriet, Duchess of Sutherland.

Primary biographical material concerning the Mossmans is extremely scant, and with a wholesale destruction of business records by the present holders of the J. and G. Mossman company name in the late 1970s, a certain trove of information has been lost for ever. John Mossman, despite the renown he enjoyed in Glasgow, remains personally obscure – a genial man, so we glean, adept in conversation, capable in society and of handsome appearance. In youth he is discovered to have been lazy, since William Mossman the elder writes to George in London of his fears that lack of industry 'will be the rock upon which your brother John will founder'.[1] Subsequently, John Mossman proved the contrary and became one of Scotland's most prolific sculptors, running a highly profitable sepulchral business, while extending his capacities in the fields of bust portraiture, pedestrian statuary and architectural decoration. By the 1870s his monopoly on sculpture commissions for the city – indeed, for the west of Scotland – was unchallenged; he was a kind of Bernini under a suitably urban Urban VIII.

It was an age blessed by an absence of full-time art schools, where, in order to become a sculptor, one must commence a slave. In 1840 John Mossman executed his masterpiece (true sense) in the monument to the stonemason Peter Lawrence – an exquisite figure of winged Death holding a dashed torch. Flaxman is the ruling influence on this work, and although the great designer is explicitly invoked in many of Mossman's later emblematic sculpture schemes, the Glaswegian never again approached the level of Flaxmanesque purity of form exhibited in this early work. But tastes

The production of sculpture traditionally takes place in rough, often *ad hoc* surroundings. Much will be produced on the very scaffoldings surrounding buildings in the course of their decoration. Studios are generally wretched; Robert Forrest of Lanark (1790–1852) worked for the first part of his career in the uncovered jaws of a Clyde Valley quarry; then upon the inhospitable crag of Edinburgh's Calton Hill. Lockhart, nephew of Sir Walter Scott, records the latter's visit to another 'emergent' artisan sculptor, John Greenshields (*c.*1792–1838), where a similarly 'doric' scene transpires. For John Mossman the situation was to be entirely different. Reckoned by Thomas Gildard to be an unsurpassed work of architecture, the studio which Mossman was to occupy from 1856 until the end of his career was designed by none other than Alexander 'Greek' Thomson. Long demolished, the exterior of this building remained entirely unrecorded until the recent discovery of a measured drawing of one elevation (see FIGURE 7.14). Otherwise, an interior photograph of *c.*1875 and a tantalising description, by Gildard, of 1888 are all that remain.

In quality of composition, if not also of detail, I do not know if, in any of his [Thomson's] subsequent works, he has surpassed it. The site, the corner of two streets [Cathedral and North Frederick], one of which is level, the other having a considerable inclination, is taken advantage of with consummate skill as regards both artistic design and utility. Along the level street the walling is of cyclopean masonry, pierced by a doorway which, from its sill being on a level with the surface within, serves the purpose of 'bank' loading, and on each side of it, by three openings, have broad dwarf pilasters between them, also on each side of the doorway, the extreme piers being of cyclopean work, part of the general walling. On the inclined street the composition is in four parts: the first, a continuation of the cyclopean wall, with its somewhat horizontal openings and their dwarf pilasters; the second, the gateway, with its piers 'growing' from the general walling: the third, the screen between the gateway and the studio proper, with its doorway crowned by a block cornice and acroterion, and having honeysuckle-and-lotus enrichment extending from each end of this cornice; and the fourth, the studio proper, composed of four pilasters and two extreme piers carrying a block

pediment, between the pilasters a dado on a level with, and continuing the honeysuckle-and-lotus enrichment on each side of the door the whole standing on a cyclopean basement.[2]

We must presume a superiority of Thomson's architectural structure over that of Gildard's sentences, yet, in all, the building *sounds* magnificent. Internally there is nothing other than a sound sufficiency of provision, with a generous double course of skylighting opening a broadly pitched roof, and an immense rolling gantry capable of lifting weights from and to any point on the studio floor. The introduction of large blocks of stone into the studio is facilitated by a set of iron rails.

Who could doubt that, in this design, the very closest collaboration between architect and client prevailed, and this not merely in the regions of functionality? It is fascinating to note that nowhere in Gildard's description is there any mention of the involvement of architectural sculpture, which one would have thought entirely appropriate. There was only a splendid freestanding Grecian urn celebrating the single-storey street corner. This building, the first article in the apparently scant list of Thomson/Mossman collaborations, commences a generally paradoxical relationship.

While the Mossman studio secured, for the sculptor, amiable premises in which to commence his stupendous programme of works for the city of Glasgow, it also secured the architect's famed 'cyclopean' idiom. Ninian R. J. Johnston, in his prize-winning essay of 1933, reports that 'the uncompromising boldness of the design ... caused a torrent of praise and condemnation at the time ... Critics were undecided whether they had before them merely a piece of *nouveau architecture* or the true spirit of Grecian craftsmanship.'[3] Notoriety, as well as notability, feeds the perennial but often disregarded factor of publicity, valuable to all; perhaps, then, the Mossman studio has its consequential part to play in the twinned rise of the reputations of both client and architect.

In the feverish climate of production which followed Thomson's work for John Mossman, the very grandest of urban designs were produced. Thomson's industry was immense, and with the Double Villa (see FIGURE 8.12) completed (a building thought to disclose something of the character of the Mossman studio) and the Caledonia Road United Presbyterian Church (see

FIGURE 7.3   Detail of the Buck's Head Building, Argyle Street.

FIGURE 5.1) commencing its resolution of a particularly awkward site, the architect was set to draw the most sublime of horizontalities into the genial elevations of the Second City. But for Mossman's involvement as an architectural sculptor, we must look first to towers and to the wearisome necessities of supposition and attribution, since the voice of primary documentation is now silent.

Mossman's practice was born of a tradition of masonry, and continued thus throughout. Indeed, towards the end of his career he had interests of a financial sort in more than one central-belt quarry. To sustain this artisan dimension, Mossman engaged numerous stonemasons, the fruits of whose labour fell, in chief, into the category of sepulchral work. Thomson could not have failed to exploit this executive resource for the purposes of the finer parts of his buildings' adornment, so it is reasonable to find Mossman's mark there. At Caledonia Road, for instance,

there are Ionic capitals to the hexastyle – all cut to the finest standard – and antifixae, and an acroterion. The ornament on the upper portions of the tower is highly wrought, in considerable relief. All, in short, is sculptural. For figure work attributable to Mossman we can resort only to two other buildings – St Vincent Street United Presbyterian Church (1857–9) and the Buck's Head Building, 63 Argyle Street, Glasgow (1863).

Certainly the most exotic of all Thomson's executed works, the St Vincent Street church (see FIGURE 7.1) includes a passage of figure sculpture carefully designed to conform to the general eclecticism of the tower's whole. A series of eight identical herm busts conclude the plinth of the tower, two to a wall, the one facing the other over a bridged void. Are they by Mossman? If so, then a strict architect's directive is being followed, for the handling both of the general composition and of the facial type is somewhat distinct from Mossman's native manner. The passage is one of static intensity, Thomson's appreciation of which will be examined in due course. The anthropoid element is highly reduced, leaving only the face (and this in the further reduction of the profile) emerging from the otherwise architectural quantities of the short herm posts beneath and the 'capitals' above. Together with the distinctive design, the perfect sophistication of the very choice of the herm-type (archaistic and paganistic in connotation, and underutilised throughout nineteenth-century neoclassicism) renders the passage Thomson's alone, with the sculptor relegated, once more, to mere fabrication. This is the single exterior specimen of anthropoid decorative sculpture in Thomson's entire extant œuvre; brilliant in conception, it positively blossoms in its isolation and brevity.

The eponymous Buck, on the Buck's Head Building (see FIGURE 7.3), seems conventional in comparison. It is firmly composed and cut, and conveys something of its species' *nerve* as it surveys Argyle Street from over the cast-iron glade of the lower structure. But as a work of animal sculpture it has significance, since Thomson was to design for this class of work rather extensively, though mainly for unexecuted projects. Again, Mossman's hand can be presumed, although he is not well known as an *animalier*. The various representations of cattle on Carrick's later Meat Market (c.1875) bear resemblances to the handling of the Buck, but they, too, are undocumented.

FIGURE 7.4   Statue of Sir Robert Peel in George Square, 1859.

FIGURE 7.5   Tomb of the Revd A. O. Beattie in Glasgow Necropolis, 1858.

And so we conclude our necessarily fleeting survey with the sole certain Thomson–Mossman collaboration, the statue of Sir Robert Peel, executed for George Square, Glasgow, in 1859. A rather poignant division of labour gives Mossman the statue and Thomson the plinth, so that the two, and very reasonably too, confine themselves to their respective disciplines. The statue of Peel (see FIGURE 7.4) is Mossman's finest pedestrian bronze, and ought to be counted among the very best statues of the nineteenth century in Britain. The prejudice against the acknowledgement of such statuary in the terms of art is still well entrenched; thus it is worth bearing in mind that, while every statue is a sculpture, not every sculpture is a statue. The Peel bronze meets both conceptual and formal demands – a modern work, in costume, natural in pose, animated in expression, the whole 'drawn' to the last nicety, the surface taut and continent. Thomson's plinth design, as a foil to this

tour de force, is utterly restrained, indeed rather orthodox; only an extended, doricising taurus immediately above the base suggests the particular powers of its designer. But there is reason to believe that this is a second design for the plinth, for a Thomson drawing of a statue, similar in pose to that of the Peel bronze and set upon a very different plinth, exists in the Mitchell Library collection – perhaps an earlier idea. This structure is evidently Thomsonesque, extending horizontals far out from the figure, and almost devoid of mouldings. It is a stepped design of extreme austerity, requiring, one feels, a properly draped, Gibsonian statue, in contrast with Mossman's documentary costume-piece.

The modern age has proven itself to be as incompetent in plinth design as it is in the design, indeed the conception, of that other work of architecture, the tomb. Both properly occupy the highest realms of design, but, in the frenzy of duct-mania that so be-

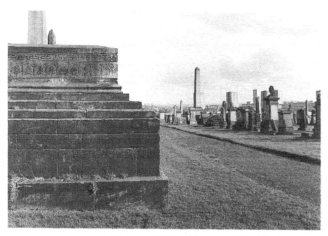

FIGURE 7.6   Tomb of William Provan in Sighthill Cemetery, the raised back of this monument has been removed.

nights the architecture of our time, they have been abandoned. The fashion is to estimate the tomb in a spirit of jocularity, as a sort of queer phenomenon, so that Thomson's sepulchral and monumental œuvre has been neglected in favour of his essays in accommodation. The configuration of Thomson–Frank Lloyd Wright, so piously repeated, is the signal manifestation of this sorry omission – sorry, indeed, and *deceiving*. The truth is that Alexander Thomson is an architect in the firmament precisely because of his permeating religiosity; that, whatever his 'skills', it is in spirit and reverence that he transcends time. The Beattie Tomb (see FIGURE 7.5) (Glasgow Necropolis, 1858) is the paradigm of Thomson's 'meta-architecture' (so to speak), yet it, like the other unauthenticated tomb designs bearing Thomson hall-marks (see FIGURE 7.6),[5] remains in the margins of critical assessments. 'His monuments are characterised by great breadth of treatment, dignity and repose',[6] writes Thomas Gildard; he might well have recommended a thorough perusal of Thomson's Haldane Lectures as an apt and informative accompaniment to their appreciation.

Any attempt to gather together the disparate elements that might combine to form a picture of the truth of Alexander Thomson's approach to the question of sculpture in architecture must entail the following identifications: that he was an 'old and intimate friend'[7] of John Mossman, sculptor; that he was a designer of sepulchral monuments (see FIGURE 7.7), the production of which is utterly dependent upon the techniques

FIGURE 7.7   Design for a tombstone amongst Thomson's drawings in the Mitchell Library.

of sculpture; that he involved figure sculpture (albeit of an unorthodox sort) in two of his executed designs. But these actualities dwindle in importance, once set against those expressions of volition manifested in the corpus of his unexecuted designs, and in the rolling text of his Haldane Lectures. For there, and most dramatically in the latter, Thomson reveals himself to be an architect positively obsessed by architectural sculpture, and one capable of its most sophisticated utilisation and contemplation. Throughout the lectures, sculpture serves to *signify*. John Flaxman is introduced early in the first lecture as an artist 'expressing the purest artistic thought with the least possible amount of material aid', the cerebral worth of which achievement is then categorically confirmed in his defence of the glyptic efforts of the Greeks:

If ever thought and being was embodied by man's art in any shape whatever, it is to be found in those

FIGURE 7.8   Perspective of obelisk tomb signed by Geo. Morrison among Thomson's drawings in the Mitchell Library.

glorious Greek sculptures ... The Greek sculptors were not contented with a sort of something like their ideal; they hewed and rasped and smoothed until they had got quit of the last particle of extraneous matter, and nothing remained but the perfect reflex of the artist's mental conception. Not a mere face, however expressive, surmounted a mass of drapery under which a figure is more or less traceable or to be accounted for, but an entire being, soul and body in the most perfect harmony ...[8]

Thomson is certain that with the addition or inclusion of aesthetic ornament the sufficient structure becomes architecture. Fondness for the structure and its purposes is the motivating cause of this adornment – a devotional impulse; consequently ('Religion being the soul of art from the beginning'), 'in the grand old days ... architecture, sculpture and painting were not regarded as sister arts, but, along with others, as one glorious art – the combined labor [*sic*] of all who had the heart and skill to do it'.[9] The entrancing power of sculptural repetition of sphinxes in Egyptian proces-

FIGURE 7.9   Tomb of the Revd George Marshall Middleton in Glasgow Necropolis, *c.*1866.

sion-ways Thomson supposes to have been developed for liturgical purposes, calculated to produce a direct and deliberate effect upon the celebrant – one, paradoxically, of increasing obliviousness to material surroundings, so that the approach towards statuary of colossal dimensions (presumed to thunder at the temple entrance) might be all the more stupefying (see FIGURES 7.8 and 7.9). The Egyptians, indeed, devised the unfenestrated character of their salient architecture precisely for the purpose of leaving ample scope for sculptural decoration, since it is exactly that element which will disclose, in explicit terms, the religious and historical import of the general precinct. The architecture, in short, is literate, rather than merely gesticulative. And Thomson closes the Egyptian lecture with a quotation from Thomas De Quincey's impression of an Egyptian *sculpture* fragment, the Memnon head in the British Museum, describing its 'peace which passeth all understanding'; its 'eternity which baffles and confounds all faculty of computation'; its 'diffusive love – a procession, an emanation from some mystery of endless dawn ... the holy thing seemed to live by silence'.[10]

Thomson's position relative to the use of the Doric order is inextricably linked to the question of figure statuary in his œuvre, indeed it is the key to the mystery of this void. Thomson, as is well known, never built in the pure Doric – some say because he was not entrusted with a building of sufficient worth; others that he never received a commission on the correct scale. In the third lecture, Thomson declares that this 'noblest style of architecture with its complete complement of sculpture and painting'[11] is, in fact, too sacred, too high for utilisation in the commemoration of anything we have yet done, so holding it in precious reserve, as it were, to flower only in the long-awaited time of moral recovery. Meanwhile, he implies, its frame is taken in vain. And what is the Doric's chief distinction?

> *The Doric is the only (order) that is in strict and perfect harmony with the delicacy of outline, the subtle gradations of light and shade, and the justness or truth of the relative proportions of parts which characterise the human frame. ... The human figure is the true proto-Doric ... the type of that Ideal perfection which, in a variety of phases, was the great end of Greek effort, the guiding star of Greek genius. ... All the mouldings of the Doric style are of a fineness corresponding to the gentle swellings and depressions of the muscles of the human frame.*[12]

The conclusion might well be drawn that Thomson, prostrate before the Doric, is likewise prostrate before its principal source and glory – the human form in sculpture.

Notwithstanding this modesty, Thomson, in unexecuted designs, proves his willingness to engage statuary in buildings. The famous perspective of St George's church, Edinburgh (1858) includes a circular porch-like structure on the turn of the podium, its entablature supported by six caryatid figures, no doubt intended to

evoke the Athenian precedent on the Erechtheum. It is a source discussed by Thomson in the third lecture, where he notes the general approval of the self-sufficient forms of the figures, and also the disapproval of the purpose they serve (of labour, and function) with which he disagrees, detecting rather the reverse of any degradation in their 'easy grace'.[13] But the two great sculptural schemes occur in the designs for the Albert Memorial Competition (1862) (see FIGURE 7.10) and the South Kensington Museum Competition (1864) (see FIGURE 17.7). At once rich and chaste, the Albert Memorial design is a catalogue, in itself, of the several potentialities of architectural sculpture. The horizontal principle is developed in deliberate collaboration with the chosen sculptural forms, so that, in the case of the lions *couchant* looking out from the side elevations, the solid stone banisters flanking the side steps mimic the form of the front limbs of the beasts, extended before their terrific busts. The main entrance cuts down through the upper body of the podium, flanked by a frieze running to the extreme edge of the first load-bearing wall, reminding us of Egyptian examples such as Thomson lectured upon. The apex of each pylon is surmounted by a seated figure in the round, behind which, in sublime and detached distance, a further flurry of sculpture is set around the base of the monument's tower.

This last passage of sculpture is almost beyond comprehension in the awful brilliance of its conception, for it amounts to a great hidden work, redolent of the Egyptian vault, decorated for endless night. For the detail, a frieze circulating the tower base, with group projections at the centre of each wall, would confound close scrutiny and remain – from the immediate orbit of the monument's bulk – virtually invisible. Yet Thomson would have refused to allow distance to permit lax design or workmanship. Rather, he is transfixed by the implications. Of the figure of Illisus from the Parthenon he writes that

> *the back of the figure ... which Canova and Flaxman declared to be unrivalled, was turned to the wall of the tympanum, and never seen by mortal eye from the time that it was put up under the direction of Phidias until it was taken down under the direction of Lord Elgin. But the Greeks did not do these things merely to be seen by man, for they said 'The gods see everywhere'.*[14]

FIGURE 7.10   A drawing of Thomson's original damaged perspective in the Glasgow School of Art of his design for the Albert Memorial, 1862.

For unspeakable, Semitic majesty, this design has no equal; in its ideal shadow, the executed design by Sir George Gilbert Scott appears a cuckoo clock.

At last, in the design for South Kensington Museum (1864) (see FIGURE 7.11), Thomson dares the Doric. In conformity with his reading of the order, the scheme entails extensive sculpture, not only in the pediments – of which there are twelve (calculating from the giant perspective drawing in the Mitchell Library) – but also on the metopes, the surrounding plinths, and in the doorways. Again, lions commence the scheme, flanking the three great stairways on to the main elevation. As this view of the building presents three temples, the central one of which is raised on a higher level, so the lions correspond: those before the lower side temples lie down, while the central pair stand on all fours. Six vast stone elephants support the lintels beneath each of the temples, and a more suitably 'trabeated' creature could not be imagined for the purpose. Thomson must

have known of the elephant sculptures of India, most notably those at the Temple of Khanakha, which also appear in a processional repetition, similar to that of the previously mentioned Egyptian sphinxes. Over the central pediment of the museum is a seated figure, possibly Brittania, while the outer temples receive substantial acroteria. The long, rhythmic side elevations start and finish with pedimented structures, tetrastyle *in antis*. These, too, are supported from beneath by works of statuary, each having a pair of Atlantes lifting the mighty lintels on their shoulders.

The type of the Atlantic figure is referred to in the third Haldane Lecture, in a detailed account of those appearing in the temple at Agrigentum in Sicily. They are

of very good design. Their arms are raised so as to bring the elbows level with the top of the head – which is thrown forward, and the hands are clasped at the back of the neck. In this position they are made to

FIGURE 7.11 Detail of the perspective in the Mitchell
Library of Thomson's design for the South Kensington
Museum, 1864.

*carry a projecting portion of the small upper entabla-
ture – probably meant to give apparent support to the
beams of the roof.*[15]

And here, in this museum design, Thomson's version
appears, frustrated for the moment, but due – a decade
later – to be given an almost exact representation, in the
concrete, in James Sellars' portico for St Andrew's
Halls (1877) (see FIGURE 7.12).

In his essay of 1933, Ninian R. J. Johnston writes of
Thomson that 'he uses the human form very sparingly
and in an archaic treatment strictly subordinate to
architectural design, so that a Greek temple of the
Periclean period would probably have seemed dis-
agreeably animistic to him'.[16] Hopefully, the myopia of
such a view, predicated upon the meanest regard of

material evidence only, is now clear. In truth, Thomson
is a most capable and careful designer and contempla-
tor of architectural sculpture, for whom this application of the glyptic art is all-important. As has been
shown, sculpture serves as a signpost throughout the
Haldane Lectures, indicating territories of high taste
and artistic intelligence, and those of lesser nobility.
(His assertion of the decline of beauty in Roman hands
is announced with a disapproving account of the increased naturalism in Roman bust portraiture.) And as
an evangelist of the 'opalescent' Acropolis of Athens –
seen from afar, at the height of its intact beauty – he
mentions, not merely in passing, the oft-neglected
statue of Athena Promachos, that 'colossal figure of
Minerva, whom the Athenians delighted to honor [*sic*],
standing in the midst, leaning upon her spear with her

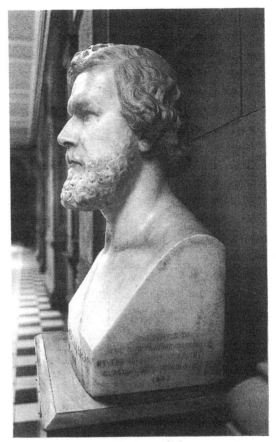

FIGURE 7.13   Bust of Thomson by John Mossman, presented to the Corporation Galleries in 1877 and now in Kelvingrove Museum.

FIGURE 7.12   Entrance to St Andrew's Halls by James Sellars, 1873–7.

hand raised pointing to heaven ... one of the most glorious sights which the human eye has ever been permitted to behold, and the like of which it will never again see in this world'.[17]

Alexander Thomson's death, in 1875, moved the Glasgow Institute of Architects to commission a commemorative bust of the architect (see FIGURE 7.13). It was executed in 1877 by Thomson's good friend John Mossman, and now resides in the Art Gallery and Museum of Kelvingrove. Although posthumous, the bust is both true and ideal, the face philosophically bearded and the shoulders nude as they terminate in

the noble truncation of the herm format. It is said that, in the days of Pericles, the streets of Athens boasted over three hundred herms of deities, philosophers, statesmen and heroes. Let us not resort to coyness, nor to any logical positivism, but imagine, truly and in the Ideal, a further herm to join that august company – one of a true Attican, an architect of genius.

NOTES

1. Uncatalogued letter, W. Mossman to G. Mossman, Glasgow University Library, Special Collections Department, n.d.
2. T. Gildard, Paper to Philosophical Society of Glasgow, 30 Jan. 1888, *Proceedings of the Royal Philosophical Society of Glasgow*, vol. XIX (1888), p. 7. This measured drawing

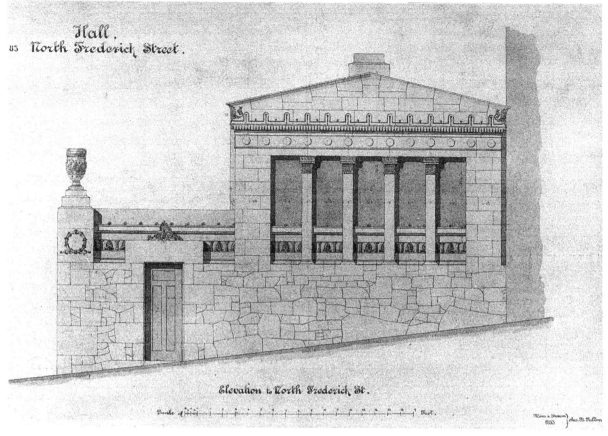

Hall.
85 *North Frederick Street.*

Elevation to North Frederick St.

Scale of ⊢⊢⊢⊢ | | | | | | | | | | | | | | | *Feet.*

Moss & Stamm
1893 } *Jas. B. Fulton*

FIGURE 7.14 Measured drawing of the east, or side
elevation of Mossman's studio in North Frederick Street,
made by James B. Fulton in 1893.

of the east elevation of Mossman's studio by James B.
Fulton of 1893 in the collection of the Glasgow School of
Art was identified by Gavin Stamp in 1993. For its
significance, see the *Alexander Thomson Society Newsletter*, no. 8, Glasgow, October 1993, and no. 9, January
1994.

3. N. R. J. Johnson, 'Alexander Thomson, a Study of the
Basic Principles of His Design', *RIAS Quarterly*, no. 43
(Sept. 1933), pp. 29–38.

4. Thomson included passages of figure decoration in the
interior of Holmwood, much of which took the form of
painted friezes derived from Flaxman's Homer illustrations (cartoons for these are in the Mitchell Library
Thomson archive). Elsewhere in the villa's interior,
friezes of scenes illustrating Tennyson's Idylls of the King
are likewise thought to lurk still under mid-twentieth-
century paint. There has been some doubt as to whether
the latter subjects were original to Thomson's design,

seeing that the Tennysonian 'culture' seems distinct from
Thomson's own. From the Haldane Lectures, however,
we discover Thomson himself quoting from the very
Idylls, and therefore must observe evidence of idiomatic
sympathy. Holmwood also contains a remarkable
chimney-piece in the hall, designed in the form of an
arch. It is topped by a marble barometer-case, itself
adorned with a very finely cut figure of a putto, winged.
Perhaps this work is by George Mossman, whose natural
proclivities towards fancy and domestic subjects could
well encompass such an essay. Thomson is known to have
worked with George Mossman on one other project, the
famous and apparently lost Garnkirk Vase, for which the
sculptor provided a processional relief.

5. The Alexander Thomson Memorial Minute Book
[Strathclyde Regional Archives] lists three monuments
by Thomson: that to Beattie, that to the Revd George M.
Middleton in the Necropolis and that to Mr William

Provan at Sighthill. There is also the tomb of John McIntyre in Cathcart Cemetery.

6. T. Gildard, Paper, p. 15.

7. Ibid., p. 7.

8. A. Thomson, Haldane Lectures, I (1874), Mitchell Library, Glasgow, p. 16.

9. Ibid., p. 6.

10. Haldane Lectures, II, p. 14.

11. Ibid., II, p. 9.

12. Ibid., p. 9.

13. Ibid., p. 19. In this context, it is tantalising and frustrating to read – in a letter written by Thomson to his brother George, *en route* for the Cameroons, on 3 June 1871 – that, 'We have begun operations at the Insurance Company – The Caryatids were objected to by the people at the head office.'

14. Ibid., pp. 12 and 13.

15. Ibid., pp. 19 and 20.

16. Johnson, 'Alexander Thomson'.

17. Haldane Lectures, III, pp. 19 and 20.

URBANISM

FIGURE 8.1   Queen's Park Terrace, Eglinton Street, 1857,
demolished 1981, photo 1980.

Chapter Eight

THOMSON'S CITY

John McKean

MAKING THE CITY MEMORABLE

Few architects inevitably stamp their mark on the city image, transforming it by their interventions. In the changing kaleidoscope of the city of Glasgow, there is no stronger individual than Alexander Thomson. It is not that he built most. There have been others who designed as much and more. It's not just that his works stand out, as figures against the grainy urban ground of the city. It is, on the other hand, that no one was better able, first, to understand the actuality of the form of the city (and therefore its image) and second, through his skill to make that clearer, stronger, and more memorable. His buildings help articulate the city form, which itself therefore becomes more clearly embedded in the *imago urbis*.

Thomson's work is memorable in that it makes the city more memorable. There are as many virtuosic architects who did not do this; indeed who shouted their individuality in contrast to their context so loudly that such was impossible. Each, of course, adds to the crystallisation of the city's *imaginaire collectif*; but Thomson's value as a lens through which to view Glasgow is in his reinforcement of the city's identity.

What was this city which Thomson knew, and whose themes he orchestrated so colourfully? Here is Glasgow when Thomson was born:

The taste of the inhabitants of this city for expense in building is well known. Travellers generally express regret that they do not show the same taste for lightness of design. They have lately built, at great expense, an extensive Infirmary, on the ancient site of the Bishop's castle; a splendid Hospital for Lunatics; a handsome

Trades-Hall; a new Prison, Town-house, and place for the county meetings, in the lower part of the Green on the brink of the river Clyde, and a monument to Nelson in the upper part of it. The latter has been unfortunately damaged by a thunderbolt. The number of the inhabitants, including those of the suburbs, is by the last calculation, made to exceed that of Edinburgh.[1]

Glasgow was on the brink of a new wave. The city which Thomson came to exemplify was indeed built upon the stones of these important buildings among which he lived – and a number of which explicitly influenced his architecture. But this 'architecture of Glasgow', as a collection of fine buildings by Adam, Stark, Hamilton (see FIGURE 2.1) or whoever, isn't what Thomson's own work amplifies. In fact it is often difficult to see how his mature buildings, always stylistically highly personal and idiosyncratic, were at all influenced by those before or around him. It is with the city rather than with individual architectural manners that his works converse. Thomson's forms, exuberant, forceful and astonishingly original, are always vigorously embedded in his city. Thus we learn about the form, structure and image of Glasgow through Thomson's 'reading' of it, shown through his buildings which catch the urban identity and articulate the forms of this city in our memory.

THE CITY FORM

This chapter suggests images of the city, at that moment – around 1860 – refracted through the lenses of five Thomson works, each with a different role as an

FIGURE 8.2 Tenement on the corner of Nithsdale Road and Darnley Street by Thomson & Turnbull, 1873–8, photo from the roof of Moray Place, 1992.

element in the fabric of the city. In sketching their context, individual buildings and architects known to Thomson seem less important than the city forms he inherited – a Glasgow characterised first, on plan, by the dominating grid-iron layout of much of its centre; and second, in reality by the sense that it was a city almost entirely of walls, largely four storeys high, surrounding back courts and enclosing streets, within which virtually the whole population lived.

Looking at any historical map of the city, the first 'urban artefact' (to borrow Aldo Rossi's word) we see is the ancient cross of Glasgow, off which runs a pattern of secondary roads and myriad tight closes and wynds. By Thomson's time these were the worst slums in the kingdom. Much of these areas were demolished between 1868 and 1877 (see FIGURE 10.2) under the City

Improvement Act, for whose trustees Thomson produced the scheme, a 'renewed' urban block, which I discuss first.

The second urban artefact, to the west and north of that centre of gravity, is the first formalised 'new town'. Its western end around Buchanan Street soon became the central commercial area of Victorian Glasgow. Embedded here is Thomson's Egyptian Halls, my second example.

The third urban artefact by the time of Thomson's birth is what most clearly stands out as the 'Glasgow grid': the rigid grid-iron, discontinuous but unified, both north and south of the river. Thomson designed many tenement blocks (see FIGURES 8.2 and 8.3) (almost all demolished now), whose strength, appropriately, is simply in their quietly reinforcing the city-dwelling form, the Glaswegian blocks of four-storey

FIGURE 8.3 Tenements at Queen's Cross by Thomson &
Turnbull, 1875, demolished, photo *c*.1960.

walls. But, where appropriate, he moulds the urban
form, reinforcing the tenement walls by punctuating
them with civic monuments. This is marvellously exemplified in St Vincent Street church, which I discuss
next.

Fourthly, new middle-class areas spread south-west
and north-west through the middle decades of the
century. That part of the grid on rising ground north of
the Clyde succumbed to commercial pressures, while
that part on the flat ground south of the river, ruined by
the railways and ironworks, was abandoned as insanitary by the middle classes (including Thomson himself)
in 1856, to become intricately subdivided and packed
by the city's exploding (largely immigrant) proletariat.

The bourgeoisie looked for housing in new, picturesquely laid-out terraced and tenemented streets as
well as, to a lesser extent, in areas of detached suburban
villas. The West End (that is Glasgow north of Argyle

Street, Partick and the Clyde, south of Maryhill and the
canal) was developed with terraced houses and spacious tenement flats. But my fourth study looks at a
new, less common suburban pattern: the detached-
villa building which had begun – some in the West End
but especially (and often more modestly) south of the
river. Thomson's Double Villa is an early and prototypical example.

Finally, if the dwellings of high-Victorian bourgeois
Glaswegians were as likely to be spacious flats as small
'villas', their other, and perhaps less typical, expression
was my fifth and final type: the terraced house. With
the opening in 1841 of the terrace-lined Great Western
Road, the grandest of Glaswegian promenades, the
West End really took off. Development was so slow that
one of these grand terraces was Thomson's last essay in
city housing.[2] But my example is his earlier, perfect,
small terrace at Moray Place (see FIGURE 17.2).

FIGURE 8.4   Reconstruction of Thomson's design for *galleria* between blocks of tenements.

These five views can fill out an image of the city: the project for working-class housing as city block; the Egyptian Halls as a commercial block deep in the first Glasgow 'order' of gridded streets; the St Vincent Street UP Church as a monumental punctuation to the pattern of the second Glasgow 'order', the four-storey tenement wall; the Double Villa as one prototypical low-density bourgeois suburban pattern; and Moray Place as a rather more urbane inner-suburban pattern.

THE CITY IMPROVEMENT HOUSING BLOCK

Victorian Glasgow's response to 'the housing question' was uniquely extreme. By the 1850s and 1860s, the hammer and chisel of the 'maker-down' (dividing and subdividing dwellings to become ever more over-crowded) sounded in the newish tenements – in Laurieston, Tradeston, and similar areas recently vacated by the middle class like Thomson – as they had long done in the old tenements around the High Street.[3]

But then came a new phenomenon: tenement blocks, which to the street appeared almost identical and which kept the similar basic common-stair design, were now being designed as one- and two-room dwellings from the start. Alongside the other architects and builders, Alex Thomson was designing single ends.[4] Of the 26,794 dwellings built in Glasgow between 1866

and 1874, half were of two rooms, and half the rest were of one room.

Certainly Thomson built many streets of tenements, containing dwellings from the reasonably spacious to the tiny. Despite irrepressible efforts to articulate the street face, he never breaks the morphological rules which would force an inappropriate 'architecture' out of this city 'building'. His response to that distinction, and the retention of an appropriate urban hierarchy, is clearest in a proposal for a renewed working-class housing form, based on the rebuilding of one of the oldest corners of the city, south-west of the cathedral.

The important City Improvement Act of 1866 argued

for the public and local Advantage if various Houses and Buildings were taken down, and those portions of the said City reconstituted, and new Streets were constructed in and through various Parts of said City, and several of the existing Streets altered and widened and diverted, and that in connexion with the Reconstruction of these portions of the City provision was made for Dwellings for the Labouring Classes who may be displaced in consequence thereof . . .[5]

The Glasgow Architectural Society was (in a context which Brian Edwards develops in Chapter Ten), approached for 'suggestions on how improvements should proceed'. The Society's subcommittee involved Alex Thomson, James Salmon, J. J. Stevenson, John Honeyman and others. Nothing survives of this subcommittee's response other than Thomson's fascinating proposal, of which we have but confused newspaper reports.[6]

Thomson, proposing a rectilinear grid of paired tenement strips with glass roofs strung between them (see FIGURE 8.4), responds to the morphology of the city. That this was an unfashionable position can be seen in a glance at his colleagues on the subcommittee: 'Salmon', in Brian Edwards' words, 'deplored the tenement and preferred English style terraced housing, Stevenson favoured conservation of the Old Town, and Honeyman too favoured conservation and the building of tall flatted blocks in "the Peabody manner".'[7] This range of views now contained the conventional wisdom, which centred on 'romantic nationalism'. Certainly in contemporary Edinburgh, the brief to designers of new housing under their High Street

Improvement Act demanded precisely that they 'maintain the Scottish character'; such a theme was surely equally forceful in Glasgow around its Improvement Act housing at this moment of antiquarian and historicist awareness.

Thomson clearly stands apart from all these voices; in tune with a different Glasgow, he responds not to a sentiment of 'character', but to the city and its abstract grid. The even carpeting of the gridded city block goes right back to the council ordinance in August 1782 which authorised 'Two streets sixty feet wide east-West and three streets North to South, parallel to Queen Street, forty feet wide and sixty feet wide . . .'.[8] South of the river, the first Tradeston blocks in the 1790s were 250 ft by 300 ft, with generous back courts soon filled with noxious industry; in neighbouring Hutchesontown, narrower blocks of 150 ft by 500 ft helped the residential character last longer; the Blythswood blocks were 200 ft by 250 ft, with central east–west lanes.

Thomson's proposal,[9] echoing the Glasgow grid rather than the taste of his colleagues, takes a huge grid, 330 ft wide – that is more or less the length of his built Queens Park Terrace tenement – but 1,104 ft long. Between major streets 60 ft and 80 ft wide, he strings a ladder of tenements, offering their ends only to the main streets. Blocks are paired; a narrow entrance between them opens to enclose 32 ft-wide courts from which the dwellings in the dozen tenements off each court are entered. The startlingly original idea is that these courts become atria, open at both ends, covered with a shimmering veil of glass, permeable to the city streets. Each great galleria provides a warm, safe, healthy social environment. Building them in 9-inch brickwork, rather than the usual stone facing to the street, pays for the 40 ft-high glazed court.

The variety of types of urban place, an ambiguity about 'fronts' and 'backs', enrich the traditionally monovalent experience of the tenement form. But it still offers separate places (a) for 'public' urban life – all the public faces on the ground floor being lined with shops and pubs which encourage an adult public street life; (b) for service, in its narrow lanes between blocks; and (c) for 'domestic' urban life – its courts provide a temperate environment, in Thomson's words, 'as playgrounds for the young, where they may run about under shelter. Glasgow is notorious for the mortality amongst children. But the warmth which would result from this method of building would be conducive to the health and comfort of all.'[10]

The huge city block is developed as eight pairs of typically sized and shaped tenements spaced along the two long sides, the parallel main streets. As the paired rungs of a ladder, double rows of five tenements, between which the space widens into the long glazed court, join the end tenements on the main streets. Dividing the block there are two cross-streets. Each tenement is about 40 ft by 50 ft on plan, and four storeys high. Facing all the surrounding streets, the ground floors are given to shops, two per tenement. On each floor are six or seven rooms (Thomson says each is at least 10 ft by 10 ft), which might be one two-bedroom flat and one four-room dwelling; some, as Thomson says, are one-room homes.[11]

The remarkable strength of this rational plan – its order, and its scale (it was designed as housing for over ten thousand people), its potential to create a really new urban artefact out of housing for the poor – is difficult to appreciate from reconstruction. For it is the link with topography and real lives, the making into actual substantial building, its detailed reality working out that breathes life into these dry bones. And that opportunity never came. Without the specific locus, without the architectural actuality to give form to the individuality of the project, it remains a potent but typological idea soon erased from the city's memory. We must move to the real fabric and its less conjectural interventions.

THE EGYPTIAN HALLS

The urban warehouse and office building was a new type which took form, in the cities of Europe and eastern USA, in the third quarter of the century. Up till then the grand ones had taken their form from town hall, market hall or palace; the smaller from urban domestic blocks. As one of the first office designers said, looking back to the 1830s from 1864, 'merchants dwelt in the City over their counting houses and next to their warehouses'.[12] But by the 1850s, suddenly, a new urban commercial architecture of cast-iron and glass was beginning to appear in New York, Glasgow and then in other industrial centres. Bogardus' work in New York was pioneering; Gardner's 1855 warehouse

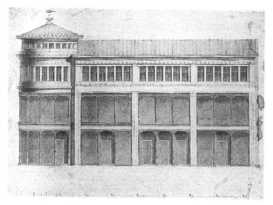

FIGURE 8.5   Elevation of a project for a commercial building at the corner of Howard Street and Dixon Street, probably mid-1850s.

FIGURE 8.6   Egyptian Halls, Union Street.

in Jamaica Street, Glasgow (by John Baird's office where Thomson had earlier been chief assistant) was among the most elegant. Over two decades, embedded deep in the first Glasgow 'order' of gridded streets, around the edge of the Merchant City, Thomson built a considerable number of warehouse and office blocks; and in the second order, the Blythswood grid, he built a few more.

One of Thomson's early designs is also one of the most uncompromising: for a corner site just to the south of St Enoch's Square, Thomson lined both streets with long colonnades to meet in a drum at the corner. (It was never built; probably designed very much at the same time as Gardner's warehouse, with which it is closely comparable,[13] it is known today from surviving elevation drawings of two different versions (see FIGURE 8.5). The building is very simple. Formed by its cast-iron frame, its wide bays are articulated by a two-storey masonry order. This supports a fully glazed cornice band of windows (and, in one version, an attic) under a shallow pitched roof. The colonnade below is filled with a filigree order of slender cast-iron mullions and very large panels of plate glass. The corner drum, which is nearly cylindrical, has a squat extra masonry storey, ending under a flat conical hat: quiet, social, commercial street architecture, but far from simply an essay in glass and iron. The qualities of iron and glass, of masonry and pitched roof are composed with care. Trabeated, sharply cut masonry, balanced precariously on delicate iron and glass, somehow contrives to become a Glaswegian stoa. With its even rhythm (6 bays above 3; or 4 above 2), it is potentially endless, a composition located only by the focus on the corner.

Nothing like this was ever built. Perhaps Thomson's most inventive actual warehouse was the Cairney Building, built on Bath Street in 1860 and demolished seventy years later. Here the surface of an even, potentially endless, street wall is articulated with unusual energy to produce five different layers of building. The ground floor is a wide colonnade with minimum-section glazing bars holding maximum-size plate-glass sheets. At first-floor level, a row of windows in elegant aedicules is formed by free-standing cast-iron columns. At the second, tall windows are joined by a zigzaging string with acroteria which bounce up and down across the façade, holding it all together. Then, from behind the second floor, between the windows, rise elegant square columns holding up the hefty cornice and attic floor of continuous angled glazing. Behind these columns, and now literally detached from them, the third-floor façade is a continuous band of timber-framed glazing.

So much to introduce the Egyptian Halls (see FIGURES 8.6, 8.7 and 9.6), designed in 1871 at 84–100 Union Street, and described at the time as 'probably the architect's most successful effort'.[14] (That comment, one of his very few English press notices, was proudly quoted by Thomson.) Fully-glazed, wide bays face a ground floor of shops; there are three main commercial levels, and an attic which, as with the Cairney, is lit by a continuous row of sloping skylights; floors are only interrupted by the necessary cast-iron columns and central staircase. That is all. There is no exercise in planning; no attempt to divert the blank plan from being undifferentiated lettable space – the direct response to speculative capitalism.

The street and the city, however, are enriched by the exuberant and richly articulated façade, a great area of glass set within a complex masonry frame. From the light and fully glazed ground floor, the building becomes heavier with each storey, ending in squat stone columns, bulging under an immensely heavy cornice – diverting our attention from the unbroken sheet of iron-framed glazing behind. A sense of indeterminate length is again felt here, but the horizontal layers are, now unlike in the Cairney Building, unambiguously clear. They precariously pile one colonnade on top of the other, the details a highly personal invention. Capitals could have vegetable inspiration, but whether in cast iron or (as here) carved masonry, Thomson makes them his own – as Horta was to do in Brussels half a century later. The eaves gallery (in front of the continuous glazing) supports a gigantic entablature as deep as itself, all producing an effect of sublimity only comparable to Chicago a generation later. It glories the strutting promenade of high-Victorian commercial Glasgow.

As Andor Gomme and David Walker rightly say: 'The peculiar triumph of Egyptian Halls is to combine a sense of personal style unexcelled by any other Scottish architect with the detachment from mere idiosyncracy which not only gives the building a compelling visual logic of its own but makes it so convincing a part of the street and city in which it stands.'[15]

FIGURE 8.7   Detail of first-floor colonnades of Egyptian Halls.

ST VINCENT STREET CHURCH

The third example moves to a less rhetorical context, to the gridded city of dwellings, with its evenness of image. Individual buildings silently mass into walled streets. Apart from the clue of a rolling topography, within this urban artefact – the grid – we locate ourselves primarily by abstract processes: reading, thinking, remembering – they are all in the head.[16] Embedded in this pattern, but articulating a unique form out of the amorphous grid, the St Vincent Street church (see FIGURE 4.1) puts the body back into the gridded city.

Virtually at the same moment, around 1856–8, Thomson designed three remarkable churches for the dissenting Church to which he belonged, the United Presbyterians. Despite their obvious family resemblances together, the churches remain very unlike any other building before or since.[17] They are the Caledonia Road church (designed early in 1856, built 1856–7) (see FIGURE 8.9), St Vincent Street church (designed towards the end of 1856, built 1857–9), and an unbuilt project for St George's Church, Edinburgh (designed in 1858).

In each, a given urban corner is exploited as Thomson 'builds the site' (if with a rather different rhetorical strength to that of Mario Botta, who originated that felicitous phrase). Thomson's theme is the romantic-classic one, whose image from the antique was the Athenian Acropolis rather than the single temple, the Parthenon atop it. On each site, Thomson builds his own acropolis, yet each composition is dominated by a

FIGURE 8.8 Caledonia Road and church, photo 1950s.

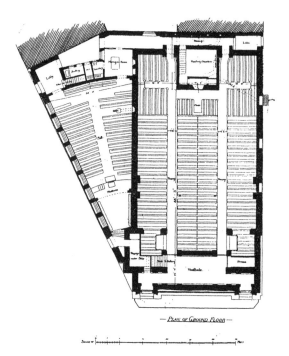

— PLAN OF GROUND FLOOR —

FIGURE 8.9 Ground plan of the Caledonia Road church.

tall tower which manages to diminish the dominance of the main temple mass and, with a leap of scale, address the town directly.

For the first church, the absolutely flat urban-edge landscape offered no hint of picturesque topography: simply a hairpin-shaped plot at the meeting of two offset grids (see FIGURES 8.9 and 8.10). The extreme end of the acute angle was cut off by a new east/west street (Caledonia Road), giving a narrow southerly frontage from which diverging lines of tenements would run to the north and north-east.

To achieve his remarkable scale, and for the architecture to speak appropriately (for it is *une architecture parlante*[18]), the 'acropolis' and its surmounting group of forms is built up with a controlled formality, based on rhetorical elements balanced with precision (and modified by optical corrections). Out of the ground grows a base of random cyclopean polygonal masonry, from which rises an ashlar cliff, on the top of which stands an Ionic temple. With this precisely sized, inaccessible portico and cella, the sense of a distant view of acropolis is implied most subtly. The scale is enhanced (and the composition saved from being toy-like or naïve collage[19] by the dynamic balance of the fine tower, standing exactly on the hinge of the two urban

geometries.[20] Like a prow to the city-ship, its diverging sides stretch back as far as the eye can see. As if to reinforce this unity, to make the church/city transition smoother, the first tenement blocks on each side are also designed by Thomson (see FIGURE 8.10).

For the St George's project, again elements bunch together on top of an 'acropolis' which is built up to form a plinth on a level with the highest part of the sloping site. Here more elements are added, including a fascinating semi-circular caryatid porch, beyond which the cliff is built up and topped with a virtually complete temple form, again offset by a tall and exotic tower.

But at St Vincent Street itself, the steeply sloping location is handled with spectacular drama. This corner site on the Blythswood grid slopes steeply down to the west and even more dramatically down Pitt Street to the south (see FIGURE 8.11). Here Thomson builds up a great square plinth to 20 feet above the highest point on the site, making a gigantic substructure nearly 40 feet tall to the south. On this, free-standing and with a portico at each end stands a mighty Ionic temple. Its form is seen from the south (to quote the words of a

friend of Thomson) 'as in a Turneresque picture dominating a series of streets rising above streets like rock-
hewn steps of some titanic staircase.'[21]

Once again, the abutting grid's street housing is
Thomson's. The tower this time, placed with unerring
compositional care on the highest point, helps set the
church apart and balances rather than overstates the
street corner itself.

The interior space of each of Thomson's churches is
powerful and architectonic; volumes and structure are
directly expressed and handled. St Vincent Street (see
PLATE IV) is a large square auditorium perfectly fulfill-
ing the Presbyterian liturgical requirement, uninterrupted save for six slender cast-iron columns rising
through the space to carry gallery and then roof. But it
is buried in the artificial hillside, with its upper galleries appearing from outside as low flanking buildings to
the temple which sails above, flooding in light from the
portico ends and clerestory sides. This magnificent,
light and powerful 'real interior architecture' is far
from a reflection of the architecture of the city being
built outside.[22]

The exterior scale is handled very differently: the
form is majestic but without being monstrous. Where
one great mass, reflecting the interior, would have
drowned the tenemented streets, Thomson's composition has a grandeur which is appropriate rather than
overwhelming. This approach is clear when he explains how he dislikes the Gothic because 'it does not
express greatness; it is only grand when it is actually
of large dimensions. Small Gothic buildings are not
impressive.'[23] On the other hand, many classic Greek
buildings were small, he argued, claiming them to be
'intellectually not materially great'.[24]

Here Thomson has added a recognisable and particular physiognomy to the city grid, one which clearly
responds both to the topography and to the dominant
morphology of street-lining walls. It animates the soul-
less grid; it articulates the town, not by contradicting it
(wounding, disfiguring, amputating it), but by giving
it memorable form.

In this, Thomson's churches are what Aldo Rossi
calls 'primary elements', in that 'they characterise the
process of spacial transformation in an area ... They
play an effective role in the dynamic of the city, and as a
result of them, and the way they are ordered, the urban
artefact acquires its own quality, which is principally a

FIGURE 8.10   Caledonia Road church and adjacent tenement
by Thomson in Hospital Street, photo 1961.

function of its placement, its unfolding of a precise
action, and its individuality. ... Primary elements are
characteristic or, better, *that which characterise* [his
italics] a city.'[25]

THE DOUBLE VILLA

My last two examples are rather different, being what
Rossi calls 'dwelling elements'. Each is an attempt,
more or less, to propose a particular type. While the
urban fabric of residential Glasgow was being renewed
and, of course, from the mid-century onwards enlarged
beyond the grid with fine streets of four-storey tenements, a new suburban fabric was beginning to be
strung together by the proliferation of 'villas'.

FIGURE 8.11 The Pitt Street entrance to the St Vincent
Street church.

Thomson's own account of his Double Villa (written a decade after it was built) begins:

Langside, where, in 1856–57, this double villa was erected, is about two miles south of Glasgow, and adjoining what is now Queen's Park. With other lands adjacent to the Park the locality is becoming an important offshoot, or suburb, of Glasgow. The Langside lands consist chiefly of the pleasure-grounds surrounding the old mansion of that name, which are now laid out for building purposes, with drives formed through the woods and shrubberies. The views obtained from the more elevated portions of Langside are extensive and fine.[26]

When Thomson built his Double Villa, the detached suburban ideal was still the exception, town street housing still the norm, in the cities of Europe. In Britain, this was especially true north of London, and particularly in Glasgow, where the commuting pattern was to become almost a reverse of the convention, in that the inner-urban tenement house remained the norm for all classes, while the new heavy industries were located further out.[27]

But from mid-century, the European bourgeoisie's flight from their mercantile and industrial city centres can also be seen here – and in Glasgow local reasons are not hard to find. In 1850, half of all children born in this city died before their fifth birthday. Glasgow had three severe epidemics of cholera, in 1832, 1848–9 and finally in 1853–4 when one in ten of the city's population died; inner-urban cholera and typhus do not respect social divisions. But the suburbs offered higher ground, fresh air and clean drinking-water. By the mid-1850s, the up-and-coming young architect Alex Thomson, whose neighbours in Hutchesontown had been lawyers, teachers, doctors and skilled tradesmen, had moved to a cottage in the dormitory village of Shawlands, close to where the Double Villa was under construction.[28]

This flight to suburban 'villas' invokes anti-urban memories right back to Vitruvius, who talks of the *villa suburbana* as the urban man's resort. The first-century Romans, with their clear urban types of *domus* and *insula*, invented the *villa* as an escape from their teeming city of a million inhabitants, a city seen as unhealthy and dangerous – mid-nineteenth-century Glasgow exactly.

The new Victorian reinterpretation of the suburb of villas had the twin aims of show and separation, of pomp and privacy. Thomson's Double Villa precisely reflects those goals, while also containing strains of all the classic 'villa' connotations from Alberti's prescriptions onwards. He forms the building picturesquely, for it to appear much grander and more imposing than the size of dwelling warrants, sitting in its arcadian terraced gardens. With this building, on the hilltop of Langside, Thomson provides the required home, the dwelling place, where the culturally anxious *nouveau riche* merchant and his family can relax and assume the social role which the architect's costume so appropriately suggests. It is a form to typify an attitude to the city; it is speculatively designed for unknown inhabitants, and proposed as a type.

Thomson's double suburban house form appears unique. The concept is very simple: the two dwellings are not paired with bilateral symmetry, mirrored about a party wall, as became typical. Instead the double unit is made up in a rotational symmetry of two identical left halves, the plan of one, rotated, joins the party walls to the right of each unit (see FIGURE 8.12). The plan arrangement of the dwellings, said the published account, is

suggested by the site, which is between parallel roads, that provide approaches to each of the fronts. The effect of each of the fronts is that of a villa of good size. . . . In this way each house looks much larger than it really is, greater variety is imparted to the design, and greater privacy is gained for the occupiers of the houses. . . . The front of the one house faces east, and the other west, and the views from them are equally good in both directions.[29]

In fact, as built, this description considerably idealises the location to fit the abstract planning concept. Thomson is consciously suggesting a model of development for the suburb. The account goes on to suggest that this reversed double plan might be an ideal solution for 'a limited piece of suburban land, too narrow for four rows of good houses, and too wide for two rows'. Here the two parallel roads could have inward-facing houses on their outer sides and 'semi-detached houses arranged like this example at Langside' as a central row, each half having access from opposite sides and

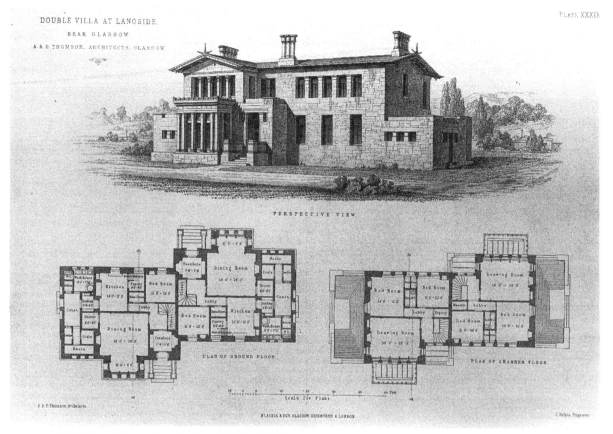

FIGURE 8.12   Perspective and plans of the Double Villa,
plate from *Villa and Cottage Architecture*.

thus enhancing the deceptive impression of grandeur
and isolation.

Once again, Thomson's dynamic composition,
precisely geometrical[30] yet picturesquely satisfying,
fulfills the urban – or rather suburban – task brilliantly.
The smaller ('back') windows fit a geometric order
rather than respond to the varied occupation behind
them – for that is all of minor importance. While his
major ('front') rooms, by contrast, have no windows at
all but rather are formed by colonnades, sealed from
the Glaswegian weather as unobtrusively as possible. It
is both these together, of course, which form the identical, opposite, elevations (see FIGURE 11.6).

Inside, there is nothing particularly striking about
the layout: a compact and directly arranged three-
bedroom house, on a two-storey plan about 33 ft
square, with a little single-storey service extension.
The main rooms, the dining-room to the left of the hall

and the drawing-room above it, are treated with lavish
care in articulation and definition of surface and space.
While the other, lesser rooms are formed with a plain-
ness which can be forcefully, brutally direct.

The Double Villa is a proposed type, to colonise
suburban land with a low-density carpet of objects in
landscape, potentially building a new 'suburban artefact'. But if it is generalised, that does not make it just a
background for bourgeois life to fill out. Thomson, in
his domestic interiors (to quote from his obituary)
'considers architecture to be total design, inside and
out'.[31] A social context which asks for this 'lifestyle
design' from its architects leaves no space for clients to
take a creative role in their own inhabitation; and leaves
little to the imagination, or indeed their action.

Here the designer self-consciously attempts to perform, in a pluralist age, the task assumed in more
settled, earlier times to result from consensus. In his

interiors, Thomson takes on board the role of provider of culture, and is valued more for his sensibility than his skill. It is a central problem of the nineteenth century. In a tone of powerful irony, he said: 'We are told that our chief business is to embody the prevailing taste of the time – to adapt our designs to the sympathies of our clients. High art is said to be irksome, and a style based upon what is called common sense and homeliness is specially recommended.'[32] Thomson, by contrast, offers a total identity, with an art work which may seem to disregard the client's self. But it may also be the strongest response to the dominant need of a culturally deprived client for stable respectability – of the socially insecure merchant for instant culture – for a persona behind which he can relax. The crisis of urban unity, from which the 'villa' fled, feels a correspondence with that form in its need to endow the individual dwelling with such emblematic significance.

MORAY PLACE

Further north, down the bosky hill on which stood the still isolated Double Villa (later to be slowly surrounded by other villas in their suburban plots), Glasgow's southern park, Queen's Park, was soon laid out. Just beyond this park, that short distance closer to the city and now on the Clyde Valley floor, Thomson next built Moray Place (see FIGURE 17.2); a rather different statement on the central tension – between the social city and the private family – of that time. A tiny, perfect terrace of houses; formal, geometrically uncompromising, yet delicately suburban. Henry-Russell Hitchcock calls it 'the finest of all Grecian terraces'.[33]

Moray Place was probably designed while St Vincent Street church and the Double Villa were both under construction, in 1857 or 1858, but its own building was delayed. A start was made in 1859 and the Thomson family moved into the completed No. 1 in 1861. Thomson was involved in commercial speculation with two friends, a builder and a quarrymaster, to develop a large tract of fields to the south of Glasgow as a new residential suburb, just north of Langside hill where he had built the Double Villa. For whatever reason, no more than this first terrace, on the edge of the development, was undertaken to his design.[34]

If my earlier examples showed Thomson's sensitive articulation of Glasgow's *existing urban* artefacts, these last two examples (the Double Villa and this two-storey terrace) show his attempts to model *potential suburban* artefacts. Moray Place is quite unlike the known morphological pattern of Glasgow, where two-storey terraces were almost unknown. The new sense of scale he explores – coherent yet intimate, mid-way between the communality of the four-storey urban walls and the individuality of suburban villas – is quite original.

Between pedimented pavilions, with their delicately incised detail and still domestically scaled double-height order, runs an even colonnade. The weighty ground-floor pattern, with its equal steps of solid and void, is surmounted by an elegant row of fifty-two sharply cut square columns. It is all scaled to obscure the fact that this plane encloses eight modest dwellings. The individual dwellings are indistinguishable in perspective, as the severe simplicity of openings masks, on the ground floor, the difference between the deeply set windows and doors; and, on the first floor, the difference between the deep-set windows and the almost identical blind panels covering party walls between the dwellings. The shallow-pitched roof and concealed rainwater removal allow a precise and simple low cornice to mark the edge with the sky (see FIGURES 8.13 and 17.1).

Inside, the dwellings are small. Similar in arrangement to the 2,200 sq. ft Double Villa, here the 1,600 sq. ft terraced houses have a dining-room below a magnificent full-width drawing-room, one large and one small bedroom, a kitchen and maid's room. Outside, the effect is of calm, of the precise and remarkably well-proportioned colonnade – humanised as so often in Thomson's work by utterly appropriate, light-hearted, linear decorative patterning. It is less a front to individual privacies, more a cover to a community; the 'stoa' memory, after all, refers to a public, social place. It offers a potential form for a new suburban balance between the household and society. But it is one which was not developed.

URBAN TRANSFORMATION

Thomson's career trickled to its end just as a deep economic depression was starting to take its grip. After his death, the Great Depression was highlighted in Scotland by the spectacular collapse of the City of Glasgow Bank in 1878. But building work had already

FIGURE 8.13   The western end of Moray Place in c.1930.

virtually stopped by 1877 and remained at a standstill for a decade. When it was taken up again, perhaps it was protesting its virility just a bit too much. That mood may perhaps be typified by the City Chambers, but even Sellars (often described as a follower of Thomson), with his magnificent individual buildings, was no longer building the city. No one took on Thomson's project.

The form of the stern, classic city of four-storey walls was held to, right up to 1914. Indeed, in many ways, it was in the forty years after Thomson's death that the city of today's Glaswegians[35] was formed. There was still urban coherence, good manners and order in the town's making, if more bombast than refinement in the monuments to the capital's self-confidence. The difference is that no one again made the *transformations* which gave definition to the ordinary pattern; which offset and identified the city for their moment, as Thomson so brilliantly had articulated Glasgow in the earlier generation.

Just when building-work was picking up again in the later 1880s, an English architectural magazine first hinted at my theme. It wrote of Thomson: 'The strong influence of his work is apparent in nearly all Glasgow architecture, giving to it – the city – a character unique among the large cities of the country.'[36] Thus Thomson did not stand against the city, but his work *gave the city character*. And that is why we can fairly call this chapter 'Thomson's City'.

NOTES

1. Dr Jamieson, 'Illustrations', in John Slezer, *Theatrum Scotiae*, London, 1814.
2. Decimus Burton had been brought in as master planner for the Kelvinside estate as soon as it was bought by developers in 1840. Hillhead terraces began building in the 1840s; but it was not until 1860 before land west of the Kelvin began to be developed with any speed. See M. A. Simpson, 'The West End of Glasgow, 1830–1914', in M. A. Simpson and T. H. Lloyd (eds), *Middle Class*

FIGURE 8.14   Part of Queen's Park Terrace, Eglinton Street,
photo 1980.

Housing in Britain, Newton Abbot, 1977, p. 65. Thomson's Great Western Terrace dates from 1867 and his adjoining Westbourne Terrace from 1871.

3. I paraphrase G. F. A. Best, 'Another Part of the Island', in H. J. Dyos and M. Wolff (eds), *The Victorian City*, London, 1973, vol. 1, p. 296.

4. 'Single-end' is a Glaswegian typology, the single-room dwelling built, within the consistent morphological pattern of four-storey tenements; 'tenement' being a number of dwellings off one stairwell giving direct access to the street, built as a city block usually of four storeys.

5. From The Minute Book of trustees under the Glasgow

Improvements Act, 1866, 'Anno Vicesimo nono Victoriae reginae, cap. LXXXV'.

6. On 16 Dec. 1867 Thomson and J. J. Stephenson were to lead a discussion on 'The City Improvement Scheme'. Only 10 people turned up, and it was postponed until 20 Jan. 1868 when 15 people heard Thomson talk on the problems of the City Improvement Scheme, followed by animated discussion. The Minute Book says no more, except that the subject was taken up again on 16 Mar. 1868 when, with Honeyman in the chair, Thomson read the paper reported in the next day's *Glasgow Herald* and the *Morning Journal*. Neither Thomson's paper nor the

obviously fully worked-out drawings survive. The plan was favourably discussed (we are told), and remitted to the subcommittee to prepare a report for the Commissioners under the Improvement Act. There is no record of this report. The Glasgow Architectural Society (GAS), itself on the point of collapse and unable to hold quorate meetings, finally dissolved at the end of 1869.

7. Brian Edwards in a letter to the author, 9 Sept. 1987.

8. The Glasgow grid is exhaustively studied in Frank Arneil Walker's paper of that name in T. A. Markus (ed.), *Order in Space and Society*, Edinburgh, 1982, p. 155.

9. Thomson, as Brian Edwards shows, is closer to the city architect's own plans at that time for new streets, which clearly show rectangular blocks extending the grid eastwards to the High Street. I am grateful to Brian Edwards for information on John Carrick's proposals.

10. From Thomson's talk to the Glasgow Institute of Architects (GIA) as quoted in the *Morning Journal*, 17 Mar. 1868.

11. I have reconstructed this project from the brief report in the *Morning Journal*. It is quoted almost complete but virtually without comment by R. McFadzean, *The Life and Work of Alexander Thomson*, London, 1979, pp. 204–5. There are clearly misprints (yards for feet at one point); equally clearly other information does not tie together. It is obvious from the description that Thomson had worked out the project in drawings of considerable detail. My proposed layout seems best to fit the clues given; my detail-planning and imagery is based very conservatively on various tenements Thomson built; I expect Thomson's design would have been startlingly original. (I have been helped slightly by Brian Edwards's own schematic reconstruction which is rather different from my own, and am grateful for his thoughts. My arrangement almost precisely fits the few figures we do have from Thomson, such as 3.83 sq. yd per person or 124 shops per super-block.)

12. Edward l'Anson, 'Some Notice of Office Buildings in the City of London', lecture at RIBA, published in their *Transactions* (1864–5), pp. 31 f.

13. Andor Gomme and David Walker, *Architecture of Glasgow*, London, 1968, suggest 'before 1853' (p. 147) but in a caption state '*c*.1851' (p. 148). McFadzean, *Alexander Thomson* states that 1851 is wrong (p. 38) and proposes 1856 in a caption (p. 39).

14. 'He [the client] is very proud of his building – a writer in the *Architect* says of it – "This is probably the architect's most successful effort, and we doubt if its equal, for originality, grandeur of treatment, or imposing effect, could be found in any city, not excepting the Metropolis itself".' From a letter Thomson wrote to his brother George, 20 Sept. 1872; quoted in McFadzean, *Alexander Thomson*, p. 183.

15. Gomme and Walker, *Architecture*, p. 149.

16. As Camillo Sitte put it, 'A network [grid] of streets always serves only the purposes of communication, never of art, since it can never be comprehended sensorily, can never be grasped except in plan', in *City Planning According to Artistic Principles*, London, 1965, p. 91.

17. A decade later he built one more, Queen's Park church, which was rather different.

18. And in that sense there is strength in Nikolaus Pevsner's linking of Thomson with Ledoux: N. Pevsner, *Some Architectural Writers of the Nineteenth Century*, Oxford, 1972, pp. 183–7.

19. Very much parallel to the design skills used by J. F. Fischer von Erlach in composing the Karlskirche façade in Vienna 140 years earlier.

20. The tower is often considered the maverick element in Thomson's church designs; of this one, Henry-Russell Hitchcock says: 'this superb tower reduces the temple front to a subordinate element' (*Architecture: Nineteenth and Twentieth Centuries*, Pelican History of Art, Harmondsworth, 1959, 3rd edn 1969, p. 100).

Understanding where the idea, which seems without precedent, came from would be instructive. Its location exactly at the junction of the two geometries, I believe, developed precisely for that (urban) purpose. Early sketches (which survive in the Mitchell Library) show the church and hall virtually as built, but without the tower. These have an awkward lack of resolution caused by the site shape; moreover, the view north, down Cathcart Road towards the city, with the tenemented streets but without the tower (and therefore with the four-storey tenement to the left, beyond the single-storey hall, seeming to collide with the portico in this view), would be unacceptably awkward and confused.

21. Thomas Gildard, paper to the Philosophical Society of Glasgow, 30 Jan. 1888 (from unpublished MSS collection in Mitchell Library).

22. 'This is real interior architecture, not just a gallery-surrounded hall like the Grecian churches in England' says Hitchcock, *Architecture*, p. 100.

23. 'An Enquiry into the Appropriateness of Gothic and Mr Scott . . .', lecture by Thomson as critique of G. G. Scott's project for Glasgow University, 7 May 1866, *Proceedings of the Glasgow Architectural Society* (1865–7), pp. 43–70.

24. Third of four lectures to the Glasgow School of Art and Haldane Academy, 1874; published in *British Architect*, vol. 2 (1874), pp. 50–2, 82–4.

25. Aldo Rossi, *The Architecture of the City*, New York, American edn 1982, pp. 87 and 99.

26. Blackie (publisher), *Villa and Cottage Architecture*, Glasgow, 1868, p. 45. The Preface, pp. viii and ix, explains that the written material was 'furnished by the architects who had in every case submitted to them proofs of the letterpress, before publication, in order that any additions or corrections might be made'.

27. 'Glasgow itself was the dormitory, the Singer works at Clydebank, or the various steelworks at Newton and

PLATE I   Entrance to 'Ellisland', Nithsdale Road,
Pollokshields.

PLATE II   Staircase in the narthex of the St Vincent Street
church.

PLATE III   Interior of the St Vincent Street church in 1992.

PLATE IV   Tor House, Rothesay, Isle-of-Bute.

PLATE V   Surviving stencilled decoration outside the
parlour at Holmwood.

PLATE VI   Entrance Hall of No. 4 Great Western Terrace in
1992.

PLATE VII   Thomson's own dining-room sideboard, now in
the Kelvingrove Art Galleries.

PLATE VIII Sketch design for a china cabinet by Thomson(?) in pencil and watercolour.

PLATE IX Pencil and watercolour record drawing of the decoration of the base of the pulpit and font in the Queen's Park church, by A. Rollo, 1899.

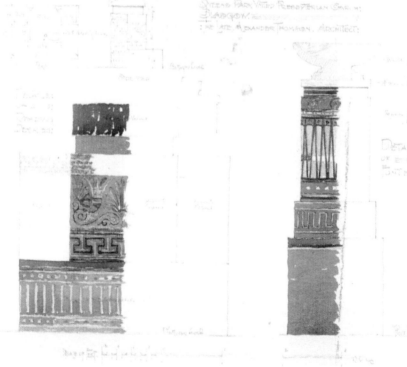

PLATE X *Belshazzar's Feast*, steel engraving, by John Martin.

PLATE XI *Ideal View of the City of Athens*, by Leo von
Klenze, 1846. As Thomson wrote in his Haldane Lectures,
'... look for a moment at the Acropolis of Athens, as it
appeared when Greece was the light of the world ... we have
one of the most glorious sights which the human eye has ever
been permitted to behold, and the like of which it will never
again see in this world.'

Coatbridge were the work destinations', John R. Kellett, *The Impact of Railways on Victorian Cities*, London, 1969, p. 355.

28. Within three years of the cholera outbreak of 1853–4, by the time Thomson was 40, four of his (then) five young children were dead.

    The fullest account of the Double Villa is in the 'Masters of Building' series, J. McKean, '"Greek" Thomson's Double Villa', *Architects Journal* (19 Feb. 1986), pp. 36–53.

    Gavin Stamp now tells me that the building was originally known as 'Maria Villa, Langside Hill' and that, at the time of the 1861 Census, the occupants were Henry Watson ('Clothier') and his wife Maria in one house, and James Gibb ('Landed Proprietor') and his wife Marion in the other half.

29. Blackie (publ.), *Villa Architecture*, pp. 45-6.

30. Thomson's geometric obsession, with 3:5 proportions and with root-two geometry, is clearly seen in plan, elevation and perspective of this building.

31. I quote Thomas Gildard, 'Obituary: Alexander Thomson', *British Architect* (16 Apr. 1875). 'If you want pictures on the walls, have a picture gallery', Thomson is said to have told a client who complained (quoted by Gildard, in MSS and cuttings collection in Mitchell Library).

32. Alexander Thomson, Presidential Address to the Glasgow Institute of Architects, 7 Apr. 1871, as reported in the *Glasgow Herald*, 8 Apr. 1871.

33. Hitchcock, *Architecture*, p. 114.

34. The facts of the story remain considerably, and rather mysteriously, cloudy; for this, and for the answer to the problem of whether the terrace or the railway in front came first, see Ch. 17, n. 1.

35. Or more precisely those of us whose memories stretch earlier than the destruction of the 1960s and 1970s.

36. The *British Architect* (28 Sept. 1888), p. 222.

FIGURE 9.1 Detail of the façade of Egyptian Halls.

Chapter Nine

·

EXPLORING THE WALL
THE URBAN FAÇADES OF ALEXANDER THOMSON

Mark Baines

*The aesthetic faculty appears to serve three purposes –
the perceptive, the selective, and the creative.*

(Alexander Thomson, Haldane Lectures, I (1874), p. 15)

These words, spoken by the Scottish architect Alexander Thomson, provide one of the most apposite and succinct summations of his own remarkable architectural career in Glasgow. There, between 1850 and 1875, he designed a large number of buildings, which in capturing the very essence of an urban architecture stand amongst the most profound and powerful architectural statements of that century. They additionally provide an appropriate point of departure for an appreciation of a particularly significant aspect of his buildings: the wall – the singularly most important focus of his intensive preoccupations with programme and place, historical source and personal vision (see FIGURE 9.1).

PERCEPTION AND SELECTION

Two factors are of paramount importance in the development of Thomson's architecture: the first is the urban character of the city of Glasgow itself; the second his knowledge and passion for the architecture and culture of antiquity.

The City

Glasgow at the beginning of the nineteenth century was a city confidently committed to its impending growth; an event overtly anticipated in the scale of its newly laid-out gridiron of streets to the west and to the south of the city. Substantially based on American examples,

they were the first of many similar, though smaller, planned extensions which progressively contributed so much to the emergent character of the city. It was ably assisted in this dramatic period of expansion through the wealth historically accrued from the entrepreneurial efforts of its merchants and manufacturers. They exploited the rich reserves of local and imported raw materials made available to them by virtue of the city's location on the River Clyde on Scotland's west coast which, not without considerable effort, afforded them access to foreign markets, especially those of the New World. During the course of the nineteenth century Glasgow increasingly became the focus for one of the most intense concentrations of both commercial and industrial activity in Europe – a phenomenon which in turn incurred a correspondingly dramatic explosion in its population. In this evolving society, virtually every individual's skills and interests were, in one way or another, either engaged in or harnessed in support of the vast enterprises of industrial mass production and world-wide distribution of all manner of goods. By the end of the nineteenth century Glasgow's status as a commercial crossroads had been additionally transformed into that of a heavily industrialised centre – the second city of the British empire – the so-called workshop of the world. Like the experience of many cities this was not achieved without human cost. In certain sections of the city, economic pressures arising out of the very speed with which it grew, forced many of its poorer work-force to live in insanitary and overcrowded housing conditions. Polluted air and the lack of an adequate water supply allowed cholera and other diseases to repeatedly take their toll of all sections of society before scientific advances could begin to

FIGURE 9.2   Walmer Crescent.

identify their causes, devise solutions and instigate re-
medial action. Victorian Glasgow emerged as a city of
extremes: robust and dynamic, rich and poor, uncompromising yet vulnerable. Standing in stark contrast to
the verdant, picturesque landscape of the Clyde Valley,
it was a city fashioned in stone. The slated roofs and
continuous sandstone walls of the buildings flanked
long streets of granite sets and flagstoned pavements,
their all-encompassing surface textures rapidly smoked
into blackened uniformity. The whole conspired to
create the impression of a seemingly monolithic mass of
masonry – the entire city and its buildings apparently
hewn and modelled from the various strains of this one,
singularly versatile material.

The near unprecedented pace and extent of such
developments in Glasgow did, however, provide the
necessary stimulus, demand and opportunity for gen-
uinely original thought in many fields of activity, including architecture, in a continuous effort to relieve
the constant strain on the city's infrastructure and
provide for the increasingly diverse needs of its many
inhabitants.

Society and Building Type

It was within this context that Alexander Thomson
both lived and worked, and in association with his
three successive partners (John Baird, 1849–56; his
brother George, 1856–71; and Robert Turnbull, 1871–
5) executed for that time a prolific output of buildings –
some 100 are recorded in this 26-year period – the vast
majority located within the centre of Glasgow, the

remainder in its immediate suburbs or along the Clyde
Estuary. As an architect, he was also a member of the
newly emergent, urban middle class whose varied
ambitions, prosperity, professional and entrepreneurial skills enabled them to become not only the educated recipients of, but also, importantly, the major
patrons of architecture, individually and collectively
commissioning a wide range of buildings in order to
accommodate their various domestic, commercial and
institutional requirements. His three city churches
aside, the most significant and by far the most numerous of Thomson's commissions were those of a specifically urban nature – terraces, tenements, offices and
warehouses – which, unlike the private villas, were all
speculative ventures in that they were multi-storey
buildings of multiple occupancy or ownership, intended to provide equal or equivalent standards of
space and amenity in repetitive accommodation for
sale, or rent, and to suit the varying incomes of a largely
anonymous clientele. Although some established precedent existed for these building types and their repetitive programmatic content, they were still in an evolutionary stage of development. Thomson both adopted
and evolved a set of generic typological solutions to this
recurrent set of building programmes, to the extent
that each building – though complete and self-contained in itself – may be seen to be partially prototypical
of another of its type, engendering in turn a corresponding cross-fertilisation of ideas between different
types (see FIGURES 9.2 and 9.3). His familiarity with the
various programmes, enhanced by the great number of
commissions he undertook, facilitated their continuous
re-examination, leading to their constant development
and refinement. In this way typologies, like the constituent elements of his buildings, are constantly recycled, adapted and occasionally augmented so as to fit
their specific locations, producing a series of unique
architectural solutions which represent a continual re-
statement and reinterpretation of a limited number of
compositional themes. The individual buildings, like
the city blocks they are located on, seek to achieve a
necessary autonomy, whilst embodying a number of
principles that are capable of a more general and widespread application.

The partnership between repeating building type
and Glasgow's gridiron – itself a timeless planning
typology of almost universal application – is of equal

importance, in that the symmetrical shape of the individual rectangular block, and its multiple repetition, offers a recurring set of predetermined, dimensionally co-ordinated locations for building. Like many of its historical predecessors, the Glasgow grid is correspondingly predisposed towards commercial speculation and development as a consequence of its general ease of buildability, its particular plot subdivision encouraging the development of more or less continuous perimeter buildings. Equally, the ubiquitous order of the gridiron pattern of streets with its characteristic of open vista and uniform repetition, and the circumstantial geometric variations occurring as a result of its fragmentation at points of intersection constitute an imposed order that controls, but barely modifies, the variability of the undulating terrain upon which it is overlaid. These forces resonate with Thomson's persistent preoccupation with the aesthetics of symmetry and serial repetition as well as his concern for the special, or unique condition (see FIGURE 9.4). It is therefore of little surprise that Thomson's buildings appear to be highly conditioned by, if not actually attuned to their urban context of regular grid street layout with its unequivocal discipline of route, domain and building line – a hierarchic order which emphatically predetermines the alignment of the building's front, back and side – conventional relationships within which he worked. The affinity between Thomson's buildings and the city grid is additionally exhibited in the geometric precision of the buildings' cubic massing, plan organisation and detailed execution, all of which respectfully acknowledge and reinforce the established order of the city.

Thomson was therefore concerned with the search for an appropriate architectural language that would conceivably be capable of meaningfully embracing a wide range of building types of different size and purpose, a language which could also encompass their evolving programmatic and technological requirements and serve to give appropriate public expression to the individual, and combined, values and aspirations of a new and forward-looking, urban society. In response to these circumstances Thomson elected to explore the primacy and totality of the building form as having a greater longevity, and embodying a more lasting expression of the collective values of society as a whole. For this, he turned to the architecture of antiquity.

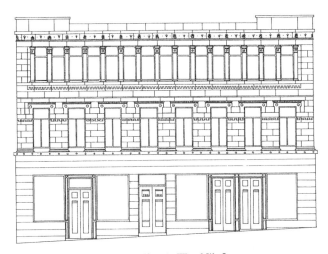

FIGURE 9.3   Elevation of the offices in West Nile Street.

Architecture and Antiquity

There can be little doubt that Thomson's primary source of inspiration was empirically founded on the basic formal and structural principles of Greek and, importantly, Egyptian architecture, in that both exhibited a trabeated structural and constructional system of material discipline, comprising an assembly of podium, column, beam, wall and pedimented roof which, through the application of sophisticated proportional geometry was capable of achieving a monumental presence. To Thomson this represented the root source of a civilised architecture, retaining eternal values, and imbued with a historically accumulated immunity to transitory and changing circumstance. It was the alluring tangibility and power of these idealised images – for he never travelled to see them – which he sought to transpose to his own era. Appreciative as he was of the contemporary resurgence of interest in classical architecture in Glasgow and Edinburgh, he chose to reject the obvious folly of attempted archaeological reconstruction and the encumbrance of academic dogma and, eschewing historical accuracy, embraced its principles, distilling them to their essence and applying them with an objectivity and intellectual detachment uncharacteristic of his peers.

It is evident that Thomson made the intellectual distinction between the architectural image and its essential construct whilst perhaps identifying an empathy within each towards the nature of the architectural problems with which he was actively

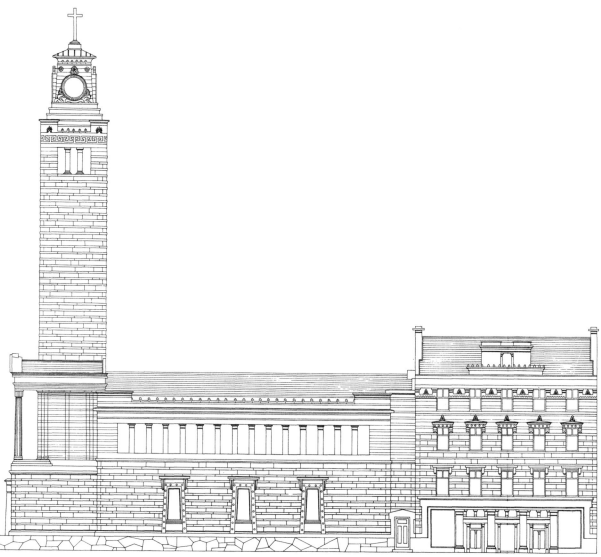

FIGURE 9.4   East elevation of the Caledonia Road church
with Thomson's tenement in Hospital Street.

engaged. This allowed him to abstract a series of
architectural elements and compositional devices from
their original context with a knowledgeable but daring
impunity, treating them as formal or operational access-
ories subservient to the greater priority of his personal
architectural intentions. Equally this suggests that the
architectural elements, images and devices he did
select were chosen, not for their historical associations
but primarily in consideration of their abstract, formal
qualities and their relative compatibility with one

another, a kit of parts with the inherent capacity for
multiple and incremental assembly in different combinations (see FIGURE 9.5). The architecture of antiquity was, quite simply therefore, his preferred architectural language, selected from all that was available to
him through contemporary literary and pictorial documentation of both recent and historical architecture,
both real and imaginary.

Consequently, Thomson sought to avoid unnecessary innovation and, in building upon received

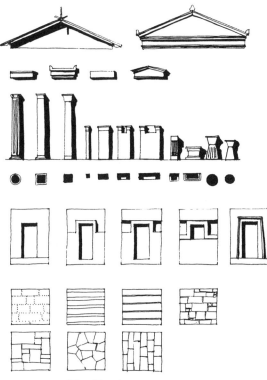

FIGURE 9.5 'Kit of Parts'.

tradition and accepted convention, employed a number of elements, compositional devices and techniques which, although not new in themselves, were constantly recycled and only occasionally augmented. Each became dynamically reinvigorated through the ingenuity and rigour that underpinned their reinterpretation and repeated application producing, as a result, a series of unique architectural solutions of rare originality. By these means, Thomson forcibly and convincingly confronted the self-imposed dilemma of preserving the original innocence and potency of his chosen architectural image, whilst coping with the various complexities of mid-nineteenth-century buildings of quite different purpose in the northern European city of Glasgow.

CREATIVITY

In pursuit of his idealised vision, Thomson embarked upon a fertile architectural dialogue between the part and the whole, solid and void, structure and light, a dialogue which he opened in 1856 with the design of Caledonia Road church and the Double Villa (see FIGURES 11.6 and 8.12), and conducted thereafter with a remorseless and unremitting intensity. Its developing theme arises out of Thomson's interest in devising the means with which to cope with the necessary penetration of the wall thickness for light, ventilation, view or means of access, whilst controlling the openings' potentially debilitating effect on the monolithic integrity of the masonry wall. His investigations invoked the use of the structural plasticity of the wall, punctured by openings, transitionally integrated with, and ultimately transformed into, the wall as a rhythmically modelled, structurally autonomous, repetitive assembly of masonry components – a fenestrated screen, simultaneously both window and wall. Throughout these investigations Thomson repeatedly attempted to achieve a physical and spatial relationship between solid and void that conspired to maximise the all-round performance of every individual masonry component and minimise any sense of physical redundancy, or extraneous detail, to the extent that window apertures are evolved conceptually, and appear figuratively, as the direct if not the inevitable consequence of the structural interval of column and beam and requiring little or no transitional constructional detail. Consequently, a number of innovative details were evolved in order to actively sustain and support the purity intrinsic to the overall architectural intention of his buildings. This involved a continuous process of physical reduction and visual simplification that was intended to preclude the interference of extraneous detail which would trivialise the building's integrity. The result of empirical thought and an inventive technical proficiency, his was the detail of effect as opposed to the pragmatic aesthetic of the craftsman, designed to ensure that his buildings maintained their formal clarity and sense of monumentality – qualities essential to Thomson's aesthetic ambitions.

The wall as the simultaneous resolution of structural principle, its physical elements, construction method, and the window opening is continually developed in all of Thomson's buildings, achieving its most powerful and succinct expression in the Egyptian Halls (see FIGURE 9.6).

The Egyptian Halls is the largest, and the most exceptional of all Thomson's commercial buildings, the impeccable logic and geometric precision of its

FIGURE 9.6   Egyptian Halls, Union Street, photograph
c.1872.

execution embodying the very essence of the industrial gridded city in an eloquently ordered synthesis of historical inspiration, programmatic determinants, structure and light, window and wall, all of which are encapsulated in the sophisticated orchestration and originality of its singularly memorable façade. Rich in historical association, the façade is an architectural celebration of Thomson's perceptive, if eclectic, sensibilities in its highly individual fusion of Greek, Roman, Egyptian and Romanesque references which collectively place it outwith normal categorisation. The building is both conventional and innovative, clearly demonstrating his skill and ingenuity in the three-dimensional organisation of the street elevation in response to its commercial programme and within the predetermined constraints of its location.

The Building Programme

The characteristic Victorian commercial building was both office and warehouse and was more often than not a multi-storey, cast-iron framed structure supporting a number of levels of continuous, largely undifferentiated floor space of almost equal height giving them an equivalent capacity for multiple subdivision into separate compartments of different size, and facilitating their potential for changing patterns of occupancy (see FIGURES 9.7 and 9.8).

Built in 1871 for James Robertson, a Glaswegian businessman, the Egyptian Halls is a five-storey cast-iron framed structure, its deep, rectangular plan extending to the maximum limits of the site, as determined by the street, the rear service lane and the adjoining buildings. At ground level two pairs of shops flank a centrally located entrance which provides access to a stair which rises directly to the first floor and subsequently returns on itself to serve the remaining floors. Two lightwells of timber construction, which also act as ventilation shafts, descend, in the centre of the plan, from the flat roof and terminate in two rooflights above first-floor level. The rear elevation is constructed of coursed rubble with paired windows separated by a single cast-iron column. The original interiors are substantially decayed. The linear and vertical organisation of the building in plan and section indicates Thomson's willingness to accept, and work within, the general constraints imposed upon him by the client's requirements and the building type, freeing him to concentrate on the three-dimensional organisation of the external wall and its fenestration.

In the interests of maximising the amount of available natural light and ventilation to the depth of the plan, and ignoring the internal column spacing, a close and regular spacing of windows and columns is established along the entire length of the wall. The regular interval of the fenestration internally allows for a greater flexibility in the location of partitions without any loss of an individual room's spatial integrity than might have occurred otherwise had Thomson adopted the more usual division of the elevation into larger and smaller bays in accordance with internal structure. The significance of this is that it also encourages each level of the façade to be read externally as a single bay, and without any intermediate punctuation which would interfere either with the notion that it serves a functionally continuous space or with the totality of the building's appearance externally.

Thomson's acknowledgement of the importance of the programmatic content and purpose of buildings consistently informs their outward appearance as well as their internal organisation. Thus he heralds the emergence of the building programme as a major determinant of built form in that the building enclosure is no longer the inanimate recipient of an arbitrarily imposed aesthetic order but rather that it derives its

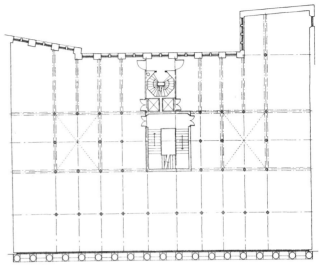

FIGURE 9.7   Plan of the third floor of Egyptian Halls.

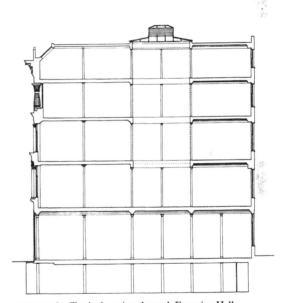

FIGURE 9.8   Typical section through Egyptian Halls.

own aesthetic integrity through a balance of internal function and outside condition. Thomson recognised that the reconciliation of the buildings' programmatic requirements with their surrounding context had profound implications for the building enclosure, and placed an even greater burden on the wall in its role as a regulating device by demanding that it sympathetically mediate between two, distinctly separate, spatial conditions simultaneously. Fundamental to his conception of architecture is a conscious manipulation of internal space consistent with external condition that allows the wall to be informing of, and responsive to, the local hierarchies of both, and requiring the sensitive adjustment of one to another.

The hierarchical sequence of internal spaces and the degree of fit between them give rise to an internally generated, three-dimensional, volumetric disposition of space, the controlled proportions of which – although physically conditioned by outside constraints – are variously given full external expression in the compositional massing and formal articulation of the building enclosure, the latter serving to locally modify and bind together its various parts. Thus, if the Egyptian Halls reflects its mid-street location and the repetitive and non-hierarchical content of its programme, the highly articulated massing of the St Vincent Street church is hierarchically evolved in direct response to its greater programmatic complexity as well as to the topographical and dimensional constraints of the corner position it fully commands.

Each of Thomson's buildings – villa, church, terrace, tenement or office – demonstrates the variety of ways by which the particular and variously demanding requirements of the given, or client, programme are skillfully accommodated to their locations within what might be legitimately described as Thomson's personal architectural programme.

The Architectural Programme

Thomson's concern with the building programme is endorsed in his overriding interest in, and persistent striving for, an all-encompassing totality of form in the overall massing and composition of his buildings, which effectively renders the building enclosure as three-dimentionally definitive, and therefore incapable of further extension (see FIGURES 9.14 and 9.15). The notion of totality exists in apparent contradiction to those buildings which in plan and section are of a serially repetitive nature – tenements, terraces and offices – a conflict between the asymmetrical unit of accommodation and the building as a whole, and one which he continually tries to resolve. Thomson therefore recognised that serial repetition of both building type and constituent part necessitates their inherent

capacity not only for repeated multiple assembly, but also, given that their infinite extension is unlikely, an equal necessity for devising the means by which they might be self-regulating with respect to beginning, middle and end, as well as top and bottom. In the linear and vertical organisation of the elevation Thomson employs two devices – symmetry in the former, and in the latter the separation of the façade into a series of horizontal planes.

Symmetry

With respect to the beginning, middle and end, Thomson's application of symmetry is critical, in that it supplies the principal means governing the linear composition of the building façade and its constituent elements, synchronising them with the building's internal subdivision at each level. Consequently each façade unfolds as a hierarchical assembly of, or subdivision into, a number, or sequence of repeated, local symmetries, determined by the relative location and frequency of a series of vertical axes distributed along the length of the wall. These axes determine the interval between the individual symmetrical element, solid or void, and the symmetrical grouping of elements, ensuring that they each retain their physical or spatial autonomy relative to one another. The relative status of each axis consequently depends upon the degree of emphasis it receives within the overall composition.

Arising out of this was a preferred tendency to deny the façade of a dominant, central focus, choosing instead to divert the emphasis laterally, towards the extremities of the building so as to physically stabilise and visibly resist the rhythmic orchestration of the intermediate wall surfaces, thereby enhancing the perceptible totality of the whole. The essential natures of the various parts are, consequently, inextricably linked with one another and with the whole by virtue of their mutual, though not exclusive, dependence on this single device, in that the symmetrical and thereby autonomous character of the part is embodied the character of the whole. In this situation the asymmetrical juxtaposition of elements only occurs as a result of the adjacency, or superimposition, of two separate axial compositions, and might appear to announce the termination of the building, or a repeated sequence of symmetrical elements, in which case it is inevitably

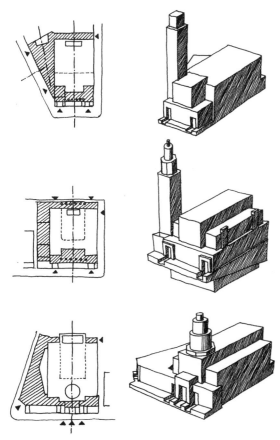

FIGURE 9.9   Diagram of Thomson's churches.

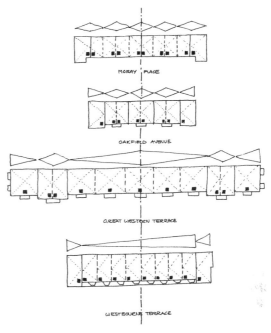

FIGURE 9.10   Diagram of Thomson's terrace plans.

reciprocated in an equal and opposite location within the confines of the façade thereby creating a larger symmetrical figure.

Alternatively, in the planning and massing of a building, a series of juxtaposed symmetries occurs as a result of accommodating an exceptional condition, as evidenced in Thomson's churches, which are invariably adapted to their location by an asymmetric disposition of the secondary parts of the programme, to preserve and protect the symmetrical organisation of the principal volumes (see FIGURE 9.9). In the case of the terrace and tenement the use of symmetry is employed to link a number of repetitive units of asymmetrically planned accommodation in various combinations of alternately handed or serially repeated units behind the wall surface, so as to allow the wall's visual release from any dependence upon the position of the party walls and internal partitions (see FIGURE 9.18). Although a

guiding influence, Thomson consistently denies a building's internal structure, party wall or frame any significant visual impact upon the continuity of its external appearance. Great Western Terrace (see FIGURE 17.3) is a singular exception to this in the positioning of two pairs of three-storey terraced houses – of the same overall accommodation as the other seven – providing a penultimate termination to the building's length. A measure of Thomson's fascination with symmetry is the fact that no two terraces are organised in the same manner with respect to handed or serial repetition of the house type (see FIGURE 9.10).

Symmetry and axiality was, for Thomson, a means of helping to determine the character of a building – monumental, formal, informal or in combination – signalling, through selective compositional emphasis on the different organisational axes, the building's relative status in the public domain.

The elevation of the Egyptian Halls (see FIGURES 8.6 and 9.6) displays an overall symmetry which is subdivided equally into nineteen vertical axes which determine the spacing of the identical sets of columns on each of the upper-level colonnades. Six of these axes are extended to locate the divisions of the shop frontages

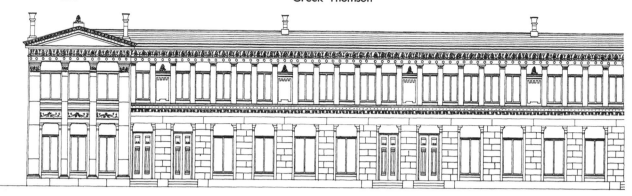

FIGURE 9.11   Elevation of Moray Place, Strathbungo.

and the central extrance door, this being the only
unique focal point in the linear extent of the elevation.
Apart from the cornice return, and its own innate sense
of proportion, the ends of the building receive only
minor recognition, relying instead on the buttressing
effect of the adjoining buildings; and in implying its
potential for infinite extension, the elevation is, in this
instance, tantalisingly suggestive of a much larger
urban idea.

Base and Top

In dealing with the top and bottom of a building,
Thomson invariably employs the classically inspired
convention of the tripartite subdivision of a building's
elevation into the base, the middle – or piano-nobile –
and the top, or attic storey. This, coupled with the use
of differently articulated wall surfaces, and the inherent
gravitational orientation and proportional discipline
derived from the classical ordering of individual elements, generally lent itself to the control of the vertical
organisation of the two- and three-storey building.

In support of this idea, each of the buildings is built
off a podium that accommodates any topographic
variations, establishing a strong horizontal base which,
if necessary, is physically extended beyond the building
line as a series of level planes and low screen walls that –
in territorially defining the site perimeter – serve to take
command of it by directing and controlling the
approaches and means of access to the building, segre-
gating public and private while firmly integrating it
into its immediate surroundings (as Great Western
Terrace or Holmwood exemplify). In front of the
Egyptian Halls, Thomson had originally positioned six

FIGURE 9.12   Detail of elevation of West Nile Street offices.

cast-iron Doric columns, surmounted by lamps, on the
pavement edge and located by the axes of the divisions
between the shop frontages and the entrance in order to
engage the building with the street in plan and elevation. These have, however, long since been removed.

Invariably, the buildings then emerge from the base

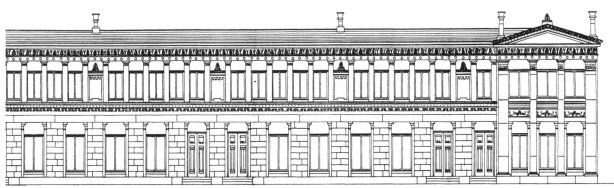

as a vertical sequence of horizontal bands of masonry of different height and further differentiated one from another by the detailed articulation of the wall surface and the nature and frequency of openings within it. Each layer bears physical witness to the accumulated gravitational load imposed upon it from the layers above, which – coupled with the application of local symmetry previously referred to – effectively locks each into position one above the other in such a way so as to highlight their progressive dependency upon each other for support. The greater proportion of the mass of the building is therefore concentrated towards the base and is progressively reduced towards the top.

The articulation of the different levels of the wall is both spatial and physical. In some instances continuous string courses serve to exaggerate the separation of the wall into a series of gradually receding planes, their combined action binding the fenestration pattern together and emphasising the horizontal thrust of the building. This is typical of the terrace elevation of two, three or, as in the case of Westbourne Terrace, four storeys. As the hierarchical nature of their domestic programmes naturally lent itself to the vertical gradation of base, middle and top, Thomson could allocate a separate band to each, with minimal external adjustment to the diminishing floor levels, and further distinguish one band from another by a different window interval.

Alternatively, as in the case of the office building in West Nile Street (see FIGURE 9.12), this was achieved by the inventive exploration of the wall depth between openings by means of precise incisions into the wall surface, the intervening masonry excavated to create a number of pockets, or continuous horizontal aper-

FIGURE 9.13 Detail of the south elevation of the St Vincent Street church.

tures, to receive the placement of a number of structural components at regular intervals – stepped mouldings at the first floor, and columns at the second in this instance – which support a series of lintels, visually

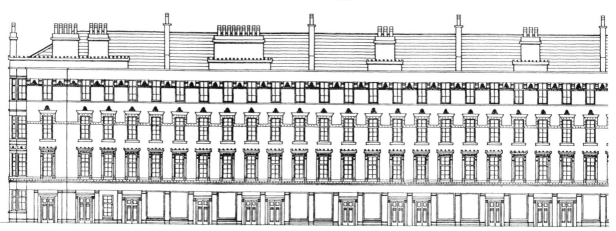

FIGURE 9.14   Elevation of Queen's Park Terrace, Eglinton Street.

fused together by seamless joints and incised or embossed surface decoration to create the effect of their carrying a continuous beam. The load carried by the hooded moulding is subsequently offset on to the intervening piers it sits on, enhancing the rhythmic continuity, and creating the effect of a structurally supportive window surround. The recessed masonry plane between the stepped mouldings was thereby acknowledged as construction skin contained between points of support, encouraging the aesthetic intention that it should be read as void, becoming rhythmically engaged with its glazed counterpart, through the effects of light and shadow.

The long horizontal aperture and a similar use of this offset, stepping device also appear in the St Vincent Street church (see FIGURE 9.13), where in order to accommodate a regular series of windows, Thomson inserts a visually continuous, highly abstract, orthogonal coil of masonry which appears to grow out of its masonry surround, and act in its support. Below, an entrance door is carved out of the massive base, with an equally massive beam supported by four large capitals, expressively carrying the wall above. The sense of abstraction is enhanced by Thomson's use of plate glass fixed directly into the masonry frame, its translucent properties giving it a dulled luminosity and, paradoxically, the appearance of a thin film of stone, which internally provides an undistracting, even diffusion of light across its surface.

If the serially linked terraced house lent itself more readily to the conventional tripartite subdivision of a building façade, then the problem posed by the fourstorey tenement, and the four- or five-storey commercial building, demanded a more radical solution. The solution appeared in the tenement design for Caledonia Road and developed in Queen's Park Terrace, where it extended the entire length of the block (see FIGURE 9.14).

In an attempt to give the elevation a similar hierarchical order as that of the terrace to the building's four equal floor levels, Thomson renegotiates convention, and boldly superimposes three receding wall planes over the four more or less equal storey heights and a regular grid of equally proportioned windows. Each plane is separated by a continuous string course which at first-floor level carries a series of attached aediculae to the windows, while at the intermediate floor level it accommodates second-floor windows by stepping over them to carry a small entablature. A third and final string course at third-floor cill level carries a series of piers the upper part of which is cut out to receive dwarf pilasters, which creates the effect of carrying a continuous entablature on a series of point supports at eaves level. The interlocking of each successive level eases the visual transition between the upper and lower parts of the building obscuring the precise junction of the floors with the inner face of the wall.

The physical vitality and visual intensity of Thomson's façades executed in this manner give them the impression of having been carved in low relief with an illusion of great depth suggested by the way in which one plane appears to rise from behind the one below, its

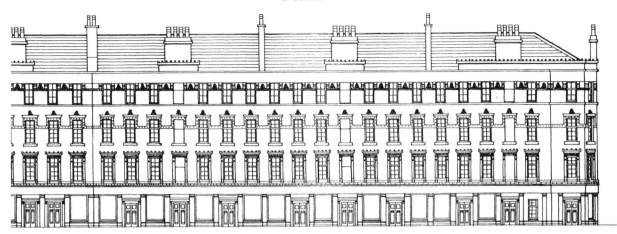

profile 'silhouetted' against the one above. By this process of addition and subtraction, the depth of the wall is fully exploited to accentuate its thickness, and by virtue of the pronounced vertical accents ensures its visual release from the controlling, and potentially divisive, influence of both party walls and the regular spacing of intervening floor levels, enabling Thomson to positively emphasise the linear rhythm of the elevation and the totality of the overall composition.

The progressive reduction of the interval of solid and void along the building's length was always tempered by the domestic programme of the terrace as well as the tenement, with their fixed spatial subdivision and need for privacy. The commercial office or warehouse building, however, presented Thomson with the opportunity for reducing this interval, opening the wall to the development of the masonry screen. At the same time Thomson begins further to explore the vertical interpenetration of the separate wall planes in an attempt to visually integrate separate floors of the same function. What was largely a descriptive treatment in the tenement wall now becomes a fully three-dimensional feature. It is noticeable too that Thomson's attitude to the fenestration changes in that the increased frequency of the window openings between points of structural support implies a sense of continuity to the planes of the fenestration set within the wall. Consequently, the fenestration seems to have been cut from a single sheet of glass, subdivided into different sizes, captured by the masonry frame but appearing to run continuously behind it, an illusion fostered by the detailing of the

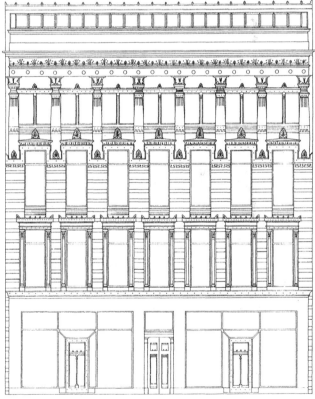

FIGURE 9.15 Elevation of the Cairney Building, Bath Street.

timber frames to provide fixed and opening lights and which tends to conceal all but their necessary moving parts. Where their visual presence is unavoidable, their

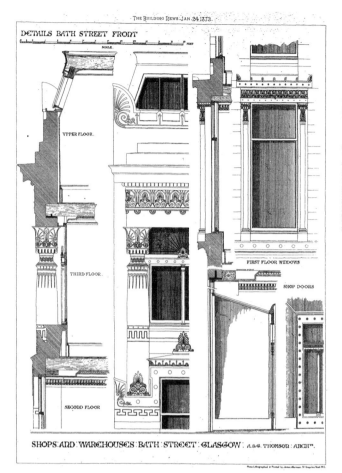

FIGURE 9.16   Sections and details of the façade of the
Cairney Building, from the *Building News*, 24 January 1873.

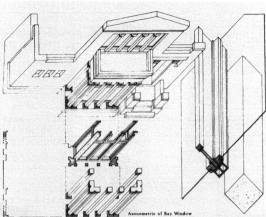

FIGURE 9.17   Axonometric study of the bay window of the
Double Villa.

detailed profile is derived from that of their masonry
counterparts. The illusion of the continuity of the
fenestration, both horizontally and vertically, and its
sense of independence from the masonry screen becomes a reality with the introduction of the timber and
glass screen positioned behind the columns at the attic
storey, allowing them their full three-dimensional freedom.

The Cairney Building (see FIGURES 9.15 and 9.16)
effects the transition from the four-storey tenement to
the five-storey commercial building. The windows of
the first and second floors are combined in the same
manner as Queen's Park Terrace, although at a closer
spacing, determined by the structural interval of free-
standing, square section columns at the third-floor

level. The gravitational thrust of these columns is
expressively received between the raised window surrounds and on to the horizontally banded masonry wall
below. The problem of the fifth and final floor is
resolved by accommodating it within the cornice,
which projects over the colonnade and free-standing
glazed screen below, prefiguring their combined use in
the Egyptian Halls. This building also sees the first
large-scale use of the independent glazed screen,
adapted from smaller scale predecessors in the projecting bays of the Double Villa (see FIGURE 9.17) and
Holmwood, and here deployed at second-floor level,
and later in the Egyptian Halls.

The Grosvenor Building (see FIGURES 9.18 and 9.20)
develops the two-storey colonnade of the earlier Dunlop Street warehouse (see FIGURE 9.19), and is a major
advance for Thomson in that the two-storey screen of
columns is far more three-dimensional and so closely
spaced that the first-floor aediculae are forced out from
their conventional position between the columns to be,
instead, partially attached to their face, forming an
almost continuous screen, gripping the base of the
all-containing proscenium-like frame within which the
whole ensemble is placed, and which serves to integrate
the components with the wall. The close proximity of
the attached aediculae and their superimposition over
the base of the frame seem to supply the means of the
building's possible linkage to its immediate neighbours, implying that the façade is both open and closed

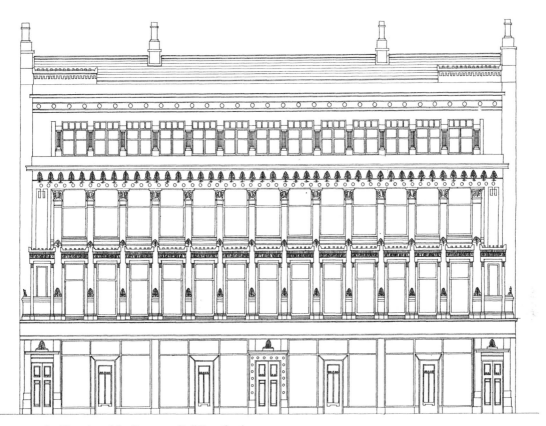

FIGURE 9.18   Elevation of the Grosvenor Building, Gordon
Street, as originally built.

at this level. Above the framed screen, a long horizontal opening is cut out of the wall surface, and large consoles – subdividing an otherwise continuous window opening – are positioned into this. In this elevation Thomson emphasises the vertical interpenetration of the horizontal layers of the wall, as though to suggest the functional continuity of its single occupancy. Here too, he manages to further exaggerate the rhythmic intensity of the elevation through the almost equivalent interval of solid and void, encouraging the eye to focus primarily on the object character of the structure and only secondarily upon the recessed interval of the glazed voids between. In this way the attached aediculae and the columns are the principal focal points as they become physically more pronounced through the depth of shadow between them, creating a series of alternating rhythms in both the vertical and horizontal expanses of the elevation.

In the Grecian Chambers (see FIGURES 9.21 and 9.22) Thomson returns to the wall to deal with the building's corner condition. The wall extends through two floors and expressively stands on its base and supports a continuous entablature by his cutting up into the lower and down into the upper extremities of the wall surface. At the ends of the building the rhythm of window openings is relaxed to allow a greater expanse of wall surface to rise around a larger window opening, separated by a single column, creating an asymmetrical pair of end bays, further accentuated by a stacking of smaller entablatures and a low pediment surmounting the continuous entablature. On the first floor, the centre section of the wall is occupied by such a closely spaced sequence of openings that it is virtually submerged behind a series of inclined pylon window surrounds, so much so that the intervening wall surfaces read as inverted columns as they are co-planar

FIGURE 9.19 Detail of the elevation of the Dunlop Street building.

with the faceted bases of tapering cylindrical columns above. These columns themselves sit in a continuous horizontal aperture cut out from the top of the wall and are the forerunners of the upper colonnade of the Egyptian Halls. The corner façade of the Buck's Head Building (see FIGURE 9.23) is, by contrast, a response to the tightened constraints of the building's location, and appears as a flat façade bent – almost literally – around the corner, an impression encouraged by the rhetorical use of external cast-iron columns and frieze.

In the Egyptian Halls, Thomson – perhaps in late recognition of the futility of attempting to build a load-bearing masonry structure of conventional arrangement over a transparent base of shops – attempts the total inversion of the proportional distribution of the mass of the building by placing it at the top.

From Union Street, the building rises from its base of shops through three levels as a vertical sequence of progressively receding bands of masonry (alternately colonnade and entablature) and is terminated by a massive, projecting cornice (see FIGURE 9.1). At first-floor level the foremost plane is established by a colonnade of slender, square section columns attached to a broader colonnade of piers, the two fused together by a continuous capital. The foremost column is then extended vertically and horizontally by means of an expansive scroll or bracket in order to support its narrower entablature. The combined effect of this is to structurally and visually stiffen the piers behind and visibly enhance the scale and depth of the window embrasure. At second-floor level – and on the same plane as the piers below – shorter paired columns of the same square section support a deeper entablature which in turn carries shorter, tapering cylindrical columns with inversely tapering capitals that stand forward, and thus independently of a continuous timber and glass screen that runs the entire length of the building. The geometric profile of these columns allows the final entablature, which carries the cornice, to be set back to a third and final plane. Above the cornice, a low parapet wall, barely visible from the street, rises to conceal a continuous gutter and sloping rooflight which lights the fifth and final floor – the whole visually concealed within the total depth of the cornice assembly. The interval and spacing of incised, embossed or projecting detail is located by a further subdivision of the column interval, visually fusing together and emphasising the linear continuity of the entablatures in strong contrast to the varying staccato rhythms of the supporting colonnades. Appropriately enough in a city which had dedicated itself to large-scale, industrial manufacturing the whole assembly appears to be the product of machine tooling or moulding, like the cast-iron façades of New York.

In this façade Thomson suspends both gravity and all previously held convention, as the rising walls of glass first dominate, engage, then disengage themselves from the descending masonry structure. He achieves this by the mutual adjustment of the relative proportions and dimensions of the columns to the entablatures they support in such a way that for each successive increase in the height and weight of the horizontal mass, there is an appropriately expressive decrease in the column height and corresponding adjustment of their profile in both plan and section.

FIGURE 9.20   The Grosvenor Building before the addition of
additional floors in 1907.

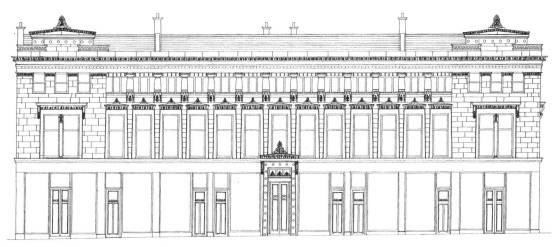

FIGURE 9.21   Elevation of Grecian Chambers, Sauchiehall
Street.

FIGURE 9.22   Detail of the façade of Grecian Chambers.   FIGURE 9.23   Buck's Head Building.

Thus, the foremost element of each colonnade – whether 'cylinder' or paired or single pier – constitute a descending columnar order of apparently increasing slenderness effortlessly effecting the graduated transition from masonry top to glazed base, as though each layer is successively suspended from the other. Viewed obliquely from the street, however, the receding planes of the elevation retain the conventional impression of progressively diminishing columnar order. This is street architecture at its best, and Thomson personified in the mature recognition and insight into the nature of visual perception and its underlying reality.

That all of these buildings combine a legitimate and meaningful complexity with such economy of means is derived from the fact that within each Thomson sought, with repeated determination, to purposefully extend the limits of a conceptually finite, or at least limited, amount of material and space. In the three-dimensional subdivision of both, he displays a con-

scientious awareness of an imperative for minimising any residual loss and for maximising their overall effectiveness through their interdependence upon each other. This is matched by an equal respect for the nature of the building programme, the expectations of its occupants and its location in the city. In aspiring towards a holistic, architectural synthesis of all these factors, Thomson with singular intellectual force marshalled all their respective energies alongside his own and expressively channelled them through one medium: stone – a material with which he had progressively acquired a knowledgeable intimacy, and which was indivisible from the architecture of both Greece and Egypt and Glasgow.

In so doing, Thomson's buildings retain an indelible affinity with the architecture of the past, but in their inspired abstraction and explicit rigour, they anticipate by twenty or thirty years the iconoclastic architectural events which occurred around the turn of the century

FIGURE 9.24   St Vincent Street looking west towards the church.

and which were subsequently to have such profound effects on the nature of the city. In this context, the architecture of Alexander Thomson seems to be of continuing relevance in any pursuit of an urban architecture, for there is a sensibility exhibited in his buildings that is able to confer an equal dignity upon all sections of society without unnecessary distinction. It was, and remains, an architecture of unqualified urbanity (see FIGURE 9.24).

FIGURE 10.1   Buck's Head Building, Argyle Street, in the
1950s.

.

Chapter Ten

ALEXANDER THOMSON AND THE GLASGOW IMPROVEMENT SCHEME

Brian Edwards

Alexander Thomson was at the height of his powers when in 1866 Parliament approved the Glasgow City Improvement Bill. Promoted by Provost John Blackie and master-planned principally by the City Architect, John Carrick, the Improvement Scheme held the prospect of a considerable body of work for local architects. Under the Act, the Glasgow City Council was given compulsory purchase powers to remove the homes of about 50,000 people crowded into an urban slum of some 80 acres. The central slum areas were concentrated into a corridor which ran from the cathedral to just south of the Clyde at the Gorbals. The spine of dilapidated, overcrowded and insanitary houses represented the remains of Glasgow's once handsome Old Town. Daniel Defoe had described the area in 1715 as having its principal streets 'the fairest for breadth and the finest built I have ever seen'[1] but by 1866 they had become a nestbed of prostitution, drunkenness and, most importantly, disease.

THE GLASGOW IMPROVEMENT SCHEME

The Glasgow Improvement Scheme was the most ambitious yet undertaken by a city council in Britain (see FIGURE 10.2). The planned urban reconstruction was based upon the imposition of a largely gridded network of streets upon the labyrinthine pattern of wynds and closes which made up the Old Town. The new straight streets, of which there were to be nearly fifty, held the prospect of an orderly reconstruction. In the eyes of Carrick and his large staff of officials, the streets provided the means to thread the health-giving public services of water and sewerage through an area almost totally bypassed by whatever rudimentary ser-

vices the city had. By 1855 the forming of Loch Katrine had promised to give Glasgow one of the purest supplies of water in the kingdom: the improvement streets were to be the channels by which the mains reached the central slums.

One cannot overemphasise the importance of the new streets to Glasgow's urban reform (see FIGURE 10.3). Almost every improvement sought stemmed from the construction in the first instance of new, wide and orderly streets. Below ground, Carrick's streets provided the servicing channels not just for water and sewerage, but later for gas pipes and underground railways. Above ground, the streets were ventilating channels; grids of light, air and sunshine. The configuration of streets encouraged the 'fresh breezes from Glasgow Green'[2] to penetrate into the densely packed housing areas along High Street and Gallowgate. Carrick knew the sanitary and engineering benefits which flowed from street construction, having visited Paris in July of 1866 to inspect Haussmann's reconstruction. Like Haussmann, Carrick regulated the renewal of the central areas around the dominating presence of municipal road construction, and sought to use the streets as a means to achieve other objectives such as the opening-up of new vistas of ancient buildings. The cathedral, restored by the Englishman Edward Blore between 1842–7, was the major focus for Carrick's sense of antiquarianism. He removed countless lesser historic buildings to ensure the cathedral was viewed in splendid isolation. His plans opened up vistas of the Tolbooth, encouraging later improvement schemes to isolate the Steeple in the centre of Glasgow Cross. Likewise, the portico of St Andrew's church was exposed to view fresh views. These activities were the

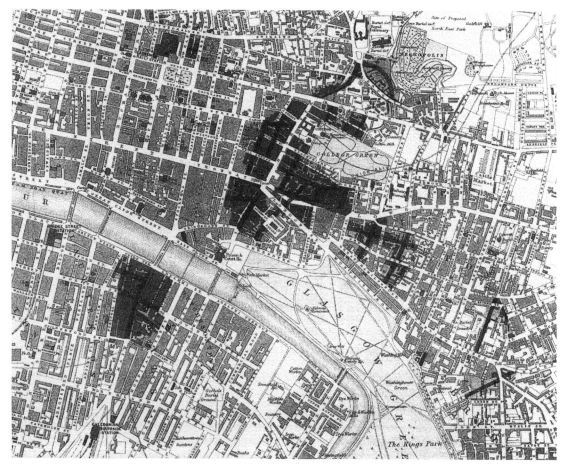

FIGURE 10.2 The general plan of the Glasgow Improvement Scheme of 1866 with the lines of new streets delineated in black. The Town Council had powers of compulsory purchase in the shaded areas.

secondary benefits which Carrick skilfully engineered on the back of street plans approved by Parliament – principally as a sanitary measure. A clause within the Improvement Act restricted the number of people in any quarter who could be made homeless without alternative accommodation being provided for their needs.[3] The provision led to much discussion within the Improvement Trust as to the form the new housing should take, and even whether the Improvement Trustees themselves were under an obligation to provide this. It should be remembered that until 1885, neither local authorities nor railway companies were required to rehouse those made homeless by municipal or railway activities. The debate within Glasgow over the design of working-class housing, its location and method of provision concerned the Glasgow Archi-tectural Society (GAS) and its members – including Alexander Thomson.

IDEAS ON URBAN HOUSING

The Improvement Trustees contributed to the debate by seeking the views of six 'eminent Glasgow archi-tects' including Thomson. They also built model housing (see FIGURE 10.4) and developed suburbs as an example for private builders. These exemplars of good practice, designed by Carrick and his assistants, drew upon the Glasgow tradition of four-storey tenements constructed as perimeter blocks around the edge of largely square urban parcels. Few fellow architects accepted Carrick's premiss that the improved tenement was the sole path to housing reform. Even within the

Improvement Trust itself, opinions were expressed in favour of English-style terraced housing and two-storey flatted blocks. The chief advocate of a more radical pattern of urban housing was the Glasgow architect and Improvement Trustee James Salmon. As a member of the Town Council, elected in the first instance in 1860, Salmon served on the Improvement Trust and acted as an essential link between the private architectural profession in Glasgow and the many public officials seeking to implement Britain's most ambitious urban reconstruction.

Salmon opposed the tenement, likening its amassing of flats into a dense and overcompacted area to the way the captains of the immigrant ships dovetailed together the various families and their freight *en route* to America.[4] To Salmon the traditional tenements were the prime source of the city's sanitary problems. They not only prevented light and air reaching into the open courts, but being densely packed together made the solving of the disposal of human waste almost impossible. Like John Honeyman, Salmon was much interested in earth closets and how human effluent could be kept away from water supplies. His answer, to spread it on the farmland of Ayrshire in order to improve the fertility of the soil, was not a path favoured by fellow Trustees. Instead of the tenement, Salmon argued for close, parallel blocks of terraced housing, no doubt under the influence of the model dwellings constructed to designs by Henry Roberts at the Great Exhibition of 1851. His ambitions did not appear to concur with those of the City Architect whose own preference for the tenement typology was given an air of legitimacy by the visit to Paris in 1866. The municipal report, recounting the lessons and observations to be drawn from a close examination of Haussmann's reconstruction, speaks specifically of the favourable impression given to the Glasgow delegation by the new Paris tenements. Their arrangement was, the report explained, not very dissimilar from those of our common stairs.[5]

The debate in Glasgow about how best to deal with the slum areas had concerned the Town Council and local architects since at least 1851. In that year the Council sought the advice of three Glasgow architects – Charles Wilson, John Herbertson and John Rochead. Their subsequent report under the title 'The Sanitary Improvement of Glasgow' was prophetic in certain

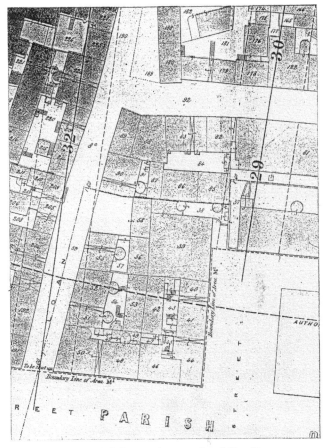

FIGURE 10.3   Detail of a large-scale 1:500 plan of *City of Glasgow Improvements and New Streets*, 1865, Sheet no. 13, Area M1 in the Gorbals area. The new streets are numbered, as is each property. Building no. 39 in Govan Street (renamed Ballater Street) is the Chalmers Free Church designed by Thomson in 1858 and demolished in 1971. Its church hall, added in *c*.1872, would follow the frontage of new street no. 29.

regards. The authors called for the opening-up of new thoroughfares through the slum areas, and the building of squares, circuses and parks in central areas for 'physical and moral well-being'.[6] These authors did not want streets alone but a collection of streets, squares and parks to make the city more beautiful and healthier. Nothing appears to have stemmed directly from the report, though fifteen years later the Improvement Act did propose the construction of Alexander Park in the east of Glasgow to complement Kelvingrove Park in the west.

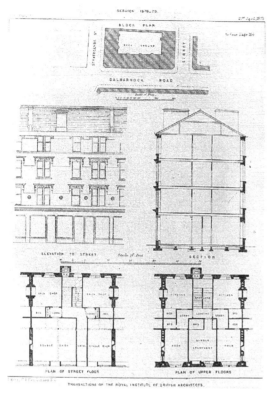

FIGURE 10.4 Example of one of the model tenements
constructed by the Improvement Trust in the early 1870s,
from the *Transactions of the R.I.B.A.*, April 1875.

A later commentator, whom Thomson himself acknowledged, was John J. Stevenson. Stevenson gave
two papers to the GAS: 'The Laying out of Towns and
Villages' in 1865 and 'Labourers Dwellings' in 1868
just before Thomson's own proposals for the City
Improvement Scheme were made known. Stevenson
had two likely influences on Thomson: he condemned
the rectangular gridded streets of central Glasgow,
arguing that they raised objections not just with regard
to architecture but also in 'matters of health, air and
convenience'.[7] The problem with the design of city
streets, Stevenson said, was that you cannot see the
buildings, only their fronts and these were only visible
if you 'squeeze yourself against the opposite side of the
street and strain your neck looking up'.[8] This unhappy
arrangement meant that architecture had become an
'unsatisfactory and imperfect art' with architects forced
to search out corner sites where one 'gets two sides of a

building – and if it runs up a lane behind, even three
sides'.[9] The argument led Stevenson to propose that
sides of long street blocks should be 'lined with the
ends of building blocks butting on them – narrow
blocks and narrow streets between them'.[10] Such an
arrangement, he said, was 'infinitely better architecturally, as it gives a series of distinct and separate blocks,
each a proper size for a single building, which would be
complete all round'.[11]

The justification for Stevenson's rejection of the
Glasgow grid and the related provisions of the Glasgow
Police Act of 1862 was both architectural and sanitary.
Instead of the parallel sides of streets being of uniform
height and unbroken, Stevenson wanted variety and
spatial permeability. In place of streets of even width,
he argued for streets, lanes, courts, squares and parks
of different sizes. This, he said, would improve both
the architecture of our cities and public health since the
sun would heat the open spaces creating air currents
which will 'do more for the ventilation of the town than
uniformly wide streets'.[12] A similar point was made by
Stevenson in his paper 'Labourers Dwellings' given to
the GAS just two months before Thomson's Improvement Scheme proposals. This time Stevenson said that
variety of town layout with narrower streets opening on
to wider spaces and squares would cause drafts and
movements of the atmosphere because of the effect of
the sun.[13]

Stevenson was not alone in expressing criticism of
the provisions of the Glasgow Police Acts. Introduced
in 1862 as a means of regulating a rapidly growing city
and reducing the level of occupation of much of the
older slum property, the Police Acts forbade residential
buildings from being higher than the width of the
streets they faced. A 45° angle of space at the front of
properties (from ground to opposite cornice) was
matched by an angle of space of about 37° to the rear in
hollow-cored tenements. The spatial parameters of the
Police Acts of 1862 and 1866, coupled with the ubiquitous right-angled grid, led to a city which the more
romantic and ambitious Glasgow designers found
seriously wanting. Stevenson was not alone in debating
alternatives, he was supported by John Honeyman and
James Cousland amongst others.

Cousland, a lesser-known mid-Victorian Glasgow
architect and former pupil of Charles Wilson, proposed
the building of healthy courts penetrating behind the

long street façades of central areas. The small squares were to be constructed behind a linking colonnade. Thomson was vice-chairman of the GAS when Cousland's paper was presented in 1860, and had by then lost four of his first five children to the cholera epidemics then spreading through the city.[14] His own personal tragedies would no doubt have strengthened his resolve to tackle the problem of the insanitary slums by whatever architectural means were available to him.

The various proposals for rebuilding the central slums made by Salmon, Stevenson, Honeyman and others took advantage of the GAS as a forum for inter-professional debate. The GAS formed in 1858 by a committee of local architects including Thomson, deliberately sought members from outside the narrow ranks of the architectural profession. Other building professionals including heating engineers, measurers and structural engineers were invited to join, as were local artists and craftsmen, and those involved in manufacturing. As a result the list of early members included the ventilating engineer John Hay, the iron-founder Walter Macfarlane, the developer John Cairney (for whom Thomson designed the Cairney Building at 42 Bath Street in 1860), the sculptor John Mossman and the interior decorator Daniel Cottier. The broad representation ensured that architecture was considered as much a building science as an artistic endeavour. The early published papers deal with questions of the design of foundations as well as aesthetic theory. Hence Thomson, who was president of the Society in 1860–1 had a wide range of expertise upon which to draw.

Thomson's involvement in the GAS helped establish the intellectual climate for his later proposals. He was active on many fronts: as a member of the library committee which negotiated the purchase of the books and the collection of plaster casts from the estate of Charles Wilson on his death in 1863; and as a member of the committee looking into the Improvement Scheme; and as one of three members who liaised with the photographer Thomas Annan in 1860 over the forming of an archive of views of selected Scottish buildings. The latter proved less than successful as Annan's prints quickly began to fade. Thomson along with Thomas Gildard (Thomson's subsequent biographer) and the measurer Thomas Howatt selected three buildings as a start to the photographic archive.

These were Melrose Abbey, Holyrood Palace and the Royal High School in Edinburgh. Thomson's influence in the choice of Hamilton's design is obvious, but the selection of Melrose and Holyrood should dispel the myth that Thomson had no time for Scotland's Gothic or Baronial past. Such buildings were, according to Thomson, not to be despised but there for dissection – to place upon us 'an elevated starting point for yet higher attainments'.[15]

The culture of the GAS was both progressive and socially democratic. It was an unusual forum in terms of British professional institutions whereby engineers, artists and architects could exchange views over a dinner table at the George Hotel or sit on committees seeking to influence local affairs. For many architects, a broadly based society undermined their sense of detachment from other building professionals. Some eminent Glasgow practitioners never joined, or let their membership lapse, such as John Burnet and the City Architect John Carrick. Increasing division and jealousies led to the setting-up of the Glasgow Institute of Architects (GIA) in 1868, exclusively for architect members.

Until the fragmentation of the GAS in 1868, the Society was an influential body and one which the Town Council and other professional societies turned to for advice. Two principal concerns occupied the attentions of members – the Glasgow Improvement Scheme and the relocation of the University from the High Street to the West End. Thomson became heavily involved in both, arguing that George Gilbert Scott's Gothic design at Gilmorehill was quite unsuitable for the needs of a modern university such as Glasgow, and putting forward the most inventive proposals for treating land cleared by the Improvement Trustees.

As chairman of the GAS in 1866, John Honeyman remarked at the annual dinner that although about a million and a half pounds was about to be spent on city improvements, the plans were likely to be carried out without a single Glasgow architect being employed.[16] The observation was based upon an understanding at the time that Carrick and his staff of surveyors and clerks were to oversee the whole operation. Where designs were to be carried out by others, the restraints of the Police Acts, feu conditions imposed by the Improvement Trustees, and models of what to construct collectively inhibited invention. Amongst the audience at the dinner was Bailie James Salmon who responded to Honeyman's remarks by suggesting he would use his influence 'in the highest possible quarters'[17] to redress the matter. Eighteen months later, in March 1868, the City Improvement Trust appointed 'six eminent Glasgow architects [to] consider and give blocks plans for the realising and laying out'[18] of specified areas of the Improvement Trust estate in the region of Gallowgate, High Street, St Andrew Square and Trongate. Salmon, as Improvement Trustee, and Carrick, as City Architect, were to meet the architects individually on site. The six appointed architects, each of whom was to receive a fee of 50 guineas once the report and plans had been submitted, were Alexander Thomson, John Honeyman, John Burnet, David Thomson, Clarke & Bell, and John Rochead (who had made proposals with Wilson and Herbertson to the Town Clerk some fifteen years earlier).

A month later, the *Glasgow Herald* elaborated on why the architects had been appointed. It was because the Trustees required 'some additional assistance … with a view to an efficient and renumerative realisation of some of the blocks where the property had been nearly or altogether acquired'.[19] Thanks perhaps to Salmon's efforts, the Improvement Trustees were now receptive to proposals for block layout and building design other than those furnished by Carrick. In parallel with this initiative, the GAS had established its own committee with the intention of advising – as a body – the Trustees. This committee included Stevenson (surprisingly omitted from those appointed by the Improvement Trustees), Honeyman, Thomson, the ironfounder Walter Macfarlane, the engineer Alexander Watt and three others. No record exists of any subsequent report but one must assume that the committee met, perhaps in the democratic and inspiring light of architects, engineers and tradesmen collaborating. The inclusion of Macfarlane, Glasgow's premier ironfounder, may be a pointer to Thomson's subsequent proposal to form Crystal Palace-like glass streets across the centre of the city blocks of the Improvement Trust's estate.

Mention has already been made of Salmon's preference for parallel streets of two- and three-storey flats. As chairman of the Glasgow and Suburban Dwellings Company with a share capital amounting to £15,000,

Salmon had not only advocated the construction of model working-class neighbourhoods but built such estates as Hutchesontown Gardens and Bunhouse between the Old and New Dumbarton Roads.[20] Thomson was no doubt aware of Salmon's preferences and this may help explain his own proposals to the Improvement Trustees for close parallel rows penetrating through the centre of the blocks. However, Thomson (with John Baird No. 2) had himself followed a similar urban layout in 1856 at Crossmyloof near Langside. Though suburban in spirit, the Baird and Thomson design for 'model working-men's houses'[21] consisted of two rows of twenty and twenty-four dwellings. Like the 'Colonies' in Edinburgh, the two-storey flats were entered from opposite sides of the block, and each flat consisted of just one room and a kitchen. Built in the cottage-style with zinc lattice-work windows in arched openings, steeply pitched roofs and projecting eaves supported on cantilevers, the architecture is reminiscent of Thomson's Woodside Cottages at Langbank, Renfrewshire. Both the Crossmyloof terraces were terminated by projecting gables, a common theme of Thomson's later classical terraces and a feature to reappear in his proposals to the Improvement Trustees.

THE GLASS-ROOFED STREET PROPOSALS

By the time of Thomson's appointment by the Trustees in March of 1868, he had wide experience of the design of both working-class tenements and terraced housing. His prime task was to propose solutions based upon the 'efficient' and 'renumerative' development of certain unspecified parcels of the Improvement Trust estate. Although the bones of Thomson's report survive in the form of journal accounts, the plans do not. The dimensions provided by Thomson go some way to allowing a reconstruction to be undertaken, but much remains speculative. Two assumptions have been made: first, that Thomson was aware of the provisions of the Police Acts and was advised to work within their constraints and, second, that he was familiar with the feuing conditions applied as a matter of course on land sold for development by the Improvement Trustees. The latter normally specified two development codes of a largely aesthetic nature, and others concerned with meeting parliamentary conditions. The first covered matters of height and finish: buildings were required to be 'four square storeys high' and constructed on the street elevation of 'polished ashlar of a white pile'.[22] Other areas frequently covered by way of feu conditions required the construction of housing of a working-class character with specific provision for one- and two-apartment flats. The setting of building lines, access to public services, and sometimes elevations were to be approved by the City Architect. Hence, one should assume that any visionary proposals were tempered by these rather sobering constraints.

In his proposals, Thomson acknowledged his debt to Stevenson. Specifically the employment of streets, courts and lanes of varying widths deliberately sought to exploit Stevenson's observation that sunlight penetration into spaces of different dimensions led to air currents and hence urban ventilation. To those familiar with Glasgow it may seem bizarre that to increase air movement was considered desirable, bearing in mind the frequent gales to which the city is prone. But medical opinion at the time, particularly that of Glasgow's Medical Officer of Health, Dr Gairdner, believed that a reduction in residential density, an increase in ventilation, and the installation of new water and sewage supplies were the corner-stones of sanitary reform.

Thomson seeks to make a virtue out of the question of ventilation by adopting the glass-roofed street as a means of accelerating solar gain and hence the stack effect of forced ventilation. Here he was taking Stevenson's argument a big step further forward, perhaps encouraged by the iron-founder Macfarlane who sat on the GAS committee. With the glass and steel arcades of the Crystal Palace arguably in Thomson's mind, he proposed an alternating pattern of glazed residential courts and service lanes running at right angles to the leading streets. Again we find Stevenson appearing as a likely source of the idea. In his published paper 'Laying Out of Towns and Villages' Stevenson had proposed the building of workmen's houses around a 'green grass square, making access for carts and vehicles from a paved lane behind'.[23] In the green in front, Stevenson said, the children could play without risk of being run over, and Thomson says that his covered streets are 'intended chiefly as playgrounds for the young, where they may run about under sheltered and out of danger from carts and other vehicles'.[24]

What Thomson had skilfully done was to transfer Stevenson's ideas to the central area of Glasgow, transforming them by way of a fusion with the engineering prowess of the Crystal Palace. In the process he had also sought to accommodate Salmon's ideas for parallel blocks which are now proposed as closely spaced as the Police Acts would allow.

Although the provisions of the Glasgow Police Acts as administered by Carrick (as Master of Works) led to the development of a city of hollow-cored, spatially well-structured tenements, the wording of the Acts required only cones of minimum space outside windows and cubes of space at the front and rear of properties. The assumption that rectangular – as against parallel – layouts were preferred led to much debate and even legal challenges. If one assumes that Thomson worked within the wording of the Acts (although maybe not their spirit), then the courts at 32 ft wide as proposed were contained by terraces no higher than three storeys. This assumption may be misplaced but it receives some credence from the form of construction. Thomson tells us that the housing was to be built of 9-inch brickwork, a practical impossibility at four storeys high, especially with the walls perforated with ventilating flues as proposed.

Before we look closer at how Thomson's scheme was to work, it is necessary to describe his proposals in full. They consisted of an area 330 ft by 1,063 ft divided by two cross-streets 50 ft wide, thereby making three urban blocks very nearly 330 ft square. The streets around the edge of Thomson's blocks were 80 ft and 60 ft wide in deference to Stevenson's proposals. Across each block Thomson proposed an alternative pattern of glass-roofed streets 32 ft wide with openings 16 ft wide, and service lanes of unspecified width. The perimeter of each block was made up of detached tenements 48 ft in length containing both shops and apartments, whilst the interior glazed courts consisted only of residential accommodation. Instead of a continuous cliff of tenements lining the perimeter streets, Thomson gives us separate pavilions with alternate openings into glazed courts. And instead of an abstract, equally weighted grid, Thomson proposed streets of different width suggesting varying levels of civic importance with the 50 ft streets for 'local traffic only'.[25]

Thomson's proposals contained in a paper to the GAS on 16 March 1868 under Honeyman's chairmanship

were illustrated by way of a diagram. These were not
fully developed architectural plans but broad brush
proposals based, no doubt, upon achieving an 'efficient
and renumerative' development of a portion of the
Improvement Trust's estate. Thomson had sought to
reconcile conflicting interests. The perimeter block
assumption in Carrick's master-planning of the whole
area had made the provision, according to Glasgow
architects, of truly working-class housing unattainable.
Only by penetrating into the rear courts or exceeding
the height limits of the Police Acts and feu conditions
could the cost of building be brought down to a level
which made house-building for the poorest classes
viable. Unlike in more peripheral areas under the
Trustees' control, such as at Bridgeton or Gorbals
Cross, central land being sold to the highest bidder
tended to be used for warehouses, department stores or
artisan housing. Thomson, realising the predicament,
proposed a radical remedy – the occupation of the
centres of the urban block. Only in this way could he
achieve a population of 10,224 within the three urban
blocks which Thomson believed was essential to maintain the commercial health of central areas.

Using the minimum space provisions of the Police
Acts, Thomson proposed apartments 10 ft square with
ceilings 9 ft high. In parts of his scheme, he said, such
single rooms would represent a whole house for a
family of three adults or 4.5 individuals if children were
accommodated. Elsewhere one suspects two-apartment flats were to be used, making a typical tenement
on Thomson's proposals a mixture of one- and two-
apartment houses. Such an arrangement would have
met the Trustees' ambitions at the time to rehouse
as many of the displaced people in central areas as
resources allowed.

We do not know how high the tenements were to be.
Two obvious constraints would have limited vertical
living. The Police Acts would have limited building
height to three storeys in the glazed courts and five
storeys in the two cross-streets. Moreover, the standard
feu condition of the Improvement Trustees would have
restricted Thomson to four storeys even along the
widest streets. If Thomson was familiar with the then
current building codes in Glasgow (and one must
assume he was), it seems likely that his proposals were
for four-storey detached tenements facing the main
streets and three-storey-high terraces of flats inside the

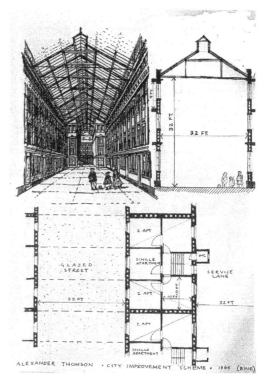

FIGURE 10.5   Reconstruction of Thomson's 'glass-roof
streets', proposal submitted to the City Improvement
Trustees in 1868.

rear courts. Such a speculation gains support from
Thomson's proposal – already mentioned – to 'build
the walls of these roofed streets of nine-inch
brickwork'.[26] The technology of brickwork in mid-
nineteenth-century Glasgow had not achieved a four-
storey brick tenement of 9-inch construction, and bearing in mind the walls were to be perforated with
ventilating flues, three- (or even two-) storey ranges
seem more likely. As for the detached tenements at the
street edges, these are likely to have been built of stone
since the feu conditions required, as a matter of course,
'polished sandstone of a white pile'. One suspects,
therefore, that Thomson's proposals were based upon
rather traditional four-storey sandstone detached tenements at the edge, and highly unusual brick-built,
glass-roofed streets inside.

The most adventurous aspect of the proposals was
without doubt the use of glass-roofed streets (see
FIGURE 10.5). Although they had been employed
in Glasgow in commercial shopping streets, such as

Argyle Arcade (1827), the source of inspiration for Thomson was probably the Crystal Palace constructed for the Great Exhibition in 1851. Thomson had designed the Garnkirk Vase for the Garnkirk Fireclay Company which was exhibited at the Great Exhibition.[27] We do not know whether he travelled to London to visit Paxton's building, but even if he did not, Thomson would have been familiar with its structural system through articles and periodicals. Judging by his enthusiasm for Paxton's glass and steel innovations elsewhere (for example, the cast-iron Howard Street warehouse), it seems likely that the health- and comfort-giving opportunities of glass-roofed streets were directly inspired by the Crystal Palace. After all for speed and cost of construction, Paxton's great structure was held up as an exemplar of the prowess of the engineer. The Crystal Palace took the aesthetic possibilities of new materials to their logical conclusion, just as Thomson sought to do in his proposals.

Thomson's justification for residential courts roofed in glass was that they would provide shelter for children, but more than that, 'the warmth which would result from this method of building would be conducive to the health and comfort of all'.[28] Here we see the legacy of Stevenson and his fascination with sun-warmed urban spaces. Thomson takes the interest in solar gain much further forward, however, by proposing the courts be roofed in glass as a health and comfort measure. The effect of the warmth generated in the glass streets would be to encourage an air flow through the flats and their staircases, thereby leading to enhanced ventilation even when the air was still. To ensure the houses were ventilated, Thomson proposed 'ventilating flues carried up in the gables beside the smoke flues'.[29] Although Thomson acknowledged the risk of the spread of contagious disease, he felt confident that the flues (and no doubt vents in the apex of the glass roofs) would be an effective safeguard.

Thomson's proposals should be seen as a well-developed system of building. He had integrated the social need to house the working classes with measures to bring about sanitary reform. He had an eye as a developer himself on commercial viability by including shops within his proposals. And he had separated the residential courts where children and mothers could meet in comfort from rear service lanes where carts posed a danger. Also, he had proposed brick construc-

tion as an economy measure to pay for the glass roofs, and finally he had sought to do this within the constraints of the Police Acts. The integrated nature of the different strands and the originality of approach confirm the 'great culture and thorough searching which characterises his work'.[30]

Nothing came of the proposals, or for that matter of the other five architects appointed at the same time. There was perhaps too much of a conflict between the brilliant individualism of Thomson and the somewhat pedestrian strait-jacket of contemporary controls. Both Thomson and Carrick were classicists, but the nature of their classicism differed enormously. Carrick had applied a largely Roman classical order upon the streets of Glasgow. In a fashion which closely parallels Haussmann's reconstruction of Paris, Carrick and his staff imposed proportional systems, elevational controls and regimentation where disorder and insanitary conditions previously prevailed. Municipal town planning, then in its infancy in Britain, spread an orderly pattern of streets and the occasional square across the face of old Glasgow. Most architects in Glasgow preferred the *laissez-faire* attitudes of earlier times to the regimented world which followed legislation in the 1860s. As Thomson's proposals testify, a conflict existed between the rational and imaginative proposals of private architects and their counterparts in public office. Even when both shared elements of a common classical language, the almost Roman *gravitas* of civic ambitions left little scope for Thomson's flights of fancy.

THOMSON AT GORBALS CROSS

This conflict may well explain why Thomson's work at Gorbals Cross in 1874 simply repeats a pattern already established by him in 1860–1. By 1872 parcels of land were being feued by the Improvement Trustees at Gorbals Cross. Carrick in characteristic fashion had straightened and widened streets, placing them wherever he could at right angles. The block size here as elsewhere was about 200–50 ft square. At the principal intersection of Main Street, Gorbals (later Gorbals Street) (see FIGURES 10.6 and 10.7) and Norfolk Street, Carrick proposed a civic square 180 ft by 150 ft. The corners of the square were splayed with its axis placed diagonally suggesting here as elsewhere the influence of Paris on Glasgow's reconstruction. Thomson did not

FIGURE 10.6   Main Street, Gorbals, looking north, before
the urban reconstructions of 1866–75.

have a significant hand in affairs, only a chance to
extend his design at 26–44 Norfolk Street northwards
into Gorbals Street and thence to Oxford Street. Why
Thomson chose to simply repeat an earlier design, with
the only major modification consisting of creating a
garden at first-floor level on the roof tops of workshops
projecting behind the ground-floor shops, remains a
mystery. Perhaps by 1874 Thomson was overworked
with Robert Turnbull enjoying increasing influence.
Perhaps Carrick had suggested the earlier design
should be extended, rather than modified, thereby
creating further order and uniformity. Carrick maintained the power to approve plans on the Improvement
Trust estate, and here as elsewhere imposed the standard feuing conditions already described. As a result, a
long terrace four storeys high of polished ashlar stone
extended right along the block and around both corners. The published view of 1875 in the former Provost
Sir James Watson's paper to the RIBA (Royal Institute
of British Architects) shows well the nature of Carrick's
urban intentions in the Gorbals. The only building to
break the four-storey height rule is the Royal Princess
Theatre (now the Citizens') which rises imperiously
about the cornice level of the adjoining Improvement
Trust tenements. None of Carrick's construction of
the Gorbals survived the slum clearance programmes
of the 1960s and 1970s, leaving only photographic
records of Thomson's terraces in the area.

No record exists to suggest Carrick thwarted Thom-

son's invention. It seems more likely that his glass-
roofed streets proposal proved too adventurous for an
Improvement Trust barely two years old, and when
Thomson did get a chance to build for the Trustees his
partner Turnbull had by then taken an upper hand.
Thomson did, however, allude to the difficult climate
for architecture at the time. His presidential address to
the GIA in 1871 on the theme of why there is no modern
style in architecture concluded that architects 'are
regarded as mere agents, and instructed what to do
within certain recognised limits of commonplace'.[31]

For those architects anxious to build housing in
central areas, the financial priorities of the Trustees
proved an increasing obstacle. For two years after
1866, the Improvement Scheme developed on the
assumption of residential, mainly working-class, rede-
velopment. However, it became quickly evident that
only by encouraging commercial development could
the high cost of land clearance be recouped. With
central sites costing up to £7 per square yard to acquire,
level, causeway and service, Carrick was under increasing pressure to sell the land not to tenement builders
but commercial developers. Moreover, with railway
construction penetrating into the area the pressure for
warehouses, offices and shops proved overwhelming.
The Improvement Trustees welcomed the activities of
the railway companies (in spite of the visual impact of
their structures which Carrick in particular regretted)
since they pushed up the value of the cleared land. As
a result, some of the central land was sold at a profit,
but only if it moved from residential land uses to
commercial ones. Although Thomson, Honeyman and
Stevenson continued to argue for working-class housing provision on central sites, the reality of the market
place meant that the Trustees built just a handful of
model tenements and a collection of working-men's
hostels in the former Old Town. In more peripheral
areas, where land was cheaper to acquire and service,
housing was constructed. The policy of suburban relocation of the working classes gained a boost in 1872
with the construction by the Improvement Trustees of
the two model estates at Overnewton and Oatlands.
Both involved Salmon as an Improvement Trustee
and Carrick as master-planner. No record survives of
Thomson's involvement in tenement design in either,
but again the controls introduced by Carrick restricted
freedom of design.

FIGURE 10 7   Drawing of Main Street, Gorbals (renamed
Gorbals Street), in 1875 looking north towards Gorbals Cross

with the Royal Princess Theatre on the right, from the
Transactions of the R.I.B.A., April 1875.

THE BUCK'S HEAD BUILDING
AND CARRICK'S INTERVENTION

Carrick was not only City Architect but also Master of
Works. In the latter capacity he advised the Dean of
Guild Court on drawings submitted for building con-
sent and on wider questions of the structural and
sanitary condition of existing buildings. In 1863, when
the Buck's Head Building (see FIGURE 10.1) on Argyle
Street was under construction, Carrick wrote to Thomson expressing concern over the delay in finishing the
building and its precarious structural state. 'I am really
ashamed at the delay at the Buck's Head Building'[32]
opened Carrick, who went on to warn that there was a
rumour of a petition to the Town Council because of
fears over the 'stability of the structure'. Carrick concluded by saying that as the Fiscal was 'threatening to
raise an action', he wished to know what steps Thomson was going to take. The lack of diplomatic language

in a copy letter which is by no means clear today
suggests that Carrick felt uninhibited to use his powers
even when dealing with one of the most senior
architects of the city. Too much should not be read into
a single hand-scribbled letter, suffice to establish Carrick's authority over so much of the building of the city.
The Buck's Head Building was one of Thomson's
experiments in mixing iron and masonry construction
where the walls were reinforced by iron columns enclosed within the stonework. The outer iron columns
and projecting balcony are said to be merely decorative, but could they have been in response to Carrick's
forthright letter? Had fear of imminent collapse per-
suaded Thomson to add a further structural system to
placate Carrick and put an end to the Fiscal's threaten-
ings? It was quite unlike Thomson to use materials
without structural justification, especially an iron
frame which orders so much of the aesthetics of the
building.

FIGURE 10.8   The Watson Street warehouses seen from
Gallowgate.

THE WATSON STREET WAREHOUSES

Within the Improvement Trust estates, one range of
warehouses with shops beneath bears the hallmarks
of Thomson, yet until recently no evidence could be
found to link it to him or his partner, Turnbull.
Standing at the junction of Watson Street and Bell
Street are two nearly identical ranges of warehouses
(see FIGURE 10.8) divided by a narrow service lane
called McPherson Street. Both are in the style of
Thomson's Dunlop Street warehouses which date from
about 1860. They could not, however, have been built
until after Thomson's death in 1875 because of delays
caused in the development of the land by the Glasgow
and South Western Railway Company. Watson Street,
named after Provost Sir James Watson, was intended to
run northwards from Gallowgate to the College lands
east of the High Street. The simple gridded layout of

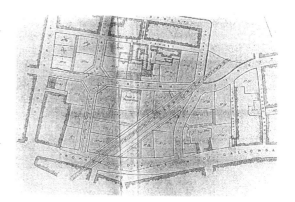

FIGURE 10.9   The Feuing Plan of 1872 prepared by John
Carrick on behalf of the Improvement Trustees for the area
east of High Street and north of Gallowgate. The pencilled
alterations to Watson Place follow the abandonment of the
northern part of Watson Street after the sale of land to the
Glasgow & South-Western Railway Co.

FIGURE 10.10   Elevations for the Watson Street warehouses almost as executed, dated Nov. 1876 and probably by Robert Turnbull.

the Parliamentary Plans of 1866 had been refined by 1872 to include a diagonal square known as Watson Place at its junction with Bell Street (then called Graeme Street) (see FIGURE 10.9). This square, like that at Gorbals Cross and Bridgeton Cross, was inspired by Haussmann's pattern of streets and intersecting squares which the Glasgow delegation had so admired during their visit to Paris in 1866. However, the implementation of the square required the participation of all the landowners, and it had become evident by 1875 that the railway company did not wish to build their side of the square, or even to construct a northwards extension of Watson Street. Although Carrick and the Trustees were firm in their dealings with local architects and developers, when it came to the powerful railway companies they seem to have lost their resolve. As a result, Watson Place was not built,

and in place of four-storey tenements and the grid of parliamentary streets, the Glasgow and South Western was permitted to construct the six-storey range of heavily rusticated warehouses in the style of an Italian Renaissance *palazzo*, which currently occupies the north side of the street.

In 1874, a year before Thomson's death, the engineer and shipbuilder Robert Barclay sold land and buildings in the Watson Street area to William Millar, warehouseman of Glasgow Cross.[33] Two years later, his brother Gavin B. Millar, merchant and shipowner, applied to the Dean of Guild 'to erect two tenements of shops and warehouses' at a cost of £20,000.[34] No architect is given in the index to Dean of Guild applications and no plans survive at this source. However, a single drawing deposited at the Scottish Record Office, labelled 'For Gavin Bell Millar' and inscribed

FIGURE 10.11   Detail of the Watson Street warehouses:
porch in Bell Street.

FIGURE 10.12   Detail of the Watson Street warehouses.

'122 Wellington Street, Glasgow: November 1876'[35] is
clearly a design prepared at the time. The address on
the plans is that of Thomson and Turnbull's office and
hence removes any ambiguity over the authorship of
the design. Although Thomson has died a year earlier,
the watermark on the Whatman paper is 1873, suggesting that Thomson himself may have had a hand in the
evolution of the design – perhaps when the land was
first transferred from Barclay to the Millar family in
1874. Most probably, however, Turnbull fashioned the
design himself, using drawings in the office – such as
those for the Dunlop Street warehouses – as his guide.
Looking closely at the drawing, there is nothing to
suggest that it is in Thomson's hand. In all probability
Turnbull, or an assistant, prepared the fine ink elevational drawing, modifying the model of the Dunlop
Street range to suit the dimensions of the Watson Street
site. There are signs on the drawing of contemplated

alterations to add a glazed attic storey not unlike the
additions provided by Thomson to his office in Bath
Street. The recent discovery of the drawing removes
any doubt which existed linking the Watson Street
warehouses to the Thomson office (see FIGURES 10.10,
10.11 and 10.12).

In 1886, the architect Henry B. W. Steel of 196 St
Vincent Street applied for permission to carry out
alterations to the southern-most block. The staircase
was to be enclosed and new brick-built toilet accommodation constructed to the rear. One surprising
aspect of Steel's application is the comprehensive nature of the submitted drawings. For relatively minor
works we have complete elevations, plans and a section
for the whole building. Drawn on tracing paper, they
are clearly copied from the original. They show a
warehouse of seventeen bays facing Watson Street with
(unusually for Thomson) the street façade taken

around the corner and extended for a further eleven bays into McPherson Street. The first-floor windows receive exaggerated importance, again a slight departure for Thomson where, in his four-storey buildings, the first and second floors are usually given equal importance.

Thomson was given little opportunity to design the corners of city blocks and when he did, one finds a flourish of one kind or another. His Howard Street and Dixon Street warehouses have corner rotundas but here, in spite of the importance of the Watson Street/ Bell Street junction, the building façade turns the corner almost unaltered. Also, there is no difference in treatment between a major street junction (that with Bell Street) and a minor one (that with McPherson Street). In spite of the recognisable brush strokes which give us the familiar detail of giant order pilasters enclosing secondary pilasters on the first floor and direct glazing on the second (a detail borrowed from Dunlop Street), circular incised decoration, five-sided stars (from Egyptian Halls) and much else, the detailed handling suggests that Turnbull rather than Thomson prepared the design. If, as seems most likely, Turnbull was approached by Millar after Thomson's death, there remains the possibility that earlier, maybe sketch proposals were furnished by Thomson when the land was sold by Barclay in 1874.

THOMSON'S CONTRIBUTION TO REBUILDING CENTRAL GLASGOW

Thomson's work for the Improvement Trust poses several dilemmas. With the loss of so many of his drawings and office records, much of Thomson's professional life, particularly his involvement with the Town Council, remains a mystery. If many of his buildings and designs have been lost, by his own admission Thomson sought to give Glasgow a 'style of architecture suited to the circumstances of the present day'.[36] His proposals for glass-roofed streets were the result of an architect who said that thinking men should value the 'suggestions of progress, which lead upwards into the light of the future'.[37] For Thomson, architects should avail themselves of the products of 'machinery and every contrivance to cheapen and facilitate the spread of correct forms'[38] rather than concern themselves with historical style. Unfortunately, Thomson's

individualism and search for novel solutions came up against the City Architect's more conservative vision. Carrick expected architects and builders to line up their cornice levels and adopt his rationalist perimeter blocks. For Thomson, the Glasgow Improvement Scheme was one area where the collective might of the Police Acts and feu conditions thwarted the most imaginative architectural minds of his generation.

Although Glasgow benefited from the imposition of Carrick's vernacular classicism, architects of the calibre of Thomson were left with mainly churches and suburban villas to provide the opportunity for inventive forms. Being outside the influence of contemporary building legislation, Thomson's churches and villas flourished whilst his tenements subsided into orthodoxy. Two different classical traditions are represented by Carrick and Thomson – a Roman urban tradition of regulation on the one hand, and a free-style Greek one on the other. If Glasgow benefited from Carrick's lengthy tenure as City Architect, Thomson was arguably one of the principal losers. Had the roles been reversed and Thomson appointed as City Architect in 1862, one wonders what fusions of Greek Revival and Modernist thinking would have resulted.

NOTES

1. Daniel Defoe is quoted by Andor Gomme and David Walker in *Architecture of Glasgow*, Glasgow, 1968, p. 51.
2. *The Scotsman*, 6 Dec. 1869.
3. Preamble to the Glasgow Improvement Act. 29° Victoriae, cap. lxxxv.
4. James Salmon, 'Workmen's Houses', paper to the GAS, published in the *Glasgow Herald*, 19 Mar. 1860.
5. (no author), 'Notes of Personal Observations and Inquiries ... on the City Improvements of Paris' (1866), Municipal Report D-TC 14.2.2 Report 27, p. 7, Strathclyde Regional Archives.
6. Charles Wilson, John Rochead and John Herbertson, 'Report on the Sanitary Improvement of the City of Glasgow', *Architectural Institute of Scotland Transactions*, vol. 2 (1850–1), p. 47. See also *The Builder*, vol. 9 (1851), p. 813.
7. John J. Stevenson, 'On the Laying Out of Towns and Villages', *Proceedings Glasgow Architectural Society* (1865–7), p. 5.
8. Ibid., p. 6.
9. Ibid., p. 6.
10. Ibid., p. 12.
11. Ibid., p. 12.
12. Ibid., p. 10.

13. *Glasgow Herald*, 22 Jan. 1868.
14. Ronald McFadzean, *The Life and Work of Alexander Thomson*, London, 1979, p. 62.
15. *Glasgow Herald*, 7 Apr. 1871.
16. *North British Daily Mail*, 16 Oct. 1866.
17. Ibid.
18. Minutes of the City Improvement Trust, Glasgow, 1868, vol. 1, p. 162.
19. *Glasgow Herald*, 2 Apr. 1868.
20. *Glasgow Herald*, 4 Mar. 1868.
21. *Building Chronicle*, 1 June 1855, p. 79.
22. See the book of Feuing Conditions, CIT Miscellaneous Papers, Box 1, F 14.13, Strathclyde Regional Archives.
23. Stevenson, 'On the Laying Out', p. 15.
24. *Morning Journal*, 17 Mar. 1868, see also *The Builder*, vol. 26, 1868, p. 234.
25. Ibid.
26. Ibid.
27. McFadzean, *Alexander Thomson*, p. 14.
28. Ibid.
29. Ibid.
30. John Keppie, *The Story of the GIA for the First 50 Years*, Glasgow, 1920, p. 8.
31. *Glasgow Herald*, 8 Apr. 1871.
32. Letter Book, D.OPW 3.3, p. 521, Strathclyde Regional Archives.
33. Minute Book of the Register of Sasines, Edinburgh, 1874, no. 103, pp. 22–4.
34. Dean of Guild Court Index, Glasgow, 1876, no. 7, p. 174.
35. Scottish Record Office, Edinburgh, RHP 14756.
36. *North British Daily Mail*, 17 Mar. 1869. The paper quoted is Thomson's 'Obstacles and Aids to Architectural Progress' given to the GAS.
37. Ibid.
38. Ibid.

INTERIORS

FIGURE 11.1 Drawing of wall decoration with instructions about colours for No. 8 Rosslyn Terrace, among the Thomson drawings in the Mitchell Library.

Chapter Eleven

.

DOMESTIC INTERIORS

Ian Gow

Anyone embarking on a discussion of Thomson's domestic interiors must be conscious of being on the brink of exciting discoveries as the foundation of the Alexander Thomson Society flushes out examples of his furniture and textile designs. There is a strong sense of frustration with the realisation that we know much more about the interiors of Pompeii and Herculaneum – from almost two thousand years ago – than those of Glasgow a century ago. We can only look at Thomson's interiors in monochrome, through nineteenth-century engravings, or muffled under the bland colour schemes of late twentieth-century emulsion paint. However, even before the Society began its mission, Glasgow Museums and Art Galleries had put in hand the restoration of the splendid mahogany cabinet that is now one of the glories of Kelvingrove and was his only surviving piece of furniture until a rumour of a carpet surfaced recently.

In spite of the lack of flesh upon the bones, there can be no doubt of Thomson's stature as one of the greatest innovators in the history of nineteenth-century interiors in Britain. Although we possess only one cabinet from his pencil, it is obvious that it belongs in the first rank of Scottish furniture. No designer, however brilliant, works in isolation, and before turning to Thomson it is worth examining those developments that had made Scotland surprisingly receptive to innovative interior design.

First, good design was a national concern pursued by the Board of Manufactures. The Board's monument is its headquarters, the Royal Institution (now the Royal Scottish Academy) on the Mound, in the heart of Edinburgh. This was begun in 1822 by W. H. Playfair, the Board's architect, as a model of good taste and was

extended and further ornamented by him in 1829 to provide more space for its expanding activities. Although the loss of almost all the visual, as against its written, records makes its success difficult to assess, there can be no doubt that during the energetic secretaryship of James Skene it was a powerhouse of design concern. The Board ran its own art school – whose students had access not only to artistic masterpieces in the form of both sculpture and painting but also to a library comprising both books and a very large collection of design drawings. Domestic textiles for linen, upholstery and carpets were a primary concern of the Board and improvements were encouraged through annual competitions with premiums for innovation and excellence.

It is perhaps a measure of the Board's success that D. R. Hay (1797–1866), Scotland's first interior decorator, was firmly within its orbit as both contract painter to the Board and decorator of Skene's private house in Princes Street. Hay probably owed his introduction to Skene to the latter's friendship with Sir Walter Scott. As a protégé of Scott and through his influence, Hay had been admitted to the Board's art school and set out to reward his patron by becoming not only the best decorator in Scotland but also in Britain. In this endeavour he was assisted by an astonishing burst of creativity within his chosen trade during the second decade of the nineteenth century. The key to this change was the introduction of graining and marbling. In Edinburgh, the accurate imitation of woods and marbles was pursued with a scientific zeal that befitted the 'Modern Athens', which not only helped to raise the status of the house-painter but also acted as springboard to a more 'artistic' form of house decoration.

FIGURE 11.2 The Royal Medical Society Hall, Melbourne Place, Edinburgh, by Robert MacFarlane, a pupil of D. R. Hay, showing a range of Hay's decorative techniques including imitation damask and gold stencilling.

FIGURE 11.3 Sir Walter Scott's entrance hall at Abbotsford, 1822, with recycled panelling and decoration by D. R. Hay, photo 1880.

Having taught his men the necessary manual dexterity to replicate satinwood or a rare marble, Hay found it was possible to encourage the ablest to produce interiors imitating the great historic styles of decoration then recognised as the Pompeian, the Raphaelesque grotesque of the Vatican Loggia and the Watteauesque. Hay was also active in technical and scientific experiments with textured paints, colour theory and pure aesthetics. An anathema to the use of wallpaper in Scotland had been one of his conclusions. The putrefaction, inevitable in our damp climate, of the animal glues and vegetable pulps made it an unhealthy choice for domestic rooms. In its place he devised a gamut of decorative techniques which raised stencilling – par-

ticularly in gold size which could subsequently be gilded – to an unparalleled height and made it a staple of Scottish decoration well into the twentieth century. Hay's influence was felt not only through his extensive publications – which his profits enabled him to supply gratis to anyone who expressed a mild interest in his ideas – but also through his firm, D. R. Hay and Co, which trained almost two generations of Scottish decorators on whom their master's pride in his new profession and self-confidence brushed off (see FIGURE 11.2).

Hay's success, however, had depended on his ability to make his own opportunities, because Scotland conspicuously lacked the patronage that could give expression to its able young designers. Hay had been lucky to gain the support of a small circle of scientifically inclined 'Modern Athenians', including W. H. Playfair, but the doors of Scotland's territorial aristocracy remained firmly shut against the new type of decoration.

It is perhaps no accident that Hay's first big chance was Abbotsford, then the modest villa of a successful Edinburgh professional citizen rather than the world-famous literary shrine it was soon to become (see FIGURE 11.3). Artistically it might be considered a failure because as an antiquarian house it was necessarily a composite jigsaw comprising pieces from quite different jigsaws – like the bosses from Melrose Abbey or the circular pulpit from Dunfermline Abbey – which could never be brought together to fit smoothly. It is significant that in order to satisfy his personal inclinations in decoration, Scott had sought the help of off-beat craftsmen like the sculptor-turned-furnituremaker, William Bullock, or his own failed-artist-turned-housepainter, D. R. Hay, rather than the established Edinburgh firms.

Even in a country villa like Abbotsford there was a limit as to how far innovation could be pushed because interior decoration was necessarily a branch of etiquette and social convention. In Edinburgh, because he was very rich, Sir John Robison could risk having his drawing-room painted by Hay so that it 'gave the appearance of a lace dress over satin and spangles',[1] but even at Abbotsford, where Scott achieved the ultimate in self-dramatisation with a Gothic library – significantly relieved of practicality by the existence of a very functional adjoining study – Lady Scott was responsible for the adjoining highly fashionable and almost Brighton Pavilionesque drawing-room with its Chinese painted wallpaper and 'summer sky' ceiling.

If Hay, as Thomson afterwards, was to enjoy a degree of freedom to experiment in villas, throughout his career he had always to offer to paint over any of these experiments when his ideas did not give satisfaction to his patrons. Country houses tied up so much family capital that they were particularly resistant to decorative experiment and its social risk. In 1843 Hay became embroiled in a battle at Falkland House with its architect, William Burn, then at the head of the profession in Scotland. Burn attempted to slam its door in Hay's face by writing to their employer Onesipherous Tyndal-Bruce on 6 March:

> I regret your employment of Hay, because he is not so good a painter as Chalmers, and you should have nothing fanciful at Falkland House, where good and substantial work, and nothing else is required – the latter is also a person of high respectability as a tradesman, while the former deserves no encouragement, and I cannot do business with him, as I may satisfy you when we next meet.[2]

Burn's odious letter, with its threat of further damaging information which could not be committed to paper, was possibly occasioned not so much by a personal dislike but by the fear that this new profession of interior decoration posed a threat to the hard-won late Georgian assumption that the architect was the captain of the building trades. It must have been particularly galling for Burn – with his professional supremacy and secure in the patronage of the Duke of Buccleuch – that Hay could not be so easily discounted as a 'tradesman', with his string of publications, the patronage of the Board and support of W. H. Playfair behind him. Hay kept the job. Again, it is perhaps relevant that Thomson's interior success arose from his possessing a mastery of ornamental design which enabled him to embrace both the architect's and the decorator's role, allowing him to exert the total control that had eluded Burn at Falkland.

In his dispute with Burn, Hay responded with a five-page appeal, citing historical authority because historical fancy dress dominated interior decoration. When Hay went so far as to introduce a new system of decoration – suited to the nineteenth century – in the Hall of the Society of Arts in London, he had to finance the experiment himself. Although architects had welcomed graining and marbling – which were essential to create the necessarily Picturesque and theatrical effects in their Gothic Revival houses – the decoration of the rooms of Greek Revival houses proved more intractable to design than their temple-fronted exteriors. While the Greeks may have possessed the purest taste, there was precious little archaeological evidence beyond the calligraphic squiggles on Greek vases. The severest ridicule of the archaeological approach to interior design – as codified in Thomas Hope's furniture designs – came from Scotland, in Lord Jeffrey's famous dismissal published in the *Edinburgh Review* of 1807:

> *In the* first *place, the articles are in general too bulky, massive, and ponderous, to be commodious for general use – There are arm chairs, whose cold hollow square would contain a woolsack, – and couches which could not be moved by a dozen of Irish chairmen. A considerable number of articles of this kind are copied from antient monuments in marble. But Mr Hope should have known, that sculpture requires a mass and breadth in its representations, which must be*

FIGURE 11.4 Proposal for the drawing-rooms at Springwood Park, Kelso, by James Gillespie Graham, *c.*1822, showing a typical Greek Revival scheme with voluminous draperies and a dado-less wallface.

extremely inconvenient, and therefore unbecoming, in utensils of ordinary use. . . . Now, in chairs, tables, footstools, &c. it is a substantial part of their convenience, to be easily moved; and accordingly, the improving luxury of the age, has gone on to make them lighter and lighter for the greater part of a century.[3]

Archaeology had even kicked the Pompeian crutch away with the realisation that this was a bastardised Roman version of the Greek. Thus, for architects, the design of Greek Revival rooms – although bearing the cynosure of the purest taste – had all too often resulted in interior disaster. Bland surfaces, voluminous draperies continued across the entire window wall, and

fitted carpets had created huge blocks of crude colour where pictures floated; and the final punishment was conferred by museum replica furniture. It was a dilemma which had dogged the Greek Revival from the outset. When 'Athenian' Stuart had sought to bypass the dearth of Greek interior detail by free invention of his own to create a highly marketable synthetic approximation, Robert Adam had not unnaturally responded with 'It may be Greek to the teeth but by God it is not handsome.'[4] It may be significant, therefore, that for Thomson's biographer Ronald McFadzean, his first success as a designer of interiors had come with the rather academic 'Greek' showroom in the Scottish Exhibition Rooms of 1855 – which thus lay outside domestic norms (see p. 18).

FIGURE 11.5 Drawing-room at Cairns House, Cambuslang, by John Burnet, c.1858, photo c.1875, showing the wallface divided by decorative painting to create both a dado and frieze.

If Thomson's freedom to experiment in real houses rather than exhibition spaces was perhaps facilitated by the public's reflex approval of almost anything 'Grecian', his success in pushing beyond the norms of convention was surely also facilitated by the peculiar conditions of Glasgow. Although it has become a cliché, there was a very different spirit in entrepreneurial Glasgow than in the careful professional conformity of Edinburgh, where lawyers referred all to precedent. Flamboyant displays of conspicuous consumption, like Lauriston House – designed by Peter Nicholson (grandfather of Thomson's wife) – have no parallel in the Capital. With its dominance of the textile trades, the commercial success of Glasgow depended on visual literacy in copying fashionable and often foreign pat-terns to ensure next season's sales rather than the Board's pursuit of good design. Shipbuilding de-manded innovative carpentry and well-seasoned tim-bers. Ship interiors too, as with the later Cunarders, could afford to be more experimental.

Although much research remains to be done, our scanty knowledge suggests that Glasgow was a hotbed of interior innovation at this time. Hay had enjoyed the support of the Glasgow architect David Hamilton. Photographs of 'The Cairns', an early villa by the architect Burnet, show not only highly original chimney-pieces but also a new interest in the division of the wall face (see FIGURE 11.5). Although equally uncertain in its dating, a newly discovered white and gold drawing-room scheme in No. 3, Park Terrace

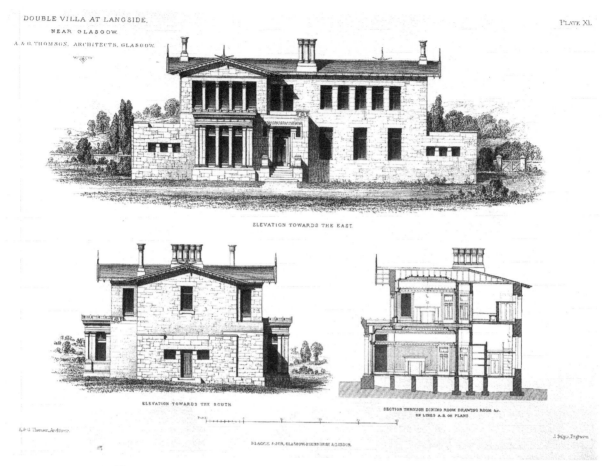

DOUBLE VILLA AT LANGSIDE,
NEAR GLASGOW.
A & G THOMSON, ARCHITECTS, GLASGOW.

FIGURE 11.6   Elevations and section of the Double Villa,
from *Villa and Cottage Architecture*.

shows pilaster strips in glittering gold leaf arising from a foliate dado. Thomson's most significant innovation also focused on the wall face. In some ways this had been left as a *tabula rasa* by the Greek Revival because late Georgian taste suppressed the Roman pedestal/dado in favour of an unbroken expanse of wallpaper or flat-painting from skirting board to cornice, and cabinets had had to be introduced to prop up the pictures which were otherwise left ill at ease.

Thomson's most doctrinaire interior is perhaps within his Double Villa (of 1856–7) at Langside (see FIGURE 11.6). If it is fascinating to see the extent to which it conforms to a standard Scottish building type, with a 'bay'-windowed drawing-room on the first floor over the dining-room (unlike English plans where the public rooms were always on the same floor), there can be no doubting the originality of its interior system (see FIGURE 8.12).

Thomson's rearrangement of the wall face began with the voids of doors and windows being made equal in size. It is difficult to find any parallel for this, although the idea of glazing a window as a single void and minimising visible framing had been an ideal of the Greek Revival elsewhere. The doors and windows were then framed by pilaster strips which support their own entablature. In a sense, this restored the architectural integrity of Scotland's first classical interiors where paired pilasters on either side of the chimney-piece raised on pedestals, controlled the room and supported a correctly detailed classical cornice. Indeed, in his use of timber he effectively reintroduced panelling (see FIGURE 11.7). Happily, the plates in *Villa and Cottage Architecture* (1868) are accompanied by explanations which draw on their designers' own words, so we can follow Thomson's intentions:

> *The whole of these interior finishings are of carefully selected yellow pine, the enrichments being frets of mahogany planted upon it. The wood is varnished, preserving its natural colour and markings, no stain of any kind being used. The object of this mode of treatment is to unite together the several parts of the room, thereby giving an effect of increased extent.*[5]

Although a taste for wood-effects must have been promoted by a familiarity with extensive graining, it is extraordinary how close this is to a panelling revival.

The intermediate door and window cornice (so close to eye level) produces a remarkable visual effect – even allowing for most modern Thomson rooms having unauthentic colour schemes – and immediately recalls a similar device used by Mackintosh to unify his previously very ordinary drawing-room, which has now been reconstructed at the Hunterian Museum. Thomson goes on to explain that: 'The apparent height of ceiling is also enhanced by giving force to the lower mass of walls, and so making them serve as does a foreground to a picture.' It is tantalising not to know how this upper zone was decorated.

Through being lower in height, the drawing-room of the Double Villa is perhaps the more perfect of the two public rooms in its equality of windows and doors. In the dining-room, and perhaps to compensate for its greater height and depth, Thomson introduced an upper attic tier of windows, but these were distinct through being glazed with coloured glass. If the interior system was architectural, Thomson displayed great ingenuity in the design of his joinery. His revised system for constructing his panelled doors may prove to be an archaeological quotation, like his frieze zone which may derive from antique murals. The technical ingenuity of the carpentry, which concealed the moving parts of the sashes and played up the expanses of glass, was thoroughly modern and may have been inspired by the kind of encyclopaedic classification of building methods illustrated in the textbooks of architects like Peter Nicholson – who had devised the techniques of draughtsmanship to display construction

FIGURE 11.7   Perspective view of the council room of George Heriot's Hospital, Edinburgh, by R. W. Billings, 1845–52, showing the architecturally ordered panelling of *c*.1690.

vividly. The purity of his window solution 'allowed space for the working of blinds and curtains' which were normally left to the whim of an upholsterer. This was a remarkable achievement in a potentially limiting commission.

Holmwood Villa (1857–8) at Cathcart was Thomson's dream ticket (see FIGURES 11.8, 16.2, 16.4 and 17.5). The patron, James Couper, traditionally gave the architect free rein with what must have been a generous budget. Again, it is characteristic that its innovation is within a villa context, but nothing demonstrates the degree of experiment and necessary social risk more than the extraordinary Bernini-esque top-lit sideboard which effortlessly allowed the dining-room to be converted to a chapel when the house became a convent. Happily, the Sisters of Our Lady of the Missions have maintained the house in good condition and most of Thomson's interior architecture – shown in the plates in *Villa and Cottage Architecture* – has survived. The plates are sufficiently detailed to help one visualise the stencilled wall patterns, and by a miracle a small section of the staircase dado alone has never been painted over and perhaps packs an even greater chromatic punch now that it is surrounded by bland modern tones (see FIGURE 11.9). The accompanying text makes clear that the plates are '– wanting, however, the colour – which, in this house, plays an

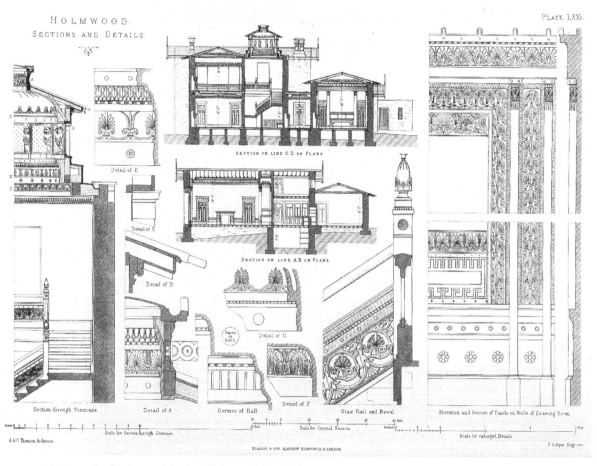

HOLMWOOD.
SECTIONS AND DETAILS.

PLATE LXXI.

Section on Line C.D. on Plans.

Detail of E.

Detail of C.

Section on Line A.B. on Plans.

Detail of B.

Detail of D.

Section through Staircase.   Detail of A.   Cornice of Hall.   Detail of F   Stair Rail and Newel.   Elevation and Section of Panels on Walls of Drawing Room

Scale for Section through Staircase.   Scale for General Sections.   Scale for enlarged Details.

A.&G. Thomson Architects.   BLACKIE & SON GLASGOW EDINBURGH & LONDON.   J. Sulpis Engraver

FIGURE 11.8   Sections and details of Holmwood, from *Villa and Cottage Architecture*.

important part in the internal effect'.[6] The surviving fragment, with its bold primary colours, demonstrates Thomson's ability to revitalise nineteenth-century interiors by drawing on fresh archaeological discoveries of Greek polychromy. Thomson is said to have cut his own stencils (see PLATE VI).

The text also explains that 'in decorative character, and in some of the structural arrangements, it resembles the villa at Langside' and this is perhaps most evident in the drawing-room. Although the house was apparently designed so that the four main rooms (dining-room, parlour, drawing-room and top-lit stair) would be visually distinct – showing that Thomson was aware of the conventional hierarchy inherited from the late Georgian period of fitting up different rooms in

different degrees of richness – the arresting feature of Holmwood was the all-pervasive interior splendour.

Conventionally, the drawing-room (see FIGURE 11.10) stood at the pinnacle, attracting the largest budget for the costliest contents – comprising pure white sculpted statuary marble for the chimney-piece, silk upholstery, gold enrichments and the finest cabinetwoods like rosewood. Dining-rooms, by contrast, were plain-painted with black marble chimney-pieces and black horn door and shutter handles, cloth curtains with morocco or horsehair upholstery, and mahogany furniture. Parlours were midway between the two, while circulation spaces were sufficiently plain and robust to give an almost external effect. At Holmwood, although there remains some lip-service to this

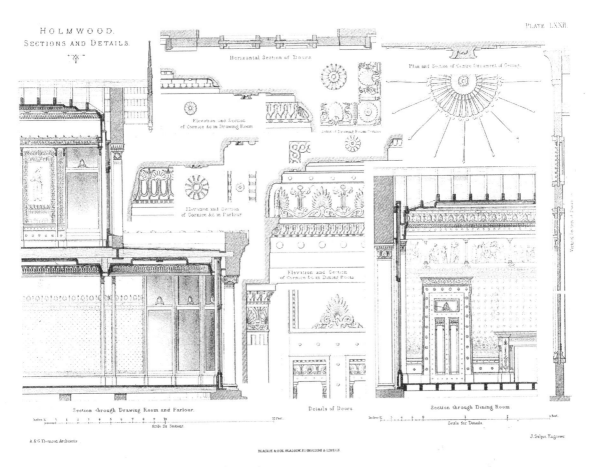

HOLMWOOD.
SECTIONS AND DETAILS.

FIGURE 11.9   Sections through drawing-room, parlour and
dining-room at Holmwood, from *Villa and Cottage
Architecture*.

ideal, probably backed up by colour differentials, the
expanse of painted decoration suggests that the rooms
shared an equality of decorative pitch. The prevailing
varnished yellow pine of the joinery throughout the
rooms must have been the only note of sobriety.

The dining-room certainly had a chimney-piece of
black marble but this had been 'enriched with gilded
incised ornament', while the now missing sideboard –
does it lurk in pieces in the convent basement? – 'is of
white marble, with enrichments incised and gilt; and
the back and ends of the recess have mirrors in mahogany framing, decorated with rosewood frets. The glass
of the mirrors has a surface enriched with gilded ornaments.'[7] By late Georgian conventions this is anarchic
or rather the best kind of egalitarianism where the

FIGURE 11.10   The drawing-room at Holmwood in 1992.

lowest has been raised to the rank of the highest. The rooms have all been designed at a drawing-room setting. The three-dimensional anthemion frieze – reminiscent of a Napoleonic tiara in its elegance – crowning the dining-room was also of drawing-room quality and conspicuous expense. High-art murals 'in brown on a blue ground' selected from 'Flaxman's illustrations of the Iliad', the figures being about '2 feet 6 inches in height, sharply defined in outline' ornamented the dining-room, while upstairs in the drawing-room 'the pannels thus formed are filled with paintings by H Cameron A.R.S.A., illustrating *Tennyson's Idyls of the King*'. The drawing-room therefore just retained a decorative edge through being decorated by a fully fledged professional artist. Interestingly, both Flaxman and Tennyson were singled out by Thomson in his Haldane Lectures.

The final polish was given to these rooms by his meticulously controlled draperies, for which the joinery had been planned, and presumably toning upholstery and carpets to his design. It is remarkable to see such careful thought being given to the furniture placement in his description. The twentieth-century mythology persists that Victorian rooms were a mindless sea of clutter but recent research shows that, at least at a middle-class level, mid-Georgian traditions of formal arrangement persisted in Scotland. The upper classes employed London firms to inject a planned informality into their drawing-rooms. Even allowing for a certain stiffness in Scottish interiors, it is surprising to read of such precision as the recess for the hatstand in the hall, while the 'ladies' work-table' was to be established in the almost full-circle of the parlour bay – like a mini-conservatory – with its circular curtain box. The sideboard was a proto-altar in its formality. This system continued upstairs where light was bounced off carefully placed mirrors which set up infinite perspectives. A mirror-topped piano balanced the chimney-piece with its glass above, while 'another large mirror' answered the window. This architectural equilibrium, underlined by harmonised textiles, must have been a striking feature of Holmwood.

In pursuit of total control, Thomson even seems to have wanted to discipline the few personal knick-knacks left to the family's choice as he explained in the passage describing the inspiration of his incised gilt chimney-pieces: 'The object in view, in adopting this mode of ornamentation, was to establish a harmony between the broad marble surfaces of the chimney-pieces and the decorated walls, and also with the various articles of taste usually arranged upon the mantel-shelf.'[8]

How is one to classify Holmwood? In a sense it is *sui generis* and this seems to have been recognised from its inception, as *Villa and Cottage Architecture* makes plain: 'We illustrate, with some minuteness a house that is remarkable for the amount of study manifested in its details.'[9]

While J. Jeffery Waddell in his brief account of Thomson describes it as having been 'designed down to the proverbial doormat',[10] even glancing no further than the other plates in *Villa and Cottage Architecture* it rapidly becomes clear how little interest the average Victorian architect took in interiors. This was not simply a question of cost, for Robert Kerr's *The English Gentleman's House* (1864) – which was intended as an etiquette book for parvenu millionaire industrialists – vividly demonstrates how even a Burn-trained Scots architect could duck the problem and pin the fault on his tradesmen:

The architect ought never to allow himself, except in extraordinary cases, and with a very clear understanding in the matter, to make unusual provision for furniture. Even in the case of mirrors, for example, although there are instances when an architectural effect may be aimed at, the architect must not venture to reckon without in the first place his client, and in the second his client's upholsterer. At the same time it must be admitted that if an architect and upholsterer can be made to work together intelligently and artistically, very charming effects can be realised; the architect's decorations bearing to the hangings, mirrors, and the like, the relation of a framework whose own integrity is left untouched, and the work of the tradesman serving to fill up all gaps of design, and give richness to the architectural arrangements.[11]

Writing of Thomson in 1888, Thomas Gildard recorded:

The Holmwood Villa, made familiar to us by Messrs. Blackie's book, has deprived us of either asking or answering the question, Is an architect an artist? If architecture be poetry in stone-and-lime – a great temple an epic – this exquisite little gem, at once classic and picturesque, is as complete, as self-contained, and polished as a sonnet. ... By the kindness of Mr Bowie, I had an opportunity of seeing the interior. I need scarcely say that it was worthy of the remarkable picture I had been studying outside. Unique beauties and ingenious devices were to be seen everywhere. Of the polychromatic decoration of the walls, ceilings, doors, I might almost say 'it beggar'd all description'. Mention is made in the 'Spectator' of a lady who could not place a patch without spoiling a beauty, and to hang upon these walls a mirror or a picture would not be merely 'a wasteful and ridiculous excess,' but a disturbing impertinence. Thomson's idea was to make a room so perfect, so satisfying as a work of art, that it was independent of all adventitious means and appliances. 'If you have pictures, have a picture gallery'. Besides the decoration, much of the furniture, solid and textile, was designed by Mr Thomson.[12]

(It is interesting to speculate if Gildard's obliging Mr Bowie is Campbell Tait Bowie, the leading Glasgow house-painter. Juliet Kinchin has noted this Bowie among Thomson's creditors at the time of his death. If these two Bowies are one and the same, it not only suggests who carried out the painted decoration in Holmwood but also provides a direct link with D. R. Hay's decorative studio – as C. T. Bowie had been apprenticed to Hay in 1846 at a time when he was decorating Hamilton Palace and the Hall of the Society of Arts in London.)

Gildard's ideas belong in the mainstream of the Aesthetic movement but it is important to recollect that he is describing rooms designed over thirty years before and it is in this ethos that Holmwood belongs and its design prefigures. This is the world also of the 'house beautiful' and the perfection of 'The Smaller English House' that inspired Hermann Muthesius's admiring volume.[13] This is surely something infinitely more subtle and complex than McFadzean's view of Thomson as a proto-modernist anticipating Frank Lloyd Wright, but who needs must be failed for his ornamental excess:

Admittedly, his design was based on the principles and structure of Greek architecture coupled to the picturesque qualities of the Italian Romanesque style, but he had forged his own interpretation of modern

FIGURE 11.11   Detail of the staircase in No. 4 Great Western Terrace.

architecture, and seemed to be looking into the future, seeing a new architecture based on function and the elimination of extraneous decoration. But he recoiled from his great vision and left the development of true modern architecture to a later generation. This appears to have been the turning point of his career as one would have expected him to contrive to simplify and refine his design but he turned, perhaps prematurely, to his Greco-baroque phase and this has led to some misunderstanding of his achievement.[14]

Had there been a set of full-colour lithographs of this voluptuous villa's interiors, such wilful misunderstandings would have been less easy to pass of than in black-and-white plates whose intricate spiky Grecian detail is rarely picked up by modern reproduction techniques.

With Holmwood, far from reaching the end of Thomson's career as an architectural decorator, we are merely on the brink of the final phase, with potentially even richer effects attained through his collaboration with the young Daniel Cottier. Trained as a stained-glass artist, Cottier – who worked with Thomson on the Queen's Park church – developed into a decorative artist of outstanding ability, although his work shows an artistic looseness very different from the careful technical perfection pursued by Hay and his craftsmen. He appears to have worked with an English architect called Middleton on the unlikely Gothic rooms for James W. Macgregor in No. 4 Great Western Terrace,

FIGURE 11.12   The first-floor gallery in the hall of No. 4
Great Western Terrace, photo taken in 1983.

a house in which Thomson's magnificent double-height galleried hall survives largely intact (see FIGURES 11.11, 11.12 and PLATE V).

Unfortunately, no evidence seems to exist of the original internal appearance of the houses Thomson completed in Great Western Terrace between 1867 and his death. In No. 7, which Thomson designed for the publisher Robert Blackie, the stencilled decoration of the entrance hall and staircase has long been painted over. However, a full-size design for the stencilled decoration in No. 8 Rosslyn Terrace survives amongst Thomson's drawings in the Mitchell Library (see FIGURE 11.1): an extremely rare drawing which also contains information about the colouring of windows and walls.

There is still a great deal to learn about this remarkable architect.

NOTES

1. I. Gow, *The Scottish Interior*, Edinburgh, 1992, p. 52.
2. Scottish Record Office, Edinburgh, GD152: letter from William Burn to Onesiphorous Tyndal-Bruce, dated 6 Mar. 1843.
3. Francis, Lord Jeffrey, *Edinburgh Review*, vol. 10 (1807), pp. 478–86.
4. John Fleming, *Robert Adam and His Circle*, London, 1962, p. 258.
5. Blackie (publisher), *Villa and Cottage Architecture*, London, Glasgow and Edinburgh, 1868, p. 49. For modern photographs and drawings of the interiors of the Double Villa, see John McKean's article in the *Architects Journal*, vol. CLXXXIII (19 Feb. 1986), pp. 36–50.
6. Blackie (publ.), *Villa and Cottage Architecture*, p. 93.
7. Ibid., p. 94.
8. Ibid., p. 113.
9. Ibid., p. 91.
10. Pamphlet by J. Jeffrey Waddell, *'Greek' Thomson*, Aberdeen, 1925.
11. R. Kerr, *The English Gentleman's House*, London, 1864, p. 124.
12. T. Gildard, Paper to the Philosophical Society of Glasgow, 30 Jan. 1888, *Proceedings of the Royal Philosophical Society of Glasgow*, XIX (1888), p. 12.
13. H. Muthesius, *Das Englische Haus*, Berlin, 1904–5, transl. *The English House*, London, 1979.
14. R. McFadzean, *The Life and Work of Alexander Thomson*, London, 1979, p. 283.

FIGURE 12.1   The mahogany cabinet (*c.*1859) Thomson
designed for himself, probably for the dining-room at No. 1
Moray Place, now at Kelvingrove Art Gallery.

Chapter Twelve

ALEXANDER THOMSON'S FURNITURE

Juliet Kinchin

It is almost unnecessary to observe that the principle of unity of expression requires that the style of furniture should correspond with that of the house; but it cannot be superfluous to remind ... the young architect of the necessity of the building and furnishing of a house being under the control of the same mind, and that this mind should be equally conversant with both departments.

(J. C. Loudon, *An Encyclopaedia of Cottage Farm and Villa Architecture and Furniture*, London, new edn 1839, p. 1039)[1]

In early nineteenth-century Scotland, the design of fashionable furniture was dominated by cabinetmakers and upholsterers whose views on matters of style and taste did not necessarily correspond with those of the architects. In fact the gulf between the two groups appeared to be widening. In an effort to redress what he perceived as 'lapses in taste', Loudon, like many subsequent 'reformers', advocated greater involvement in furniture and interior design on the part of architects. This advice was clearly not lost on Alexander Thomson, although tantalisingly little is known of the architect's furniture, and as yet very few examples have been located. 'With Mr Thomson the designing of a building did not cease with the plasterwork and joinery', commented the *Building News*, 'It extended to the coloured decoration. ... Furniture, even carpets are indebted to a pencil that charmed alike by its novelty and grace.'[2] The aim of this chapter is to piece together what scanty information there is relating to Thomson's furniture, and to explore the significance of his designs both in relation to the development of Glasgow's furnishing industry and to the formulation of middle-class values in the city.

The single most spectacular item which can be confidently attributed to the architect is the towering two-stage cabinet currently on display in the Glasgow Art Gallery and Museum (see FIGURES 12.1, 12.2 and PLATE VII). Its design is thoroughly thought through and original in conception, indicating the kind of detailed attention that furniture might receive from this exceptional architect. Whatever its past history, the cabinet leaves no doubt in the minds of Thomson specialists that on stylistic grounds alone, it is his work. In terms of form, ornament and construction, the attribution withstands detailed scrutiny: the distinctive overall pylon shape surmounted by a spiky-leaved anthemium, and the projecting table-altar form of the cupboards below are immediately reminiscent of Thomson's architectural repertoire. The same could be said of the ornamental features which duplicate those to be found in his extant buildings, both externally and internally: the applied discs, paterae and palmettes; the incised Greek key pattern; the three-quarter-turned and dentil mouldings. Echoes of the spiky ivy leaves in the door panels also reappear in a Thomson drawing in the Mitchell Library collection.[3] In terms of construction, the idiosyncratic joinery relates to the detailing of surviving interior woodwork (doors, skirtings and fitted cupboards), one of the most distinctive features being the stepped, square-edged framing around the door panels.

The unusual design of the cabinet reveals the preoccupations of an architect-designer, in that it relates primarily to building types rather than to any conventional notion of a sideboard formulated by a cabinetmaker. Viewed negatively, it is a classic example of what one nineteenth-century critic termed 'wooden

FIGURE 12.2   Detail of the Thomson cabinet.

drawing out the front drawers in these sideboards without the aid of knobs, by avoiding the necessity of introducing these, adds much to the massive and architectural character of furniture.'[5]

A vivid description given by the architect's grand-daughter, Jane Nicholson Thomson, suggests that a likely provenance for this spectacular object was the dining-room of the Thomson household at 1 Moray Place. 'The sideboard was enormous, reaching to the ceiling, lavishly embellished with Greek key pattern. It had fascinating cupboards on each end at the back. They were really a set of pigeon holes which were revealed on opening a tall narrow door.'[6] While it is just possible that more than one version of a design with this unusual cupboard formation was made, this seems unlikely in view of its costly and unconventional character. According to Jane Thomson, her grandfather had designed and made furniture both for the dining-room and his bedroom when the family moved to Moray Place. The dining-room suite was passed on to his daughter Nell (Mrs J. B. Anderson), who died without issue in the 1930s. It remains to be discovered who her heirs were, and what happened to the furniture at this point. According to Thomson's biographer Ronald McFadzean, however, a Thomson cabinet and bookcase were transferred from the Glasgow School of Art to the Glasgow Museums' collections in the early 1950s.[7] Unfortunately, this predated the formation of the Decorative Art Department, and documentation of the acquisition has not come to light, nor has it been possible to identify a bookcase of an appropriate style or date in the Museums' reserve collections.

The fate of the bedroom furniture from 1 Moray Place is somewhat easier to disentangle. 'The wardrobe stood in my Father's bedroom all my life', recalled Jane Thomson,

building masquerading as furniture'.[4] It certainly has all the grandeur and presence of a scaled-down temple, and in its present location (which gives no sense of its function or relation to an overall interior scheme), the piece stands marooned like some altar to a long-forgotten cult. Plan and elevation are conceived in three dimensions so that its impact is not merely full-frontal. Indeed, the decorative elements and subtle planar modulation are carried through to the side elevations, where the canted pylon shape is offset against the rectangular panels of the sides and front (see FIGURE 12.2). All possible excrescences and distractions are deliberately eliminated: hinges are neatly concealed within the channels of incised decoration, and no unsightly handles protrude to disrupt the flush surfaces. Cupboard doors are opened with purchase-on keys in the discreetly placed locks, and the drawer in the lower section can be pulled out from beneath. In Loudon's words, 'We may observe that the plan of

It was enormous and occupied one wall of quite a large room. At each end were hanging cupboards which enchanted me as they were lined with red moire silk and in the centre was a series of drawers with cupboards above. In my Father's room also was a Spanish mahogany pelmet decorated with the greek key pattern from which hung deep red face cloth curtains with a border of greek key pattern in gold and black. These were cherished because they came from Moray Place and were only replaced when they quite literally

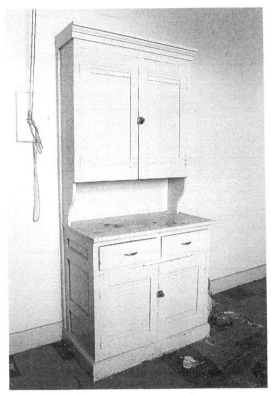

FIGURE 12.3   Kitchen dresser (c.1859) formerly in No. 1 Moray Place.

FIGURE 12.4   Sheet of sketches of furniture etc., among the Thomson drawings in the Mitchell Library.

fell off the windows. When my Father died the wardrobe presented a problem as none of the family could house such a massive piece comfortably. I therefore decided to present it to Queen's Park Church. . . . Unfortunately it perished with the building.[8]

The only piece of Thomson furniture to have remained in Moray Place up until very recently was a pine kitchen dresser (see FIGURE 12.3). This may once have been fixed to the wall, which would explain why there is no mention of a free-standing cabinet in the inventory of furnishings made in 1875. The design is very plain, and of straightforward frame-and-panel construction. However, even this relatively unimportant cabinet, originally located behind the scenes in Moray Place, incorporated details relating to the internal architecture of its setting. The cupboard doors are put together in the same distinctive way as many of the door panels in this and other houses, combining plain vertical stiles with an additional moulding on the horizontal

muntins. In this respect it resembles the fitted cupboards in the corridor behind the altar in St Vincent Street church.

Amongst the drawings now held in the Mitchell Library (see FIGURE 12.4) is a sheet with rough pencil sketches for a sloped lectern and a church settle.[9] Apart from these, the only furniture design attributable to Thomson is a tiny watercolour and pencil sketch for a rectangular china cabinet, which has been passed down through the family. (On the reverse is a chair or cabinet leg with a few simple ring-turnings.) The sketch indicates oriental and blue-and-white ceramics in a range of colours, shapes and sizes, all regulated and contained within a clear rectilinear structure. The cabinet was presumably intended either to hang on the wall, or to sit on a separate stand in a drawing-room. This type of open shelving with innumerable nooks and crannies for the display of 'artistic' ceramics was evolved in response to the growing 'chinamania' of the 1870s and 1880s. Similar display units were designed in the early

1870s by architect-designers such as E. W. Godwin and Thomas Colcutt.

Within the full range of furniture types, large-scale cabinetwork and fixtures such as overmantels or pelmets were widely viewed as more suited to an obviously architectural treatment than movable items such as chairs and occasional tables. The former, being relatively fixed features of the interior, were perceived as 'belonging more to the permanent or constructive architecture of a room than to the furniture'.[10] They were designed for a specific location, and in terms of proportions, ornament, materials and colour were intimately related to the immediate setting and composition of the wall elevation. The descriptive notes in Blackie's *Villa and Cottage Architecture* certainly stress the architectural character of items designed for Holmwood, such as mirrors, side-tables and a sideboard. These pieces of furniture were evidently styled to correspond with other elements of the interior such as the plasterwork, the architraves of the doors and windows, or the fire surrounds. Exact location was of paramount importance. The sideboard, for example, was designed to fill a top-lit recess in one wall of the dining-room so as not to disrupt the flow of the interior space. Ingenious fitted features such as the niche for visitors' hats, built into the hall fireplace, also helped to reduce the clutter of free-standing objects in the interior.

What we cannot yet establish is how much *movable* furniture Thomson might have designed, or what it looked like. In 1888, Thomas Gildard remarked that Thomson was responsible for 'much of the furniture, both solid and textile'[11] at Holmwood (see FIGURES 11.8 and 11.9), but this is virtually the only evidence which might indicate that Thomson's repertoire extended to designing furniture of a 'non-architectural' character. It brings into question the extent of Thomson's interest in, or opportunities for furniture design. Was he simply unconcerned with the 'minor', less architectural types? There would not have been much call for bespoke furniture in his speculative housing developments, and even his wealthier clients were unlikely to have wanted to furnish their new houses from scratch. As discussed above, Thomson designed certain key items for his own home, but it is clear both from furnishings which have remained in the family, and from the inventory taken at the time of his death in

1875, that a good deal of the movable furniture was in a restrained neoclassical style dating from the late eighteenth to early nineteenth centuries.[12] The Thomsons presumably could not afford new furniture throughout their house, and in any case this would have meant disposing of the many handsome pieces they had inherited. Another consideration might be that an item such as a Thomson chair could prove difficult to distinguish on purely stylistic grounds from the more routine Grecian and Egyptian furniture available from many other cabinetmakers. A chair by its very nature does not allow for a particularly architectonic treatment, so perhaps we should not expect to find movable furniture which closely parallels his architectural style. As an example of this problem one might look at the rosewood circular pedestal table reputed to have been designed by the architect Peter Nicholson, Thomson's grandfather-in-law.[13] While handsome in its proportions and construction, there is little to distinguish it from much other Regency furniture.

Unlike other media he designed for, such as cast iron, wallpaper or textiles, there is no evidence to suggest that he designed furniture for sale outside his architectural schemes. For general middle-class taste, his creations were perhaps too uncompromisingly architectural to have been taken up as models for batch production by local firms. The vogue for 'Art Furniture' designed independently by architects and artists does not seem to have caught on in Glasgow until the early 1870s, and even then tended to be confined to a small middle-class élite with self-consciously 'advanced' tastes. A manufacturer like Walter Macfarlane was operating in a relatively new area of production which was less hidebound by public expectations than cabinetmaking, and was therefore in a position to see the potential application of Thomson's designs for cast iron to a wider market. Cabinetmakers still viewed themselves as socially superior to artisans working in many other areas of the applied arts, and as a group also resisted interference from the architectural profession.

The calibre of joinery and woodwork in Thomson's buildings demonstrates that he was working within a well-established cabinetmaking tradition, and that he could call on a range of highly specialised and skilled craftsmen. It is also clear that Thomson's specifications were sensitive to the quality of the materials being used, and the constraints or potential of available production methods. The *Picture of Glasgow*, published in 1812, drew attention to the various branches of woodworking in the city, 'particularly that of the cabinet makers, which is, in general, executed in a style of exquisite elegance and taste',[14] and illustrated the stylish showroom of Cleland and Paterson in the Trongate (see FIGURE 12.5). From this point on there was a rapid proliferation of both cabinetmakers and furniture warehouses in the city to feed the phenomenal growth in demand, both in terms of local consumption and products for export. The boom in domestic furnishings was complemented by the increase in commercial, institutional and recreational interiors. A further area of demand which was to prove crucial to the way Glasgow's furnishing industry developed in the mid-nineteenth century was the kitting-out of the ships and trains which were beginning to pour out of yards along the Clyde. Not only was there a multiplication of suppliers, but the industry as a whole was becoming increasingly specialised and sophisticated. As in other large centres, it was characterised by intensive division of labour, and the larger factories were being 'scientifically' organised to attain production levels far exceeding local demand. Along with cabinetmakers, a whole host of mutually supporting trades contributed to the Glasgow interior. Thomson would have been able to call on lighting, fireplace and bathroom specialists, in addition to the more traditional skills of plasterers, stained glass artists, ironmongers, painter-decorators and paper-hangers.

In his furniture and woodwork Thomson deployed many of the colourful and rich timbers imported down the Clyde. Throughout the nineteenth century virtually all fashionable furniture produced in Glasgow would have been made from trees which grew abroad. The city was in fact a major entrepôt for timber being brought into Britain. Clyde-bound cargoes and timber sales advertised in local papers indicate the range and quantity being imported from Scandinavia, the Baltic and the West Indies in particular. Thomson clearly revelled in the use of high-quality, machine-cut timber, as one senses looking out over the banks of solid golden-pine pews in St Vincent Street church (see PLATE IV), or looking at the glorious flame veneers of the Glasgow Museums' cabinet. He advocated a philosophy of 'truth to materials', very much in keeping with that of the design reformer A. W. N. Pugin.

FIGURE 12.5   Interior view of ware-rooms of Cleland Jack, Paterson & Co., Trongate, from R. Chapman, *The Picture of Glasgow or Stranger's Guide*, 1812.

Thomson used wood as the key material with which to unite his schemes, just as an upholsterer would have manipulated textiles in many eighteenth- and early nineteenth-century interiors. His intentions in this respect are made clear in notes accompanying the illustrations of the Double Villa in *Villa and Cottage Architecture*: 'The whole of these interior finishings are of carefully selected yellow pine, the enrichments being frets of mahogany planted upon it. The wood is varnished, preserving its natural colour and markings, no stain of any kind being used. The object of this mode of treatment is to unite together the several parts of the room.'[15] Even from the limited evidence which survives, one can see that he exploited the available repertoire of woods, carefully selecting according to colour, grain and expense to complement the character and function of particular rooms. At Holmwood, for example, in keeping with established conventions expressed in the growing body of literature on household taste, he favoured the darker hues of mahogany offset by rosewood for the dining-room, as opposed to the lighter glowing tones of American yellow pine with mahogany detailing in the drawing-room. Pine came in a range of qualities, and the type selected for the public rooms was distinct from the cheaper deal used in the kitchen dresser and fitments in the service areas, or from the more robust red pine from Canada used on the exteriors.

There were numerous yards and sawmills which were quick to assimilate the new steam-powered technology such as circular and band saws, and planing machines from the 1840s. The average turner's output was at least doubled by the introduction of steam-powered lathes, and die-stamping and moulding machines facilitated the production of ornamental features. In Glasgow there were soon steam-powered factories specialising in wood-turning, fretwork and veneer-cutting, all techniques on which Thomson relied extensively. The production of veneers, formerly labour-intensive and highly skilled, had been transformed by this time. Large, uniformly wafer-thin sheets were made available in huge quantities and at reasonable prices. The thickness of the veneers and pierced fretwork employed by Thomson, for example, was little more than 1 or 2 mm. He made bold and extremely effective use of simple machine-cut and -turned mouldings, put together in unusual combinations (FIGURE 13.2). Another hallmark of his style was the pierced fretwork ornament stuck onto a ground of contrasting coloured wood, creating an effect in shallow relief which did not disrupt the bold outlines of the furniture or panelling. In the case of the large sideboard, panels pierced with a design of ivy leaves and berries were let into the upper doors. The effect was further enhanced by very low relief carving and a lining of crimson silk behind. Both the technique of pierced fretwork and the practice of displaying it against crimson silk were extremely popular in furniture of the mid-Victorian period throughout Britain.[16]

The importance attached to a piece of furniture such as this cabinet reflected the emphasis on visual identity and patterns of socialising within the Glasgow middle classes. The city within which Thomson lived and worked was at the centre of a buoyant regional economy in which the furnishing industry was one of many to thrive. In describing Wylie & Lochhead's Buchanan Street showrooms in 1859, one guide remarked,

The surprising display of house plenishing to be seen in these galleries furnish an unmistakable proof of the luxurious habits and refined taste that have grown up among the middle classes in the west of Scotland during the last quarter of a century. The fact is, the house of a respectable tradesman now in Glasgow, is equal if not superior, to the halls of nobles a few years ago. The sense of vision would seem to be consulted in the decoration of the homes of people at the expense of all the other senses, and in this there is a growing rivalship. ... in a thriving population where the genius of trade and manufacture is continually creating material wealth.[17]

Glasgow's burgeoning middle classes were certainly fashion-conscious in the extreme, and high-profile expenditure on houses and their contents helped to reinforce the group perception of a distinctive civic and class consciousness. Thomson's clients shared in this strong middle-class identity, and his domestic architecture ranged from villas and houses down the Clyde for members of the manufacturing and mercantile élite to flatted dwellings for the less affluent middle classes. Through the range of his architectural and interior work he offered them a unified aesthetic vision which held the different spheres of their urban experience together – the commercial, spiritual and domestic – thereby helping to play down the potential conflict between an aggressive search for wealth on the one hand, and living in a moral society on the other. Thomson's style was rooted in the recognition of shared values which spanned the public–private divide.

In such an economically volatile and densely populated city, the need for visual recognition of prestige and class was more marked than, for example, in Edinburgh. Indeed, as early as 1809 the taste of the Glasgow's new rich was noted as being somewhat extravagant and theatrical: 'Observing the weight attached to what are termed fashionable accomplishments they conceived the idea that to excel in these areas was the only way to public estimation. They accordingly ... made fashion their model in everything – in their house and furniture, their dress, their taste.'[18] The opulent interiors of Lauriston House, designed by Thomson's grandfather-in-law, Peter Nicholson, certainly give credence to this view. Throughout the nineteenth century, style and taste were to prove an important mechanism through which the middle classes could restrict contact with their social inferiors. So how did Thomson's furniture and interiors capture the dominant bourgeois ethos of the city?

In Thomson's lifetime, Glasgow assumed industrial

pre-eminence world-wide. A sense of calculated risk and experimentation was implicit in the city's rapidly expanding capitalist economy – qualities which were conveyed through the self-assurance and drama of Thomson's interiors. It was an economy which favoured entrepreneurs, and fortunes were rapidly made and lost – as Thomson himself would have known through personal experience of speculative building projects. In this urban context, modernity and functionalism were highly prized. Survival required an innovative approach to materials and new technology; profits could also be maximised through streamlining factory production and administration, or through an emphasis on uniformity, consistency and repetition of product types. It is difficult to document or prove a direct link between such concepts and style, particularly as such connections were often made at a subconscious level. Nevertheless, it seems relevant to suggest that Thomson somehow translated these priorities into his interiors, not only through the application of new technology, but also on a more abstract level, through alluding to mechanised production in the uniformity and repetitive detailing of his style, or the flush surfaces, high finish and clean-cut forms of his furniture.

As many of Thomson's clients were involved in manufacturing and trading, it is small wonder that such as range of skills and materials were deployed within the interiors they commissioned. Their villas and townhouses were designed as showpieces of the most sophisticated industrial art and high-quality materials, expressing not only wealth but also an identification with the city's technological progress, scientific achievement and artistic traditions. This point is eloquently demonstrated by one of Thomson's clients, the gas-fitting manufacturer William Johnson. Johnson had very clear views on the subject of lighting interiors, and was proud of his products which Thomson was doubtless asked to incorporate in designs for Ellisland (1871). In a lecture on 'Gas Lighting and the Best Mode of applying it to Buildings', Johnson proudly announced,

Glasgow and Edinburgh have now the best and purest supply of gas in the kingdom, probably the best in the world, hence its use in every apartment of our houses [whereas] people in London have to tolerate the most clumsy and ill-fitting gas appliances in their shops and houses – gas so foul and coarse, and street lamps of such imperfect construction, as would not be tolerated in any third-rate town in Scotland . . . why is it that so many people in London decline to have gas in their rooms? Better fittings and better gas would soon cure this.[19]

The front door of Ellisland (see FIGURE 14.10 and PLATE II) is again now flanked by two magnificent gas lamps designed by Thomson. He used cast iron, a material with strong associations of industry and modernity, both inside and outside in the form of balustrades, finials and lamp standards.

Design was particularly important within the context of the home, as a good deal of business-related socialising was carried on there to reinforce professional networks outside the family. Owing to the pattern of industry and commerce in Glasgow, lavish expenditure on dining-rooms and entertaining seemed to have been correspondingly higher than in a city such as Edinburgh, where the concentration of landed wealth and middle-class professionals created slightly different social structures and patterns of patronage. 'Entertainments are now given more frequently and the mode of giving them is materially changed', wrote Cleland in the *Statistical Facts of Glasgow* (1837), 'Persons who formerly gave supper parties and a bowl of punch are now in the habit of giving sumptuous dinners, . . . The value of the table service and the style of furniture in the houses of many of the Glasgow merchants, are inferior to none in the land.'[20] A memento from one such 'sumptuous dinner' hosted by the publisher Robert Blackie still survives in the Thomson family – the handpainted gilt plate off which the architect himself had eaten.[21] The public rooms of Thomson's own home at 1 Moray Place must also have been a point of discussion with potential clients, many of whom seemed to have moved in similar social circles. It is surely no coincidence that the massive and stunning sideboard described above appears to have been situated in the dining-room. Entertaining in this interior must have helped to cement the network of contacts made initially through organisations like the United Presbyterian Church, or the Masonic brotherhood to which Thomson almost certainly belonged. What better advertisement for his aesthetic vision?

It is clear that in some respects Glasgow's municipal

élite still took their cue from London fashions, but at the same time there was growing resistance to metropolitan influence. 'Fortunately Cockneydom is not Britain', was William Johnson's retort; 'This tendency of most Londoners and London writers to ignore or undervalue anything not "town", is a serious disadvantage to themselves.'[22] No one could accuse Thomson of replicating London fashions or aping aristocratic taste, and clearly his distinctive style appealed to someone of Johnson's independent and civic-minded outlook. Within such circles there was a sense that it was not necessary to filter standards through London, since both economically and culturally Glasgow operated in an international rather than a narrowly British context. The growing network of rail and sea links centred on Glasgow ensured that connections with world-wide markets were being made direct. Thomson did not need to travel outside Scotland; the world came to Glasgow. As discussed elsewhere in this book, Schinkel, for example, visited in 1826 (see Ch. 14). The classical and exotic sources of Thomson's style would have had a particular resonance in the context of Glasgow, arising from the city's extensive commercial dealings with the Near and Far East. Explicit Egyptian references are as apparent in Thomson's furniture and interiors as in his architecture and theory – for instance, the pylon shape of the cabinet, or the star-studded blue ceilings which recall Egyptian tomb paintings. In terms of Freemasonry, the Egyptian reference in the pylon shape of the cabinet would have been particularly appropriate (see FIGURE 12.2).

Inevitably, all such discussion is somewhat tenuous and speculative. The fact remains that, at present, only one major piece of furniture can reliably be attributed to Thomson. In terms of this category of design, however, it is as original, cosmopolitan and stylish as his architecture. Indeed, it was not just as an architect, but as a designer of furniture and interiors that Thomson was revered by succeeding generations. It is significant that the designer John Moyr Smith concluded his influential publication on household taste, *Ornamental Interiors*, with a eulogy to his hero Thomson.[23]

ACKNOWLEDGEMENTS

I am very grateful to Ann and Duncan Hutcheson for all their help in unravelling the family traditions relating to Thomson's furniture, and to Sheenah Smith and Paul Stirton for their encouragement and patient comments.

NOTES

1. A copy of this widely read manual was lodged in the Library of the Glasgow Architectural Society.
2. *Building News* (26 March 1875), p. 357.
3. Mitchell Library, Glasgow, Dept of Rare Books and Manuscripts, Thomson drawing 28 v.
4. Cited in J. Lever, *Architects' Designs for Furniture*, London, 1982, p. 14.
5. Loudon, *An Encyclopaedia*, p. 1046.
6. Quoted from unpublished manuscript notebook (n.d.) of Jane Nicholson Thomson (Mrs W. L. Stewart) – private collection, Mrs Hutcheson. The 1875 inventory of household furnishings for 1 Moray Place lists a mahogany 'pedestal' sideboard, which seems an inappropriate term to describe the cabinet now in the Glasgow Museums.
7. Letter from Dr R. McFadzean to the author, 14 Aug. 1982, Glasgow Museums furniture correspondence.
8. Jane Nicholson Thomson manuscript notebook.
9. Mitchell Library, Glasgow, Dept of Rare Books and Manuscripts, Thomson drawing 28.
10. Loudon, *An Encyclopaedia*, p. 1073.
11. T. Gildard, 'Greek Thomson', *Proceedings of the Royal Philosophical Society of Glasgow*, XIX (30 Jan. 1888), p. 12.
12. Inventory of furnishings for 1 Moray Place, March 1875, in the *Trust of Alexander Thomson 1875–1895*, Strathclyde Regional Archives T-MJ 143, pp. 19–22.
13. According to family tradition, the table was designed for Michael Angelo Nicholson's house in Melton Mews, Euston Square, London.
14. R. Chapman, *The Picture of Glasgow or Stranger's Guide*, Glasgow, 1812.
15. Blackie (publisher), *Villa and Cottage Architecture*, Glasgow, 1868, p. 49.
16. See manuals such as Blackie's *Cabinetmakers' Assistant*, London and Glasgow, 1859.
17. *Illustrated Railway Guide Glasgow–Edinburgh*, Glasgow, 1859, p. 328.
18. L. Smith, *Northern Sketches or Characteristics of Glasgow*, Glasgow, 1809, pp. 152–3.
19. W. Johnson, *Proceedings of the Glasgow Architectural Society* (1865–7), pp. 96–7. Johnston's firm, Johnston Fraser & Co., operated from 78 Gordon Street in Glasgow. They manufactured and installed chandelier and gas fittings.
20. J. Cleland, *Statistical Facts of Glasgow*, Glasgow, 1837, p. 39.
21. Thomson designed 7 Great Western Terrace for Robert Blackie in 1872, and remodelled Lilybank for John Blackie jun. in 1869. Their professional relationship was not

merely one-way, in that Blackie's firm published *Villa and Cottage Architecture* (1868), which featured Thomson's work so prominently; also the *Proceedings of the Glasgow Architectural Society*.

22. W. Johnson, *Proceedings*, p. 97.

23. J. M. Smith, *Ornamental Interiors*, London, 1887, p. 219. As editor of the short-lived magazine *Decoration*, Moyr Smith published various references in the 1880s to Thomson's buildings and designs. In the June 1881 issue, he remarked of a Grecian design for a chimney-piece with adjoining mural and frieze decoration submitted by John Thomson: 'The son could have no better model than his father, Mr Alexander Thomson, who was the first architect of the age if originality, refinement and pure artistic feeling count for anything.' (The design was published the following month.) Thomsonesque stencil, fabric and furniture designs also appear under the names of Thomas Gildard and Alexander *A*. Thomson, a furniture designer based in Glasgow in the 1880s, who is not to be confused with his namesake.

FIGURE 13.1 Interior of the Queen's Park church in 1881.

Chapter Thirteen

ALEXANDER THOMSON, DANIEL COTTIER AND THE INTERIOR OF QUEEN'S PARK CHURCH

Sally Joyce Rush

The interior of Queen's Park church (see FIGURE 13.1) was decorated between 1867 and November 1869, when the church was opened for worship.[1] Fourteen years later, in December 1883, the London artist Ford Madox Brown (1821–93) lectured in Glasgow. His hosts correctly anticipated that he would admire the interior of Queen's Park church. When Madox Brown died in 1893, the *Glasgow Herald* published – as an obituary – what he had said on seeing the interior:

The Queen's Park United Presbyterian Church – the work of Greek Thomson and Daniel Cottier, two fitting representatives of Modern Glasgow – was a revelation to him. His first questions were, Why didn't Thomson come to London and why did Cottier leave it for New York? . . .

Mr Madox Brown, with a feeling of pride, claimed Mr Cottier, who had attended a course of his lectures to art students, as a pupil, 'I might' he continued, 'have instructed; and doubtless did instruct, Cottier in general principles, but Cottier, as a colourist has a range of performance beyond that of any other modern artist. Here line and colouring are suggestive of paradise itself. I now know what all along has been wrong with my ceilings. Well done Glasgow! I put . . . this Thomson–Cottier church above everything I have seen in modern Europe.'[2]

The dramatic statement that no building in modern Europe compared to Queen's Park church (see FIGURE 13.2) is often used creatively out of context to underline Thomson's importance as an architect. McFadzean opens his book accordingly. This is misleading. Madox Brown was an artist, designer and interior decorator. Most importantly in this context, he was an associate of the pioneering William Morris (1834–96). Avant-garde interior design was his point of reference. First he compared the interior of Queen's Park church to his own work, and then to modern interiors in Europe generally. Significantly, he identified Thomson's unprecedented dependence upon the decorator Daniel Cottier (1838–91), and the innovative talent underlying the colour scheme of Queen's Park church.[3] Cottier's contribution was so conspicuous to him that he praised Thomson and Cottier alike. That Glasgow also awarded Thomson and Cottier equal credit implies that the interior of Queen's Park church was a significant departure from the church interiors Thomson had previously designed alone.

Cottier studied under Madox Brown in London in the early 1860s. He was in close proximity to Morris and obviously learnt from the latter's experimentation with colour harmonies. In turn, innovative colour harmonies were Cottier's most significant contribution to the Aesthetic movement in the 1870s. Madox Brown implies that, as early in his career as 1867, Cottier had left Morris behind. Exactly why the interior of Queen's Park church was still above anything in modern Europe to Madox Brown in 1883 begins to become clear.

Thomson's collaboration with Cottier has been accepted without question. In fact, it was unprecedented and surprising. It identifies that Thomson was interested in innovative colour harmony but was unable to master it for himself. The established and independent architect modestly sought the assistance of an unknown and much younger man. Presumably Cottier introduced Thomson to Morris's colour harmonies, and it was Cottier's Glasgow interiors that made Thomson

FIGURE 13.2   The Queen's Park church, Langside Road.

dissatisfied with his own. The colour scheme at Queen's Park church was a subtle departure from the archaeological primary-colour schemes of Thomson's earlier buildings.

Thomson, as his obituary confirms, was himself an innovative master of interior design, including colour:

With Mr Thomson, the designing of a building did not cease with the plaster-work and joinery. It extended to the coloured decoration, and this was as original, beautiful and characteristic as were the groupings or the mouldings. In some instances he painted the figure with his own hand, and in many he drew all the stencils. Furniture, even carpets, are indebted to a pencil that charmed alike by its novelty and grace. His interiors, with which the public is necessarily less familiar, are as subject to beauty, the offspring of originality and truth, as are his façades.[4]

There is no evidence that Thomson ever collaborated with anyone other than Cottier. Thomas Gildard's description of Queen's Park church – in a lecture given to the Glasgow Architectural Society in 1888 (by then amalgamated with the Glasgow Philosophical Society) – confirms Thomson's control of the decoration. Although Cottier executed the mural decoration, Thomson collaborated with him on one aspect only: colour harmony. As Gildard knew both Thomson and Cottier well, all three being members of the Glasgow Architectural Society, his account can be trusted. Seemingly the colour scheme was outlined by Thomson but detailed by Cottier:

the polychromatic decoration ... is rich and brilliant. It decorates surfaces, but in no wise disturbs an architecture that is independent of it. When it is said that it is from the pencil of Thomson himself, the severity, the delicacy, the power, the grace – in a word, the beauty and the appropriateness of the lines may be readily conjectured. In the colours, or rather in the harmonising of some of the tones, he had the assistance, frankly acknowledged, of the contractor, Mr Cottier, now of London. The scheme of this decoration is as unique as original, as is purely the architecture. Throughout the Church there is not even one cubic inch of plaster, and the natural colour of the wood – yellow pine – contributes its tone towards the general harmony.[5]

Thomson's readiness to participate in the experiments of a younger generation is surprising. Cottier completed his first polychrome church interior only one year before he collaborated with Thomson on Queen's Park church. In 1867, Thomson was well established while Cottier had only just moved his business from Edinburgh to 47 Carrick Street, Glasgow.[6] Cottier was only 31, while Thomson was 52. Cottier began his own business, at the age of 26, as a glass-stainer and mural decorator at 24 George Street, Edinburgh in 1864.[7] While still based in Edinburgh, Cottier designed and executed his first polychrome church interior, that of Townhead church on Garngad Hill, Glasgow (1865–6) by the 34-year-old John James Stevenson (1831–1908) of Campbell Douglas & Stevenson. In 1867, Cottier was perhaps still finishing his second interior, that of Dowanhill United Presbyterian Church, Glasgow (1865–6), by William Leiper (1839–1916). Leiper was only 26 when he designed Dowanhill church, his first commission on leaving Campbell Douglas & Stevenson.

Perhaps Thomson's collaboration with Cottier had a history and is not as surprising as it first seems. It can be suggested that Cottier worked on Thomson buildings during his apprenticeship as a glass-stainer and decorator in Glasgow in the 1850s. Thomson's innovative polychrome interiors perhaps inspired the young Cottier who later, as with Morris, passed him by.

To whom Cottier was apprenticed in Glasgow is open to question. Gould says that he 'served an apprenticeship in glass-painting with Kearney & Co. of Glasgow ...' but does not quote a source.[8] There was no glass-painter by the name of Kearney in Glasgow at the time. Perhaps because for a few years before this the glass-stainer David Kier (1802–64), and his sons William and James, had also worked from 47 Carrick Street, both Donnelly and Harrison have concluded that Cottier was apprenticed to Kier.[9] Neither quote a source, but Kearney could be a misconstruction of Kier. More likely, it is a misconstruction of Cairney.

The glazier, glass-stainer and decorator John Cairney was seemingly a client of Thomson's. Certainly, Cairney knew Thomson socially as he too was a member of the Glasgow Architectural Society. Cairney resigned from the Glasgow Architectural Society on 20 June 1860, due to ill health.[10] If he was also Thomson's decorator before Cottier – and Cottier trained under Cairney – Thomson's immediate employment of Cottier on his return to Glasgow in 1867 becomes more understandable. Presumably it was the same Cairney who in 1860 commissioned Thomson to design Cairney Buildings, 42 Bath Street (now demolished). That same year he was advertising as a glass-stainer, with premises at 46 Bath Street.[11] Cairney Buildings was substantial and presumably incorporated 46 Bath Street (see FIGURE 9.15).

Apparently Cottier was born in Dumbarton, and his father was from a traditionally seafaring family of Manx – and perhaps originally French Huguenot – extraction. In 1851, at approximately the time when Cottier would have begun his apprenticeship, John Cairney was already trading from 46 Bath Street.[12] A contemporary advertisement states that he was not only a glass-stainer but also a glass merchant and glazier, and a house painter and decorator. Significantly, he was an agent for the London and Manchester Plate-Glass Company.[13] Considering that expanses of plate glass and rooflights are design features of Thomson buildings,

FIGURE 13.3 Detail of stencilled wall decoration in the Caledonia Road church.

FIGURE 13.4 Detail of stencilled wall decoration in the Caledonia Road church.

and that Cairney was also a house decorator, he could have been very useful to Thomson.

McFadzean writes of Cairney Buildings:

> growing out of the masonry between the second floor windows, was a range of slender, square columns with bold entasis which flowered into exotic capitals ... Behind the columns was something new – the windows were treated as a continuous glazed timber screen which was completely independent of the columns ... Hidden from view was an attic storey which was set back with a continuous row of sloping windows.[14]

This new feature was perhaps conceived by architect and client as an advertisement of the product on sale, plate glass. Also, in the case of the attic, it was as a facility for a stained-glass studio where work in progress could be assembled against the backlight of an uninterrupted expanse of glass.

Gould says that Cairney's apprentices 'learnt to grind and mix their own colours'.[15] This implies that Cairney was a house painter as much as a glazier, and that Cottier was a colour boy entrusted with the nauseous task of mixing paints. If so, and Cairney was Thomson's contractor, Cottier perhaps assisted with the painting of Thomson's earlier interiors and Caledonia Road church (1856, gutted in 1965) (see FIGURES 5.4, 13.3, 13.4, 13.5 and 13.6) was perhaps his introduction to polychrome church decoration. Knowing this would have contributed to Thomson's appreciation of what Cottier subsequently learnt from Morris in London.

Thomson's mural decoration at Caledonia Road church completed the introduction of polychrome into Scottish Presbyterian churches, while Cottier's schemes later realised its artistic potential. After the division of the Scottish Presbyterian Church in 1843, architecture became the vehicle of inter-denominational rivalry. Decorative features of English Gothic Revival churches, particularly stained glass, were adapted to Presbyterian use; ideological objections quickly disappearing.[16] Generally, however, taste had become accustomed to the incomplete survival of medieval church interiors; stained glass and tiles had survived time and the Reformation, while painted decoration had not. In the case of Neoclassical churches, the weathered white marble of the Parthenon was precious to the Romantic imagination. Not until the 1850s was the archaeological argument in favour of painted architecture generally accepted.

Taste apart, Glasgow lacked skilled mural decorators. It is no surprise that Thomson drew his own stencils, and on occasion took up a brush. In Edinburgh, the Trustees' Academy of Design had taught trade apprentices Ornamental Design since 1832 and by the 1840s this included 'Ornamental Design in form and colour, including architecture, perspective, modelling and fresco painting.'[17] Glasgow's Government School of Design (from 1840), however, had no equivalent training to offer. In 1848, The Builder remarked that 'Polychrome decorations do not appear to be very general in Glasgow ... Our readers will scarcely believe, that in the school for a place like Glasgow, to say nothing of there being no class for design, there is

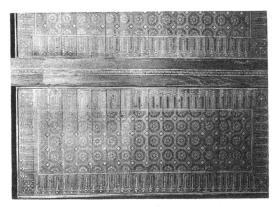

FIGURE 13.5 Detail of decoration on the ceiling of the Caledonia Road church.

FIGURE 13.6 Detail of stencilled decoration on the underside of ceiling beam in the Caledonia Road church.

actually no class for mechanical drawing or architectural ornament.'[18]

Not a traveller, Thomson's knowledge of ancient architecture was gained from secondary sources. It can be suggested that Thomson's use of polychrome decoration was encouraged by the publication of *The Grammar of Ornament* by Owen Jones (1809–74), in 1856. Thomson would certainly have empathised with Jones's ideas. These were disciplined by Jones's architectural training, and validated by his travels in, amongst other places, Greece and Egypt. He taught at the newly established Government School of Design in London. Disturbing to the Romantics, archaeological investigation proved that ancient architecture was painted in primary colours. Jones argued that the legibility of contemporary architecture would be enhanced by corresponding systematic decoration in primary colours.

Seemingly, Thomson referred to *The Grammar of Ornament*. Close equivalents of all the stencilled patterns Thomson used in Caledonia Road church can be found in Jones's chapters on Egyptian, Assyrian, Persian and Greek ornament. Caledonia Road church was designed the year *The Grammar of Ornament* was published. The introductory 'Propositions' were published separately by the government Department of Practical Art, for the bargain sum of one penny.[19] In 1851, as superintendent of the International Exhibition and Co-Director of the decoration of Crystal Palace, Jones was able to put his arguments into practice.[20] The colour schemes of St Vincent Street church and Holm-

wood House (see PLATE VI) correspond to Jones's identification of archaeological Greek colour schemes. Certainly by 1861, Jones's proposed system of decorative colouring was familiar to the Glasgow Architectural Society.[21]

Fortunately, it is now possible to do more than guess Cottier's colours at Queen's Park church, and to informatively compare them to those of St Vincent Street church, Holmwood House, Townhead church and Dowanhill church. A watercolour dated 1899 has come to light, recording areas of the colour scheme: the base of the pulpit and the font (see PLATE IX).[22] How true to the original this is cannot be confirmed.

Evidence of the colour scheme of Caledonia Road church would be more accurately informative than the restored interior of St Vincent Street church, opened in 1859.[23] Apparently, Thomson was not allowed to determine the colour scheme of the latter;[24] who did is unknown. Presumably it is close to that of Caledonia Road church, which must have been considered when Thomson was awarded the St Vincent Street church commission. The absence of stencilled mural decoration is in marked contrast to the interior of Queen's Park church, and perhaps this is where the church authorities drew the line. The stencilled decoration at

Caledonia Road church was modest in comparison to that of Queen's Park church.

The St Vincent Street church colour scheme is archaeologically Greek bright red and blue, and close to that of the hall at the contemporary Holmwood House, Cathcart, of 1857–8.[25] In both cases, flat scarlet and sky-blue are in brilliant contrast to yellow-pine woodwork. This suggests that Thomson was allowed to outline the colour scheme at St Vincent Street church. However, his contemporaries regretted that the legibility of the architecture was veiled by the colour scheme as executed.

As the Church is a building only he himself could have designed, only he himself could have completed it – by the colour – 'decoration;' only he himself knew what it required, or what was from the very first intended; why this was designed a carved convex, or that left a plain concave. The 'decoration' by colour is as essentially a part of the building as is the decoration by carving or moulding . . .[26]

The suggestion is that Thomson would have comprehensively followed Jones's Proposition 21: 'In using the primary colours on moulded surfaces, we should place blue, which retires, on the concave surfaces; yellow which advances, on the convex; and red, the intermediate colour, on the undersides; separating the colours by white on the vertical planes.'

The restored executed colour scheme at St Vincent Street church merely shadows the relief decoration in blue and is predominantly unbroken red. In outline, the colour scheme at Queen's Park church is also archaeologically Greek red and blue against yellow pine. What seems to have changed is that the colours are deeper, more complex and more in harmony with the woodwork. Cottier's colours at Queen's Park church were tertiaries: sky-blue became deep-turquoise blue and scarlet became russet against its opposite olive green, all harmonising with the ochre of the yellow pine.

The colour scheme at Townhead church was seemingly also archaeologically Gothic red and blue.[27] It was more likely that the colour scheme at Dowanhill church was the precedent for Queen's Park church one year later. Cottier came to Glasgow from Edinburgh to be better placed to work for Stevenson and Leiper, and to exploit a more adventurous patronage. His application for membership of the Glasgow Architectural

Society on 23 October 1865 was no doubt motivated by commercial interests and perhaps targeted Thomson as another architect interested in polychrome decoration. Stevenson and Thomson were friends and perhaps Stevenson personally introduced Cottier to Thomson. Thomson no doubt closely followed Cottier's lecture, 'Colour the Handmaid of Architecture', given to the Glasgow Architectural Society on 19 February 1866. Frustratingly, no transcript of this has been traced.[28]

The *Building News* gives some insight into their experiments, in its report on Dowanhill church, stating that 'The architect's aim has been to build a Presbyterian church which might have some claim to be reckoned artistic.' The description of Dowanhill church as 'artistic' is significant. It refers to the decoration rather than the architecture, and introduces the Aesthetic movement of which Cottier was to become a pioneer in the 1870s. Stevenson, like Cottier, moved permanently to London in 1869 and became an exponent of the 'Queen Anne' style.[29] Cottier and Leiper continued to work together on Scottish commissions.[30] After London, Cottier branched out internationally at 144 5th Avenue, New York, USA and in Sidney, Australia in 1873. By this time he was also an enlightened picture dealer and his firm was furnishing complete Aesthetic interiors. As Mark Girouard has recognised, it was Cottier – not Oscar Wilde – who introduced the Aesthetic Movement to America. Wilde did not lecture there until 1881.[31]

That Thomson, perhaps encouraged by Stevenson, paid attention to the innovative decoration of the 'Queen Anne' style is confirmed by an interesting letter written to his brother George, dated 3 June 1871:

When I wrote to you last I was on the point of starting for London ... I called upon Sandy Skirving [a former assistant] ... He took me to see his employers place – Messrs. Heaton – they are glass stainers and decorators. They and some others seem to be adapting Japanese art to their Gothic things with great success. While some that were strong Goths a short time ago are now as zealous for what they call the Queen Ann [sic] Style.[32]

Central to the work of Morris and his associates was 'artistic' colour. The insensitive and flat primaries of the Gothic Revival were replaced by subtle and resonant tertiaries. As architecture became eclectic in style, so decorative colour was no longer determined by archaeology. The mural painting at Dowanhill church shows that Cottier was experimenting with non-primary-colour harmonies as early as 1866–7. As Madox Brown, who would have known Cottier's later work well, was unaware of any discrepancy between this and the colour scheme at Queen's Park church, Cottier seemingly mastered artistic colour precociously early.

When recently the original mural decoration at Dowanhill was recovered from beneath subsequent dreary layers, the colours found were surprisingly subtle: resonant tertiaries; various russets, dark-turquoise blue and ochre, harmonise, significantly, with the yellow-pine roof members and gallery fronts. Brighter red and green highlight the tertiary colours and edge the roof members. Black and gold define the patterns. The foil for the mural decoration is a very dark indigo.[33]

From the beginning, Cottier was obviously determined to be among the avant-garde. When he had completed his apprenticeship as a glass-stainer and decorator in Glasgow, some time towards the end of the 1850s, he took himself to London. Madox Brown no doubt introduced him to Morris. What Cottier was doing during the day is unknown, but he attended night classes at The Working Men's College in Red Lion Square in the East End of London. This was opened on 31 October 1854 by the Christian Socialist F. D. Maurice. John Ruskin taught drawing and design. He recruited Dante Gabriel Rossetti, who was then replaced by Ford Madox Brown towards the end of 1858.[34] Practical classes were supplemented by lectures on science, history and art. Cottier could not have been closer to the Pre-Raphaelites and the stirrings of the Arts and Crafts, and Aesthetic movements. For the first time, his experimental creativity would have found sympathetic encouragement.

The recollections of another pupil, perhaps a contemporary of Cottier, are informative as to what Cottier learnt from Madox Brown. J. Philips Emslie recalled: 'Mr Brown several times invited us to his studio when there was an exhibition of works by himself and friends. Here we saw the "Work" while it was in progress, also "Lear" and "Cordelia", "Out of Town", "Autumn Afternoon".'[35]

When Madox Brown praised the colour scheme of Queen's Park church, he confessed to teaching Cottier

no more than 'the basic principles' of colour. Madox Brown did not introduce the colour harmonies associated with his circle. Rather, he too learnt from Morris. Madox Brown's early colours, before his association with Morris, were deliberately discordant rather than harmonious. In the 1860s, they became more subtle. *Work* (1852–65) is a transitional painting. It was more likely the other paintings Cottier saw in Madox Brown's studio which influenced him.

In April 1861, Morris, Marshall, Faulkner & Co. began operation at 8 Red Lion Square. The tertiary harmonies typical of Morris & Co. stained glass of the 1860s are repeated at Queen's Park church and eventually in Cottier's own stained glass. Although Madox Brown designed stained glass for Morris & Co., Morris decided the colours.

As seen, Thomson's collaboration with Cottier was limited to colour harmony and the execution of the mural decoration. It is no surprise that Thomson did not risk the discipline of the Queen's Park interior to Cottier's spontaneous invention. However, comparison of their interiors identifies a similar experiment with decorative motifs which might also explain Thomson's immediate collaboration with Cottier. Their motifs are similarly eclectic and conventional. Both took advantage of Scotland's impoverished medieval Gothic heritage and the consequent absence of preconceived ideas regarding appropriate styles for church decoration.

We do not know what Thomson thought of the anarchic Cottier on a personal level. However, professionally, Cottier possessed in measure the three faculties Thomson attributed to the gifted artist: 'the perceptive, the selective and the creative'.[36] In his Presidential address to the Glasgow Architectural Society in October 1861 Thomson said: 'I hope to see the day when it will not be considered necessary to answer the question "What style do you call that?" but when every man will have his own style . . .' In every respect, Cottier had 'his own style'. Perhaps it is not unfair to say that this was deliberately contrived, and to compare Cottier to the younger Oscar Wilde (1854–1900). Cottier enjoyed a certain infamy of his own. According to Andrew Wells:

Cottier was, like William Morris, one of the chief pioneers in the Revival of Decorative Art in this country; a man of strong individuality of character, brimming over with interesting talk and humorous anecdote, who spoke a strange mixture of good English and quaint broad Scotch. The more punctilious his auditors the broader Scotch he affected. He laid himself out to be odd and remarkable. When surrounded by a sedate church committee, he would cry to one painting the ceiling such directions as 'Andra, slabber on some broon there, just beside the wibble-wabble' – his name for wave ornament. On one occasion he wrote a tender for the painting of a church on the back of a soiled theatre bill.[37]

Thomson's design is creatively eclectic within an archaeological discipline. There is a relationship in principle between the ancient architectures he selected for adaptation. Jones proposed in *The Grammar of Ornament* that use of conventional plant motifs associated the decoration of ancient architectures.[38] Thomson's juxtaposition of Egyptian, Assyrian and Greek plant motifs in the surviving decoration of the St Vincent Street church follows Jones.

This argument was expanded by Jones's pupil, Christopher Dresser (1834–1904). Dresser studied under Jones at the Government School of Design from 1847–54, and lectured there from 1855–68.

Conventionalised nature, we say, will be found to consist in the delineation of nature in its purist or typical form; hence it is not imitation, but consists in the embodiment in form of a mental idea of the perfect plant; but this ideal figure is subject to a process of adaptation ... We are now enabled to classify ornaments by affinities resulting from equality in respect to the embodiment of mental power. Thus we have as examples of the first, or most exulted grade of ornament, the Greek, the Moorish, the Early English, much of the Indian, many features in the Japanese, and some parts of the Egyptian and Renaissance.[39]

Accordingly, Dresser designed decorative schemes which combined all the above. His designs were first published in *The Art of Decorative Design* in 1862. Towards the end of 1861, he gave a series of lectures to the Royal Society of Arts, and these were published in the *Building News* and *The Builder*.[40]

Thomson and Dresser agreed on many points; Dresser also admired the Greek civilisation, disliked

stylistic imitation and considered the Gothic style inappropriate for Protestant churches. It is perhaps due to Dresser's influence that, as McFadzean remarks, Thomson completely abandoned abstract pattern in favour of complex schemes of eclectic and conventional plant forms at Queen's Park church.[41]

James Mavor wrote an informative recollection of Cottier's interior for Townhead church.[42] Although this building still stands, it has yet to be investigated.

Undoubtedly the decoration was striking enough. Great masses of positive colour, red and blue with figures of dense black – the motif was Egyptian and the design might have found a fitting place in a great hall of the Pharaohs. In an ecclesiastical building it was inappropriate; in any building in Western Europe the effect would have been bizarre; the design was out of scale and wanting in the repose indispensible in church architecture. Nevertheless, the decoration was bold and in its way original. I felt at once, here at least is the work of a designer with brains and courage.

It can be suggested that Thomson would have agreed with him; that he would have admired Cottier's 'brains and courage' as an expressively colourful and eclectic designer, but would have had reservations regarding the autonomy of the decoration. At Dowanhill church, also Geometric Gothic, Cottier used Egyptian, Assyrian and Greek motifs. Close equivalents to Cottier's decorative scheme at this church can be found among Dresser's *Studies in Design*.[43] The decorative scheme is more Greek than Gothic in character. Interestingly, the Greek-derived ray and dot motif (it is found on the tapering areas of Greek vases) used by Dresser and Cottier is also used by Thomson for the font at Queen's Park church (see PLATE IX).

Today, Glasgow is beginning to appreciate Thomson's genius. However, the name of Daniel Cottier – which was once coupled with that of Morris, and famous not only in Britain but also in America and Australia – still means nothing in the city where he began his career. Even his collaboration with Thomson is overlooked. Queen's Park church (see FIGURE 13.7) is lost, but other internationally significant Cottier interiors survive in Glasgow – just. For a long time now, The Four Acres Trust have been struggling to restore Dowanhill church. The future of the vandalised Townhead church is far from secure. Recently, the

FIGURE 13.7   Interior of the Queen's Park church following
the lowering of the choir gallery and alteration to the organ
case in the 1890s, photo *c*.1900.

building sustained damage from the explosive demolition of an adjacent tower block. It has been necessary
for Glasgow District Council to compulsorily purchase
Thomson's No. 4 Great Western Terrace, which has
one of Cottier's earliest domestic interiors. Perhaps
the 1990s will see a return to the appreciation of Cottier
as when – a hundred years before, in 1893 – Thomson
and Cottier were together proudly considered to be
'fitting representatives of modern Glasgow'.

NOTES

1. J. Logan Aikman (ed.), *Historical Notices of the United
   Presbyterian Churches of Glasgow*, Glasgow, 1875, pp.
   215–17.
2. *Glasgow Herald*, 9 Oct. 1893.
3. Ronald McFadzean, *The Life and Work of Alexander
   Greek Thomson*, London, 1979, p. xiii.
4. *Building News* (25 Mar. 1875), p. 357.
5. Thomas Gildard, 'Greek Thomson', *Proceedings of the
   Royal Philosophical Society of Glasgow*, vol. XIX (30 Jan.
   1888), pp. 191–210.
6. *Glasgow Post Office Directory*, 1867–8, p. 116.
7. *Edinburgh Post Office Directory*, 1864–5, pp. 57, 243 and
   324.
8. Brian Gould, 'Two Van Gogh Contacts: EJ Wisselingh,
   Art Dealer; Daniel Cottier, Glass Painter and Decorator',
   London, 1969, p. 1 (typescript at Glasgow Art Galleries).
9. Michael Donnelly, *Glasgow Stained Glass*, Glasgow,
   1981, p. 8, n. 22; Martin Harrison, *Victorian Stained
   Glass*, London, 1980, p. 47.
10. Donnelly, *Glasgow Stained Glass*, p. 6, n. 12.
11. *Glasgow Post Office Directory*, 1860–1, pp. 72 and 467.
12. Ibid., 1850–1, pp. 69 and 465.

13. Ibid., 1851–2, p. 130.

14. McFadzean, *Alexander Thomson*, p. 137 and pl. 98.

15. Gould, 'Two Van Gogh ….', p. 1.

16. Renfield Street United Presbyterian Church (James Brown, 1848) was the first Glasgow church to have stained glass. This was by Ballantine & Allan of Edinburgh, and contemporary with the building.

17. Esmé Gordon, *The Royal Scottish Academy of Painting, Sculpture and Architecture, 1826–1976*, Edinburgh, 1976, p. 69.

18. *The Builder*, vol. 6 (28 Oct. 1848), p. 517.

19. Christopher Dresser, *The Development of Ornamental Art in the International Exhibition*, London, 1862, p. 32.

20. *Journal of Design*, quoted in B. Denvir, *The Early 19th C: Art, Design and Society, 1789–1852* (Mar. 1851).

21. David Haire (of Hugh Bogle & Co.), 'Decorative Art', a lecture to the Glasgow Architectural Society, printed in the *Glasgow Herald*, 17 Apr. 1861.

22. This is by A. Rollo. The watercolour is now in the National Monuments Record for Scotland, Edinburgh. It is possible that the restoration was undertaken when the organ gallery was lowered and other alterations made to the interior.

23. See n. 1 above.

24. [T. Gildard], 'The Late Alexander Thomson', *British Architect*, vol. 3 (16 Apr. 1875), p. 211.

25. Thomson's colours can be seen in a surviving strip of the original dado decoration and the floor tiles in the hall.

26. [T. Gildard], 'The Late Alexander Thomson', p. 211.

27. James Mavor, *My Window on the Street of the World*, London, 1923, vol. 1, pp. 227–8.

28. I am grateful to Fiona Sinclair for scanning the surviving records of the Glasgow Architectural Society.

29. Mark Girouard, *Sweetness and Light: The Queen Anne Movement, 1860–1900*, Oxford, 1977, pp. 38–40.

30. e.g. Colearn House (1870–1), Auchterarder, Perthshire for Alexander MacKintosh and Cairndhu House (1872–3), Helensburgh for Provost John G. Ure of Glasgow. See Donnelly, *Glasgow Stained Glass*, pp. 11–12 n. 44 and 45.

31. Girouard, *Sweetness and Light*, pp. 210–11.

32. McFadzean, *Alexander Thomson*, pp. 227–8.

33. I am grateful to Allan Ferdinand of The Four Acres Trust, Dowanhill church and Robert Snowdon, Principal Conservator at the Stenhouse Conservation Centre, Edinburgh for their generous assistance in analysing Cottier's mural decoration.

34. Ford Madox Hueffer, *Ford Madox Brown: A Record of his Life and Work*, London, 1896, p. 159.

35. Ibid., app. A, pp. 425–7.

36. Alexander Thomson, the Haldane Academy Lectures, published in *British Architect*, vol. 1 (1874), pp. 274–8.

37. *Journal of Decorative Art and the British Decorator* (May 1902), p. 145.

38. Owen Jones, *The Grammar of Ornament*, London, 1987 (first published in London, 1856), Proposition 13, p. 6.

39. *Building News* (3 Jan. 1862), pp. 8–9.

40. *Building News* (20 Dec. 1861), pp. 997–8 and (3 Jan. 1862), pp. 8–9; *The Builder* (15 Mar. 1862), pp. 185–6.

41. McFadzean, *Alexander Thomson*, p. 159.

42. Mavor, *My Window*, p. 40.

43. C. Dresser, *Studies in Design*, London, 1875–6.

THE INTERNATIONAL DIMENSION

FIGURE 14.1   The Caledonia Road church from the north-east in *c.*1960.

Chapter Fourteen

THE GERMAN CONNECTION

David Watkin

In the debate conducted in the first half of the nineteenth century about the direction of the Greek Revival in Britain, France and Germany, Greek Thomson was a latecomer, though a very powerful one. The leaders of this debate had originally been Cockerell in England, Hittorff and Labrouste in France, and Schinkel and Klenze in Germany. Their questioning of the path the Greek Revival was taking was particularly challenging since they were themselves products of the Greek Revival and had accepted without question the Enlightenment or Winckelmannesque conception of fifth-century Greek architecture as the summit of cultural achievement. It was precisely because they held the monuments of the Acropolis in such, arguably, exaggerated esteem, that they were disturbed by the failure of modern architects to understand those monuments, still less to equal them.

Urban expansion in the immediately post-Napoleonic period led, on the Continent, to small Residenz or court towns – like Karlsruhe or Munich – being transformed into modern cities with neoclassical abattoirs and museums, court-houses and schools. But the Greek Revival, from Stuart and Revett to Wilkins, had provided no urban imagery to fire the imagination of architects confronted with these new tasks. Schinkel, with his topographical awareness, and his experience as a diorama and panorama painter, provided compelling images in paintings such as his Poussinesque *Antique City on a Hill* (1805)[1] and his *Glimpse into the Flourishing of Greece* (1825). His *Gothic Cathedral on the Water* (1813)[2] also shows his ability to create a heightened sense of urban experience, of the close juxtaposition of buildings on steep sites. In this, he was followed by British architects such as C. R. Cockerell

in his *View of an Ancient City* (1819)[3] and James Pennethorne in his *Imaginative Reconstruction of the Forum at Rome* (1825).[4] The dense and exciting urban landscape they created was later realised in the development of cities such as Glasgow.

We know that Thomson admired continental architecture and the work of Schinkel in particular.[5] Indeed, he gave two volumes of Schinkel's *Sammlung architektonischer Entwürfe* to the Glasgow Architectural Society in October 1863. Why did Thomson feel that on the Continent the art of architecture was 'more generally appreciated than with us'?[6] He cited as evidence that foreign architects had not taken up the Gothic Revival. The irony was that the elevated conception of the role of architecture, which he shared with Schinkel, had in his own day in Britain largely passed from adherents of the classical tradition to the Gothic Revivalists. In Glasgow, moreover, he saw little evidence that his predecessors had much understanding of what he saw as the principles of Greek architecture.

Thomson was, in addition, impatient with the limited understanding of Greek architecture presented in its chief record: the four volumes of Stuart and Revett's *Antiquities of Athens*, published from 1762 to 1816. In their engravings, Greek architecture seemed reduced to a series of isolated monuments, distinguished only by varied decorative details, and insulated from the world (see FIGURE 4.2). It was also felt that Stuart and Revett failed to provide a coherent account of the principles which underlay Greek design.

Thomson's elevated, indeed divine, conception of the place of architecture in the scheme of things led him to claim that 'the laws which govern the universe, whether aesthetical or physical, are the same which

189

govern architecture'.[7] He was influenced by the synthetic historical vision of the new science of comparative world architecture, enshrined in Fergusson's *Illustrated Handbook of Architecture* of 1855. Thomson wrote of architecture that 'gradually developed is the noble series beginning with the dawn of human intellect and diffused over distant parts of the world – in Central America, India, Syria, Egypt, and reaching its climax on the Acropolis in Athens'.[8]

He believed that the trabeated architecture of the ancient Near East was the fundamental principle from which we should never deviate, as the Romans and the Goths had done. 'The laws of architecture', he wrote, 'were not invented by man, but were discovered by slow degrees.' The essential Egyptian elements are the pylon and the 'sloping wall, bound at the corners with a roll-moulding and surmounted by a horizontal cornice.'[9] He was totally opposed to the arch, writing,

Can anything be more absurd than to rear a fabric with the very agents of destruction? Every stone in an arch is a wedge, and every stone upon it is a hammer, slowly, it may be, but surely, driving those wedges home. All the parts in Gothic architecture seem to aspire at standing upon end ... the introduction of the arch into architecture has strewed Europe with ruins; whilst in Egypt and Greece, except where deliberately injured or destroyed, we have lintelled structures which have stood the test of thousands of years ...[10]

Thomson saw that the attempt to revive Grecian architecture had been based on imitating a small number of structures, known through the plates in the *Antiquities of Athens*. He said of these that, 'Like the Muses they are nine',[11] seven of which he said appeared in Glasgow. He cited Stark's Court House of 1807 for imitating the Parthenon; the Wellington Street UP church (see FIGURE 14.2) for copying the temple on Ilissus; Elliott's Royal Bank of Scotland of 1827 for the Erechtheum Ionic order; Taylor's Clarendon Place of 1839–41 with its capitals from the Tower of the Winds; Taylor's Custom House of 1840 with the Theseion Doric and an attic from the Choragic Monument of Thrasyllus; and finally Clarke and Bell's County Buildings of 1842 (see FIGURE 2.6) for the order and frieze from the Choragic Monument of Lysicrates.

These, he admitted, were 'all very good, but promoters of the Greek Revival could not see through the

FIGURE 14.2   The Wellington Street United Presbyterian Church by John Baird I, 1825, demolished 1884, photo from J. L. Aikman, *Historical Notices of the United Presbyterian Churches in Glasgow*, 1875.

material into the laws upon which that architecture rested. They failed to master their style and so became its slaves.'[12] Feeling that London had been even less fortunate in this respect than Scotland, he complained that 'The three windows in the wall of the Erechtheion, though unusual in Greek architecture especially for incorporating engaged columns, yet served as models for all street houses in Glasgow for the last 60 or 70 years.' None the less, Thomson admired what he called the glory of Edinburgh, Hamilton's Royal High School (1825), which, with Elmes's St George's Hall, Liverpool, he described as the 'two finest buildings in the kingdom'.[13] At St George's Hall, the walls are, indeed, articulated in a powerful Egyptian manner.

Although, as we have noted, Thomson saw more hope in continental than in British architecture, his surviving writings on architecture do not, unfortunately, contain references to specific foreign architects or buildings. It is striking that, failing to admire most modern British architecture, he found more to excite him in modern painting. This, ironically, made him a close parallel to Ruskin whom otherwise he totally condemned.[14]

Thomson also resembled Schinkel in finding inspiration in paintings of imaginative architectural panoramas. He singled out for praise 'the magnificent architectural compositions of Turner and of the late

FIGURE 14.3   *The Seventh Plague*, steel engraving after John
Martin by J. Godfrey, 1865.

John Martin' in which features were 'united by
terraces'.[15] It is possible to compare the sublime
architecture in paintings such as Turner's *Decline of the
Carthaginian Empire* (1817) and Martin's *Pandemonium*
(1841), with buildings such as Thomson's Moray Place
of 1859. The architecture in Martin's *Seventh Plague of
Egypt* (1820) (see FIGURE 14.3) can be compared with
Thomson's Great Western Terrace of 1867 and his
Egyptian Halls of 1871. Further Thomsonian architecture in Martin's *Belshazzar's Feast* (1820) (see
PLATE I and FIGURE 5.2) includes Babylonian capitals
supporting an Egyptian entablature, while another
arcade features Indian capitals, and the three stepped
arches in the centre distance have stones joined in the
apparent strength of the arch without being one.

The composition is close to stage sets by Schinkel,
such as his 'Temple of the Sun' for *The Magic Flute* of

1815, Schinkel later echoes the profile of these stepped
arches in this temple in the museum of his Orianda
Palace of 1838 with its Assyrian flavour. Like Martin,
Schinkel was moved by the prodigious scale and repetition, the fire, smoke and artificial light of buildings
associated with the Industrial Revolution – like railways and factories. Indeed, the French found England
'martinien', Michelet describing Nash's Regent Street
colonnade in 1834 as 'un monument babylonien, à la
Martin'.[16] The heady expansionist flavour of post-1815
London is conveyed in J. M. Gandy's visionary designs
for imperial palaces for George IV. In Glasgow, Thomson captures this pictorial splendour in romantic compositions such as his St Vincent Street church (see
FIGURE 4.1), which is close to the tradition of topographical paintings by Turner, Schinkel and Klenze.

A key Greek building which for many architects,

FIGURE 14.4   The Choragic Monument by Thrasyllus, from volume II of the *Antiquities of Athens*.

In his *Sammlung architektonischer Entwürfe*, in which he recorded his executed and projected works, Schinkel cited the trabeation of the Thrasyllus monument as a source for the fenestration of his Berlin Schauspielhaus of 1818–26 (see FIGURE 14.5), claiming that it admitted the maximum amount of light. Thomson knew Schinkel's designs, for, as we have already noted, he gave two volumes of his *Sammlung* to the Glasgow Architectural Society, which he had founded in 1848.[17] It is not clear when Thomson first became aware of Schinkel's work, but the 174 plates of the *Sammlung*, with accompanying commentary, were issued intermittently in twenty-eight parts in 1819–40, with later editions in 1843–7, 1852, 1866 and 1872.

In fact, Wilkins had used the Thrasyllus form as early as 1809 at Grange Park, while Cockerell made it the basis of his Hanover Chapel towers of 1823; Goodridge took up the theme in 1824 for his Lansdown Tower, Bath; Donthorn developed an austere trabeated architecture, as in his Bure Homage of 1835; while George Smith's Corn Exchange, Mark Lane, London, is a little-known example from 1827. Charles Barry also incorporated these themes in the 1820s in Manchester: in his Schinkelesque house at Buile Hill and in his Institution, now the City Art Gallery.

In the mean time, Cockerell had made the remarkable discovery that the temple of Olympian Zeus at Agrigentum on Sicily incorporated engaged columns and piers which took Egyptian or Greek trabeation a step in the direction of the moulded wall mass of the Romans.[18] Cockerell developed this technique in the 1830s in the side elevation of his Westminster Life and British Fire Office, and in his London and Westminster Bank. Barry, in his offices in Pall Mall of 1833, devised another Schinkelesque trabeated façade which was echoed in 1862 by Thomson in his Buck's Head Buildings. Thomson here produced a skeleton of cast-iron colonettes with winged brackets in Schinkel's manner. Schinkel had initiated his own trabeated brick architecture in 1817 with his Lindenstrasse barracks in Berlin, which were in part a return to the medieval brick buildings of the Hanseatic tradition. Among those who had discovered this tradition was his mentor, Friedrich Gilly, who made a celebrated set of drawings in 1794 of the fourteenth-century Schloss Marienburg.

Both Schinkel and Thomson were faced with the problem of designing classical churches at a time when

including Thomson and Schinkel, seemed the perfect expression of the rational trabeated architecture of the Greeks was the Choragic Monument of Thrasyllus in Athens (see FIGURE 14.4). Before its destruction in the nineteenth century, this had been recorded by Stuart and Revett in their *Antiquities of Athens* (1789), vol. II, and by J.-D. Le Roy in his *Ruines des plus beaux monuments de la Grèce* (Paris, 1758). Both Schinkel and Thomson were impatient with those modern architects who thought they could make a building Greek simply by clapping a portico on to a box. Schinkel and Thomson saw in the Choragic Monument of Thrasyllus a clear demonstration of the post-and-lintel construction of the Greeks in which the inert mass of the wall was abolished. They knew from the plates in the *Description de l'Égypte* (1809), such as that of the temple at Elephantine in vol. 1, that the ancient Egyptians had followed similar principles. What Thomson ultimately made of this we can see in buildings such as his Walmer Crescent of 1857.

a church was expected to have a tower, an essentially medieval feature. As a result, there are close links between Thomson's Caledonia Road church of 1856 (see FIGURE 5.1) and Schinkel's church at Charlottenburg of 1822. In 1816, Nash, who was close in a number of ways to Schinkel, had added a Schinkelesque Grecian tower to the medieval parish church at East Cowes on the Isle of Wight. To compare it with Thomson's Caledonia Road church is to remind us that Schinkel's opposite number in Munich, Leo von Klenze, also used these trabeated pilastrades, as in his Propylaea of 1846 in the Königsplatz. The trabeated form which dominates Schinkel's Schauspielhaus constantly recurs in Thomson's work, for example in his Caledonia Road church and Oakfield Avenue of 1865 (see FIGURES 4.4 and 14.1).

Thomson's St Vincent Street church of 1856 may be compared with the origin of the dreams of Greek temples raised on high platforms: Gilly's design for a monument to Frederick the Great of 1797, which sets the monument in an essentially urban context. Much later, in 1846, Klenze – inspired as a young man by Gilly's design – produced a painting called *Ideal View of the City of Athens with the Acropolis and the Areopagus* (see PLATE X).[19] Incorporating new archaeological discoveries such as polychromy, this image was still portrayed with a fiery romance. We may compare this vision with the Caledonia Road church in its urban setting, though Hamilton's Royal High School, Edinburgh, also inspired Thomson's brilliant handling of Greek forms so as to create their own landscape.

The great stepped podium of the St Vincent Street church (see FIGURES 17.4 and 18.11) also recalls the spirit of that at Klenze's great national shrine, the Walhalla near Regensburg (1830–43). The discovery of Greek polychromy also features strongly in the interiors of both the Walhalla and of Thomson's St Vincent Street church (see PLATE IV), as well as in the palace Schinkel designed in 1834 for the king of Greece on the Acropolis. Once again, Egypt is not far away, as can be seen by comparing a capital from the St Vincent Street church with a coloured detail from the temple at Philae, as recorded in the *Description de l'Égypte* (Paris, 1809–28). The study of Egyptian architecture had encouraged the notion of polychromy as part of an architectural language which can express life and meaning, a theme which requires further exploration.[20]

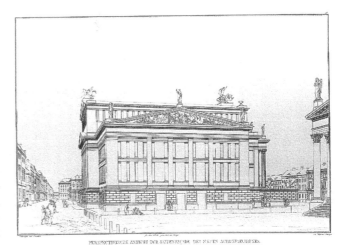

FIGURE 14.5   The side elevation of the Berlin Schauspielhaus, engraving first published in 1821, from Schinkel's *Sammlung architektonischer Entwürfe*, 1866.

Thomson's unexecuted design of 1858 for St George's Free Church, Edinburgh featured an open curved portico in which caryatids took the place of columns. This was a synthesis of various features on the sea-front of the unexecuted palace at Orianda in the Crimea (see FIGURES 14.6 and 14.7), which Schinkel designed in 1838 for the Empress of Russia.[21] This included a square portico of caryatids as well as two curved Ionic porticos where the space between the columns was replaced by glass. Such a dissolution of the wall mass through the handling of glazing was a key feature of Thomson's own architectural thinking and practice. It had been prefigured in neoclassical theory by Laugier who envisaged a rational architecture of load-bearing columns separated by glass. Thomson introduced further curved glazed porticos in the parlour of his villa, Holmwood, Cathcart Road (1857) (see FIGURE 16.2) and in his now demolished house at Busby (1856) (see FIGURE 14.8).

This leads us to Thomson's domestic work. In discussing its relation to the German tradition, we should note that whatever Thomson owed to German work, German architects were themselves inspired by English Picturesque practice. Pioneering British designs in the Picturesque tradition include J. B. Papworth's asymmetrical towered villa, a residence for an artist. This was published in 1818, at about which time a version of it was realised at Deepdene, Surrey, the

FIGURE 14.6   Project for a palace at Orianda by Schinkel:
elevation of the sea-front, 1838.

country house of the connoisseur, designer and collec-
tor Thomas Hope. Thomson may have known Playfair's design of 1829 for Drumbanagher (see FIGURE
3.21), which – with its low-spreading, far-flung office
wing – has features in common with Thomson's own
Craig Ailey, Dumbartonshire, of 1850.

As taken up in Germany, this subtle asymmetrical
method of composition is well typified in a design for a
duck decoy at Potsdam by Schinkel's collaborator,
Ludwig Persius. This was one of a number of similar
designs published in the *Architektonisches Skizzenbuch*
from 1852. It may be compared with several Thomson
designs, including his Green Bank, Bothwell Road,
1856–8, and his Holmwood, Cathcart Road, 1857 (see
FIGURE 17.5). That Klenze could work in the same
manner can be seen from his unexecuted design of 1835
for the Pantechnion, a museum in Athens. Klenze
included this in his own *Sammlung architektonischer
Entwürfe*, which he began publishing in 1830. One can
compare the Pantechnion with Thomson's Howard
Street warehouse (1851) (see FIGURE 8.5) and with a
detail from his Double Villa of 1856. Holmwood is
close to Schinkel's Court Gardener's House (see
FIGURE 16.10) and Roman Baths complex at Schloss
Charlottenhoff of 1829–33, and to plates from the
Architektonisches Skizzenbuch showing a villa of c.1858
near Trier by the architect J. Emmerich (see FIGURE

14.9), and a house of c.1855 for a vineyard near Sans-
souci by L. Hesse.

The Picturesque element in Thomson's villas relates
to a softening of the Greek tradition, which reminds us
that Klenze – who shared Thomson's passion for fifth-
century Athens – made a greater compromise than
Thomson ever did. If Klenze's heart was in his trabeated Propylaea in Munich and in his Walhalla, he
worked for a patron, King Lugwig I of Bavaria, with a
far more eclectic approach, Klenze thus convinced
himself that the Greek spirit was equally expressed in
the round arch as in the post-and-lintel system. He
developed this curious argument in the preface to his
Sammlung, and thus designed neo-Renaissance buildings such as the Königsbau at the Residenz in Munich
(1826), and the Catholic cathedral of St Dionysius
(1844) in Athens of all places, works of which Thomson, understandably, would not have approved.

But the old Grecian trabeated image always tugged
at Klenze's heart, as in his Hermitage Museum, St
Petersburg (1842–51). Klenze's handling of forms
in this building may be compared with Thomson's in
works such as his Oakfield Avenue (see FIGURE 4.4)
and Grecian Buildings (see FIGURE 9.21), both of 1865.
Further analogies suggest themselves if we compare
Thomson's Moray Place (1859–61) (see FIGURE
17.2) or Walmer Crescent (1857–62) with Klenze's

FIGURE 14.7   Project for a palace at Orianda by Schinkel: perspective of the terrace, 1838.

FIGURE 14.8   Busby House, Busby, extended by Thomson, 1856–7, and demolished in 1969.

Propylaea or with the kind of architecture he portrayed in his *Athens in Ancient Times*, a magnificent image painted as late as 1862.[22]

In the mean time, Berlin was being developed in like manner by Schinkel's pupils who were inspired by his urban vision.[23] A plate from the *Architektonisches Skizzenbuch* showing the Viktoria Strasse (1855–9) in Berlin by Hitzig may be compared with Thomson's more imaginative Great Western Terrace of 1867. The development of Berlin was also illustrated in the publications from the mid-1830s of the Berlin Architekten-Verein, which had been founded in 1824 as one of the earliest associations of practising architects.

Thomson's powerful entry in the Albert Memorial competition of 1862 (see FIGURE 7.10) has a giant podium recalling that of Klenze's Walhalla and of Klenze's Peace Memorial of 1815. James Pennethorne had much in common with Thomson as can be seen in his entry of 1838 in the competition for the Royal Exchange.[24] Pennethorne's entry in the Albert Memorial competition, based on the Mausoleum at Halicarnassus, also had a Germanic flavour.[25] Thomson's design of 1864 for the South Kensington Museum (see FIGURES 7.11 and 17.7) may be compared with Schin-

kel's reconstruction of Pliny's villa for the Crown Prince of Prussia, or, perhaps more appositely, with Hamilton's Edinburgh High School.

But let us return, finally, to the topic on which we touched at the start of this chapter: Egypt, the influence of which always gave a compelling strength to Thomson's work. The temple of Hathor at Dendera was raided by Thomson for two late works of 1871: his Egyptian Halls (see FIGURE 9.6), and his villa, Ellisland, in Pollokshields (see FIGURE 14.10). Yet at Ellisland there is so individual a language that any parallel with contemporary Europe is no longer relevant. That there are close parallels between Thomson, Schinkel and Klenze – in terms of urban imagery, trabeated Grecian vitality and Picturesque composition – is unquestionable. Thomson, we know, was aware of

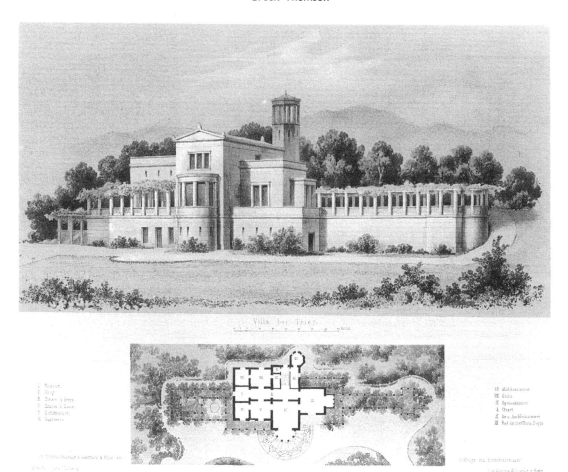

FIGURE 14.9   Design for a villa near Trier by Joseph
Emmerich, from the *Architektonisches Skizzenbuch*, 1858,
p. xxxvi, pl. 5.

Schinkel's work, but there is an internal logic in Thomson's own development which accounts for his personal language: indeed, he found in German work what he wanted to find.

NOTES

1. Now in the Nationalgalerie, Berlin.
2. Schinkel's *Glimpse into the Flourishing of Greece* and *Gothic Town on the Water* are known from copies by Wilhelm Ahlborn in the Nationalgalerie, Berlin.
3. Sotheby's sale catalogue, *Early English and Victorian Watercolours, Architectural Drawings and Watercolours*, London, 30 April 1987, Lot 561; and *Architectural Drawings*, The Clarendon Gallery, London, 1987, p. 23.
4. Illustrated in G. Tyack, *Sir James Pennethorne and the*

Making of Victorian London, Cambridge, 1992, pp. 14 and 178.
5. Thomson did not visit Germany but, apart from owning Schinkel's *Sammlung*, he may have seen accounts of Schinkel in architectural journals. For example, the 23rd volume of the *Sammlung* was reviewed in Loudon's *Architectural Magazine*, vol. II (1835), pp. 365–7; and G. F. Waagen's lecture of 1847 on Schinkel was printed in the *Civil Engineer and Architect's Journal*, vol. X (1847), pp. 226–7.
6. Cited from a summary of Thomson's lecture at the Glasgow Architectural Society, 7 May 1866, 'An Enquiry as to the Appropriateness of the Gothic Style for the Proposed Buildings for the University of Glasgow', in *The Builder* (19 May 1866), p. 370.
7. Ibid., p. 368.
8. Ibid.

FIGURE 14.10   Ellisland, Nithsdale Road, Pollokshields,
photo *c.* 1930.

9. Cited from Thomson's course of four lectures on 'Art and Architecture' at Glasgow School of Art and Haldane Academy, 1874, as printed in the *British Architect*, vol. I (1874), p. 354.

10. *The Builder*, 19 May 1866, p. 368.

11. *British Architect*, vol. II (1874), p. 51.

12. Ibid.

13. *The Builder* (19 May 1866), p. 370.

14. Thomson wrote of Ruskin, 'I know no one who has done more to mislead the public mind in matters of Art than he' (Haldane Lecture, *British Architect*, vol. I (1874), p. 275).

15. *The Builder* (19 May 1866), p. 369.

16. Cited from J. Seznec, *John Martin en France*, London, 1964, p. 29.

17. The volumes of Schinkel's *Sammlung* given by Thomson cannot now be traced.

18. See D. J. Watkin, 'Archaeology and the Greek Revival: A Case-study of C. R. Cockerell', in *Late Georgian Classicism*, Georgian Group Symposium, London, 1987, pp. 58–72.

19. Bayerische Verwaltung der staatlichen Schlösser, Gärten und Seen. See N. Lieb and F. Hufnagl, *Leo von Klenze: Gemälde und Zeichnungen*, Munich, 1979, catalogue no. 655. On Klenze as an archaeologist, see *Ein griechische*

Traum: Leo von Klenze der Archäologe, exhibition catalogue, Glyptothek, Munich, 1985.

20. But see D. Van Zanten, 'The Architectural Polychromy of the 1830s', Ph.D. Thesis, Harvard University, 1970 (Garland Publishing Inc., New York and London, 1977). Cockerell's opinions on Klenze's polychromatic buildings in Munich are recorded in his MS 'Notes on German Architecture', Cockerell Papers, British Architectural Library, London, Cock 1/199–102.

21. This parallel was first noted in J. McKean, 'Trabeated Essence and Frosted Glass', in the 1984 exhibition catalogue, *Alexander 'Greek' Thomson: Architect 1817–1875*, Architectural Association, London, 1984, p. 32. Schinkel's designs were published posthumously in obscure German publications which Thomson might conceivably have seen.

22. See Lieb and Hufnagl, Leo von Klenze, catalogue no. G73.

23. See E. Börsch-Supan, *Berliner Bauten nach Schinkel, 1840–1870*, Munich, 1977.

24. G. Tyack, *Sir James Pennethorne and the Making of Victorian London*, Cambridge, 1992, p. 41.

25. Ibid., p. 275.

FIGURE 15.1   Detail of the south-west corner of the
Caledonia Road church.

Chapter Fifteen

·

AN AMERICAN FORERUNNER?
MINARD LAFEVER AND ALEXANDER THOMSON

Andor Gomme and Gavin Stamp

Does this door (see FIGURE 15.2) look familiar? A delicately battered architrave frame punctuated by rosettes; a concave frieze with alternating anthemia and palmettes above running scrolls – where might one have seen those before? Try the entrance doors of the Caledonia Road church (see FIGURE 15.3) – although the architraves there have small but unmistakable lugs at the top corners and a beaded frame, while an akroterion in the form of another anthemion sits on top of the whole thing. So it does in another door design (see FIGURE 15.4), albeit with scrolls running off either side into rinceaux; and, though the frieze has gone, along with the rosettes down the sides, the lugs are here and the architrave frame is nearly identical with that in Caledonia Road. Or compare the 'pylon' windows at the ends of the galleries in St Vincent Street, or the slightly enriched versions once on the front of the Queen's Park church (see FIGURE 13.2). The frame is simplified and the rosettes are reduced to roundels, but nevertheless they are strikingly like our first design (see FIGURE 15.2).

Of course, what happens inside the architraves is quite different: subordinate antae and a meander-fretted lintel at Caledonia Road; a square pilaster-like mullion carrying a beam below a transom light at St Vincent Street. And surely our engravings are of designs for internal doors? Indeed they are – remarkably like (to take three random examples) those in the dining-room at Rockland, or at the foot of the main staircase in No. 1 Great Western Terrace, or that in the Holmwood dining-room published by Blackie (see FIGURE 11.9).

These engravings, however, do not come from *Villa and Cottage Architecture* but from the American

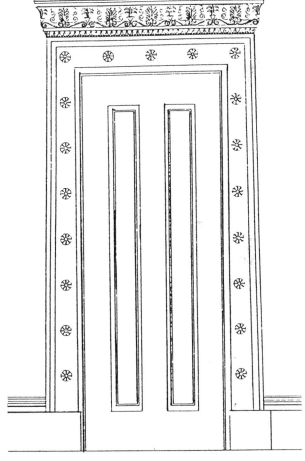

FIGURE 15.2 Design for a parlour door by Minard Lafever, from *The Modern Builder's Guide*, 1833, pl. 160.

architect Minard Lafever – little known in Britain but, especially through his pattern books, once widely influential in the eastern United States. Lafever was born

FIGURE 15.3   The eastern entrance to the Caledonia Road church.

FIGURE 15.4   Design for a door by Lafever, from *The Beauties of Modern Architecture*, 1835, pl. 14.

in 1798 and trained as a carpenter but, by 1830, appeared as an architect.[1] This was a year after the publication of his first book (in Newark, New Jersey), *The Young Builder's General Instructor*, which was largely derived from Peter Nicholson and which he later withdrew. In 1833, in New York, Lafever produced *The Modern Builder's Guide* which was reprinted six times between 1841 and 1855. It was followed in 1835 by *The Beauties of Modern Architecture* (also several times reprinted in New York)[2] – the most finely executed and best-considered of Lafever's books in which designs for doors, windows, chimney-pieces and

so forth are accompanied both by descriptive explanations and by large-scale details giving 'all the particulars necessary to render [their] execution . . . intelligible to the understanding of every workman'.[3] These are thought through with the understanding of a true craftsman; and the designs themselves, in the words of Lafever's editor, D. P. Myers, show 'mastery of proportion and [an] ability to combine restrained simplicity with delicate exuberance'.[4]

In the later years of his life (he died in 1854), Lafever gave up neo-Greek and designed a number of Gothic churches, while for cottages and villas he turned to the widely fashionable and less demanding Italianate. This he illustrated in his posthumously published *Architectural Instructor* (New York, 1856), a latter-day swim-of-the-tide book of no special distinction which lacks the thoughtful refinement of detail which so strongly characterises Lafever's Greek work. However, this book illustrates Lafever's Neo-Egyptian project for a Washington Monument in New York City, which is curiously reminiscent of Thomson's designs for rather smaller obelisk gravestones in Glasgow's cemeteries (see FIGURE 7.8).

Our hunch is that, by the mid-1850s, Thomson owned or had access to both *The Modern Builder's Guide* and *The Beauties of Modern Architecture*. Influences are notoriously difficult to confirm and we have not yet identified any single large feature of a Thomson building which exactly replicates a Lafever engraving. Rather, they play variations on several Lafever designs, mixing motifs to create something new and characteristically Thomsonian. The main doorcase of Grecian Chambers (see FIGURE 9.22), for example, suggests FIGURE 15.7 with the sidelights removed and battered architraves and brackets from other Lafever plates topped by Thomson's favourite cresting of a bold anthemion on top of a shallow pediment. Transom lights (as at Grecian Chambers) are common features of Thomson front doors, though rarely accompanied by the sidelights which Lafever added to enrich his larger examples, but the frontispiece of the Queen's Park church (see FIGURE 13.2), with its main architrave carried on two great antae through which the subsidiary entablature is threaded, could be seen as a magnificent enrichment of several Lafever designs based on the same formal skeleton. The front doors at Westbourne Terrace, on the other hand, which have sidelights, are recessed behind pairs of conventional Ionic columns *in antis* which closely reproduce – though without framing antae or overall worked entablature – another engraving in *The Modern Builder's Guide*.

The lesser antae which typically flank Thomson's front doors, as in Moray Place (see FIGURE 8.13), could – though they need not – come from those included in numerous Lafever designs, sometimes given with details for capital and base moulds. Such details are at times remarkably close: the base moulds of the antae which act as mullions to the great ground-floor windows on the Double Villa are identical with those shown in large scale on Plate 16 of *The Beauties of Modern Architecture*. This is an engraving which also gives fully worked-out detail for antae capitals decorated with anthemia and palmettes in a form which appears in close replica, whole or in part, on many and various Thomson buildings – Holmwood, Moray

FIGURE 15.5   Detail of the west gallery of the St Vincent Street church.

Place, Caledonia Road, Oakfield Avenue, Dunlop Street and Norfolk Street.

The ultimate source of all such ornament is, of course, the Ionic of the Erechtheum (see FIGURE 4.2), where bands alternating in Lafever's and Thomson's way form the necking of the capitals. These are shown in large scale in Stuart and Revett's *Antiquities of Athens*, from which Lafever gives a selection of redrawn examples in *The Beauties of Modern Architecture*, together with some fresh adaptations of his own. Thomson naturally used Stuart and Revett and could just as well have developed his ornament in parallel

FIGURE 15.6   Design for a door by Lafever, from *The Modern Builder's Guide*, 1833, pl. 66.

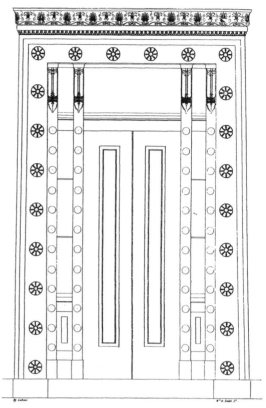

FIGURE 15.7   Design for a door by Lafever, from *The Modern Builder's Guide*, 1833, pl. 80.

with Lafever. But if other evidence is felt to be suggestive, he might also have gone to the secondary source for the ornament.

None of this – need we add? – is intended to cast Thomson's originality in question. Mature architects, like mature poets, don't borrow; they steal.

But how, and why, did Thomson consult Lafever? The publications of Minard Lafever were rare in Britain, which makes Thomson's knowledge of them remarkable. Henry-Russell Hitchcock, who ought to know, detected the influence of American pattern books on the early work of Cuthbert Brodrick but, surprisingly, not in Thomson's buildings.[5] Yet the vaguely American character of much of Thomson's work has often been commented on while many Americans – above all Hitchcock – respond positively to his architecture. This may well be owing to the long-established links between the West of Scotland and North America (exemplified both by the later career of Daniel Cottier and by the Audsley brothers taking Thomson's style to

New York (see FIGURE 16.13) and the Mid-West), together with the pronounced American flavour of the city of Glasgow. Nevertheless, the suggestion that the nineteenth-century transatlantic cultural traffic might have been two-way and that Thomson was influenced by American sources is surely a novel and an intriguing one.

As Thomson's library is dispersed, unrecorded, we cannot establish whether he acquired copies of Lafever's books, nor, if he did, how he came by them. Nevertheless, there were particular family reasons why these volumes may well have reached Thomson's Glasgow office. Thomson may have had distant American relations, bearing his surname, who left Scotland for New York in 1847, some of them eventually reaching California. Greek Thomson was in correspondence with these Thomsons in the 1870s, but although one was a cabinet-maker and sometime builder, none was an architect.[6] In fact, the contact who is most likely to have come across Lafever's books in the United States and sent them to Glasgow was Thomson's other architect brother-in-law: Peter Angelo Nicholson, who emigrated to the United States at the age of sixteen in *c*.1845 and worked in Philadelphia for the Scottish-born architect John Notman (1810–65). Later he moved to Chicago but, in 1867, returned to Philadelphia, where he died in 1902.[7]

Peter Angelo Nicholson had been born in 1829. He was one of Michael Angelo Nicholson's ten children and thus the younger brother both of Thomson's wife Jane and of Jessie, the wife of his sometime partner, John Baird – both architects married in a combined ceremony in 1847. And Michael Angelo Nicholson, of course, was the draughtsman son of that great producer of architectural books, Peter Nicholson, whose widely influential titles were also published in the United States. The first of several American editions of *The Carpenter's New Guide* appeared in Philadelphia in 1818 and Nicholson's other principal books were published in either Philadelphia or New York over the following two decades. As Talbot Hamlin, the historian of Greek Revival architecture in America, has written, 'It is difficult to overestimate the great debt which the American architectural builders owed Nicholson for the excellence of much of their technical equipment ...'[8]

This debt was usually acknowledged but seldom paid, in cash. British books were regularly pirated in the United States in the absence of effective copyright law, as many Victorian writers such as Dickens and Ruskin had cause to complain. Peter Nicholson suffered similarly. American architectural authors, not least Minard Lafever, made good use of his texts and illustrations, notably in *The Modern Practice of Staircase and Handrail Construction* of 1838. In his first book, *The Young Builder's General Instructor*, published in 1829, Lafever acknowledged a debt to both Stuart and Revett's *Antiquities of Athens* and Nicholson, while in *The Beauties of Modern Architecture* of 1835 he praised Nicholson's *Carpenter's New Guide* as having 'none superior to it' as well as acknowledging the usefulness of Elmes, Gwilt, Stuart and Revett and the *Encyclopaedia Brittanica*. When, following the death of Michael Angelo Nicholson in 1842 and of old Peter Nicholson two years later, Peter Angelo Nicholson arrived in Philadelphia, he must soon have become aware of the good use Minard

Lafever had made of his grandfather's books – to the possible pecuniary disadvantage of the Nicholson family. It is likely, therefore, that young Nicholson would have acquired copies of Lafever's publications in Philadelphia and then sent them to his brother-in-law in Glasgow, who was, through marriage, the Nicholson dynasty's principal architectural legatee in the British Isles.

Alexander Thomson seems to have made productive use of those books. He surely recognised in them the innovations of an imaginative architectural mind. For Minard Lafever was no copyist, nor an ordinary plagiarist. Hamlin describes him as 'fertile in imagination' and 'the greatest designer of architectural decoration of his time in America'.[9] It was the ability of pattern-book makers like Lafever and Asher Benjamin to develop Antique precedents, to invent and to stretch the conventional rules of proportion, that gave the peculiar rustic vigour to the American Greek Revival, which distinguishes it from run-of-the-mill European neoclassicism. Hamlin notes how the designs for doors, windows and other details reflected 'Lafever's true sense of Greek refinements expressed in new ways'.[10] The same could so often be said of Thomson.

This controlled originality surely appealed to the great Glaswegian. He was well familiar with the work of modern Scottish architects who made scholarly and appropriate use of the plates in the *Antiquities of Athens* but, while he insisted that such buildings in Glasgow were 'all very good', he complained that 'the promoters of the Greek revival ... failed; not because of the scantiness of the material, but because they could not see through the material into the laws upon which that architecture rested. They failed to master their style, and so became its slaves.'[11] Thomson, in contrast, was not a slave to Stuart and Revett – nor even, in the end, to Lafever – though he was clearly inspired by the happy invention displayed in the American's plates. Lafever, like Schinkel and John Martin, surely suggested possibilities.

The problem with Lafever, and Thomson, is only today's problem, for we have a crude and unsophisticated notion of originality in architecture. We overvalue the self-consciously inventive, even if it is inappropriate, vulgar and unsophisticated; often, we do not even recognise that it has been done before. Living in an ill-educated and unscholarly age, we do not know our precedents and so misinterpret unfamiliar gestures. So we vaunt the apparent originality of Mackintosh, choosing not to recognise his roots in multifarious traditions, while undervaluing Thomson both because of his unashamed eclecticism and his employment of apparently conventional Classical forms. But because we have forgotten how to speak that language well, we often do not recognise brilliant innovation and sophistication when it appears.

To understand that Thomson's stealing from Lafever indicates high sophistication and originality on the part of *both* designers, it is perhaps necessary to see this architecture through the eyes of his contemporaries. Towards the base of the west face of the campanile of the Caledonia Road church (see FIGURE 15.1) is a window bisected by a central square pier supporting an intermediate transom. This is a developed form of a conventional Thomson motif and one which may have been influenced by Lafever (like the main doorcases). Ultimately, however, it was inspired by Stuart and Revett's plate of the Choragic Monument of Thrasyllus – except that it is placed within a Lafeverish architrave frame and enhanced by a superimposed cornice on flanking console brackets. Description makes the motif seem complex, yet it may appear to be comparatively unremarkable and certainly attracts little notice or comment these days compared with the surviving abstracted Schinkelesque elements of that sad ruin.

Yet, for his contemporary Thomas Gildard, it was a 'boldly-designed window which, when the works of Thomson were few, I looked upon as the grandest individual architectural mere part that I had ever seen either on paper or in execution'. Praise indeed; and we need the learned and informed eloquence of Gildard (who may, or may not, have known his Lafever) fully to understand what Thomson was about. For he continued, 'It is not a two-light window, but a one-light window divided into two by a pilaster with antae supporting a cornice which serves as a transom. This pilaster, with antae and cornice within a magnificent architrave, with frieze and cornice supported by trusses, is characterised no less by great power and beauty than by novelty.'[12]

Novelty! True novelty: invention and unprecedented combination within a tradition and informed by function and propriety. That is what Thomson must have recognised in the felicitous mutations found in Minard

Lafever's books. And it is the quality that distinguishes Thomson's work from the noble but chilling correctness of so much British neoclassicism. All architects, ancient and modern, must be judged by their cribs, for no architect, ever, anywhere, is uninfluenced by the work of others. Nothing can come of nothing. Thomson evidently chose his sources well; perhaps it was he who suggested to Blackie, his publisher client, that a telling quotation from Sir Joshua Reynolds' *Discourses* should be printed on the title page of *Villa and Cottage Architecture*: 'Invention is one of the great marks of genius; but if we consult experience, we shall find that it is by being conversant with the inventions of others that we learn to invent; as by reading the thoughts of others we learn to think.'

ACKNOWLEDGEMENT

The link between Minard Lafever and Alexander Thomson was suggested by Andor Gomme, who wrote the first part of this essay.

NOTES

1. For Lafever, see Jacob Landy, *The Architecture of Minard Lafever*, New York, 1970.
2. Lafever's books were catalogued by Henry-Russell Hitchcock in his *American Architectural Books*, New York, 1976. That they were little known in Britain is suggested by the fact that the RIBA Library seems to have acquired any in the 19th century.
3. M. Lafever, *The Beauties of Modern Architecture*, New York, 1835, p. 38.
4. Ibid. (1968 facsimile reprint, New York), p. vii.
5. Henry-Russell Hitchcock, *Early Victorian Architecture*, London and New Haven, 1954, vol. I, p. 341.
6. Tom Thomson, architect in St Louis, Missouri, possesses a New Year card sent to George Alexander Thomson – from Glasgow, in January 1874 – by an Alexander Thomson whose signature could well be Greek Thomson's. Mr Thomson also has a coloured hand-drawn sheet of Greek ornament which may have come from the same source. However, these American relations must have been distant ones as the Thomsons identified by the Genealogical Society of the Church of Jesus Christ of the Latter Day Saints do not seem to connect with Greek Thomson's family in the immediately preceding generations. Tom Thomson kindly informs us that his forebear, George Alexander Thomson, seems to have been both a cabinet-maker and builder in New York (and so might have used

Lafever?) before he moved to California where he was living in 1874; later he moved back to Wisconsin.

7. According to an unidentified obituary pasted into Mrs W. L. Stewart's MS memoir of the Thomson family.

8. Talbot Hamlin, *Greek Revival Architecture in America,* London and New York, 1944, p. 340.

9. Ibid., pp. 349 and 147.

10. Ibid., p. 353.

11. A. Thomson, Haldane Lectures, III (1874), Mitchell Library, Glasgow, p. 8.

12. Thomas Gildard, 'Greek Thomson': paper read before the Architectural Section of the Philosophical Society of Glasgow, 30 January 1888, *Proceedings of the Royal Philosophical Society of Glasgow*, vol. XIX (1888), pp. 191–210; and published as pamphlet, pp. 7–8.

FIGURE 16.1   The St Vincent Street church, Bath Street and
the grid street plan of Glasgow.

Chapter Sixteen

FRONTIERS OF THE WEST – GLASGOW AND CHICAGO

THE PIONEERING ARCHITECTURES OF THOMSON, MACKINTOSH AND WRIGHT

Andrew MacMillan

A tight and most un-English tenement town, Glasgow can be seen to be Scottish in the totality of its stone fabric, European in its urban pedigree, and American in its gridiron plan (see FIGURE 16.1). It has a unique integrity and singular identity among the cities of Britain, which may stem from the fact that it is almost entirely a Victorian and Edwardian construct.

Streetwise in every sense, uncompromising in the rigour of its hard-nosed, hard-surfaced fabric, and ventilated in the Haussmann tradition by great urban parks, its greatest period of building occurred in Victoria's reign when the city expanded explosively to meet the needs of its burgeoning engineering and chemical industries and its empire-wide commerce.

New buildings proliferated to suit and serve its emerging industrial society, and much of historic Glasgow disappeared at that time as the city fathers – responding simultaneously to the growing demands of commerce and industry, and a desperate need for modern hygiene in the wake of horrific cholera epidemics – swept away the twisting streets and overcrowded slums of the old city, and inserted a rationally planned fabric, a fresh-water supply and sewage system, public utilities and a public transport system which all made it, for a time, the finest provided-for modern city in Europe.

At precisely the same time on the western plains of America, the city of Chicago was being built in response to similar pressures, this time in a 'green field' rather than a *tabula rasa* situation, but employing the identical urban devices of grid and block, and exploiting the same modern technologies in the doing.

Both cities too, hard cored and densely built up, were constructing new leafy suburbs for an enlightened middle class demanding a healthier disease-free environment, made possible initially by horse-drawn trams and later the steam commuter trains and electric trams and subways, which encouraged the wider colonisation of the surrounding countryside.

Uncoincidently, in each city, architects of stature arose whose works responded to and in turn shaped the new urban lifestyle which was evolving. Glasgow's Alexander Thomson (1817–75) and Charles Rennie Mackintosh (1868–1928), and Chicago's Frank Lloyd Wright (1867–1959) stand out – even in a milieu of talented and innovative architects of the stature of Burnam, Root and Sullivan in Chicago, and Salmon, Miller and Burnet in Glasgow – as figures who grasped the architectural implications in the frenetic building of the times.

Thomson was the earliest, a mid-century front runner, interpreting the needs of Glasgow's new industrial society within the terms of reference of a rationalised traditional construction and the tenets of classical architecture, adhering as he thought, to the 'principles' of Greek architecture, rather than indulging in an 'exquisite' architecture involving the replication of Greek temples adapted to secular or Christian use. In his many tenement and terrace blocks, he brought the art of street architecture and the development of the serial urban façade to a fine pitch and his 'landmark' churches rank as major monuments of the Romantic movement.

He developed the concept of what, in the twentieth century, came to be called the curtain wall in his great Victorian office and warehouse developments (Dunlop Street (1859) (see FIGURE 3.7), the Grecian Chambers (1865) (see FIGURE 9.21), the Egyptian Halls (1871)

FIGURE 16.2   Holmwood, Cathcart.

(see FIGURE 9.6), etc.), and effectively anticipated Wright's Prairie House of the 1890s in Holmwood House (1857) (see FIGURE 16.2) and the Double Villa (1856) (see FIGURE 8.12).

Mackintosh, at the turn of the century, was arguably the most significant modern architect in Europe, and Windyhill (1900) and Hill House (1902) are among the greatest houses of the twentieth century; his Art Lover's House portfolio (1901) (see FIGURE 16.12) decisively influenced the development of 'Functional Architecture' in Europe, while in his Glasgow School of Art he exhibited, unequivocally, a true modern architecture, free of historic precedent or canon, deriving solely from purpose, context and the nature of the building process itself.

In Chicago his great contemporary, Frank Lloyd Wright, consciously rejected history (European history in particular) to seek an American architecture which would grow out of the American prairie, responding to America's egalitarian society and its means of construc-

tion. Unlike the Glaswegians, his was an entirely suburban architecture. Wright never seriously engaged with the concept of urbanism, though in his later Broad Acre City proposals he demonstrated the implications of the motor-car suburb in possibly a truer understanding of mid-twentieth-century urban development than that of the more persuasive 'Heroic Moderns'.

It is especially useful to consider the work of these three men at this present time of cultural retrenchment and loss of faith. Belief in the causal nature of architecture is reaffirmed by the discovery of significant commonalities in their works, despite on the one hand an ocean, and on the other a generation separating them. The nature of architecture, its role in the ordering of the human habitat, and its importance in the manifestation of cultural values is seen to follow from principle rather than aesthetic whim, and clear anticipation of the social and technical thrust of the later Modern movement can be seen in their intentions.

In discussing them, it is interesting too, to relate

FIGURE 16.3 Nithsdale Street and Nithsdale Road,
Strathbungo; the tenement with the cylindrical acute corner
was by Thomson & Turnbull, 1875.

their work to the contemporary English House movement, generally held to be the precursor of the Modern
movement proper. Philip Webb's and William Morris's seminal Red House was built in 1859, two years
after Holmwood, and three after the Langside Double
Villa. The Red House has been hailed as revolutionary,
marking the real start of a movement which stimulated
the search for modern architecture throughout Europe
and America, but which had run its course by the turn
of the century and was sinking into the picturesque – or
even returning to historicism with Webb and Lutyens's
'Wrenaissance'. At this point, as Muthesius has
pointed out, Mackintosh and his group took up the
baton for progress, with Windyhill and Hillhouse,
while in America, Wright's Prairie Houses entered
their classic phase.

THOMSON AND WRIGHT

Thomson's creative peak extended from the mid-1850s
to the mid-1870s, a period of intense building activity

in Glasgow, which not only saw the reconstruction and
densification of the city centre but the development of
outer suburbs and an outreach of commuting along the
down-river banks of the Clyde.[1]

The architectural offices of the time, particularly
those in which Thomson gained his training, and later
his own practice, were at the forefront of innovatory
developments in building, busily evolving the new
plate-glass, gas-lit, commercial offices, wholesale warehouse buildings, suburban terraces and villas, as well
as developing an urban vocabulary in the volume
production of Glasgow's traditional urban housing –
the tenement. A major building of churches was also
taking place as a consequence of the schismatic nature
of the Church of Scotland of the day. It was a busy and
fruitful time for architecture.

At the same time, building methods were also subject to great innovation: the introduction of machinery
in the wake of steam, the use of blast furnace cement as
a consequence of iron production, and the use of iron
itself. New concepts of servicing also proliferated:

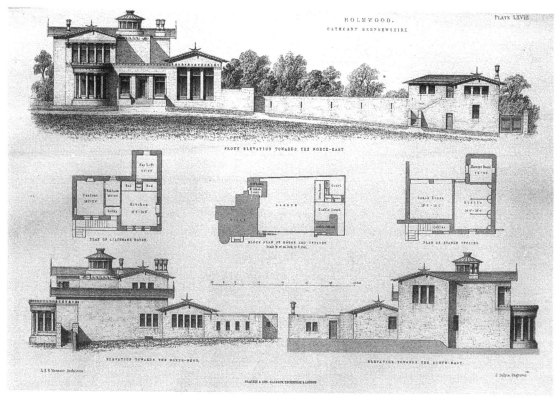

FIGURE 16.4   Elevations and block plan of Holmwood, from *Villa and Cottage Architecture*.

piped water, town gas, central heating and efficient sewage disposal were seen as essential to modern town life.

Thomson's suburban villas, although serving a new social class, were evolved within the context of traditional architecture; Thomson applied his interpretation of the principles of Greek architecture by developing a trabeated 'tectonic' system of ordering. He rejected the moralising and nostalgic craft-centred 'Gothic' revivalism of Ruskin and his followers in favour of a rational approach to masonry construction, which could accept the use of machinery and the structural possibilities of the new technologies and materials. This was an attitude also to be adopted by Mackintosh and Wright, but by 1869 Thomson was confidently looking forward to an end to revivals and styles, when, in his own words, 'Architecture would be judged on its own merits, for a change is not only quite practicable but absolutely inevitable.' He went on to say that 'the architect would avail himself of the pro-

FIGURE 16.5   The Darwin D. Martin house, Buffalo, New York, by Frank Lloyd Wright, 1904–5.

ducts of machinery and every contrivance to cheapen and facilitate the spread of correct forms'.[2]

In the field of urban architecture, he had a grasp of the essential nature of street architecture within the European urban tradition, and in his tenements and terraces he continuously experimented with the elevational implications of longer streets and the need for a

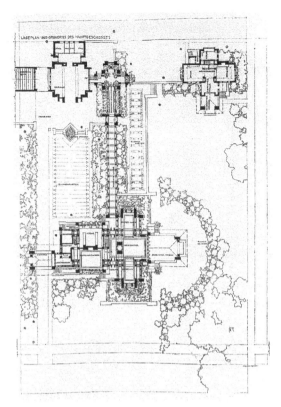

FIGURE 16.6   Ground plan of the Darwin D. Martin house.

naturalistic garden of the plot, and in the case of the bigger houses – e.g. Holmwood (1857) (see FIGURE 16.4) and Darwin D. Martin (see FIGURES 16.5 and 16.6) (1904) – to thrust out connections to the smaller buildings and gateways to organise and control the entire site. Reciprocally, both men intended the landscape to be part of the interior through large-window screens, often with similar planting outside and inside (for example, early photographs of the Double Villa, see FIGURE 8.2).

The internal arrangements of their houses employ strikingly similar devices, and there are unusual similarities of planning in the placing of the kitchens and dining-rooms on the ground floor, with the living-rooms above. The explicitness with which both use a string or cornice at door head height – to establish a horizontal datum above which the volumetric developments of the larger rooms can be fully developed and appreciated – is uncanny; both, too, utilise timber trim to make major and minor and sub-spaces specific places in a total spatial composition. Similar exploitation of toplit double-height volumes can also be seen in the circulation spaces.

Thomson's churches exhibit some of the same massing and geometric patterning of flat wall surfaces perforated by large trabeated openings and smaller linked windows, found in the Textile Block houses of Wright's 'Mayan' period in the 1920s. This is particularly noticeable in the St Vincent Street church (see FIGURE 4.1) and above all in Ballater Street church (see FIGURE 16.7), where the resemblance to Unity Chapel (see FIGURE 16.8) is striking.

This is a most interesting comparison and, sadly, one that we can now make from the few remaining photographs only. The formal similarities are immediately perceivable. Each consists of a larger and a smaller block, connected by a lower entrance wing, the blocks largely blank faced, with large central trabeated openings. The building was initially built in 1859, but was altered in 1872 when a wing was added and in 1896 after the new railway was widened across the site. Unfortunately there are no extant drawings of Ballater Street, the Dean of Guild record copies having been destroyed to make space for newer records – just before the value of such historic archives was realised.[3] The design for a small church and manse at Balfron (see FIGURE 16.9) show that Thomson was experimenting

city scale ordering. He was a magnificent player of the 'Glasgow Game', the camouflage of the serial imposition of identical floors behind an articulated, spectator-responsive exterior, inventively conforming to the classical *parti* of Base, Piano Nobile and Attic. Like Wren, he also recognised the role of the monument as a 'landmark' in the vast urban fabric, as the unique compositions of the towers of his city churches show.

It is in his response to the new problems of surburban building, however, the design of the individual family house on the leafy plot, that his approach to a modern architecture and the formal similarities of his building to Wright's are seen at their most striking.

Both Wright and Thomson, in their classic innovatory periods, employed low pitched roofs with wide, overhanging eaves, a horizontal emphasis in both massing and fenestration, and a geometric *parti* of major and minor axes. They both allowed their houses to reach out to possess the landscape through a series of low walls which engage, like jeweller's clasps, with the

FIGURE 16.7   The former Govan Street Free Church in
Ballater Street, photo c.1930.

with the idea of a total building subsuming the public as
well as the less public and private parts of the complex
in a single articulated mass.

Coming almost twenty years after Thomson, Wright
had overt intentions to create an American architecture. In this he was responding to the *Zeitgeist*, to
the spirit of the times, with Mackintosh in Scotland,
Guimard in France and Gaudi in Barcelona, for example, all explicitly seeking a new architecture appropriate to Scotland, France and Catalonia respectively,
following the example of the 'English House' in England.

Yet his resulting Prairie Houses bear an extraordinary resemblance to the mature Thomson villas.
Was this purely a coincidence; in his search for a 'new'
architecture, could Wright have been influenced by an
earlier architecture? In 1925, in the Dutch magazine
Wendingen, Louis Mumford perceptively remarked
that Wright's architecture struck a particular chord 'in

the Netherlands and on the plains of Prussia'.[4] Was this
a subconscious reference to Schinkel, whose trabeated
buildings also have similarities to those of Thomson
and Wright, particularly his Roman Bath and the
Gardener's House at Charlottenhof (1829–40) (see
FIGURE 16.10)? This is perhaps Schinkel's most striking 'romantic' image, possibly deriving from the plains
of Italy, but of particular interest in its adoption of
vernacular rather than classical form – a significant
innovation.

Thomson certainly, and Wright surely, must have
been aware of Schinkel, but whether or not the borrow-
ings were conscious is difficult to assess. These obvious
similarities, though, demand to be more fully explored.

THOMSON AND MACKINTOSH

It is relatively easy to see and develop similarities
between Thomson and Wright, and even between

FIGURE 16.8   Unity Temple, Oak Park, by Frank Lloyd
Wright, 1904–7.

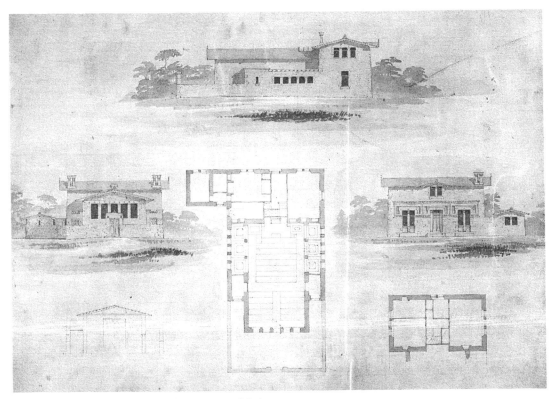

FIGURE 16.9   Elevations and plans of an unexecuted design
by Thomson for a combined church and manse, possibly at
Balfron.

FIGURE 16.10   The Court Gardener's Houser at Potsdam,
perspective and plan, first published in 1821, from
Schinkel's *Sammlung architektonischer Entwürfe*, 1866.

Mackintosh and Wright, but what of the two Glaswegians themselves (see FIGURE 16.11)? How do Thomson and Mackintosh relate?

Mackintosh had the early good fortune to tour Europe in the traditional way, sketch-book in hand, as a consequence of being awarded the Alexander Thomson Travelling Studentship of the Glasgow Institute of Architects (still available today for the study of Classical Architecture). His consciousness of Thomson's work would surely have been heightened by his applying for the scholarship, and perhaps this explains his concern not only with architectural form and space but with the 'elevation', that vital interface between the building and the public domain to which Thomson devoted so much energy.

Mackintosh's elevational approach normally goes unremarked, but the use of four different systems in four different elevations in the same building is not uncommon in his work (Glasgow School of Art and Windyhill, for example). Indeed, it may be a polemic characteristic of his work. Perhaps too, his high sensitivity to traditional architectural phenomena, his concern for the elaboration of the entrance, the base, the roof or top, the gable with its peak and shoulders, etc., also came out of his study of the older master.

Mackintosh's and Thomson's plans share a common, rational approach. Simple and direct, they constitute a mapping of carefully observed social activity rather than a canonic statement of architectural intent, lending themselves to an equally rational constructional development or, perhaps more strongly, deriving from an interaction of rational construction and human use.

FIGURE 16.11   Grecian Chambers and the Glasgow School
of Art, the only place left in Glasgow where buildings by
Thomson and Mackintosh stand side by side.

Above all, Thomson and Mackintosh have in common a firm grasp of the urban implications of building form, the need for interaction between the spectator in the street and the architectural object, something seen clearly in Mackintosh's schools – where the manifestation of memorable image, of front and subsidiary doors, of front and back even, occurs in a socially understandable way. Thomson's street façades and landmark towers have already been remarked upon.

Wright had little real philosophy of urbanity other than the aggregation and distribution of blocks: location in Broadacre City is on a par with that of LA today, a matter of number rather than place.

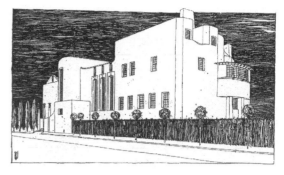

FIGURE 16.12   Perspective drawing of the unexecuted 'Haus eines Kunstfreundes' design by Mackintosh, 1901.

MACKINTOSH AND WRIGHT

In comparing the works of the Chicagoan and his Glasgow contemporary, similarities are less obvious and less formalistic than between Wright and Thomson, but fundamental parallels do appear.

Where Thomson had believed a new architecture would inevitably occur naturally, both Wright and Mackintosh consciously sought to create a new national architecture; where Thomson had pursued development within the European tradition, Mackintosh and Wright each strove to establish a modern architecture with internal rules of its own.

They were also liberated from historicism by the revelations of the newly discovered Arts of Japan. This was critical for their generation, who in Europe had also been able to read Ruskin, now in translation since his recent death, and thus similarly viewed nature as a prime source of ornament and form. They were influenced, too, by new magazines like *The Studio* and critics like Muthesius, who spread the gospel of the arts and crafts in England. Both Mackintosh and Wright flirted with the Arts and Crafts movements of their respective countries but found their attitudes to the machine unsympathetic, much in the same way as the earlier Thomson had rejected Pugin and the Ecclesiologists.

Mackintosh's solid stone and roughcast houses were in the tradition of Scotland's vertical, harled vernacular, while Wright's long horizontal timber-and-plaster villas grew out of the contemporary American 'shingle style' identified by Scully.

Both men's buildings had simple programmatic plans; both employed natural materials like brick, stone and timber (see the Bedford Lemere and Annan photographs of Mackintosh's work). Each moved towards an abstract concept of form: Mackintosh towards the cubist forms of the later Modern movement (compare the gables of the Art Lover's House (see FIGURE 16.12) with those of Hoffman or Loos); and Wright towards the destruction of the closed box, towards the hovering planes of, for example, Mies van der Rohe's Barcelona Pavilion.

Thomson's buildings contained their orchestrated spaces behind a disciplined Classical façade; Wright's within a controlled ordering of tectonic elements; Mackintosh identified the capacity of the vernacular building to allow free expression of its inner space, even to the extent of penetration or pushing through the outer skin, and raised it to a principle, which later directed the development of middle-European Modern towards a programmatic attack on form-generation.

Unity of interior space was another major characteristic, somewhat constrained by climate in Mackintosh's case, but manifestly clear in his halls and circulation spaces. His approach was freer and less obviously controlled than Wright's – perhaps a result of the greater sophistication of his formal architectural education; perhaps too of the influence of the recent 'English House' movement. Wright's more geometric approach may well have been conditioned by his early Froebel training and a resulting preoccupation with grids.

Wright also had a more developed grasp of the freedom conferred by machinery, and his employment of contemporary servicing systems permitted a more open architecture. He was able to dissolve the 'box' more thoroughly, more abstractly than Mackintosh, and like him, influenced development in central Europe – the Wasmuth portfolios confirming the direction stimulated some ten years earlier by the publication of Mackintosh's Art Lover's House portfolio in 1901.

Victorian by birth or context, all three were perhaps diverted by a belief in the necessity for ornament: trivial in Thomson's case, peripheral but not insignificant in Wright's, but curiously pervasive in the case of Mackintosh. Thomson's ornament was unsophisticated and simplistic, a repetitive use of traditional classical motifs like the anthemion and the Greek key pattern, adding little to his fame or his building. Wright and Mackintosh, on the other hand, aware of Ruskin, Morris and Japan in particular, consciously strove to develop integral ornament and decoration of their own invention.

Today, Mackintosh's decorative facility probably overshadows his (more major) contribution to the development and clarification of the direction Modern architecture took in the new century, and certainly continues to exercise the imagination of the public as well as of innovatory architects and furniture designers.

Mackintosh and Wright were both 'designers', a radical difference from Thomson. Although they shared his view of the necessity of the use of machinery, they had a much clearer understanding of the implications of machine production and the freedom it could confer on design. Trained as architects, both found a need to design everything connected with their buildings, from light switches to drapery, carpets to cutlery, even to the floral arrangements in the rooms. They employed a total, integrated approach, quite different from the *ad hoc* interior assemblages to be found in the contemporary English House. Here, the extra twenty years, the many International exhibitions and the new photogravure magazines may well have played a significant part; the pace of change in modern life was perhaps another factor.

Thus from 1893 on, working in Chicago and Glasgow (cities similar in size and nature), Wright and Mackintosh moved towards a role as designers seeking to create a new, total, architectural ambience in which their clients – the rising, liberated middle class – could flourish and live a convenient, comfortable life, a pro-

FIGURE 16.13   The Bowling Green Offices, New York, by W. & G. Audsley, 1899: Egyptian Halls taken to Manhattan and extended skywards.

cess started in Glasgow some forty years earlier by the relatively neglected Thomson.

NOTES

1. Thomson built in the inner suburbs of Langside and Pollokshields as well as fringe suburbs like Maryhill and the West End, outer commuter towns like Uddingston, Busby and Strathaven, and Clyde resorts like Langbank, Dumbarton, Helensburgh and Rothesay.

2. Thomson, 'Obstacles and Aids to Architectural Progress', 1869, quoted by McFadzean, *The Life and Work of Alexander Thomson*, London, 1979, p. 207.

3. For the enigmatic and complicated history of the Ballater Street church, see R. McFadzean and G. Stamp in *The Alexander Thomson Society Newsletter*, no. 7 (June 1993), pp. 6–9.

4. Lewis Mumford, 'The Social Back Ground of Frank Lloyd Wright', in *The Work of Frank Lloyd Wright*, New York, 1965, p. 78.

PERSPECTIVE

FIGURE 17.1   The view from the bay window of No. 1
Moray Place.

A VIEW FROM THE BAY WINDOW

Gavin Stamp

All who have studied works of art must have been struck by the mysterious power of the horizontal element ...

(A. Thomson, *Proceedings of the Glasgow Architectural Society* (1865–7), p. 54)

In the spring of 1861, Alexander Thomson and his family moved into No. 1 Moray Place (see FIGURE 17.1): one of the end houses in the remarkable terrace in Strathbungo he had designed and which had been built in the previous year next to the cutting containing the Glasgow, Neilston and Barrhead Direct Railway. He thus joined that select band of architects who have been prepared to live with their own work. 'Moray Place, Regent Park terrace' was the 44-year-old architect's first speculative venture, undertaken with John McIntyre, builder, and William Stevenson, 'quarrier', to exploit the amenity of the nearby Queen's Park – which had been acquired by the Corporation in 1857 and was being laid out by Paxton. According to local tradition, this first portion of Moray Place proved too expensive so that, although the rest of 'Regent Park' was built on the general lines established by the architect, the subsequent terraces were simpler and by another hand. The fact that Thomson took No. 1, and a friend, John Shields – a measurer – moved into No. 3 might possibly suggest that the development was not an immediate success. Nevertheless, Alexander Thomson stayed in Moray Place until he died there, on 22 March 1875.[1]

Moray Place consists of ten two-storeyed houses, with the two larger ones at the ends occupying the projecting temple-fronted bays terminating the unified composition. Behind the glazed bay of No. 1 are the large drawing- and dining-room. As elsewhere in the terrace (in which the interior details were standard and uniform), Thomson's dining-room was on the ground floor, with its black marble chimney-piece and a ceiling enlivened by a stylised sunburst. The drawing-room, with a white marble fireplace and elaborate star-spangled ceiling, was upstairs on the first floor. Moray Place faces north–north-west and for much of the year its ashlar façade is in permanent shade. In the summer months, however, the evening sun can pour through the large plate-glass windows between Thomson's giant order of square columns supporting the pediment to flood his drawing-room with golden light.

If, as I believe is the case, the sash windows here were originally hung like those in the Double Villa and at Holmwood – as Thomson describes in the text of *Villa and Cottage Architecture*[2] – the architect could have thrown them up some 4 feet 6 inches so that they would have half disappeared behind the cornice, leaving their bases level with the transom supporting the upper, smaller, fixed pane of glass, and allowing huge voids to appear between the four projecting structural piers. So, on a balmy summer evening, if all five sashes were fully opened, Thomson could perhaps imagine that he was no longer near the Clyde but transported to an open loggia by the Mediterranean, near whose shores stood all the buildings of Antiquity he most admired but whose heat and light he never experienced.

But most compelling is the view of the rest of the terrace from this projecting bay. The glory of Moray Place – 'finest of all Grecian terraces'[3] – is its precisely considered unity. Thomson carefully designed the ground-floor window and door openings so that they are of equal width and evenly spaced, while the upper

FIGURE 17.2   Moray Place, nineteenth-century photograph.

floor is unified by a continuous and equidistant colonnade of his favourite Schinkelesque square columns, or antae. Between these, every sixth interval is filled with stone, ornamented by a palmette, rather than a window. These blank bays mark the divisions between the houses. As Thomson was not subject to such legislation as the London Building Acts, which required party walls to rise 15 inches above the roof covering, the roof plane is continuous and the distinctiveness of each individual house is minimised, so that, when seen at an angle, Moray Place appears as a unified abstracted formal classical composition rather than as a terrace of ten separate dwellings. Unity is all – a very un-Victorian concern (see FIGURES 8.13 and 17.2).

From the side-window of the drawing-room bay, Thomson could gaze at fifty-two antae receding in sharp perspective, with the horizontal lines of the terrace dramatically converging until terminated by the opposite balancing projecting bay away to the west (see FIGURE 17.1). This noble prospect exemplifies Thomson's belief in the importance of the 'principle of repetition' and his insistence on the superiority of the horizontal character of the Classic as opposed to the vertical emphasis of the Gothic. As he wrote in 1866, in his attack on Gilbert Scott's designs for the University, 'All who have studied works of art must have been struck by the mysterious power of the horizontal element in carrying the mind away into space, and into speculations upon infinity. The pictures of Turner and of Roberts afford frequent examples of this. The expanding effect which is thus produced upon the mind cannot be overrated.'[4]

It is a strange combination of circumstances that has resulted in No. 1 Moray Place being the postal address of the Alexander Thomson Society – founded on the great man's birthday, 9 April, in 1991 – and my home. It is now I and my family who have the inestimable privilege of gazing from the first-floor side bay window down Thomson's colonnade and so experiencing the mysterious power of those long converging horizontal lines – now interrupted, unfortunately, by one insufferable rogue down-pipe. I naturally never thought, when I first visited Glasgow in 1968 as a 20-year-old student, that I would ever live in the city, let alone stay in Thomson's own house. But what is gratifying to me is that, when I paid that first visit, what I sought out were buildings both by Charles Rennie Mackintosh and by

Alexander Thomson – I have faded colour-slides to prove it.

Guided by the admirable *Glasgow at a Glance*, I picked my way through the Gorbals to see the Caledonia Road church. It was three years after the fire that destroyed its richly coloured and beautifully detailed interior, and the surviving masonry structure was clothed in scaffolding to effect repairs. What is distressing is that more of that sublime masonry has disappeared since. Indeed, I am haunted by the knowledge that on my early visits to Glasgow, had I known, I could have seen more buildings by Thomson that have been so stupidly and wickedly destroyed. Every day I pass an empty site in Eglinton Street (see FIGURES 8.1 and 8.14), enclosed by advertisement hoardings, where until as late as 1981 Thomson's finest tenement stood: Queen's Park Terrace. Those fatuous advertisements are insulting: how could the responsible authorities have allowed such a building to go so recently, and only to be replaced by ... nothing?[5] Equally poignant is the nearby site in Langside Road, where a mediocre block of flats – in the repulsive yellow brick typical of modern Glasgow – stands, for here stood the extraordinary Queen's Park church (see FIGURE 13.2). At least that was destroyed by a German bomb unlike the poor Caledonia Road church, 'one of the greatest nineteenth-century buildings anywhere', as Andor Gomme put it, which, 'in a way only too characteristic of Glasgow ... after years of ill-treatment amounting to dereliction, has in 1965 been, almost casually, gutted by fire ...'.[6]

The year 1968, of course, saw Glasgow's self-hating frenzy at its height, and in the campaign to wipe out the nineteenth-century city, Thomson's work inevitably perished. His career was so much more central to Victorian Glasgow than that of Mackintosh, the tangential artistic individualist. Furthermore, the revival of interest in Mackintosh was also well under way, already eclipsing the once-greater reputation of the older architect, who was then scarcely fashionable in the city. So why did I seek out buildings by Greek Thomson on that first visit? I think it must have been Henry-Russell Hitchcock's Pelican history of *Architecture: Nineteenth and Twentieth Centuries* that stimulated my interest, and I am glad that I recognised something extraordinary and powerful in his illustration of the Caledonia Road church (see FIGURE 5.1) –

something of the quality and feeling that I then so admired in the great Victorian Goths: Street, Butterfield and Teulon – that made me want to see the sad ruin.

Russell Hitchcock deserves honorable mention in the historiography of Greek Thomson. Americans are often more responsive to his architecture than Europeans: perhaps it is owing to the American character and orientation of Glasgow as well as the American feeling of many of Thomson's buildings – or, rather, the decidedly Thomsonian air of, in particular, the early work of Frank Lloyd Wright.[7] Certainly Hitchcock provides the most hyperbolic quotations about Thomson, putting him in a global perspective when he wrote how he built 'three of the finest Romantic Classical churches in the world' (even if we might quibble over Hitchcock's notion of 'Romantic Classical'). And it is peculiarly gratifying to find that, in *Early Victorian Architecture*, Hitchcock considered that Moray Place is 'with little question the finest of all 19th century terraces, both in design and execution, and one of the world's most superb pieces of design based on Greek precedent' – although I might dispute the extent to which it is actually 'Greek' in inspiration.[8]

Glaswegians now speak of the long-awaited revival of interest in Thomson, but, from an English perspective, he has never been forgotten. The present Thomson bibliography may be small compared with the literature devoted to Mackintosh, but there is no shortage of intelligent tributes by English architects and critics. They begin at the turn of the century, which is significant. Articles on Thomson by Reginald Blomfield and David Barclay appeared in the *Architectural Review* in 1904, which was the very year when John Burnet was invited south to design the extension to the British Museum in London as no English architect seemed up to the job. It was a time when English architects were reviving the Grand Manner, after the decades of Gothic and licentious eclecticism, and they were seeking legitimacy in the missing links between early Victorian classicism and the present. It was also a time when English architects were in awe of Scottish sophistication and continuity within the classical tradition – and Thomson now seemed a crucial figure: the only man who developed the Greek Revival creatively in the mid-nineteenth century, happily oblivious of what was happening outside Scotland.

Reginald Blomfield, that architectural bruiser who was a better critic than designer, made remarkable claims for Thomson: that he 'was possibly the most original thinker in architecture of the nineteenth century ... born with a deep and tenacious instinct for form ...' and that, 'while most of his contemporaries were scratching about in the rubbish-heaps of mediaeval detail, Thomson was soaring aloft in the spacious solitudes of pure architecture ... where Thomson was strong, with a strength sometimes amounting to genius, was in his mastery of abstract form ...'.[9] This encomium was followed in 1910 by an article by Lionel Budden of the Liverpool School of Architecture, that hotbed of neo-neoclassicism; and, four years after that, by both Trystan Edwards's article and Albert Richardson's eulogy in the culminating published product of neoclassical revisionism, *Monumental Classical Architecture in Great Britain and Ireland during the Eighteenth and Nineteenth Centuries*. Both these writers used Thomson to justify the modern 'neo-Grec' they favoured.

'Neo-Grec' is a subjective, imprecise term. For Joseph Addison, the Head of the Leeds School of Architecture who had won the RIBA's Athens Bursary in 1931, it meant Greek Revival and for him, 'in the application of Greek principles of design, the Neo-Grec architects failed miserably'. Yet, in his published report on his investigations into Greek architecture, he could nevertheless maintain that, 'strangely enough, the nearest approach to the Greek ideal during the Neo-Classic period is to be found in the work of the late Alexander Thomson, of Glasgow, an architect of remarkable originality'. Having listed the 'essentially Greek characteristics' in his work, this Scottish architect could then boldly claim, even at this date, that, 'The work of "Greek" Thomson does not only mark the zenith of the Neo-Classic movement in Britain, but heralds the coming of a new age when the art of architecture will be based on a tradition of "motives" and not a tradition of "appearances" ... [his works] can be a true inspiration to the student, an inspiration more readily assimilated if less potent than that derived from study of the architecture of Ancient Greece.'[10]

It must be admitted that some commentators on Thomson – and ones I much admire – were not uncritical. Even Budden, although adulatory, considered that in the Egyptian Halls (see FIGURE 9.6), 'Thomson exhibits a depravity of taste of which he was never subsequently guilty upon so large a scale', chiefly because he had never enjoyed 'the advantage of a consistent drill in the principles of Classic design'[11] – such as he could have enjoyed, no doubt, studying under Professor Reilly in Liverpool. Trystan Edwards was more qualified in his praise and, evidently having just read Geoffrey Scott's *Architecture of Humanism* which was first published in that same year, 1914, felt it necessary to accuse Thomson of having fallen victim to 'the symbolic fallacy'. Edwards's generation was reacting violently against Ruskin and he could not tolerate Thomson's belief that certain architectural forms, like the 'pyramid, the obelisk and the rudimentary temple form', had intrinsic moral qualities and represented 'unchangeableness, justice and goodness'. Indeed, for Edwards, this was 'sheer Ruskinism' except that it was directed to justifying classical rather than Gothic architecture. (Interestingly, Edwards also compared the eccentricities of Thomson's Queen's Park church with the recent work of Joseph Olbrich at Darmstadt, describing it as 'L'Art Nouveau with a Greek or Egyptian dressing'.[12]

Thirty-five years later, in his celebrated lecture on 'Rogue Architects of the Victorian Era', H. S. Goodhart-Rendel could include Thomson (wrongly, I think) as a 'rogue elephant' along with such Gothic eccentrics as E. B. Lamb, F. W. Pilkington and Joseph Peacock, and Arts and Crafts individualists like James MacLaren and E. S. Prior. Although he admired him for his 'savage and lonely acts' outside the herd, Rendel concluded that, 'Taking his work in the mass, we cannot, I think, call Thomson a great architect, but we can call him with truth one having great originality of outlook, and great skill in architectural picture-making. With a little less attention to style and a little more attention to propriety, he might have proved no rogue but a leader.'[13] In Goodhart-Rendel's brilliant discussion of *English Architecture since the Regency*, finally published in 1953, Thomson only receives passing mention, but it is a flattering one, claiming that 'some villas designed by Alexander Thomson ... are as interesting houses as any that of the nineteenth century produced [*sic*]; they are, unhappily, few, and so peculiar to Thomson's idiosyncracy that none of the attempts of others to follow him have resulted in anything but failure.'[14]

FIGURE 17.3   Great Western Terrace, photograph *c.*1955.

The most perceptive and sympathetic English admirer of Thomson's work was undoubtedly Albert Richardson. Twenty years after he published *Monumental Classic Architecture*, he discussed Thomson and the classical tradition in the long chapter on architecture he contributed to G. M. Young's two-volume survey of *Early Victorian England 1830–1865*. 'Even towards the mid-Victorian period,' Richardson believed,

> *the classicists were tenacious of their beliefs and became more suspicious of innovations, hence the disapproval which greeted the highly original designs of Alexander Thomson, which show a wide divergence of character from those of the Greek or Italian schools. Alexander Thomson was more ambitious than his contemporaries; he attempted with some degree of force to combine Hellenic, Egyptian and Hindoo motives, and the Church of St. Vincent [sic], Glasgow, which shows the working of his mind, is an outstanding example. A master of abstract form, he outdistanced Soane in the higher flights of originality; never condescending to trivialities, he thought of details as integral to grandiose design ... His work vindicated the purpose of the earlier classic school, and at the eleventh hour, when classicality seemed finally doomed, he revived it in the streets and high places of Glasgow. A man of artistic courage, he was appalled at the confusion around him, and he sought for a way out of the maze by inventing a new classical style, never dreaming it to be an accomplishment beyond the power of a single artist ... Towards the end of his career he designed and built the fine group of Glasgow houses known as Great Western Terrace. Here he showed the greatest restraint and it is no exaggeration to say that a finer example of Victorian architecture of similar character does not exist.*[15]

This praise of Great Western Terrace (see FIGURE 17.3), together with Hitchcock's discussion of Thomson in *Early Victorian Architecture*, raises the question as to what extent Thomson's work can usefully be described as 'Victorian' in any sense other than the chronological. For the whole fascination of Thomson is that he was out on a limb, apparently unaffected by the dominant tendencies in Victorian architecture. Here we meet the fundamental divide between England and Scotland in the nineteenth century. In England, the major cultural achievement of the mid-Victorian years was undoubtedly the Gothic Revival. All the brightest and best talents joined the crusade proclaimed by Pugin. Scotland was different, however, and it seems to me that the Gothic Revival here was, if not peripheral, certainly secondary and its practitioners demonstrated none of the invention and sophistication shown by Butterfield and Street. I can admire the solidity and scholarship of Rowand Anderson's work and the medievalism of John Honeyman but, to my English eyes, the most interesting exponent in Scotland of the Gothic was the English-born F. W. Pilkington, who produced wild and highly creative solutions to the liturgical exigencies of Scottish Presbyterianism which are in marked contrast to the generally starved and miserable interiors of Gothic Protestant churches in the North. And religion, of course, is the key: Scotland was resistant to the close association between Christianity and the Gothic proclaimed by the Roman-Catholic Pugin and the High Anglican Ecclesiological movement. It is not surprising, therefore, that in the mid-century, the Episcopal Church of Scotland tended to turn to English Gothic Revivalists.

Thomson, of course, after initial and uninspired experiments in a secular Gothic mode, came utterly to despise both the style and the arrogant moral and functional claims of its proponents. Thomson's lecture attacking Gilbert Scott's design for the University of Glasgow, delivered in 1866, is not just the most trenchant and fearless criticism of the theoretical claims for the superiority of the Gothic made by Pugin, Ruskin and Scott himself, but almost the only one, for in England, classicists were of an older generation and largely demoralised. This astonishingly outspoken attack (by today's mealy-mouthed standards) by one member of the profession on another was, of course, born of outrage, for the University's choice of architect not only represented a betrayal of Scotland's dominant stylistic tradition but also denied any local architect the chance of designing one of the most important public buildings likely to be raised in Glasgow in the foreseeable future. Indeed, having disposed of the site and buildings of the second-oldest university in Scotland, the dons compounded that crime by a culpable lack of nerve – after all, even if Gothic was considered to be more learned and academical than classic, Scotland also could provide expert practitioners in Baronial.

The decision to go, without competition, to a fashionable London architect can be regarded as marking the beginning of Glasgow's long, sad decline in self-confidence even if, paradoxically, it predates the apogee of the Second City's wealth and architectural splendour.

Even though he shared with Ruskin an essentially moral and theological view of architecture, Thomson evidently regarded the English critic's pervasive influence with suspicion. Their views, indeed, of what constituted architecture were diametrically opposed – not only in terms of style but in the essential matter of the treatment of solid and void. For Ruskin, the essence of Gothic was not only naturalistic detail but also the emphasis given to the shape of a window opening. In an eloquent passage in *The Seven Lamps of Architecture*, he discussed the high point of Gothic before its supposed decline into Late Decorated and degenerate Perpendicular, and how, in the best work, 'the attention is kept fixed on the forms of the penetrations, that is to say, of the lights as seen from the interior, not of the intermediate stone'. After that, the tracery '*caught the eye* of the architect' and this was 'the great watershed of Gothic art. Before it, all had been ascent; after it, all was decline … The change of which I speak, is expressible in few words; but one more important, more radically influential, could not be. It was the substitution of the *line* for the *mass*, as the element of decoration.'[16]

In contrast, Thomson maintained that the essence of architecture was mass and structure, and in his fourth Haldane Lecture, he echoed the apocalyptic certainty as well as the eloquence of Ruskin in his contrary argument not only that 'the adoption of the arch by the Romans has strewed Europe with ruins' but also that, 'While the Egyptians and the Greeks bestowed their chief attention upon the solid parts of their buildings (see FIGURE 8.11), the Romans and Goths adopted the openings as the principal objects of their concern' . In consequence,

The progress of art was henceforth to take the opposite direction … We are inclined to think that the Romans deserve the credit of fully adopting fenestration as an architectural principle as distinguished from the columnar, which had been growing all through the early ages of the world down to its perfect development on the Acropolis of Athens. The great importance of this change will at once appear when it is pointed out to you that from henceforth the attention of the architect was to be directed to the voids instead of the solid part of his structure.

Thomson had no doubt that a straight-headed opening was always superior to the (for him) problematic arch and that, 'the lintelled window, from being the most self-contained, and at the same time more in sympathy with the prevailing horizontality of buildings in general, is by far the most tractable of the two kinds'.[17] What better proof of that than Moray Place (see FIGURE 17.2)? Furthermore, the great sheets of plate glass that afford such fine views from the bay window exemplify Thomson's belief that a void should be appreciated only as a gap between active structural elements. So the fixed upper panes run straight into the masonry while the lower sliding sashes have the narrowest possible frame and but one thin vertical glazing bar. The ultimate development of this structural aesthetic are the windows in the St Vincent Street church (see PLATE IV), which are but sheets of glass fixed directly into the masonry, and the metal-framed glazing strip placed far behind the exotic upper colonnade on the Egyptian Halls (see FIGURE 9.1). Columns must perform as columns and astragals are inimical to real architecture.

Thomson had certainly read his Ruskin and could not fail to admire much about him; after all, they had a God-fearing Protestant background in common. 'There is no writer on Art half so well known as is Mr. Ruskin,' he said in 1874,

no one more eloquent or more amiable, no one who has said more good and true things about Art, who has had a more loving regard for the beauties of Nature, or a more sincere reverence for the God of Nature, no one who can so readily, so pleasantly, and so instructively translate what he sees in Nature and Art into plain language, so that all men may read and thereby become sharers with him in those pure and noble pleasures which his sensitive and exquisitely refined mind seems to imbibe from all the springs of truth. And yet I know no one who has done more to mislead the public mind in matters of Art than he ...

Which is why he devoted so much of his first Haldane Lecture to showing 'the absurdity of the doctrines of those teachers of Art who hold that because Nature is the work of God it must therefore be perfect, and that it is impious for man to presume that he may begin where the Creator has left off ...'.[18]

For Thomson believed strongly in the creative purpose of the 'aesthetic faculty'.

Some say that man can never get beyond his experience. Whence then come Music and Architecture? There is nothing in Nature like either; for although they have been slow of growth, the fact is before us that they are something that by man or through his agency has been added to the work of God, and that, not presumptuously or sinfully, as some would tell us, but by destiny and duty; for being made in the image of God, man was made partaker of the divine nature so far as to become a fellow-worker with God – in however humble a sense, a co-Creator.[19]

This is of great importance, as it explains why Thomson believed in progress in art, in refinement and formalisation. An imitative naturalism had no place in his architecture, in contrast to that of those architects who were Ruskin's disciples.

In the work of, say, Gilbert Scott, Woodward or Street in England, or Pilkington in Scotland, immense pains were taken to employ talented artists to carve elaborate capitals and other carefully considered areas of ornamentation in a charmingly naturalistic manner – all vital and varied as illuminated by the 'Lamp of Life'. But the aims of such craftsmanship were of no concern whatever to Thomson. His ornament, whether incised, cast or painted, was deliberately repetitive. The cast plaster details on the ceilings in Moray Place, for instance, use precisely the same stock of motifs as appear in the Double Villa, Holmwood (see FIGURE 11.9) and elsewhere. Andy MacMillan aptly describes Thomson's ornament as 'trivial and mechanical'.[20] It is. What matters is the overall effect; details are secondary to the whole. There was no need to invent any new ornament (here is the fundamental contrast with Mackintosh) for that provided by the Ancient World (and so usefully catalogued by Owen Jones) was perfectly satisfactory and served Thomson's purpose. More important was the 'principle of repetition': hence fifty-two identical square columns in a row, each embellished with the same simple incised key pattern.

All this may make Thomson's work seem utterly removed from that of his High-Victorian Gothic contemporaries, yet there are intriguing similarities. These are not just in such attitudes as Thomson's cheerful eclecticism, or in his Picturesque, or 'Romantic Classical' taste for asymmetrically placed towers, but go much deeper. The 'Vigorous Style', the work of the most adventurous English Gothic designers – inspired by Ruskin and informed by French and Italian precedents – demonstrated an aesthetic that sought simplification and abstraction. There was a paramount emphasis on the integrity of the unbroken wall, accompanied by an elimination of detail proud of that plane. Ornament – and sculpture – was incised, and window openings were punched into the wall. This is an aesthetic that is concerned with pure geometrical forms. It may have been influenced, in particular, by the rugged simplicity of French thirteenth-century Gothic, rather than by the massive forms of the Egyptians, but a similarity of mood, of aesthetic intent between, say, Street and the young Bodley in England and Thomson in Scotland is discernible.

The emphasis on the integrity of the wall plane and the delight in vast unbroken masses of wall – often treated with a batter – unites Thomson with the English Vigorous Goths. This shared aesthetic produced other similar expressions. Thomson sometimes played with two wall planes on his domestic buildings, giving the lower plane a high haunch, or shoulder, sometimes not far below the eaves. This plane would then be developed into his typical pilasters, or piers, or, on side elevations, be terminated according to a personal, mannered sensibility. Yet a similar high shoulder can be found on several of Street's vicarages of the 1860s. Thomson also shared with Street at his most 'Vigorous' a predilection for short, fat columns, which appear as if compressed by the weight of masonry above. Perhaps these similarities between the lone Glaswegian neoclassicist and the advanced English Goths are not that surprising: all, after all, were not interested in the beautiful but in the *Sublime*. This may explain why Billy Burges, of all people, felt able to praise Thomson's designs.[21] Whether Thomson was influenced by their work cannot be demonstrated: we know he visited London and he cannot have failed to see illustrations of their creations in *The Builder* and other professional journals. But we have no proof, and it may be too easy

merely to attribute these similarities to the *Zeitgeist*, to the spirit of the age.

Yet there is something peculiar and remarkable about the way Thomson treats his walls, which may well result from his careful study of the massive, solid forms of Egyptian architecture. Even when treated as unbroken planes of stone, they are not static. Rather, they have a dynamic quality, which comes from performing a structural task. This is particularly evident on the side-elevation of the St Vincent Street church. Below the range of windows lighting the aisles, with their powerful rhythm created by the snaking forms of structurally distinct lintels and architraves, is a great wedge of stone taking the steep slope of Pitt Street – a man-made Acropolis. This wall is truly Sublime, composed of huge pieces of stone laid on a distinct slope, or batter. This great plane of magnificent masonry is broken at a lower level by but one architectural feature, a side-door, which serves to emphasise the bareness of the rest of the masonry (see FIGURE 17.4).

And what a door! It is a tripartite composition inspired by Egyptian precedents: a door and shorter flanking windows rising to the same lintel, all cut directly into this magnificent wall which runs continuously into the solid masonry under the windows and then up – still on the same place – into piers either side of (what should be) sheets of plate glass, so framing the door. All four tough, square piers then narrow before developing into exotic carved capitals which carry, not a simple lintel stone but an elaborate entablature supporting the massive weight of masonry above. All this is fully expressed and ornamented within a wide aperture seemingly incised into the wall. And the wonderful thing about this composition is that the resulting coved cornice emerges proud of the dominant wall plane. Here is a piece of happy mannerism, based on developed aesthetic logic, that never fails to delight once it is noticed. This door is surely one of the most inventive and powerfully composed details of the whole nineteenth century.

What, I think, makes Thomson's wall planes so dynamic is the feeling that they are not mere walls but an abstracted order, that beneath the outer skin is a hidden determining structural system of columns and lintels. Cut into that skin, and the order is there underneath, controlling and supporting. This is the essence of the door composition in the side-wall of

FIGURE 17.4 The Pitt Street entrance to the St Vincent
Street church.

HOLMWOOD,—CATHCART, RENFREWSHIRE.
A. & G. THOMSON, ARCHITECTS, GLASGOW.

FIGURE 17.5   Perspective of Holmwood, from *Villa and Cottage Architecture*.

the St Vincent Street church (see FIGURE 8.11), for the order re-emerges in St Vincent Lane on the south or back wall of the church – except that here no game is played with the three-dimensional ambiguity revealed by exposing that order. Nor is the sense that a plane is an abstracted order confined to masonry; it is surely the explanation of the unique form of Thomson's doors. No conventional framed and panelled affairs these; instead, they seem to have cornices buried within them, exposed by creating Thomson's favourite composition developed from the Choragic Monument of Thrasyllus (see FIGURE 14.4): of a single opening above a taller double opening with the lower divisions separated by a single square pier. With Thomson, doors and windows conform to the same aesthetic, an all-pervading sense of a dynamic structural system, the logic of the 'columnar effect', the 'purely structural

character, which is so distinctive of Grecian architecture',[22] worked through remorselessly.

It is this essential implicit classicism of Thomson's bare walls that make them subtly different from those composed, however simply and boldly, by his English Gothic contemporaries. The virtue of Gothic, after all, was its flexibility, both vertically and horizontally. Classicism, in contrast, depends on the structural logic of the order, and that inevitably insists upon the horizontal. Almost all of Thomson's buildings are characterised by this remorseless, logical projection of the horizontal line, whether achieved by a colonnade, as at Moray Place, or by a bare wall in which that governing order is implicit. This, I think, distinguishes Thomson's work from that of Schinkel, from whom he learned so much. Schinkel's trabeated system (in his neoclassical designs) (see FIGURE 14.5) displays the structural logic admired by Thomson but is treated only as an interpenetrating grid. On the Altes Museum, the great Ionic order of the portico reaches the corners – and then is stopped, rather unsatisfactorily, by piers of an uncomfortable width. Then, after the corner is turned, the implicit material continuity of that order as wall plane is cleverly and deliberately denied.

Thomson, in contrast, develops the logic of those abstracted orders and extends them beyond the building, whether as the great podia and plinths that distinguish so many of his compositions, or, occasionally, as walls that project into the landscape. It is this feature that seems so excitingly to anticipate the similar concerns of the young Frank Lloyd Wright (see FIGURE 16.5) – and the young Lutyens. It is evident, above all, at his finest villa, Holmwood (see FIGURE 17.5). Thomson's eloquent admirer, the Glasgow architect Thomas Gildard, was well aware of the significance of the wall which develops from the right hand side of the main elevation of Holmwood (see FIGURE 16.4) with insistent horizontality, regardless of the slope of the ground, to meet, *on precisely the same plane*, the wall of the stable-block. In his lecture on Thomson delivered in 1888, Gildard noted how,

> *The connecting of the offices with the villa by the unbroken long line of possibly a garden wall, is an impressive instance of the value of a continuous horizontality. This value may be estimated by supposing the wall away, each building apart, solitary, and unsympathetic. By this supposition it will be seen that this mere wall is one of the most important parts of the composition.*[23]

Alexander Thomson, it seems to me, is one of the very few British architects who succeeded in extending the classical language of architecture. Many others spoke it with unusually accomplished distinction, but only four men made it say original and new things. They are Hawksmoor, Soane, Thomson and Lutyens. One of these, Lutyens, was self-taught as a classicist while two, Hawksmoor and Thomson, never left the shores of Britain and so never saw at first hand the buildings of Antiquity by which they were obsessed. This seems to me a strength rather than a weakness, requiring them to exercise imagination because striving for archaeological exactitude was rendered more difficult. All four relied, to a considerable extent, on

the novelty and power of abstraction, while also adding new and peculiar motifs to the vocabulary. In his delight in the monumental and the Sublime, Thomson is certainly akin to Hawksmoor. He is, perhaps, least like Soane, for Soane's abstraction is so thin and planar, suggestive, in John Summerson's memorable words, of 'a sense of deflation, as if all *mass* had been exhausted from the design'.[24] Thomson's abstraction, in contrast, is three-dimensional and dynamic, the consequence of thinking in terms of mass and the governing columnar order. This leads to the emphasis on the continuous horizontal – which is what makes his work so similar in spirit to the later classical designs of Sir Edwin Lutyens.

Lutyens, born six years before Thomson's death, seems to have understood the possibilities of the classical language almost intuitively. Like Thomson, he was interested in the optical corrections found in Greek temples, but was more concerned with the expressive possibilities offered by Renaissance classicism. From an early stage, he treated classical details with Mannerist invention and wit; later, in his great war memorials, he added to the stock of motifs by freezing certain wooden and fabric forms in stone – a process analogous to the original development of the Greek orders. Above all, he seems to have had a feeling for the horizontal emphasis produced by the coherent use of the orders. This is particularly evident in Viceroy's House, New Delhi (see FIGURE 17.6), where many of the elevations consist of layers of massive, subtly battered wall surfaces, separated by carefully composed string courses and cornices. Like Thomson's, these sweeps of wall have a dynamic quality, stemming from the implicit control of an order. These horizontals are inexorable, like continuous strata of rock, sometimes spreading into great plinths or retaining walls with an inevitable, elemental, eternal quality. This is precisely what Thomson admired in the buildings of Ancient Egypt: 'the idea of duration ... The carefully adjusted proportion, and the thickness diminishing as the height increases, deprives the mass of any idea of weight or tendency to fall. Its poise is perfect, and we regard it as an imperishable thought ...'.[25]

Possibly Thomson would not have cared for Lutyens's employment of the arch, but he would surely have admired the smaller rectangular apertures punched directly into the superb pink-and-cream

FIGURE 17.6   The south front of Viceroy's House, New
Delhi, photograph *c*.1931.

sandstone. And what about the basement colonnades of
large squat Hindu columns bearing strange corbelled
brackets, and ending, in the forecourt, in great carved
elephants (creatures that appear in Thomson's South
Kensington Museum design, see FIGURE 7.11)? Surely
these long, powerful retaining walls would have
seemed to Thomson like nothing more than those long
terraces supported on exotic columns that appear in the
images by John Martin (see FIGURE 1.3) he so admired?
I doubt if Lutyens was influenced by Martin's work,
although William Walcot, that accomplished artist who
executed perspectives for Lutyens, shared with Martin
a taste both for Antique subject matter and the Sublime. Nor do I know if Lutyens knew Thomson's work.
When he passed through Glasgow in 1897 *en route* for
the Ferry Inn at Roseneath, he wrote to his wife only of

Miss Cranston's tearooms. Perhaps that was too early a
date for Lutyens to have seen the point of Thomson's
buildings. Besides, he was not an architect who seems
to have learned much from contemporaries and he
tended to share the conventional disparaging view of
his generation towards the mid-Victorians.

Yet, in contemplating the peculiar, Sublime character of Lutyens's classicism, it is worth remembering
that the English architect may well have learned something from the abstraction of the Gothic 'Vigorous
Style' owing to his admiration of the work of Street's
pupil, Philip Webb.[26] It must be admitted that
Lutyens's mouldings and forms are softer and more
sophisticated than Thomson's. Even so, they had
much in common. Neither had time for self-expression
by craftsmen and both required all sculpture, detail

and decoration to be under the total control of the architect. Above all, both exploited the aesthetic possibilities of the horizontal to the maximum. 'No man knew better than Thomson the value of the horizontal line,' argued Gildard (before the advent of Lutyens), 'no man has more powerfully expressed it. It is a dominant element in all his compositions ...'.[27] In Thomson's work, the levels established by lintels, entablatures, capitals and other structural elements are consistently maintained and developed, even though they sometimes interpenetrate and may, in places, disappear. This is a peculiarly satisfying aspect of his architecture, both inside and out.

Let us return to Thomson's advocacy of the horizontal in a fuller quotation. 'In a colonnade or façade,' he argued against the different character of Gothic,

the element of length is developed or suggested, and it will be readily perceived that there is no single building or combination of buildings, however great in extent, to which this element does not apply and which, with proper treatment, would not be enhanced in dignity in proportion as it is prolonged. I may refer to the magnificent architectural compositions of the late John Martin in illustration of this. A comprehensible number of columns are arranged in a compartment, then a feature projecting outwards and upwards is introduced; the columns are continued through and beyond it to the next feature of the same kind; these are repeated as often as they can be comprehended, and a feature still larger is brought in, to be repeated at greater intervals; and so on almost indefinitely; the columns are connected by their stylobates below and their entablatures above; while the other features are united by terraces – the whole producing an effect of surpassing grandeur. All who have studied works of art must have been struck by the mysterious power of the horizontal element in carrying the mind away into space, and into speculations upon infinity. The pictures of Turner and of Roberts afford frequent examples of this. The expanding effect which is thus produced upon the mind cannot be overrated.[28]

Thomson shared with Ruskin an admiration for Turner, and he is remarkable among architects for having a great love of paintings and for referring repeatedly to artists in his writings. Clearly the work of his compatriot, David Roberts, was important to him

for introducing to the insular Scot not only the forms but the colours of the ancient buildings of the Near East. But of which work by Roberts can Thomson have been thinking as an illustration of the power of the horizontal element? Surely not one of his topographical pictures but *The Israelites Leaving Egypt*, a large and ambitious canvas which now hangs in Birmingham City Art Gallery and which was painted in 1829, that is before Roberts had visited Egypt. It is an Egyptian architectural phantasy, a composition of endless colonnades seen in sharp perspective, dominated by converging horizontal lines – just as in the view of Moray Place from Thomson's bay window. This is, of course, by no means a typical Roberts but a work in which the painter emulated the apocalyptic historical paintings of John Martin, the artistic sensation of his time.

John Martin (1789–1854) was the ultimate painter of the Sublime and, what is more, he achieved this through the depiction of architecture. He specialised in depicting Old Testament catastrophes, set against colossal architectural backgrounds of massive terraces and colonnades receding into the distance where can be discerned further astonishing structures and towers, sheltering beneath massive storm clouds. Martin's first great triumph was his sensational canvas of *Belshazzar's Feast* (see PLATE I), exhibited in 1821 and this success was followed by such works as *Joshua Commanding the Sun to Stand Still*, *The Deluge* and *The Fall of Ninevah* (see also FIGURE 14.3). In his descriptive catalogue to *The Fall of Ninevah*, exhibited in 1827, the painter explained how

The mighty cities of Ninevah and Babylon have passed away. The accounts of their greatness and splendour may have been exaggerated. But, where strict truth is not essential, the mind is content to find delight in the contemplation of the grand and marvellous. Into the solemn visions of antiquity we look without demanding the clear daylight of truth. Seen through the mist of ages the great *becomes* gigantic, *the* wonderful *swells into the* sublime.[29]

It is easy to compare such compositions with the massive film sets achieved by Cecil B. De Mille or W. D. Griffiths a century later, but that does not diminish them. The achievement was prodigious and, as Norah Monckton has demonstrated, although 'Martin's stupendous reconstructions were universally supposed

FIGURE 17.7   Second, smaller, perspective of Thomson's
design for the South Kensington Museum, 1864, now at the
NMRS.

to be the creations of his own imagination. In fact, he
had taken infinite pains to ensure that they were historically correct.'[30] This he did by consulting all the
published works about the architecture of Egypt,
Mesopotamia, Persia and India. Martin's strong sense
of the architectural was also shown by his involvement
in real projects. In 1820 he submitted a strange design
for a national monument to commemorate the Battle of
Waterloo in London and he devoted much time and
money in abortive proposals to bring fresh water into
London and to embank the Thames. His was a prodigious, visionary talent.

Although Thomson reveals his admiration for Martin in his published writings, Goodhart-Rendel seems
to have been the first to point out the architect's
practical debt to the painter. 'Not that Thomson was
any disciple of Schinkel;' he said in 1948,

*it is hard to think of him of having been a disciple of
anyone unless it had been of the painter, John Martin.
In the middle distance of* The Fall of Babylon *or of*

The Last Judgement *his United Presbyterian
churches would not look at all amiss. In their architecture Egyptian, Hellenic and Hellenistic elements are
picturesquely combined in a manner that show very
little commonsense but great scenic skill.*[31]

I do not know which, if any, of Martin's great canvases
were exhibited in Scotland or whether Thomson saw
them on his visits to London; it does not matter. The
means by which Martin's architectural images reached
a wide audience were through prints. So popular were
his paintings that Martin engraved and published his
own mezzotints of them. *Belshazzar's Feast* (see PLATE
I), for instance, went into several editions and we know
that almost 600 prints were made from the plate of *The
Deluge*. It is scarcely surprising that Thomson was
familiar with Martin's work.

Thomson's obsession with Martin's architectural
imagery is evident, above all, in the astonishing façade
of Egyptian Halls in Union Street. Seen in perspective,
this towering composition of horizontal layers of exotic

colonnades seems like nothing so much as a short length of a Martin-imagined terrace. It would be a grave mistake, however, to interpret Thomson's admiration for Martin purely in terms of architectural images which he brought to tectonic reality in the streets of Glasgow. Thomson's admiration for Martin goes much deeper, for it was the subject matter of the images that surely seized Thomson's imagination. For Martin was nothing if not a *religious* painter. As well as the set pieces of Old Testament catastrophes, Martin made series of engravings of Milton's *Paradise Lost* and of *The Last Judgement*, as well as illustrations for various editions of the Holy Bible. These must have deeply impressed Thomson, who was a profoundly religious man and whose theory of architecture was moral and theological. For Thomson, the civilisations of Babylon, Egypt and Greece were all part of God's unfolding purpose, which is why it was legitimate to use their architectural styles for modern churches and why he was exasperated by the exclusive claims of the Gothicists to be building in a Christian style. Pugin

dismissed classicism as 'Pagan'; Thomson had more sense and a broader vision of religious history.

I approach the subject of Thomson and religion with trepidation, knowing so little of the history and traditions of radical Scottish Presbyterianism with which he was deeply involved. I am therefore in debt to Sam McKinstry's earlier essays which link Thomson's religious background and architectural theory. For it is inescapable that Thomson was steeped in Presbyterianism. He was an elder of the Caledonia Road United Presbyterian Church and his religious view of life is clear from reading the Haldane Lectures. His whole family were affected by the same theological outlook, and his brother George – his sometime partner – abandoned architecture for the ultimately fatal calling to be a missionary in Darkest Africa. 'Religion has been the soul of art from the beginning.'[32] It is clear to me that Thomson's architecture cannot be understood without reference to his religious outlook – but of what great Victorian is that not true?

This aspect of his character will, of course, spare him

the dreadful fate of becoming the object of selective and uncritical adulation – such as perverts our understanding of Mackintosh's genius. It is significant how all the architects who have become objects of worship in their respective countries – Mackintosh in Britain, Wright in the United States, Horta in Belgium, Gaudi in Spain – are all of the same generation, all working at a time of radical experimentation and cultural crisis, all self-consciously artistic, all perceived, whether rightly or wrongly, as misunderstood *avant-garde* innovators ahead of their time, which sometimes gives them the glamorous aura of failure in addition to the interest of an unorthodox private life. This evidently has popular appeal, unlike the notion of an architect being rather conventional, successful and serving his time and society. For this reason, great architects of earlier generations who are revered as national heroes, like Wren or Schinkel, will never attain such cult status; nor will Thomson – it is a mercy.

Unlike that of Mackintosh, Thomson's career was central to Victorian Glasgow. He designed all the types of building that the expanding city needed – warehouses and offices, houses and tenements, tombstones and villas as well as great churches – and so had a profound influence on the very character of the city – as others demonstrate elsewhere in this book. Some commentators hint that Thomson's conspicuous originality was criticised; if so, it is nevertheless much to Glasgow's credit that so independent a designer, uncompromising and yet very practical, was given so many opportunities. The only tangible blot on that record is the fact that he was denied the opportunity of undertaking a great public work; as Gildard recounted, 'I once asked Mr. Thomson why he had never used the Doric; he told me that he had never had a building whose size was worthy of it.'[33] Had he lived, what would Thomson have done with the City Chambers competition of 1881? George Square surely deserved the Doric to complement David Rhind's great column in honour of Walter Scott.

Even so, Thomson built a great deal, for the Second City then had energy and confidence. The contrast with today is painful. It baffles and exasperates me, as an outsider, that modern Glasgow is always prepared to accept the mediocre and second-best, that there is still that vein of self-hating, self-destructive shame – all too often in high places – resulting from the long years of depression and decline in what is still one of the great cities of the world. In such a climate, perhaps it is no wonder that so many of Thomson's buildings have unnecessarily perished, that others suffer intolerable neglect. The final insult is that Thomson and his family lie in an unmarked grave in the desolate, vandalised Southern Necropolis – not owing to any such mythical circumstances as surround Mozart's burial but because someone has stolen or cleared away the stone. Is this the way to treat the memory of one of the distinguished minds, one of the great artists, of the nineteenth century?

Alexander Thomson [see FIGURE 17.8] *was, in appearance, a distinguished-looking man, of a good average height, stout, well and proportionally made, a fine manly countenance with a profuse head of hair. His general appearance was, indeed, very much in harmony with the strength and elegance which he imparted to the structures he designed, while the genial smile which so often over-spread his face might be fittingly compared to the finished enrichment which was so marked and pleasing a feature of his compositions. Any intelligent person watching the stream of traffic on the pavement of a Glasgow street, and seeing Mr. Thomson passing would at once set him down as no ordinary man. The man of genius that he undoubtedly was was clearly indicated in his personal appearance, and that, without any effort, as is sometimes the case, to assume the airs of genius ... You could not say he was indolent, but there was a dreamy unrest about him even when engaged on important work ... A notable feature of Mr. Thomson's character was his social friendliness. This he displayed in no way more strikingly than the frequent occasions when he had his pupils at his house. He was a great antiquarian lore of our own country. Even ghost and antiquity of past ages, as well as the more familiar antiquarian lore of our own country. Even ghost and fairie stories were not beneath his notice, and the happiest hours upon which many of his old pupils look back were spent under his hospitable roof.*[34]

I am glad to know that. Living in the great man's own house where he stayed for fourteen years and where he died – after four months confined indoors, coughing with bronchitis and asthma during a dreadful cold, wet, dark Glasgow winter – I cannot help wondering

FIGURE 17.8 Alexander Thomson, photograph of the
1850s.

what sort of man he was. Would he approve of *me* – an Englishman and an Anglican, married to a Roman Catholic, who has written in praise of the Gothic Revival and even of the (non-Glaswegian) work of Sir Gilbert Scott? I hope so. The earlier chapters here dealing with his religious outlook reveal a wider sympathy and tolerance than, rightly or wrongly, we tend to associate with Scottish Presbyterianism. Certainly the Haldane Lectures reveal a thoughtful acquaintance with modern evolutionary and scientific thinking. More to the point, as I sit in the bay window, gazing at this supreme expression of 'imperishable thought' in Giffnock sandstone, at the converging composition of horizontals with those fifty-two square columns receding with extreme foreshortening (see FIGURE 17.1), I am in awe of the achievement of an architect who was at once so romantic and so practical, of a man who could create such comfortable, sensible, beautiful houses whose imagination was yet seething with extraordinary images of the Ancient World and the Old Testament, of great terraces and hanging gardens rising beneath storm-filled skies, with extraordinary colonnades and strong horizontal lines receding into infinity. No mere functionalist, 'In Thomson, with the severe judgement and high culture of the Greek there was combined the rich and glowing imagination of the Oriental...'[35]

Alexander 'Greek' Thomson, that insular, self-educated, widely read and brilliant Scot, is a paradox, and yet a paradigm for Scotland. He was an artist who was consciously part of a European tradition – *the* European tradition – with little interest in being distinctively Scottish in his work, and yet one who seldom ventured beyond his native land and never travelled abroad.[36] Imagination, sustained by book learning, was all – as with Hawksmoor. In common with that of Mackintosh, Thomson's achievement is open to a variety of interpretations, whether as an eclectic precursor of early twentieth-century neoclassicism or a pioneer of mid-twentieth-century modernism: a Presbyterian proto-functionalist, as some have seen him – a significant step on that direct path from Schinkel to the total abstraction of Late Mies. He was that; and yet was so much more. Surely he was, at heart, an intense romantic, steeped in history and inspired by deep religious faith, who brought exotic glamour and immense intellectual distinction to the wet, smoky streets of Victorian Glasgow. I like the fact that while he let his

mind be carried away into space – speculating upon infinity and on the splendours of Ancient Greece and Egypt, of Karnak and Jerusalem, of Babylon and Ninevah, of the Acropolis of Athens and the Temple of Solomon – Alexander Thomson was quite content to remain in Strathbungo.

ACKNOWLEDGEMENTS

I enjoyed the assistance of Thomson's great-granddaughters, Catherine Rentoul and Ann Hutchinson, in confirming biographical details in this chapter and thanks are also due to Dr David Walker and Dr Sam McKinstry.

NOTES

1. The pre-existing railway had been opened in 1848 but the dating of Moray Place is confusing. It has been generally assumed that the terrace was built in 1859 and Ronald McFadzean, in his *Life and Work of Alexander Thomson*, London, 1979, suggests that the Thomson family moved from Shawlands in 1860. However, the Feu Contract for 'that steading of ground number one of the block or range of buildings called Moray Place' between John McIntyre and William Stevenson as one party, and Thomson as the second, disposing of interests in the land by John Heys and George Heys, is dated October 1861, and states that the land had been feued by Sir John Maxwell of Pollock, Bart, to McIntyre and Stevenson in July 1860. No houses are indicated on the 1860 Ordnance Survey map of the area, nor are any recorded as being occupied in the 1861 Census, taken on 7 April when Thomson and his family were still resident at 16 Darnley Terrace, Shawlands. In the *Post Office Glasgow Directory* for 1861–2 published in 1861, the entry appears for 'Thomson, Alex. of A.& G. Thomson*; ho. 1 Moray Place, Regent's Park, Pollok-shaws Road' and John Shields is recorded as living at No. 3, although matters are confused by the fact that 'Thomson, Alex.' is listed at Darnley Terrace in Shawlands for several years afterwards. Nevertheless, as the memoir of the Thomson family written by the architect's granddaughter, Mrs W. L. Stewart (in which William Stevenson is wrongly named as Alexander Stevenson), records – 'Corrected from The Family Bible' – Thomson's ninth child, Helen, was born at Moray Place on 9 July 1861. All this suggests that the terrace was built in the autumn and winter of 1860–1 and that Thomson moved into No. 1 between April and July 1861. The precise date of the *design* remains uncertain, however. Thomson's widow lived on in the house until her death in 1899. It was then bought by Dr Thomas Forrest who, in 1900, added a wing containing a surgery and waiting

room with a separate entrance in Titwood Place, now Nithsdale Road. This was designed by the Glasgow architect John Binnie Wilson (drawings in the Strathclyde Regional Archives) and although it disturbs the overall symmetry of Moray Place, it is remarkable for the respect shown towards Thomson's design of forty years before.

Stevenson, whom McFadzean claims moved into 3 Moray Place in 1860, was in fact listed as resident at 15 Moray Place in 1862 and at 13 Moray Place in 1864 – that is, in the next terrace to the west, which was not designed by Thomson. For a summary of the history of the area, see Maurice Lindsay, 'The Fabric of Heritage. Strathbungo, Glasgow', in *Scottish Field* (Jan. 1977), pp. 26–7.

2. Blackie (publ.), *Villa and Cottage Architecture*, London 1868, p. 48. I discussed the peculiarities of the sash windows in Moray Place in the *Architects Journal* (27 Nov. 1991), pp. 46–9.

3. Henry-Russell Hitchcock, *Architecture: Nineteenth and Twentieth Centuries*, Harmondsworth, 1963, p. 72.

4. A. Thomson, 'An Inquiry as to the Appropriateness of the Gothic Style …', in *Proceedings of the Glasgow Architectural Society* (1865–7), p. 54.

5. In *The City that Disappeared*, Glasgow, 1981, p. 72, Frank Worsdall aptly notes that

> *The work of demolition began on St Andrew's Day 1980. Surely there is some significance in that choice of date? To demolish one of the treasures of Scottish architecture by Scotland's greatest architect, on Scotland's national day, seems to me to be deliberately perverse. It is, however, typical of the attitude of the District Council, which frequently shows a disregard of the wishes of those who know and love this sadly dismembered city.*

6. Andor Gomme and David Walker, *Architecture of Glasgow*, London, 1968, p. 131.

7. It cannot be proved that Wright had seen Thomson's work and the great American egotist never admitted being influenced by anyone. It is likely, however, that his knowledge of Thomson came from the plates of the Double Villa and Holmwood in *Villa and Cottage Architecture*. This, however, cannot explain the remarkable similarities between Unity Temple at Oak Park and Thomson's Ballater Street church commented on by Andrew MacMillan (Ch. 16). Another connection between Thomson and the United States is the Thomson-esque work of the brothers Audsley, two Scottish architects and organ builders who emigrated to the United States and who designed the Layton Art Gallery in Milwaukee in 1885. Wright must have known this (and its architects?) – Milwaukee is equidistant from Oak Park and the valley where Wright was born and would build Taliesin – and in 1893 he entered the competition for the Milwaukee Public Library. See the *Alexander Thomson Society Newsletter*, no. 3, Jan. 1992; and David Van Zanten in [Milwaukee Art Museum], *1888: Frederick*

Layton and his World, Milwaukee, Wisconsin, 1988.

8. Henry-Russell Hitchcock, *Architecture*, p. 63; and id., *Early Victorian Architecture*, London and New Haven, 1954, vol. 1, p. 489. In their *Architecture of Glasgow*, p. 139, Gomme and Walker dispute Hitchcock's characterisation of Moray Place as pure 'Greek' and argue that, 'What counts for the onlooker today is the severe withdrawn serenity of Thomson's building, its simplicity and absence of fuss, the uncanny accuracy of Thomson's eye in judging the proportions of his long façade, the exquisite, near mechanical precision of the incised details on the cornice and panels.'

9. Reginald Blomfield, '"Greek" Thomson. II. A Critical Note', in *Architectural Review*, vol. XV (May 1904), p. 194. For the significance of Burnet at the time, see Gavin Stamp, 'Mackintosh, Burnet and Modernity', in *Architectural Heritage III: The Age of Mackintosh* (the Journal of the Architectural Heritage Society of Scotland), vol. III (1992), pp. 8–31.

10. Joseph Addison, 'Some Aspects of Greek Architecture, Including a Study of the Neo-Grec Style in Europe', *Journal of the Royal Institute of British Architects*, vol. XXXIX (9 Jan. 1932), pp. 177–80.

11. Lionel B. Budden, 'The Work of Alexander Thomson', in *The Builder* (31 Dec. 1910), pp. 817–18.

12. A. Trystan Edwards, 'Modern Architects:-II. Alexander ("Greek") Thomson', in the *Architects and Builders Journal*, vol. XXXIX (20 May 1914), p. 350.

13. H. S. Goodhart-Rendel, 'Rogue Architects of the Victorian Era', in the *R.I.B.A. Journal*, vol. LVI (Apr. 1949), p. 254.

14. H. S. Goodhart-Rendel, *English Architecture since the Regency*, London, 1953, p. 112. The text of this book had largely been written as lectures given in Oxford in 1934 and Rendel's interest in Thomson went back further. In his introduction to *H. S. Goodhart-Rendel 1887–1959*, edited by Alan Powers (Architectural Association, London, 1987), Sir John Summerson recalled how, 'We first met at a dinner-party at Mrs Fleetwood-Hesketh's house, I think in 1928, when I was twenty-three and he forty? It was a good evening. I recall that after dinner conversation ran on to Beethoven's piano works and then shifted to the architecture of Schinkel and (of all people) "Greek" Thomson. Rendel was perfectly at ease with all three, reciting fragments of Beethoven at the piano and making acute observations on the two architects and their respective styles.'

15. A. E. Richardson, 'Architecture: The Classic Tradition', in G. M. Young (ed.), *Early Victorian England 1830–1865*, London, 1934, vol. II, p. 206.

16. John Ruskin, *The Seven Lamps of Architecture*, London, 1849, pp. 53–5.

17. A. Thomson, *Art and Architecture: A Course of Four Lectures* read to the Haldane Institute, Glasgow, 1874; Haldane Lectures, IV (1874), Mitchell Library, Glasgow, p. 11.

18. Haldane Lectures, I (1874), p. 9.

19. Ibid., p. 16.

20. Andrew MacMillan, '"Greek" Thomson, Charles Rennie Mackintosh and Frank Lloyd Wright' in *Alexander 'Greek' Thomson Architect 1817–1875*, London, 1984, p. 8.

21. 'Let me ask you to devote some time to the drawings by Mr. Thomson of Glasgow. They represent buildings in Greek Architecture, but certainly the best modern Greek Architecture it has ever been my lot to see' – William Burges at the Architectural Association, *Building News*, vol. XIV (1867), p. 374, and the *Builder*, xxviii, 1.6.1867, pp. 385–7. Burges, who cannot actually have seen Thomson's buildings as he referred to them being in Edinburgh, would seem to have admired his drawings because, ironically, he saw Gothic qualities in it: '... the most curious thing is that many of them, by a very few touches, could be most easily translated into thirteenth century French art...' In his *William Burges and the High Victorian Dream*, London, 1981, p. 308, J. Mordaunt Crook suggests that the porch of Burges' Tower House, with its square columns, recalls Thomson's work.

 The Victorian urban aesthetic of the Sublime – both Gothic and classic – was discussed by Nicholas Taylor in his essay on 'The Awful Sublimity of the Victorian City', in H. J. Dyos and M. Wolff (ed), *The Victorian City: Images and Realities*, London and Boston, 1973, vol. 2, pp. 431–47.

22. Haldane Lectures, IV, p. 7.

23. Thomas Gildard, 'Greek Thomson': paper read before the Architectural Section of the Philosophical Society of Glasgow, 30 January 1888, *Proceedings of the Royal Philosophical Society of Glasgow*, vol. XIX (1888), pp. 191–210; also published as pamphlet: p. 12.

24. John Summerson, *Architecture in Britain, 1530–1830*, Harmondsworth, 1963, p. 287.

25. Haldane Lectures, II (1874), p. 10.

26. See Roderick Gradidge, 'Edwin Lutyens: the last High Victorian', in J. Fawcett (ed.), *Seven Victorian Architects*, London, 1976, pp. 122–36.

27. Gildard, 'Greek Thomson', pamphlet, p. 11.

28. A. Thomson, 'An Inquiry...', p. 54.

29. Descriptive catalogue to *The Fall of Ninevah*, exhibited in 1827, quoted in Thomas Balston, *John Martin 1789–1854: His Life and Works*, London, 1947, p. 107; and Christopher Johnstone, *John Martin*, London, 1974, p. 12.

30. Norah Monckton, 'Architectural Backgrounds in the Pictures of John Martin', in the *Architectural Review*, vol. CIV (Aug. 1948), p. 81.

31. Goodhart-Rendel, 'Rogue Architects', p. 254.

32. Haldane Lectures, II (1874), p. 6. In 'The Awful Sublimity...', p. 443, Nicholas Taylor noticed 'the close connection that existed in the Victorian city between Sublimity in architecture and rhetoric in religion'.

33. Gildard, 'Greek Thomson', p. 8.

34. MS of 'my impressions and recollections of Greek Thomson' written for Thomas Ross in 1897 by William(?) Clunas ('The writer was for many years in Thomson's office') among MS 694 in Thomas Ross's papers in the National Library of Scotland – copy by courtesy of Dr David Walker.

35. Gildard, 'Greek Thomson', p. 9. He used a very similar phrase in his long obituary of Thomson in the *British Architect*, vol. III (26 March 1875), p. 1 (Thomson was a major shareholder in the periodical). It is not known if Thomson ever met Sir Gilbert Scott but he did encounter George Gilbert Scott junior, the subject of my Cambridge Ph.D. Thesis (1978), and in 1979 I corresponded with Ronald McFadzean to obtain a longer version of the quotation in his new book (p. 271) from Thomson's description of meeting him at dinner with Scott senior's former assistant, the Scottish architect J. J. Stevenson.

36. According to McFadzean, *Alexander Thomson*, p. 273, quoting a memoir written by a member of the family, during his long last illness Thomson planned to go abroad for the first time and travel to Italy the following winter for the benefit of his health, but it was not to be.

SELECT BIBLIOGRAPHY

PUBLICATIONS ABOUT ALEXANDER THOMSON IN CHRONOLOGICAL ORDER

A great deal has been written about Thomson, although much of it in comparatively obscure periodicals. However, as Ronald McFadzean warns in his 1979 standard work (which contains a full bibliography), 'Since Thomson's death many articles on his work have been published. Most of them derive their information from sources of doubtful authenticity or from the writings of inaccurate predecessors. Consequently an understanding of Thomson's work is obscured by a mass of poorly researched material displaying a remarkable misunderstanding of his achievement.' None the less, almost all the articles are interesting for expressing the outlook of their time on Thomson's achievement.

[Thomas Gildard] obituary, *Building News*, vol. XXXV (26 Mar. 1875), p. 357.

[Thomas Gildard] obituary, 'Mr. Alexander Thomson', in the *British Architect*, vol. III (26 Mar. 1875), and 'The Late Alexander Thomson', ibid., 16 April 1875.

Obituary in *The Evening Citizen*, Glasgow, 22 Mar. 1875.

J. Moyr Smith, 'The Style of the Future', in the *Building News*, vol. XXXV (16 Apr. 1875), p. 425; reprinted in Smith's *Ornamental Interiors, Ancient and Modern*, London, Crosby Lockwood & Co., 1887, p. 219.

[The Revd J. E. H. Thomson], *Memoir of George Thomson, Cameroons Mountains, West Africa: By one of his Nephews*, Edinburgh, Andrew Elliot, 1881.

D. Thomson, 'Greek Thomson', *The Architect*, vol. XXXIII (19 Nov. 1886), pp. 292–3.

Thomas Gildard, 'Greek Thomson', Paper read before the Architectural Section of the Philosophical Society of Glasgow, 30 Jan. 1888, *Proceedings of the Royal Philosophical Society of Glasgow*, vol. XIX (1888), pp. 191–210, and published as pamphlet [Glasgow].

Edward Irving Carlyle [information from J. J. Stevenson], 'Thomson, Alexander (1817–1875)', in *The Dictionary of National Biography*, 1900.

David Barclay, '"Greek" Thomson. I. His Life and Opinions', and Reginald Blomfield, 'II. A Critical Note', in the *Architectural Review*, vol. XV (May 1904), pp. 184–95.

Lionel B. Budden, 'The Work of Alexander Thomson', in *The Builder*, vol. XCIX (31 Dec. 1910), pp. 815–19.

A. Trystan Edwards, 'Modern Architects:-II. Alexander ("Greek") Thomson', in the *Architects and Builders Journal*, vol. XXXIX (13 and 20 May 1914), pp. 334–6 and 350–2.

[Henry Hunter, quoting, amongst others, the Revd John E. H. Thomson], 'Description of the Church Building', in *Queen's Park East United Free Church Glasgow Jubilee Book 1867–1917*, Glasgow, A. & W. Kennedy, 1918, pp. 113–20.

William Power, 'A Note on Greek Thomson', in *The World Unvisited: Essays and Sketches*, London and Glasgow, Gowans & Gray, 1922, pp. 79–95.

Malcolm Stark, 'The Work of Alexander Thomson', in *The Builder*, vol. CXXVI (11 Apr. 1924), p. 576.

J. Jeffrey Waddell, '"Greek" Thomson', in the *Scottish Ecclesiological Society's Transactions*, vol. viii, part 1 (1924–5), pp. 31–5, and reprinted as a pamphlet [Aberdeen], 1925.

Joseph Addison, 'Some Aspects of Greek Architecture, Including a Study of the Neo-Grec Style in Europe', *Journal of the Royal Institute of British Architects*, vol. XXXIX (9 Jan. 1932), pp. 165–80.

Ninian Johnston, 'Alexander Thomson: A Study of the Basic Principles of his Design', in the *R.I.A.S. Quarterly*, no. 43 (Sept. 1933), pp. 29–38, reprinted in the *Handbook of the British Architects Conference at Glasgow*, RIBA, 1935, pp. 69–80.

J. M. M. Billing, 'Alexander "Greek" Thomson: A Study of the Re-Creation of a Style', in the *R.I.A.S. Quarterly*, no. 62 (Oct. 1939), pp. 20–9.

H. S. Goodhart-Rendel, 'Rogue Architects of the Victorian Era', in the *Journal of the Royal Institute of British Architects*, vol. LVI (Apr. 1949), p. 254.

W. J. Smith, 'Glasgow – "Greek" Thomson, Burnet and Mackintosh', in the *R.I.A.S. Quarterly*, no. 85 (Aug. 1951), pp. 56–60.

Graham Law, 'Greek Thomson', in the *Architectural Review*, vol. CXV (May 1954), pp. 307–16.

Graham Law, 'Colonnades and Temples: Greek Thomson's Style', *Glasgow Herald*, 8 June 1954.

Francis Worsdall, '"Greek" Thomson', in *Scottish Field*, vol. CXXIII (Feb. 1962), p. 46–8.

Peter McNeil and David M. Walker, 'A Note on Greek Thomson', in the *Glasgow Review*, vol. II, no. 2 (Summer 1965), pp. 44–8.

Francis Worsdall, 'The Achievement of "Greek" Thomson', in *Scotland's Magazine* (July 1966), pp. 42–5.

Chapter on 'The Individual Contribution of Alexander Thomson', in Andor Gomme and David Walker, *Architecture of Glasgow*, London, Lund Humphries, 1968, pp. 123–52, revised edition, 1987.

Ronald McFadzean, *The Life and Work of Alexander Thomson*, London, Routledge & Kegan Paul, 1979.

Malcolm Holzman, 'Thomson's Glasgow', in *Progressive Architecture* (New York) (June 1982), pp. 90–5.

Andy MacMillan, '"Greek" Thomson, Charles Rennie Mackintosh and Frank Lloyd Wright'; Mark Baines, 'Form, Façade and Rhythm'; and John McKean, 'Trabeated Essence and Frosted Glass', in *Alexander 'Greek' Thomson Architect 1817–1875*, London, Architectural Association, 1984.

John Maule McKean, 'The Architectonics and Ideals of Alexander Thomson', in *AA Files (Annals of the Architectural Association School of Architecture)*, no. 9 (Summer 1985), pp. 31–44.

John McKean, 'Masters of Building: "Greek" Thomson's Double Villa', in the *Architects Journal*, vol. CLXXXIII (19 Feb. 1986), pp. 36–50.

[Fiona Sinclair], *Alexander Greek Thomson: The Glasgow Buildings*, City of Glasgow District Council Planning Dept, 1990.

The Alexander Thomson Society Newsletter, Glasgow, no. 1 (May 1991), *et seq*.

INDEX